W9-ACG-428

DANIEL

My French Cuisine

DANIEL

My French Cuisine

Daniel Boulud and Sylvie Bigar

ESSAYS BY BILL BUFORD

PHOTOGRAPHS BY THOMAS SCHAUER

GRAND CENTRAL
Life & Style
NEW YORK · BOSTON

Copyright © 2013 by Daniel Boulud, Ltd.

All photographs on page xi, the top left photograph on page xii, and all photographs on page xvi *except* the top left photo are from Daniel Boulud's personal collection.

On page xii, the lower right photograph is by Patrick McMullan.com.

On page xvi, the top left photo is by Jerry Ruotolo.

All other photographs are copyright © 2013 by Thomas Schauer.

The illustration on page 281 is by N. Ronjat, from *The Royal Cookery Book* by Jules Gouffé.

All rights reserved. In accordance with the U.S. Copyright Act of 1976, the scanning, uploading, and electronic sharing of any part of this book without the permission of the publisher is unlawful piracy and theft of the author's intellectual property. If you would like to use material from the book (other than for review purposes), prior written permission must be obtained by contacting the publisher at permissions@hbgusa.com. Thank you for your support of the author's rights.

Grand Central Life & Style
Hachette Book Group
237 Park Avenue
New York, NY 10017

www.GrandCentralLifeandStyle.com

Manufactured in the United Kingdom
by Butler Tanner & Dennis Limited.

First Edition: October 2013

10 9 8 7 6 5 4 3 2 1

Grand Central Publishing is a division of Hachette Book Group, Inc.

Grand Central Life & Style is an imprint of Grand Central Publishing. The Grand Central Life & Style name and logo are trademarks of Hachette Book Group, Inc.

The Hachette Speakers Bureau provides a wide range of authors for speaking events. To find out more, go to www.HachetteSpeakersBureau.com or call (866) 376-6591.

The publisher is not responsible for websites (or their content) that are not owned by the publisher.

Book and jacket design by Gary Tooth/Empire Design Studio

Library of Congress Control Number: 2013939294

ISBN: 978-1-455-51392-5

FSC
www.fsc.org

MIX
Paper from
responsible sources
FSC® C023561

To Julien and Marie, my parents, whose kitchen table at
the farm revolves around the seasons.
To Alix, my daughter and favorite dining companion.
To Katherine, my wife and partner in our home kitchen.

CONTENTS

IX   INTRODUCTION: AN INSIDE LOOK

XVII   A LETTER FROM PAUL BOCUSE

XIX   HOW TO USE THIS BOOK

       PART I. RECIPES FROM RESTAURANT DANIEL

3   **Appetizers**

42   Daniel on Bread

87   Daniel on Seasoning and Spicing

88   Daniel on Truffles

103   **Fish**

142   Daniel on Stocks and Sauces

145   Daniel on Wine

149   **Meat**

216   Daniel on Cooking It All

219   Daniel on Cheese

221   **Desserts**

262   Daniel on Desserts

265   **PART II. ICONIC SESSIONS**

       PART III. DANIEL AT HOME

335   **Alsace**

343   **Normandy**

351   **Provence**

359   **Lyon**

367   **BASE RECIPES**

380   **CULINARY TERMS AND INGREDIENTS**

383   **SOURCES FOR INGREDIENTS AND TOOLS**

384   **ACKNOWLEDGMENTS**

387   **INDEX**

396   **ABOUT THE AUTHORS**

Finally, on May 17, 1993, after dreaming about it since I was a boy and years of hard work and planning, Daniel the restaurant opened for business. What a whirlwind the past twenty years have been! I am thrilled to finally bring you *Daniel: My French Cuisine*.

This is not an exhaustive and exhausting encyclopedia of French food. Often what we cook at Daniel is completely novel. But more often, it has a direct link to the past. In *Daniel*, I will share with you three types of cuisine: that of Restaurant Daniel, iconic French classics, and French regional dishes I make at home. At Restaurant Daniel, my amazing brigade and I constantly play with the French recipes of the past, which allows us to move forward and develop our own. We build on prior knowledge using technique as a foundation to develop new ideas, new textures, and new presentations, always with a lighter touch. Some of the recipes from Restaurant Daniel are composed of many parts. I didn't want to keep any details from you by trying to make things simpler. You can decide how inspired you want to be: to make the whole recipe or just the main protein, or perhaps only the vegetable garnish. It's up to you. Besides cooking à la carte and creating precise, artistic plates, I enjoy revisiting historic dishes that encompass tradition and celebration with grand and soulful presentations. In the iconic section of this book, I wish to share the foundations of what makes me a French chef.

Do you know that I live twenty feet above the restaurant? Do you know that my office, called the "skybox," is a glass-enclosed den overlooking the kitchen? This is my home base, where I still move among the stations cooking, tasting, poking, and on occasion, teaching a young cook a trick I learned when I was seventeen. And as in the old French tradition, I still live above the "store," which is why I also included a section on how I cook at home. You may want to try your hand at a few of my personal recipes— the kind of regional dishes I make for my friends and family. Join me on this journey to delicious fun!

I REVEL IN AMERICA'S GENERATIONS OF CHEFS AND CUSTOMERS whose vibrant enthusiasm and passion for food support culinary talent. By sharing ideas with the ever-changing pool of emerging young chefs from around the world, I am inspired. These young cooks may not need to practice classic French cuisine anymore, but they use it as their reference. They respect it, and they know its foundations.

My connection to food is human and humble. I am a chef with soul: an American chef with a French soul or a French chef with an American soul. I have both influences in me, and that's what keeps me grounded.

In New York City, where I live, I constantly feel inspired by the bountiful markets and multiethnic culture, but deep down, I have remained quite French. In fact, I come from Lyon first, from France second. If I think back to my roots, I see a boy running around a farm, getting into trouble, helping his father sell vegetables at the market, and plunging his nose into his grandmother Francine's pot of succulent soup. Certainly, I didn't grow up around starched white tablecloths. At the Boulud farm the seasons ruled our table: We ate what we grew, when the time was ripe.

With the first money I made at age fourteen, peeling carrots and potatoes in the kitchen of Restaurant Nandron in Lyon, I bought two books: Escoffier's *Le Guide Culinaire* and Gringoire and Saulnier's *Le Répertoire de La Cuisine*. They may look like simple books, but they encapsulate what I still consider to be the code of French cuisine. It was the beginning of my now impressive cookbook collection. But trust me—at the time I couldn't collect anything; I didn't have a franc to my name!

Nandron, a famous Michelin two-star restaurant named for its chef/owner Gérard Nandron, sat almost across from Les Halles, the fabulous covered market where the country's top ingredients converged daily. Inside you would find fruits, vegetables, fragrant herbs and spices, meats, and fish. But right outside the building, along the surrounding streets, teemed the tripe sellers, the charcutiers, the oyster bars and bouchons. It wasn't Zola's *Le Ventre de Paris*, but it was close. If we needed a bunch of watercress in the middle of service, I would run there to get one that had been pulled that very morning. From the pretty, blond lady fishmonger (a favorite with all the chefs) to the paunchy butcher and the baggy-eyed baker, these characters lived together, and the cheerful camaraderie they exhibited was very similar to what I try to build with my cooks every day at Daniel.

I remember at fourteen seeing Paul Bocuse leading the pack of great chefs at Les Halles, where he shopped every day, but he also came by the restaurant to have coffee with my boss, his friend Gérard Nandron. I looked up to him as a hero. Then one day Nandron and I were driving down along the Saône River on our way back from a catered event, and he asked me:

"So, kid, have you ever been to Bocuse's Auberge?"

I hadn't, of course, so he made a right turn over the bridge and off we went to the famous restaurant, L'Auberge du Pont de Collonges. But we weren't headed to the dining room; it was in the kitchen that everything happened. I couldn't believe my eyes. Nandron's kitchen was fine, but Bocuse's was the Rolls-Royce; silver platters, shiny copper pots, cooks and waiters working like finely tuned machinery everywhere. I sat on the side of a counter taking it all in while the two friends chatted. After a while Bocuse hailed a waiter:

"Hey, bring the kid something to drink!"

What they put in front of me wasn't milk; it was a huge "communard" (Beaujolais and cassis liquor). There was no way I could say no, so little by little, I sipped my cocktail, getting drunker by the minute. And when the two elders were done, we drove back to the restaurant, where I tried to finish the dinner service, but everybody noticed how tipsy I was, and they gently sent me home. I slept well that night!

Maybe a year later, Bocuse needed cooks and called Nandron, who sent me as an extra apprentice. I showed up in the morning with sunglasses hanging on my shirt, and bumped into Bocuse in the entrance. "You're from Nandron?" he asked. "Go back, get a haircut, and we don't need sunglasses here!" At Bocuse, everybody had to follow the rules, so I left and got a crew cut!

Between the ages of fourteen and twenty-three, I worked my way through some of the best kitchens in France, propelled by my desire to learn and my hunger for new experiences and ingredients. I was always interested in cooking, but also in the entire operation of a restaurant, in how all the different parts (wine, flowers, design, service) interact with each other to create an "experience." Then I moved on to Denmark, and then America. I saw Paul Bocuse regularly at events. He took me under his wing, and over the years we developed a close bond. Today I consider him my guiding shepherd, a spiritual father. His son Jérôme is one of my best friends, and I am the proud godfather to "Petit" Paul, Jérôme's son. Now we're family.

Clockwise from top left: *on the family farm; at a garlic fair with my father (left); Copenhagen, 1977; at La Mere Blanc (on far right), 1975; as chef at Le Cirque, 1986; at Le Régence with Sottha Khunn, 1984;* center: *apprenticing at Nandron, 1970*

At Restaurant Daniel enjoying wine pairings from each of our birth years. From left: *Julien (my father), Gilles (my brother), me, Celine (my niece), Marie (my mother)*

Besides Paul Bocuse, I have been influenced and even mentored by the great chefs of the 1970s: Roger Vergé, Alain Chapel, the Troisgros brothers, Michel Guérard, Frédy Girardet, and Georges Blanc. Their cuisine, styles, and souls stayed with me and continue to inspire me.

• • •

FRENCH CUISINE WAS IN MY DNA, AND I CARRIED IT WITH ME across the Atlantic. When we first opened Daniel, everybody had an opinion about what I needed to do. We built the restaurant on a shoestring; no dream kitchen, but a good one. The goal was efficiency on a budget. But when we moved to the corner of 65th and Park, the historic spot previously occupied by Le Cirque, I felt both terrified and thrilled. I knew that such a restaurant was going to be "une maison pour la vie," a home for life. With the new Daniel, I was taking not only a huge financial risk, but a personal risk as well. There, for the first time in my life, I built a dream kitchen, a station for each position, even a Bonnet stove. I was pinching myself. The whole team was exhilarated; we were all in it together, and I had the best possible partners—Joel Smilow and Lili Lynton—who allowed me to dream big.

Today my life revolves around my amazing team and our marvelous and faithful guests. Cooking is friendship, communication, and passion, not only for the ingredients, but also for the people who cultivate them. I love to walk through my kitchen and take in our mosaic of people, cultures, regions, and tastes.

Our dishes today are vibrant, modern, and alive almost, and they constantly evolve. On the other end of the spectrum, favorites such as the sea scallop "black tie," created for the 1996/97 New Year's Eve, have become true classics and need no updates. These creations join the repertoire of our classics at Daniel, and they speak to the diverse collection of talent.

Though French cuisine is based on rules and codes, I also practice what I call spontaneous cuisine. For many home cooks today, this is the new mantra. What did I find at the market today?

What do we feel like tonight? Often purveyors push open the doors of my kitchen bearing rare treasures. Everything stops. The crew comes over to admire the new mushroom, see the live crabs, or taste an unknown spice. Excitement in the kitchen makes all eyes brighten with anticipation. How will we cook it? The energy kicks in.

Some recipes are spontaneous. They happen because an ingredient is making its short appearance on the seasonal market—think of the ovoli mushrooms with the loup de mer; but others are meant to become classics. I am as excited to work on a new dish as I am to revisit a classic. My famous paupiette of sea bass in crispy potato scales was taken off the menu and rethought, keeping the same ingredients, but in a new preparation every year at Daniel. But at Café Boulud, executive chef Gavin Kaysen insisted he wanted to bring back the original paupiette, and the diners love it!

At the James Beard Awards with my daughter, Alix (ⓒ Patrick McMullan.com)

The service team and chefs after a pre-meal meeting

One morning the kitchen is exploding with spring. Chef de cuisine Eddy Leroux shows off his scary knife skills as he dices the thickest fresh Hawaiian heart of palm. I never saw that in France! Sous chef Roger Ma is on double morel duty as he fills morels the size of small volcanoes with a morel stuffing; every single part of the huge white asparagus from Provence is going into every dish we can possibly think of; the langoustines have landed and now they crawl in the tray, red and angry; at the garde-manger station, young men and women on their externship from culinary school are busy quartering spring onions, julienning carrots, and dicing radishes. It's noon, and even though we're not open for lunch, the kitchen is teeming with whites, toques focused down, watching the clock and praying they'll get everything done before the curtain goes up with the first reservations at 5:30 p.m.

Below the dining room, in the crowded prep kitchen, the pace is getting frantic. Knives dive in and out, butchering whole animals; fish from Maine rest on cutting boards, awaiting their fate; and across the way, the pasta station is in gear, fingers pinching herb agnolottis. Next door in the pastry kitchen, Sandro Micheli, our creative pastry chef, puts the finishing touch on a passion fruit and mango parfait. My spoon darts in for a taste. Is it tangy enough? As I pass one of our assistant cooks from Mexico, I congratulate him on the fantastic cassoulet he cooked for everyone's lunch yesterday. I enjoy seeing the young, eager faces of tomorrow's great chefs as they work in our kitchen, learning what I hope will enable them to shine. They come from all over the world: There's Chris from Germany, Maria from Peru, Pat from San Francisco, Laurence from Montreal, and Jean from Burkina Faso. Today they learn from us, but tomorrow they'll be cooking the staff's family meal and we'll all learn from them!

I am thrilled to see so many cooks come to Daniel to learn the craft. Years ago, young people from all over the world went to the kitchens of France. Today they come to New York! On the wall, a poster reads "Keep calm, DB is in the house." I smile and head back to work.

• • •

LAST YEAR A COUPLE CAME INTO THE KITCHEN AND TOLD ME about the life-changing moment they experienced years ago at Fernand Point's famous La Pyramide (one of the first French restaurants to garner three stars from the *Michelin Guide*). They reminisced about the menu and the memorable bottle of Crozes-Hermitage. And this, for me, is the magic of French cuisine—the combination of great food, service, and wine—that makes an indelible impression on the senses, a meal that lasts a lifetime!

But back in New York City, our challenge is to translate

Jean François Bruel and Toto Ourzdine

traditional culinary experiences into modern recipes. With this book I want to share with you my own French cuisine: where it started and where it is today.

As a French chef in America who loves to bridge my past with the present, I am also influenced by the flavors of the countries I visit, by the cultures I encounter—from Istanbul to Singapore to New Orleans to Rio. Each trip uncovers treasures of culinary discoveries, and these often land in our New York kitchens—from the "Voyage" menu at Café Boulud to DBGB Kitchen and Bar and Boulud Sud.

• • •

OVER THE YEARS, I HAVE BEEN INCREDIBLY FORTUNATE TO WORK with great teammates, friends really, who have shared so much with me. There was Sottha Khunn, who followed me from Le Régence at the Plaza Athénée New York to Le Cirque, where we worked together for eight tough but exciting years; Alex Lee, who started as a commis at Le Cirque and became my executive chef to open the first Daniel on 76th Street in 1993 (now Café Boulud).

Today our ensemble is led by Jean-François Bruel, a 2002 James Beard Rising Star Chef, with me for sixteen years and now, for the last decade executive chef at Daniel, supervising a team of forty chefs and cooks; Eddy Leroux, his right-hand man, chef de cuisine for the last eleven years; and Sébastien Mathieu, one of our excellent sous chefs, with me for five years.

Living together the way we do, night in and night out on such a scale, is a collaborative endeavor. We sit down and share ideas and experiences to create new dishes, but during service, ideas

and techniques boil down to the precision of the finished dish in an exciting burst of pressure and adrenaline. I may be the guiding force, but everyone chimes in.

On the other side of the kitchen pass stands a loyal and disciplined service crew led by a general manager who hires, trains, and achieves the highest level of hospitality. I am particularly proud of the casual sophistication and discreet professionalism of our service team. Michael Lawrence, now our director of operations, was a masterful general manager. Today his protégé, Pierre Siue, who started as a runner at the ripe age of twenty-three and was promoted to GM only six years later, supervises a staff of sixty. He is a great motivator, and with the guests, his elegance and dedication are the benchmarks of his warm demeanor.

Often at Daniel, the staff not only feels like family; they are, in reality, family. The loyal Bernard Vrod, our dining room manager, has served seven American presidents and has worked with me for twenty-five years. His wife, Ginette, is the "gouvernante-in-chief," attending to all housekeeping matters; his sister Cécile works in the coat check; his son Yannick is a maître d'; and his brother-in-law Giovanni a captain. It's an extended Vrod clan on 65th Street! Another vital part of the restaurant, the stewarding department, is led by Toto Ourzdine, a true friend who has worked for me for the last twenty years.

We sit at the table, open a good bottle of wine, and start a vivid conversation. My love affair with wine and the vignerons is an integral part of who I am. Some of my dearest friends come from or work in the wine world. Thanks to them, I enjoy creating wonderful moments around exceptional bottles. Sharing wine with friends always makes it taste even better! Friends like Robert Parker challenge me to create lavish five-hour feasts with legendary wines and iconic dishes. In return, I challenged author/chef Bill Buford to come and cook some of these dishes with me. We had fun, and I hope you will enjoy reading his fabulous account of our time together.

After decades in the kitchen, I am happy to welcome you into our kitchen at Daniel to share our French cuisine. And by now, perhaps, you can see that the story of French cuisine is reflected in the story of my life. I want to cook for you and help you discover new tastes and new pleasures. And nearly every night, on Manhattan's East 65th Street, you will find me at Restaurant Daniel, joyfully flowing from the stove to the dining room and back again.

Clockwise from top left: *At the Citymeals-on-Wheels gala with the team led by former executive chef Alex Lee, my daughter, Alix, and my five mentors—from left in suits: Gérard Nandron, Roger Vergé, Georges Blanc, Paul Bocuse, Michel Guérard; Paul Bocuse sending a copper pot to decorate DBGB Kitchen and Bar; with the Bocuse family—from left: Paul Bocuse, "Petit" Paul, Jérôme Bocuse, and me; toasting with Paul and Jérôme Bocuse in Orlando; Paul Bocuse's sixtieth birthday— standing, from left: me, Pierre Franey, Jacques Maximin, Alain Chapel, Roger Jaloux, Roger Vergé. Sitting: Barbara Kafka, Paul Bocuse.*

Mon Cher Daniel,

It is an honor to be asked to preface what is sure to become a reference for tomorrow's chefs. Between us we share a long history—starting with your days as a young apprentice to my friend Gérard Nandron, where your talent and pugnaciousness did not escape me.

As luck would have it, we saw each other regularly in New York, where you worked for my good friend Roger Vergé at Le Polo, and where each culinary experience felt elegant and distinctive. I knew that one day you would come out of your shell, because to express yourself you just needed a nudge from destiny.

I enjoyed watching your progress at Le Cirque; always as impressive as your skills. A quiet young man with a combination of determination and simplicity, you invested yourself fully to reach the highest level of excellence.

And that is how your Restaurant Daniel, which now celebrates its twentieth anniversary, became the springboard for your spectacular international success.

Your leadership at Daniel inspires in your team the highest standards and ethics. What is most impressive is the mastery you continue to show in developing your art in the kitchen, and the whole community of French chefs is proud to count you as one of their own.

Another reason I am proud of our friendship lies in the fact that this book is also an homage to *la cuisine lyonnaise*, and to the gastronomic roots you have always cultivated so loyally. As time went by, you also became close friends with my son Jérôme, and you are practically family, since you are now my grandson Paul's godfather. I hope that your journey will inspire him.

With All My Admiration,

Paul Bocuse

Paul Bocuse

HOW TO USE THIS BOOK

HOW TO USE THIS BOOK

Restaurant Recipes

These recipes are the same ones our team prepares, but scaled down to home-friendly portions, and only slightly altered to fit most home kitchens' capacities. Start by reading the whole recipe, and as you cook, follow the order of the directions. As you will see, most restaurant recipes use what we have called base recipes—vital elementary preparations such as stock, or optional garnishes such as chips. You can reference these shorter recipes at the back of the book. Feel free to prepare individual components, base, or the complete recipes. You're the chef now!

A Note on Sous-Vide

As you will read, some of the recipes in our book are best prepared by cooking sous-vide, but when other cooking techniques can be substituted, we included those too.

Here are the essential tools for cooking sous-vide: a vacuum sealer, sous-vide bags, thermal circulator, digital thermocouple thermometer, and thermocouple tape. Using the sous-vide technique often guarantees the best, most consistent results, but also poses health risks if not utilized properly. Take extra caution to follow the instructions with precision when preparing sous-vide foods.

Ingredient Guide

In many cases, the headnotes to the recipes mention the source of the star ingredient. Specialty ingredients often include a recommended brand.

Unless otherwise noted, these are the specifics of the basic ingredients:

Butter is unsalted.

Eggs are large.

Flour is all-purpose.

Herbs and juices are fresh.

Milk is whole.

Olive oil is extra-virgin.

Salt is fine sea salt (we recommend La Baleine).

Sugar is granulated.

Gelatin sheets are silver.

Tool Guide

These tools will be helpful as you prepare the restaurant recipes:

Cake tester

Cheesecloth

Clear acetate

Digital scale

Dutch oven (6 quart or larger)

Electric stand mixer with a 4- to 5-quart bowl

Fine-meshed drum sieve (or tamis)

Fine-meshed sieve (or chinois)

Food processor

Hand blender

Heatproof glass or stainless steel bowls

Japanese Chiba Peel S turning slicer

Large, medium, and small saucepans

Rimmed baking sheets (9½ x 13-inch and 13 x 18-inch)

Mandoline

Measuring cups, spoons, and pitcher

One nonreactive baking dish, such as 9 x 9-inch Pyrex

One 8½ x 4½-inch loaf pan

Pastry bags (plastic disposable)

Pastry tips

Rolling pin

Salad spinner

Set of round pastry cutters

Sharp set of knives (at the minimum: butcher, slicing, paring, serrated)

Silpat sheets (one 8 x 11½-inch and two 11¾ x 16½-inch)

Small metal offset spatula

Stem thermometer (we recommend a Thermapen)

Stockpot

Vegetable juicer

Whipped cream maker (we recommend iSi)

At the back of the book, we list sources for tools and ingredients in further detail. You will also find a glossary of culinary terms and ingredients.

Iconic French Dishes

These laborious, traditional French classics, rarely seen on today's menus, are presented as boisterous, adventurous semitutorials in Bill Buford's voice. Cooking with Bill, with his obsessive passion for culinary knowledge, is a reminder of how the history of these grand dishes intermingles with my story and Restaurant Daniel's. I challenged Bill with these blasts from the past. These iconic dishes were researched and rehearsed, but as you will read, some components kept evolving as we went. We prepared them by remembering special meals and chefs, and we did not follow specific recipes. I hope this section will inspire you and that you will appreciate these dishes' resonance in today's cuisine. An attempt to re-create them could seem daunting to say the least, but not impossible with a little research, time, and practice.

Daniel at Home

I trust you will make some of the dishes featured in these home-cooked meals, inspired by some of my favorite regions in France. They have a special place in my heart and have been on my personal menus for friends and family for a long time. As always, take the time to read the instructions thoroughly before you start, since some recipes require marinating or other overnight processes. But don't worry; these are the types of dishes that don't require much attention once your guests arrive. This way you can enjoy the party and delight your crowd at the same time. Feel free to make just part of the menu or the whole thing. Either way, I hope my dishes will become standards in your recipe repertoire.

If you have any questions about sources, ingredients, or recipes along the way, please feel free to reach out to us by e-mailing recipes@danielnyc.com.

PART I
RECIPES FROM RESTAURANT DANIEL

APPETIZERS

PEEKYTOE CRAB ROLLS
GRANNY SMITH APPLE, CELERY, WALNUT

SERVES 6

THIS SMALL CRAB that inhabits the craggy eastern coastline rocks, and particularly the Penobscot Bay in Maine, weighs often less than a pound. It lay there, underutilized by the rest of the world, until one of my favorite suppliers, Rod Mitchell, owner of the Browne Trading Company, decided to "officialize" its slang name. Often called mud or sand crab or even rock crab, the leggy specimen was branded the peekytoe crab. Mitchell got into his truck, drove to New York, and brought us some to taste. Since that day, it has become our crab of choice.

Because they are so delicate, the crabs cannot be shipped alive, so they have to be cooked in Maine and the shells picked, often by the fishermen's wives, very carefully. At the restaurant, we pluck the remainder of the minuscule pieces of shells by placing them in a dark room and flashing a black neon light to highlight every speckle of shell.

In this recipe, the slightly tart apple exalts the sweetness of the crab. Since my days at Le Cirque, I have been playing with flaky crabmeat, celery, and apple in new ways every season, and this recipe is a variation of the original combination.

PEEKYTOE CRAB ROLLS
GRANNY SMITH APPLE, CELERY, WALNUT

Honeycrisp Apple Confit

2 Honeycrisp apples

1 teaspoon celery salt

Salt and freshly ground white pepper

¼ cup walnut oil

Apple Pickle Coins

1 Granny Smith apple

1 cup rice vinegar

3½ tablespoons sugar

Apple Cider Gelée

1½ sheets gelatin

3 cold egg whites

3 cups apple cider

½ tablespoon poppy seeds

Celery Root Chips, Coins, and Puree

Canola oil for frying

1 medium (about 1 pound) celery root, peeled

Salt

1 tablespoon butter

1 cup milk

Freshly ground white pepper

Pomegranate Reduction

2 cups pomegranate juice

½ teaspoon xanthan gum

Apple Celery Sauce

5 Granny Smith apples

1 medium stalk celery

1 teaspoon lemon juice

½ tablespoon cider vinegar
(we recommend Huilerie Beaujolaise)

½ teaspoon walnut oil

½ teaspoon xanthan gum

Crab Salad

1 pound peekytoe crabmeat, picked

1 tablespoon brunoised celery root

1 tablespoon brunoised Honeycrisp apple, reserved

1½ tablespoons Mayonnaise (page 370)

½ tablespoon Orleans mustard

½ tablespoon Dijon mustard

2 tablespoons cider vinegar

1 teaspoon walnut oil

1 tablespoon thinly sliced chives

1 tablespoon chopped chervil

Salt and freshly ground white pepper

3 Granny Smith apples

Juice of 1 lemon

¼ cup crushed walnuts

To Finish

Walnut Glaze (page 376)

¼ cup pomegranate seeds

½ ounce micro celery leaves

6 Apple Skin Chips (page 372)

12 small light green celery leaves

For the Honeycrisp Apple Confit

Peel at least six 3-inch strips from the apples and square off the edges; reserve for apple skin chips. Cut the apples into at least six 2 x ½-inch batons; cut 1 tablespoon of the trim into brunoise for the salad.

Season the apple batons with the celery salt, salt, and pepper and transfer to a small saucepan. Add the walnut oil and set over medium-low heat. Cover and cook, stirring occasionally, until the apples are tender, 10 to 12 minutes. Reserve, chilled.

For the Apple Pickle Coins

Peel the apple and, using a mandoline, cut into ⅛-inch slices. With a 1-inch ring cutter, punch out at least 12 "coins" and place in a shallow heatproof container. In a small sauce-pan, combine the vinegar and sugar and bring to a boil, stirring to dissolve the sugar, then pour the mixture over the coins. Cover and refrigerate for at least 1 hour or up to 3 days.

For the Apple Cider Gelée

Soak the gelatin sheets in a bowl of ice water for 10 minutes; squeeze dry. In a small sauce-pan, whisk the cold egg whites and cider to combine. Place over medium heat and simmer for 10 minutes, undisturbed, allowing the egg whites to cook and form a "raft" on the surface. Remove from the heat and carefully scoop the clarified cider (so as not to break the raft) with a ladle through a fine-meshed sieve. Measure 2 cups clarified cider into a small saucepan, warm to just below a simmer, and stir in the gelatin until dissolved. Cool the liquid to room temperature and stir in the poppy seeds. Pour onto a rimmed baking dish or plate to form a ¼-inch-thick layer. Refriger-ate uncovered, making sure to keep it flat, for 4 hours, or until set. Using a paring knife, slice the gelée into at least six ¼-inch-wide by 1½-inch-long batons. Reserve, chilled.

For the Celery Root Chips, Coins, and Puree

For the chips, fill one-third of a medium saucepan with canola oil and heat to 300°F. Cut the celery root in half. With a mandoline, cut nine ⅛-inch slices from a flat edge. With a 1-inch ring cutter, punch out at least 12 discs; reserve the scraps for the puree. Fry 6 of the discs until crisp but not browned. Drain onto a paper towel–lined tray, sprinkle with salt, and cool.

For the coins, bring a small pot of salted water to a boil and place a bowl of ice water on the side. Boil 6 discs for 30 seconds, then transfer to the ice water to chill. Strain, pat dry, and reserve, chilled.

For the puree, roughly chop the remaining celery root (approximately ¾ pound) from the chips and coins. Place the butter in a medium saucepan over medium heat and cook until browned. Add the celery root, milk, and enough water to cover; bring to a simmer. Cook until tender, about 12 minutes. With a slotted spoon, transfer the celery root to a blender and puree with enough of the cooking liquid to make a smooth puree. Pass through a fine-meshed sieve into a bowl set over ice and season with salt and pepper.

For the Pomegranate Reduction

Place the pomegranate juice in a small saucepan and bring to a simmer. Reduce by two-thirds, then remove from the heat and cool to room temperature. Whisk in the xanthan gum until well combined. Pass through a fine-meshed sieve into a bowl and reserve, chilled.

For the Apple Celery Sauce

Core the apples and cut them into quarters. With a vegetable juicer, juice the apples and celery into a bowl and add the lemon juice. Using a hand blender, mix in the remaining ingredients. Strain through a fine-meshed sieve into a bowl and reserve, chilled.

For the Crab Salad

Up to 1 hour before serving, in a medium bowl, combine the crabmeat, celery root, apple, mayonnaise, mustards, vinegar, walnut oil, chives, and chervil. Season with salt and pepper and reserve, chilled.

With a Japanese Chiba Peel S turning slicer, slice the Granny Smith apples and trim into twelve 8 x 3-inch sheets. On a flat surface, line the sheets of apple vertically in a single layer. Lightly brush lemon juice on both sides. Divide the crab salad on top of each apple sheet into mounds at the end closest to you. One by one, roll the apple sheets away from you into tight rolls around the crab salad. Press a celery root coin against one end of each roll and an apple pickle coin on the other end. Lightly press one end of the crab roll with crushed walnuts to coat. Reserve, chilled.

To Finish

For each serving, brush a streak of walnut glaze onto the bottom of a chilled plate. Place 2 rolls of crab on top. Spoon 3 dots of celery root puree in between the rolls and place a dot of pomegranate reduction, 1 pomegranate seed, and 1 leaf of micro celery in the center of each dot. Rest 1 baton of apple confit against 1 crab roll and 1 baton of apple cider gelée against the other roll. Garnish the rolls with 1 celery root chip, 1 apple skin chip, and 2 celery leaves. Pour approximately 3 tablespoons apple celery sauce onto the plate.

CITRUS-CURED FLUKE
SHISO BAVAROIS, PONZU GELÉE

SERVES 6

WE ALWAYS look for local Long Island fluke for this dish because when it gets to Hunts Point, the vibrant market in the Bronx, the fish literally shimmers as if it just couldn't get any fresher.

At the restaurant, we add freshly grated wasabi, shiso, and soy, an essential Japanese scenario, and then set the stage for this delicate fish cured in salt, sugar, and lemon and lime zest. A creamy shiso bavarois balances the tangy and lean petals of fluke.

CITRUS-CURED FLUKE
SHISO BAVAROIS, PONZU GELÉE

Ponzu Gelée

½ cup soy sauce

1 (2-inch-square) piece dried kombu

½ cup bonito flakes

3 tablespoons mirin

3 tablespoons lemon juice

2 teaspoons orange juice

1 teaspoon sake

2½ sheets gelatin

Roasted Beets

3 baby yellow beets

3 baby red beets

3 baby chioggia (candy stripe) beets

Olive oil

Salt and freshly ground white pepper

Shiso Bavarois

Salt

7½ ounces shiso leaves, stems trimmed

5 sheets gelatin

1 cup heavy cream, whipped to
medium peaks

Edamame Puree

Salt

2 cups edamame beans

½ cup heavy cream

Tabasco sauce

Salt and freshly ground white pepper

Beet Reduction

1 cup fresh red beet juice

⅛ teaspoon xanthan gum

Sesame Dressing

3 tablespoons olive oil

1 tablespoon sesame oil

1 tablespoon sherry vinegar

1 tablespoon lime juice

Salt and freshly ground white pepper

Cured Fluke

1 cup kosher salt

½ cup sugar

Finely grated zest of 2 lemons

Finely grated zest of 2 limes

2 (6-ounce) skinless, boneless fluke fillets

2 tablespoons olive oil

2 teaspoons grated fresh wasabi

Salt and freshly ground white pepper

To Finish

6 rectangular (5 x 1-inch) seaweed croutons
(see Melba Croutons, page 372)

¼ cup micro shiso

¼ cup red seaweed salad (aka-tosaka)

*"Whole fluke meunière was the norm during my Copenhagen days.
Then Japanese chefs taught us the pleasure of raw."*

For the Ponzu Gelée

In a small bowl, combine all the ingredients except the gelatin with 3 tablespoons water, cover, and refrigerate for 48 hours. Strain. Soak the gelatin sheets in a bowl of ice water for 10 minutes; squeeze dry. In a small saucepan, heat one-quarter of the strained liquid to just below a simmer. Remove from the heat, stir in the gelatin to dissolve, add the remaining liquid, and strain into a flat, rimmed container to reach ¼-inch thickness. Refrigerate, flat, for 4 hours, or until firm. Cut into ¼-inch cubes. Reserve, chilled.

For the Roasted Beets

Preheat the oven to 350°F. In a medium bowl, toss each variety of beet separately with olive oil to coat and season with salt and pepper. Wrap them separately in aluminum foil packets and place them on a baking sheet. Bake for 45 minutes, or until tender. Remove and, once cooled enough to handle but still warm, peel and discard the skin. Cut the beets into ¼-inch slices and cut into decorative shapes such as rectangles, diamonds, or circles. Reserve, chilled.

For the Shiso Bavarois

Bring a medium pot filled with salted water to a boil; place a bowl of ice water on the side. Boil the shiso for 20 seconds. Strain and chill in the ice water. Squeeze dry and transfer to a blender along with 2 tablespoons ice water. Puree until very smooth but still thick, adding more water only if needed. Strain through a fine-meshed sieve.

Soak the gelatin sheets in ice water for 10 minutes; squeeze dry. In a small saucepan over low heat, heat one-third of the shiso puree, then stir in the gelatin until dissolved. In a medium bowl, combine the warm shiso puree with the remaining puree. While the mixture is still slightly warm, fold in the whipped cream until no streaks remain, then season with salt. Spread the mixture onto a parchment-lined baking pan in a ½-inch layer and freeze, uncovered. Once frozen, cut into six 4½ x 1-inch rectangles, cover, and refrigerate.

For the Edamame Puree

Bring a medium pot of salted water to a boil and place a bowl of ice water on the side. Add the edamame and boil for 1 minute, or until tender. Strain and chill in the ice water; reserve 30 beans for garnish. Place the remaining edamame in a blender. Heat the cream to a simmer and, while the blender is running, stream in the cream to make a smooth, thick puree. Pass through a fine-meshed sieve; season with Tabasco, salt, and pepper and reserve, chilled.

For the Beet Reduction

In a small saucepan over medium heat, reduce the beet juice to ½ cup. Whisk in the xanthan gum until dissolved. Reserve, chilled.

For the Sesame Dressing

In a small bowl, whisk all the ingredients to combine, and season with salt and pepper. Reserve, chilled.

For the Cured Fluke

In a nonreactive container, combine the salt, sugar, and zests. Add the fluke and pack the salt mixture around to coat completely. Refrigerate for 45 minutes. Remove the fluke, rinse off and discard the salt mixture, and pat dry.

With a sharp slicing knife, starting at the tail end, cut the fillets diagonally against the grain into ⅛-inch slices. On a flat surface lined with plastic wrap, arrange the fish slices in a single layer and season with the olive oil, wasabi, and salt and pepper. Top with more plastic wrap and gently pound with a meat mallet to flatten into thin, translucent petals. Reserve, chilled.

To Finish

When ready to serve, season the beets and fluke separately with sesame dressing to taste.

For each serving, place a rectangle of bavarois at the center of a chilled plate and top with a crouton. Arrange 3 or 4 petals of fluke on top of the crouton to resemble waves. Garnish the perimeter with a line of 5 edamame puree dots, alternating with pieces of diced ponzu gelée. Top the puree dots with the reserved edamame. Swipe a line of beet reduction at a right angle to the line of edamame and gelée and arrange 3 pieces (one of each color) of beets in front. Garnish the top of the fluke with micro shiso and red seaweed salad.

NANTUCKET SCALLOP CEVICHE
BLOOD ORANGE SAUCE

SERVES 4

ON THE EAST COAST, November through March represents the blessed season of the sweet Nantucket bay scallop. Winter and its cortege of meats, stews, and deep flavors seem to plead for lighter appetizers such as this sweet and sour citrus ceviche symphony. Blood orange, lime, lemon, and one of our house favorites, Buddha's hand citron confit, all conspire to create the base for a tangy and colorful tide.

Blood Orange Sauce

½ cup blood orange juice

1 tablespoon lime juice

1 tablespoon lemon juice

2 tablespoons red verjus (we recommend 8 Brix)

1 tablespoon olive oil

1 splash of Tabasco sauce

Salt and freshly ground white pepper

Scallop Ceviche

¼ cup orange juice

2 tablespoons lemon juice

2 tablespoons lime juice

2 tablespoons white verjus (we recommend 8 Brix)

¼ teaspoon sugar

Salt

20 fresh bay scallops, muscle removed

To Finish

Good-quality olive oil (we recommend Armando Manni Per Mio Figlio)

Salt and freshly ground white pepper

1 blood orange, cut into supremes

2 red radishes, cut into brunoise

1 tablespoon brunoised celery

Freshly grated zest of 1 lime

1 tablespoon nori sheet, cut into ¼-inch squares

2 red radishes, thinly sliced

2 tablespoons Buddha's Hand Citron Confit (page 377)

¼ cup small opal basil leaves

¼ cup yellow celery leaves

12 dill leaves

Chive Oil (see Green Herb Oil, page 376)

For the Blood Orange Sauce
In a small bowl, whisk all the ingredients together; season with salt and pepper and reserve, chilled.

For the Scallop Ceviche
In a medium bowl, whisk the orange juice, lemon juice, lime juice, white verjus, sugar, and ¼ teaspoon salt until the sugar and salt are dissolved; cover and reserve, chilled. Rinse the scallops in cold water and pat dry.

Add the scallops to the juice 45 minutes before you are ready to serve and toss to coat.

To Finish
Strain the juice from the scallops, then adjust the seasoning with the olive oil, salt, and pepper.

For each serving, arrange 5 scallops and 4 blood orange supremes into a circle in a chilled bowl. Add a sprinkling of brunoised radish and celery, lime zest, nori sheet, a few radish slices, and a few slices of Buddha's hand citron confit. Garnish the top with 3 opal basil, celery leaves, and dill leaves. At the table, pour in blood orange sauce to reach halfway up the scallops and drizzle a few drops of chive oil and olive oil on top.

SPANISH MACKEREL AU VIN BLANC
POACHED WITH CARROT MOUSSELINE, LETTUCE-WRAPPED TARTAR WITH CAVIAR

SERVES 8

A TYPICAL BISTRO DISH, maquereau au vin blanc has always been an affordable staple on menus throughout France, but was certainly not the kind of fish you found in gastronomic restaurants. Since mackerel is one of my favorites at the sushi bar, I thought we could highlight its versatility by presenting it raw and poached, our own interpretation of the classic.

SPANISH MACKEREL AU VIN BLANC
POACHED WITH CARROT MOUSSELINE,
LETTUCE-WRAPPED TARTAR WITH CAVIAR

Poached Mackerel and Pickled Vegetables

1 (3- to 4-pound) Spanish mackerel

2¾ cups white wine

1½ cups white wine vinegar

1 sachet (½ teaspoon each coriander seeds and black peppercorns and 4 sprigs of tarragon, wrapped in cheesecloth and secured with butcher's twine)

¼ cup small-diced red onion, plus 3 table-spoons cut into thin ½-inch-long slices

¼ cup small-diced leek, white and light green parts only, plus 3 tablespoons cut into thin ½-inch diamonds

¼ cup small-diced carrot, plus 3 table-spoons cut into thin ½-inch discs with a ring cutter

White Wine Gelée

½ cup reserved poaching liquid from above

1 gram vegetable gelatin (carrageenan)

Carrot Mousseline

1 teaspoon butter

1 cup small-diced carrot

¼ cup fresh carrot juice

1 (¼-inch) piece ginger, peeled

⅛ teaspoon freshly ground cumin

Salt

Lettuce Puree

1 tablespoon grapeseed oil

2 ounces peeled and diced russet potato

2½ ounces small-diced onion

Salt

2 heads Bibb lettuce

Mackerel Tartar

6½ ounces skinless, boneless mackerel fillet, reserved from above

½ teaspoon lemon zest

1 teaspoon lemon juice

1½ tablespoons olive oil

½ teaspoon grated fresh wasabi

Salt and freshly ground white pepper

8 blanched Bibb lettuce leaves, reserved from above

To Finish

8 tarragon leaves

¼ cup micro celery leaves

¼ cup golden osetra caviar

2 tablespoons crème fraîche

24 Lemon Confit strips (page 377)

24 small romaine lettuce leaves, cut into 1½-inch spears

For the Poached Mackerel and Pickled Vegetables

Using a sharp knife, carve the fillets from the mackerel. Chop the bones into roughly 1-inch pieces. Rinse the bones, head, and tail in cold water, and reserve them for the poaching liquid. Trim the thin belly meat from the fillets and slice the thicker ends of the fillets into 4 approximately 1½-inch diamonds. Lightly score the skin of each diamond with 4 to 5 parallel incisions and set aside. Remove the skin from the remaining flesh. Reserve the fish, chilled.

In a large heavy-bottomed saucepan, combine the bones, head, tail, 4 cups water, the wine, vinegar, and sachet, the small-diced red onion, leek, and carrot. Simmer lightly for 35 minutes, skimming off any foam that rises to the surface. Strain the liquid through a fine-meshed sieve into a clean saucepan and discard the solids. Measure ½ cup of the liquid for the gelée and reserve, chilled.

Arrange the mackerel diamonds in a single layer in a heatproof baking dish. Bring the liquid to a simmer and add the sliced red onion, leek diamonds, and carrot discs; simmer for 1 to 2 minutes, until tender. Immediately pour over the mackerel and rest at room temperature for 5 minutes. Transfer to the refrigerator to cool completely, then cover, keeping the fish in the liquid.

For the White Wine Gelée

Transfer the reserved ½ cup poaching liquid to a small saucepan, and using a hand blender, mix in the vegetable gelatin. Bring to a simmer, then pour onto a rimmed plate or baking dish to reach ⅛-inch thickness. Refrigerate, uncovered, being sure to keep it flat, until it firms, about 2 hours. Using a paring knife, cut out 8 diamonds the same size as the poached mackerel diamonds.

For the Carrot Mousseline

Melt the butter in a medium saucepan over medium heat. Add the carrot and cook, stirring, without coloring, for 3 minutes. Add the carrot juice, ginger, and cumin and bring to a simmer. Cook, stirring occasionally, until the carrots are tender. Discard the ginger and transfer the mixture to a blender. Puree until smooth, then pass through a fine-meshed sieve into a bowl. Chill the bowl over ice, then season with salt.

For the Lettuce Puree

Heat the oil in a small saucepan over medium-low heat. Add the potato and onion. Cook, stirring, without browning, for 10 to 15 minutes, until very tender; set aside. Bring a large pot of salted water to a boil and place a bowl of ice water on the side. Separate 8 of the largest leaves from the lettuce heads. Boil for 5 seconds, strain, and chill in the ice water. Being careful not to tear, remove the leaves from the ice water, pat dry, and reserve for

the tartar. Separate the remaining leaves from the stems and boil them for 20 seconds, then strain and chill in the ice water. Squeeze dry and transfer to a blender with the cooked potato and onion. Puree until smooth, pass through a fine-meshed sieve into a bowl, and chill over ice. If needed, adjust the seasoning with salt and reserve, chilled.

For the Mackerel Tartar

Finely dice the reserved fish and transfer to a bowl over ice. Stir in the lemon zest and juice, olive oil, wasabi, and salt and pepper. Line a flat surface with a 24-inch-square double layer of plastic wrap. Arrange 4 of the boiled lettuce leaves on the plastic in a horizontal, overlapping 12-inch-long line. Arrange half of the fish tartar in a horizontal line in the center of the lettuce leaves. Using the plastic wrap as an aid, begin rolling the lettuce up and away from you, tucking it tightly against the fish, and then roll forward to completely enrobe it. Roll the tartar in the

plastic a few times to tighten into an approximately ½-inch-diameter log, then tie off the ends of the plastic. Repeat the process with the remaining lettuce leaves and fish. Chill well, at least 2 hours, and using a sharp knife, slice each plastic-wrapped roll into 12 cylinders. Gently peel off the plastic and reserve, chilled.

To Finish

For each serving, place a spoonful of carrot puree on a chilled plate and place a piece of poached mackerel, skin side up, in the center. Top the fish with a leaf of tarragon and then a gelée diamond to cover. Arrange a few of the pickled vegetables and micro celery leaves over and around the diamond. Stand 3 cylinders of tartar in a line with 4 dots of lettuce puree in between on an opposite side of the plate. Top each cylinder with a teaspoon of caviar, a dot of crème fraîche, and a small strip of the confit lemon zest. Rest 3 romaine leaves against the tartar cylinders.

CARAWAY-CURED TAI SNAPPER
CUCUMBER AND DILL BROTH

SERVES 6

I LOVE THE COMBINATION of citrusy cured fish with fresh and crisp crudités boosted with zest and spices. Here we choose tai snapper, which is cured with salt, sugar, and citrus zest and then sprinkled with citrus juice so that it retains a rather firm texture. The palette flavor in this ceviche is in fact quite Scandinavian, with dill, cucumber, and caraway, a hint of my time in Denmark. A touch of mint in the cucumber broth, poured tableside, brightens the taste. Tapioca and radish pearls provide a contrasting texture, while the briny caviar crowns the dish.

Tai Snapper Ceviche

½ cup kosher salt

¼ cup sugar

Finely grated zest of 2 lemons

Finely grated zest of 2 limes

2 teaspoons ground toasted caraway seeds

2 (4-ounce) boneless, skinless tai snapper fillets

1 tablespoon lemon juice

1 tablespoon lime juice

1 tablespoon olive oil

Salt and freshly ground white pepper

Dill Glaze

¼ cup Dill Oil
(see Green Herb Oil, page 376)

1⅔ teaspoons glycerin monostearate

Cucumber Broth

2 English cucumbers (1½ pounds), chopped

1 stalk celery, chopped

3 leaves mint, chopped

2 tablespoons olive oil

2 tablespoons white balsamic vinegar

Tabasco sauce

Salt and freshly ground white pepper

¼ teaspoon xanthan gum

Tapioca Pearls

2 tablespoons large tapioca pearls

Salt

1 tablespoon olive oil

To Finish

1 bunch red or breakfast radishes

6 Melba Croutons (page 372), cut into a half-moon shape to fit in the bowls

1½ ounces golden osetra caviar

¼ cup micro sea cress

For the Tai Snapper Ceviche

In a shallow, nonreactive dish, combine the salt, sugar, zests, and caraway seeds. Add the fish and coat with the mixture on all sides. Cover and refrigerate for 20 minutes. Remove the fish from the cure, rinse, pat dry, and cut into ½-inch cubes. Reserve, chilled. When ready to serve, season the fish with the lemon juice, lime juice, olive oil, and salt and pepper.

For the Dill Glaze

In a small saucepan, combine the dill oil and glycerin monostearate and place over medium-low heat. Cook, stirring, just until the glycerin monostearate is dissolved. Chill over ice and store, refrigerated.

For the Cucumber Broth

Combine the cucumbers, celery, mint, olive oil, and vinegar in a blender and puree on high speed until smooth. Season with Tabasco sauce, salt, and pepper. Add the xanthan gum and blend to combine. Pass through a fine-meshed sieve into a bowl set over ice and stir until very cold. Reserve, chilled, in a sauce pitcher.

For the Tapioca Pearls

Place the tapioca in a small saucepan, cover with water, and sprinkle lightly with salt.

Boil until cooked and translucent, about 20 minutes. Strain, transfer to a small bowl, and toss with the olive oil. Reserve, chilled.

To Finish

With a mandoline, thinly slice half of the radishes into a bowl of ice water. Slice 2 radishes into julienne. Use a very small Parisienne scoop to form balls from the remaining radishes, or cut them into small dice. When ready to serve, brush the inside of 6 chilled wide-rim pasta or soup bowls up to the rims evenly with dill glaze. Divide the snapper, sliced and julienned radishes, tapioca, and radish pearls (or dice) into the bowls.

Top each serving with a crouton and place a spoonful of caviar on top. Garnish with micro sea cress. Pour cucumber broth into the bowls at the table so as not to soften the bread, filling the bowls from the side to reach two-thirds of the way up the fish.

LANGOUSTINE AND UNI CHAUD-FROID

SERVES 4

ONE OF MY FONDEST memories of vacationing on the Mediterranean is picking up sea urchins and eating them raw, accompanied by a nice and fresh Blanc de Provence. Once, near Menton, one of our sommeliers, Olivier Flosse, and his parents took me to an isolated creek to fish for urchins. Well, we almost got arrested because unbeknownst to us, the legal season for picking urchins had just ended!

This chaud-froid combines creamy sea urchin custard and a flavorful langoustine broth transformed into a gelée. The Scottish langoustines, the most refined saltwater shellfish, lacquered with more gelée, support plump grains of caviar. At the center of the plate, avocado espuma, a delicate mousse, acts as the vegetable coda.

Langoustine Broth

1 tablespoon sugar

1½ tablespoons kosher salt

16 live Scottish langoustines,
in their shells

½ tablespoon minced fresh ginger

1½ stalks lemongrass, peeled
and chopped

½ teaspoon crushed Szechuan
peppercorns

½ teaspoon fennel seeds

¼ teaspoon cracked black peppercorns

¼ teaspoon coriander seeds

Leaves of 2 sprigs tarragon, chopped

Fennel Pollen Tuile

Tuile Batter (page 374)

1 teaspoon fennel pollen

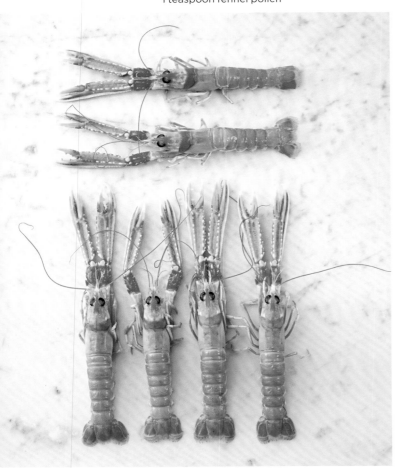

Sea Urchin Custard

1 cup heavy cream

2¾ ounces sea urchin roe

2 egg yolks

¼ teaspoon salt

¼ teaspoon lemon juice

1 splash of Tabasco sauce

1 pinch of piment d'Espelette

Glazed Langoustine Tails,
Chayote, and Fennel

Salt

1 small head fennel with stalks

1 small chayote

2½ sheets gelatin

¼ teaspoon lemon juice

Freshly ground white pepper,
if needed

¼ ounce vegetable gelatin
(carrageenan)

Avocado Espuma

1 ripe avocado

2 teaspoons lemon juice

¼ teaspoon xanthan gum

Salt and freshly ground
white pepper

To Finish

8 pieces sea urchin roe,
halved widthwise

2 tablespoons golden osetra caviar

¼ cup fennel fronds, reserved
from above

¼ cup sea cress leaves

8 oyster leaves, cut into diamonds

16 Lemon Confit strips (page 377)

1 teaspoon fennel pollen

Olive oil

2 finger limes

For the Langoustine Broth

In a large saucepan, combine 1 gallon of water with the sugar and 1 tablespoon of the salt; bring to a boil and place a bowl of ice water on the side. Twist and reserve the claws of the langoustines and discard the heads. Grasp the middle fin of the tails and gently twist and pull off to remove the veins. Boil the langoustine tails for 10 seconds, then immediately strain and transfer to the ice water to chill. Peel and discard the shells.

Transfer half of the langoustine claws to the bowl of an electric mixer fitted with a paddle and begin to mix on low speed for 1 minute to break them into smaller chunks. Add the remaining claws and continue mixing for another minute, then increase the speed to medium and mix until they break down into a mash. Add the remaining ½ tablespoon salt, the ginger, lemongrass, Szechuan peppercorns, fennel seeds, black peppercorns, coriander seeds, and tarragon and mix until well combined. Transfer the mixture to a medium saucepan and cover with 1 quart water. Gently stir a few times, then place over medium heat. Bring to a gentle simmer, undisturbed, allowing the mixture to form a solid mass, or raft. Once the raft begins to rise to the surface, gently poke a hole in the top. Continue to gently simmer for 20 minutes, occasionally basting the raft by ladling broth from the hole. Carefully strain the liquid by ladling through a fine-meshed sieve lined with 3 layers of wet cheesecloth. Reserve the liquid, chilled.

For the Fennel Pollen Tuile

Preheat the oven to 300°F. Line a baking sheet with a Silpat and, using a 1½-inch-wide teardrop-shaped stencil and a small offset spatula, spread the batter onto the sheet to make at least 4 tuiles. Sprinkle lightly with the fennel pollen and bake for 8 minutes, or until golden brown. Cool, then store in an airtight container at room temperature.

For the Sea Urchin Custard

Preheat the oven to 200°F. Combine all the ingredients in a blender, puree just until smooth, and pass the mixture through a fine-meshed sieve into a bowl. Divide into 4 serving bowls with a 4-inch inset diameter to form ¼-inch-thick layers. Cover the bowls with plastic wrap and set inside a large roasting pan. Pour hot water into the roasting pan around the bowls to reach the level of the custard. Bake for 20 minutes, or until the custard is set. Remove the bowls from the water and rest for 15 minutes at room temperature. Unwrap and refrigerate until chilled, making sure to keep the bowls flat.

For the Glazed Langoustine Tails, Chayote, and Fennel

Bring a large pot of salted water to a boil and place a bowl of ice water on the side. Trim the fennel, pick and reserve ¼ cup of the fronds, separate the layers of the bulb, and peel the outer sides of the layers. Using a ¾-inch-diameter ring cutter, punch out at least 8 "coins." Peel the chayote and cut into ¼-inch slices. Cut at least eight ½-inch triangles from the slices. Boil the fennel and chayote in separate batches until tender, then transfer to the ice water to chill. Strain and pat dry with paper towels.

Soak the gelatin sheets in ice water for 10 minutes, then squeeze dry. Pour the langoustine broth into a large saucepan and heat it to 135°F. Season the broth with the lemon juice and, if needed, salt and pepper. Submerge the langoustine tails in the broth and gently poach for 5 minutes, or until just cooked through. Pour the broth with the langoustines into a large bowl set over ice and stir until well chilled. Strain the broth through a fine-meshed sieve lined with cheesecloth and adjust the seasoning with salt and pepper if needed.

Pour 1 cup of the broth into a small saucepan (reserving the remaining), place over medium heat, and whisk in the vegetable gelatin. Bring to a simmer, while whisking, for 30 seconds, then remove from the heat and cool to 95°F. Individually dip four langoustine tails into the cooled broth and arrange on a bowl of custard. Dip 2 fennel coins and 2 chayote triangles into the gelée and set on the custard, alternating in between the langoustines. Repeat the process with the remaining 3 bowls of custard. Return the bowls to the refrigerator and chill for 15 minutes, or until set.

Pour 1 cup of the remaining broth into a small saucepan, bring to a simmer, then remove from the heat and stir in the gelatin sheets until dissolved. Cool to room temperature and pour approximately 2 tablespoons onto each bowl to cover the custard in a thin layer. Return to the refrigerator to set the gelée, about 1 hour.

For the Avocado Espuma

Pit the avocado and scoop the flesh into a blender with the remaining ingredients and 6 tablespoons cold water. Puree until smooth. Pass through a fine-meshed sieve and transfer to the canister of a whipped cream maker. Insert a nitrogen cartridge and reserve, chilled.

To Finish

For each serving, place a piece of sea urchin roe next to each langoustine and place a small spoonful of caviar on top of each langoustine. Squeeze approximately 1 tablespoon of avocado espuma in the center of the bowl and lean a fennel pollen tuile next to it. Garnish the top of the custard with 2 fennel fronds, 4 sea cress leaves, 2 oyster leaf diamonds, and 4 lemon confit strips; sprinkle some fennel pollen over the top and drizzle with a few drops of olive oil. Halve the finger limes and squeeze about ¼ teaspoon of finger lime juice pellets over the top of the custard.

CHILLED SALMON
À L'OSEILLE

SERVES 4

IN THE 1970S, Chefs Jean and Pierre Troisgros created one of the most famous recipes of the nouvelle cuisine era: escalope de saumon à l'oseille. Everything about it was revolutionary: the searing technique with no fat and no color as it warmed up in the nonstick pan, the fish cooked medium-rare only, and the extraordinary balance of richness and acidity of the sauce.

When the spring brings back the wild salmon and the harvest of the sorrel, inspired by this classic marriage, we prepare our favorite salmon three ways: raw, cured, and poached.

Luscious tartare from the belly is topped with lightly smoked trout caviar and encased in a ring of phyllo; the tail end gets cured Scandinavian style, and a log of poached salmon from the thickest part of the loin is held between two discs of hearts of palm. Fresh, vibrant sorrel finds its way onto each preparation, lending its unique tart and grassy flavor.

Crispy Phyllo Ring

3 sheets phyllo dough

3 tablespoons Clarified Butter (page 377), melted

Salt

½ teaspoon ground lemon omani

King Salmon

1 (14-ounce) boneless, skinless king salmon fillet, preferably from the thickest end

Poached Salmon

4 (3 x 1-inch) salmon batons, reserved from above

Salt and freshly ground white pepper

4 small sorrel leaves

Cured Salmon

¼ cup kosher salt

2 tablespoons sugar

Finely grated zest of 1 lemon

Finely grated zest of 1 lime

1 (4 x 2½-inch) salmon rectangle, reserved from above

1 sorrel leaf, cut into four 1½ x ¼-inch rectangles

1 tablespoon olive oil

Salmon Tartar

Diced salmon, reserved from above

Finely grated zest of 1 lemon

2 teaspoons olive oil

Grated fresh wasabi

Salt and freshly ground white pepper

Baby Turnips and Snap Peas

Salt

3 baby turnips, peeled, with their greens

2 snap peas

Lemon Crème Fraîche

¼ cup crème fraîche

Finely grated zest of 1 lemon

Salt and freshly ground white pepper

Sorrel Coulis

Salt

1 egg, in the shell

½ cup Chicken Stock (page 368)

10 ounces sorrel leaves, chopped

1 tablespoon Dijon mustard

½ teaspoon xanthan gum

Quail Eggs

4 quail eggs

Fleur de sel

Freshly ground black pepper

To Finish

Olive oil

Salt and freshly ground white pepper

2 tablespoons (1 ounce) Washington State steelhead trout caviar (we recommend River & Glen)

4 micro wood sorrel leaves

4 baby turnip leaves, reserved from above

8 thinly sliced ¾-inch diameter discs fresh hearts of palm

4 hearts of palm matchsticks

8 micro red ribbon sorrel leaves

For the Crispy Phyllo Ring

Preheat the oven to 300°F. Lay 1 sheet of dough on a cutting board and brush evenly with clarified butter. Sprinkle a pinch of salt over the top. Press a second sheet of phyllo on top and repeat the process. Add a third layer, brush with clarified butter, and sprinkle with lemon omani powder. Cut into 1-inch-wide strips. Wrap the strips with the lemon omani side out around four 1¼-inch-diameter ring molds. Transfer to a baking sheet and bake for 15 minutes, or until golden brown. Cool to room temperature, gently slide from the molds, and store in an airtight container.

For the King Salmon

Cut a 4 x 2½-inch rectangle from the center of the fillet for curing. Cut the remaining fillet into four 3 x 1-inch batons for poaching. Cut the trim into small dice for the tartar.

For the Poached Salmon

Using an immersion circulator, heat a water bath to 133°F and set a bowl of ice water on the side. *Alternately, heat a large saucepan filled halfway with water to 133°F, and maintain the temperature as best as possible using a stem thermometer.* Sprinkle the 4 salmon batons lightly with salt and pepper, and place a sorrel leaf on top of each one. Wrap each baton by laying a sheet of plastic wrap on a flat surface, setting the baton in the center, and rolling it up in the plastic into a tight cylinder. Tie off the ends to secure. Submerge in the water bath and cook until their internal temperatures reach 124°F, about 10 minutes. Chill in the ice water and reserve, chilled.

For the Cured Salmon

In a shallow nonreactive container, combine the salt, sugar, and zests. Add the rectangular piece of salmon fillet and pack the mixture around it to coat. Cover and refrigerate for 40 minutes. Rinse the salt mixture from the salmon and pat dry. Cut the salmon against the grain into 12 slices, transfer to a tray, cover, and reserve, chilled. Arrange the sorrel leaf rectangles on another tray, brush with olive oil, cover, and chill for 30 minutes.

For the Salmon Tartar

Up to 1 hour before serving, mix the diced salmon with the lemon zest and olive oil, and season with wasabi, salt, and pepper. Allow to rest for 5 minutes, then adjust the seasoning as necessary with more salt and pepper.

For the Baby Turnips and Snap Peas

Bring a medium pot of salted water to a boil and place a bowl of ice water on the side. Pick at least 4 small leaves from the turnips and reserve, wrapped in wet paper towels, for garnishing. Trim the stems and boil the turnips for 45 seconds, or until tender. Halve 2 turnips stem to tip and quarter the third. Boil the snap peas for 1 minute, chill in the ice water, and split them. Reserve the vegetables, chilled.

For the Lemon Crème Fraîche

In a small bowl, combine the crème fraîche with the lemon zest and season with salt and pepper. Keep chilled.

For the Sorrel Coulis

Bring a medium saucepan of salted water to a boil and place a bowl of ice water on the side. Add the egg and simmer in the water for 3 minutes, then remove and chill in the ice water (you can reserve the boiling water for the quail eggs). Pour the chicken stock into a small saucepan and bring to a simmer. Crack the egg and scoop it into a blender with the hot stock and the remaining ingredients along with ½ teaspoon salt. Puree until smooth. Pass through a fine-meshed sieve into a bowl set over ice and stir until chilled.

For the Quail Eggs

Boil the eggs for 2½ minutes, then submerge them in ice water to chill. Peel the eggs and slice them in half lengthwise; sprinkle with fleur de sel and pepper.

To Finish

In a small bowl, lightly season the turnips and peas with olive oil, salt, and pepper.

For each serving, place a crispy phyllo ring in the center of a chilled plate and fill two-thirds to the top with salmon tartar. Top with a layer of lemon crème fraîche, then spoon an even layer of caviar on top; finish with a leaf of micro wood sorrel. On one side of the plate, arrange 3 slices of cured salmon in a square shape and top with a rectangle of sorrel, 1 half and 1 quarter of turnip, 1 snap pea half, 1 quail egg half, and 1 baby turnip leaf. Place a poached salmon cylinder on the other side of the plate and press 2 discs of hearts of palm at the ends. Spoon sorrel sauce on top to completely cover, then top with a heart of palm matchstick and 2 leaves of micro red ribbon sorrel.

POACHED CAROLINA SHRIMP
SUMMER MELONS, LEMON BALM

SERVES 6

I HAVE combined shrimp and melon in many different ways, but sometimes, as in this simple presentation, we just let the ingredients speak for themselves. Poached lemon balm–infused shrimp seem to watch over an aureole of several different melons. My favorite shrimp come from the Gulf Coast in South Carolina. I would compare their flavor to the French crevettes roses or bouquet shrimp from the North Atlantic.

POACHED CAROLINA SHRIMP
SUMMER MELONS, LEMON BALM

Pickled Watermelon Rind (makes extra)

8 ounces watermelon rind

1 cup Pickling Liquid (page 377)

1 teaspoon Szechuan peppercorns

Poached Shrimp

2 quarts Court Bouillon (page 369)

2 ounces lemon balm sprigs

30 medium shrimp, peeled and deveined

Compressed Melons

7 (½-inch) slices of summer melons (such as watermelon, canary, cantaloupe, casaba, charentais, galia, honeydew, and orange flesh honeydew)

2 ounces lemon balm springs

Lime Sauce

8 limes

¼ cup sugar

¼ cup olive oil

Lime Gelée

1 egg white

⅔ cup lime juice, reserved from above

⅓ cup sugar

1.5 grams agar-agar

Charentais Melon Coulis

6 ounces ripe charentais melon, roughly chopped

1 sachet (½ teaspoon each fennel seeds, coriander seeds, and black peppercorns wrapped in cheesecloth and secured with butcher's twine)

½ cup heavy cream

⅛ teaspoon xanthan gum

1 pinch of salt

To Finish

Olive oil

Salt and freshly ground white pepper

¼ cup small lemon balm leaves

Lemon Balm Oil
(see Green Herb Oil, page 376)

For the Pickled Watermelon Rind
Use a small knife to trim and discard the green skin from the white part of the rind. With a mandoline, slice the white rind into ⅛-inch-thick slices. Cut the slices into 1-inch strips and then cut the strips on a diagonal into diamonds. Place the diamonds in a small, heatproof bowl. In a small saucepan, combine the pickling liquid and Szechuan peppercorns and bring to a simmer. Pour over the watermelon rind, cover, and infuse at room temperature for 5 minutes. Reserve, chilled.

For the Poached Shrimp
In a medium saucepan, bring 1 quart of the court bouillon to a boil and stir in the lemon balm. Pour the remaining 1 quart court bouillon into a bowl set over ice. Arrange the shrimp in a single layer in a baking dish and pour the hot liquid over the shrimp, making sure they are submerged. Steep for 2 minutes, or until the shrimp are cooked through. Strain the shrimp and transfer them to the court bouillon set over ice; stir until chilled. Trim the ends of the shrimp so they can stand. Reserve, chilled.

For the Compressed Melons
Place melon slices in a single layer in sous-vide bags, dividing them by variety, and divide the lemon balm into the bags. Vacuum-seal the melon and refrigerate for at least 4 hours or up to 4 days.

For the Lime Sauce
With a vegetable peeler, peel the zest from the limes in long strips. Squeeze and reserve the juice from the limes. Use a paring knife to remove any remaining white pith from the strips. Place the strips in a small saucepan, cover with cold water, and bring to a simmer. Strain and repeat the process 3 more times. Strain, return the zest to the pan, and add ½ cup water and the sugar. Simmer until the sugar is dissolved. Transfer the mixture to a blender with 3 tablespoons of the lime juice (save the remaining juice for the gelée) and puree until smooth. Stream in the olive oil until emulsified. Pass the puree through a fine-meshed sieve, transfer to a piping bag, and reserve, chilled.

For the Lime Gelée
In a small saucepan, whisk the egg white until frothy, then whisk in the lime juice. Place over medium heat and bring to a simmer, allowing the egg white to rise to the surface and clarify the juice. Strain through a fine-meshed sieve. In a separate saucepan, bring ½ cup water with the sugar to a simmer until dissolved. Whisk in the strained lime juice and the agar-agar and bring to a simmer. Remove from the heat and pour onto a rimmed dinner plate or small baking dish. Refrigerate until firm, then use a ½-inch ring cutter to punch out discs of gelée. Reserve, chilled.

For the Charentais Melon Coulis
Place the melon and sachet in a medium sauté pan over medium-low heat and cook, stirring, until the melon begins to break apart and its juice reduces to a syrup, about 5 minutes. Add the heavy cream, bring to a simmer, and reduce by one-third, about 8 minutes. Discard the sachet, transfer to a blender, add the xanthan gum and salt, and puree until smooth. Pass through a fine-meshed sieve into a bowl set over ice. Stir until chilled and thickened. Transfer to a piping bag and reserve, chilled.

To Finish
Season the poached shrimp with olive oil and salt and pepper.

Cut the compressed melon into desired shapes and divide among 6 chilled salad plates. (For the photo, the melon was cut with a ring cutter into half-crescent moon shapes and arranged into a pinwheel.)

For each serving, brush the melon with olive oil and sprinkle with salt and pepper. Stand 5 shrimp around the melon and garnish with 3 lime gelée discs, 4 watermelon rind pickles, several dots of lime sauce and charentais melon coulis, and a few small lemon balm leaves. Drizzle lemon balm oil onto the plate.

1. Canary, 2. Watermelon, 3. Galia, 4. Cantaloupe, 5. Honeydew,
6. Yellow watermelon, 7. Charentais, 8. Orange flesh honeydew, 9. Casaba

ECKERTON HILL FARM HEIRLOOM TOMATO TASTING

SERVES 6

EACH COMPONENT of this tomato tasting can be found at one or another of our restaurants during the summer, but in this Daniel appetizer, we have combined all of them to paint a summery ode to the fruit. For more than fifteen years, we have been getting our heirloom tomatoes from Tim Stark, who runs Eckerton Hill Farm in Pennsylvania. I recently visited Tim, a management consultant who left the business world to follow his passion for tomatoes. Together with his family, we cooked, ate, shared stories, and had a fabulous time around a great bottle of Châteauneuf-du-Pape.

Tim's tomatoes, all field-grown, are incredibly sweet and juicy. For each preparation, we use a different vinegar, but my favorite is the simple tomato salad drizzled with the unique honey and herb–infused Alsatian Melfor vinegar.

Chilled Tomato Soup (makes approximately 1½ quarts)

4 pounds very ripe, red heirloom tomatoes (such as Brandywine, Neves Azorean Red, or Aussie)

3 tablespoons olive oil

1 small onion, diced

½ fennel bulb, diced

1 red bell pepper, cored, seeded, and diced

⅓ small leek, white part only, diced and rinsed well

1 small stalk celery, diced

1 clove garlic, peeled and sliced

1 bouquet garni (3 parsley stems, 3 basil stems, 2 thyme sprigs, 1 bay leaf, 1 teaspoon black peppercorns, and 1 teaspoon coriander seeds wrapped in cheesecloth and secured with butcher's twine)

Salt

1 tablespoon tomato paste

¼ cup olive oil

½ teaspoon celery salt

Splash of Tabasco sauce

Freshly ground white pepper

Yellow Tomato Vinaigrette

1 large (7 ounces) yellow heirloom tomato (such as Dixie Golden, Kentucky Beefsteak, or Marvel Striped)

¾ teaspoon salt

1 small pinch of saffron threads

1 teaspoon white balsamic vinegar

2 tablespoons olive oil

Tomato and Brunet Cheese Crostini

2 thin slices olive focaccia or sourdough bread

2 tablespoons olive oil

Salt and freshly ground white pepper

3 ounces cave-aged Brunet cheese

6 petals Tomato Confit (page 376)

12 Garlic Chips (page 372)

¼ cup opal basil leaves

Heirloom Tomato Salad

1½ pounds heirloom tomatoes
(3 or 4 medium tomatoes)

2 tablespoons diced opal basil

2 tablespoons diced green basil

2 tablespoons brunoised shallot

3 tablespoons Melfor vinegar

¼ cup olive oil

Salt and freshly ground white
pepper to taste

Avocado-Stuffed Tomatoes

4 golf ball–size red heirloom tomatoes

1 avocado

Juice of ½ lemon

¾ teaspoon salt

1 tablespoon olive oil

To Finish

Grilled Eggplant Puree (page 371)

Basil Oil (see Green Herb Oil, page 376)

¼ cup bush basil leaves

3 tablespoons aged balsamic vinegar

1 cup small arugula leaves

For the Chilled Tomato Soup

Halve the tomatoes. Scoop out the insides into a sieve set over a bowl. Press to extract the juices and discard the seeds. Reserve the juice. Cut the tomatoes into 1-inch chunks. Heat the olive oil in a Dutch oven or large saucepan over low heat. Add the onion, fennel, bell pepper, leek, celery, garlic, bouquet garni, and 1 tablespoon salt and cook, stirring, for 10 minutes, or until the vegetables are tender but not colored. Stir in the tomato paste and cook for 3 minutes. Add the tomatoes and cook, stirring, for 10 minutes. Scoop the liquid that has released in the pan into a separate saucepan with the reserved tomato juice and simmer until reduced by half; set aside. Continue to cook the tomatoes, stirring, for 20 more minutes. Remove the bouquet garni and pass the tomatoes through a food mill into a bowl set over ice. Whisk in the olive oil, celery salt, and Tabasco. Add the reduced tomato juice to the desired consistency. Stir the soup until chilled, about 15 minutes, then adjust the seasoning with salt and pepper as needed. Reserve, chilled.

For the Yellow Tomato Vinaigrette

Fill one-third of a medium saucepan with water and bring to a simmer. Halve the tomato, squeeze out and discard the seeds, and chop it into small chunks. Transfer to a medium heatproof bowl and toss with the salt and saffron. Cover with plastic wrap. Place the bowl over the simmering water to warm the mixture until the tomatoes release their juices, about 45 minutes. Transfer the mixture to a blender, add the vinegar and olive oil, and puree until smooth. Pass through a fine-meshed sieve and chill.

For the Tomato and Brunet Cheese Crostini

Preheat the oven to 300°F. Cut the bread into 6 rectangles, brush lightly with the olive oil, sprinkle with salt and pepper, set on a parchment-lined baking sheet, and top with another sheet of parchment paper and a baking sheet, to keep the bread flat. Bake for 20 minutes, or until crispy and golden brown. Place a slice of Brunet cheese on the bread, cover with a piece of tomato confit, and if desired, trim the sides into straight lines. Top with garlic chips and opal basil leaves.

For the Heirloom Tomato Salad

Bring a large pot of water to a boil and place a bowl of ice water on the side. Core the tomatoes and, with a paring knife, score a small X on their bottoms. Boil the tomatoes for 5 seconds, or just until the skins start to loosen around the scored bottoms; chill in the ice water and peel the skins. Reserve the boiling water for the stuffed tomatoes.

Cut the tomatoes into equal-size wedges and lay them in a nonreactive baking dish. Sprinkle the remaining ingredients over the top and marinate, refrigerated, for 1 hour.

For the Avocado-Stuffed Tomatoes

Core the tomatoes and score a small X on their bottoms. Boil the tomatoes for 5 seconds, then transfer to a bowl of ice water to chill. Peel and slice a ¼-inch cap from the top of the tomatoes. Scoop out the insides with a small spoon into a sieve set over a bowl. Press to extract the juices and discard the seeds.

Split the avocado, remove the pit, and scoop the flesh into a blender with the lemon juice, salt, olive oil, and 2 teaspoons of the tomato juice. Puree until smooth. Transfer to a piping bag. Fill the cherry tomatoes with the avocado mixture up to 1 hour before serving.

To Finish

Spoon a thin layer of grilled eggplant puree into the bottom of 6 small soup cups and fill with tomato soup; garnish with a few drops of basil oil and small leaves of bush basil.

For each serving, arrange one-quarter of the heirloom tomato salad and a crostini on a chilled salad plate. Drizzle aged balsamic next to the crostini. Swipe a spoonful of yellow tomato vinaigrette onto the plate and top it with an avocado-filled cherry tomato. Garnish the salad with arugula.

VENISON AND DAIKON RADISH MOSAIC

MAKES ONE 16-INCH TERRINE, OR APPROXIMATELY
30 SLICES (15 PORTIONS)

CHARCUTERIE, AN essential part of the Lyon cuisine, has always been one of my passions. Since 2007, third-generation Parisian charcutier and friend Gille Vérot oversees tradition and innovation in an elaborate charcuterie program for our casual restaurants.

For executive chef Jean-François Bruel, aka JFK, the annual pig slaughter at his parents' farm near Saint-Étienne in France meant he would be allowed to help with the making of terrines, one of his favorite childhood memories. Fast-forward to his head post at Daniel, where each season we offer at least two terrines and where JFK often takes the creative lead to craft new combinations, such as this saddle of venison cooked sous-vide and paired in a perfect miniature checkerboard made of squares of foie gras, daikon radish, and venison en gelée.

VENISON AND DAIKON RADISH MOSAIC

Poached Venison Loin

1 (5-pound) venison loin

Seasoning mix per pound of trimmed venison:

1½ teaspoons (7 grams) salt

¼ teaspoon (1 gram) freshly ground white pepper

⅛ teaspoon (½ gram) ground juniper

Daikon Radish and Foie Gras Batons

1 (14-inch) daikon radish, peeled

Salt

1 pound Foie Gras Terrine (page 375)

Assembling the Mosaic

7 sheets gelatin

2 cups plus 2 tablespoons Venison Consommé (page 368)

Salt and freshly ground white pepper

Plum Coulis

4 red plums, pitted and chopped

2 tablespoons butter

2 tablespoons sugar

2 tablespoons Sauternes wine

Daikon Radish "Tubes" and Pickles

1 (12-inch) daikon radish, peeled

1 cup rice vinegar

1 tablespoon sugar

1 tablespoon honey

3 tablespoons grenadine syrup

½ teaspoon mustard seeds

½ teaspoon black peppercorns

½ teaspoon coriander seeds

Prune Paste Coins

4 sheets gelatin

2 cups (12 ounces) prunes, pitted

6 tablespoons almond oil

5 tablespoons Sauternes wine

4 grams agar-agar

Compressed Red and Yellow Plums

3 red plums

6 tablespoons sugar

3 yellow plums

1 teaspoon lemon juice

To Finish

2 tablespoons almond oil

Fleur de sel

Mostarda Cremona (page 376)

¼ cup micro pepper cress

15 micro mustard leaves

For the Poached Venison Loin

Using an immersion circulator, preheat a water bath to 139°F. Trim the loin of any fat or sinew, weigh it, and measure the seasoning according to the seasoning ratio listed in the ingredients. Sprinkle the seasoning over all sides of the meat, transfer to a sous-vide bag, and vacuum-seal. Submerge in the prepared water bath and cook for 24 hours. Cool the bag at room temperature for 1 hour. Press between baking sheets with a weight on top, such as canned goods, and refrigerate overnight. Remove from the bag and cut the loin into ¼-inch-wide, long batons and reserve, chilled.

Alternately, season the loin and rest for 2 hours in the refrigerator. In a large saucepan, heat 2 quarts Venison Consommé (page 368) or Veal Stock (page 368) to 160°F and maintain the temperature as best as possible using a stem thermometer. Poach the loin for 25 to 30 minutes, until the meat reaches 139°F. Cool the loin at room temperature in the liquid for 1 hour. Remove the meat, wrap tightly in plastic wrap, and press between baking sheets with a weight on top, such as canned goods; refrigerate overnight. Cut the loin into ¼-inch-wide, long batons and reserve, chilled.

For the Daikon Radish and Foie Gras Batons

Cut the radish into long batons, ¼ inch wide and as straight as possible. Bring a large pot of salted water to a boil and place a bowl of ice water on the side. Boil the batons until they are tender, about 30 seconds. Chill in the ice water, dry, and refrigerate.

With a sharp slicing knife rinsed in hot water after each use, trim off the outer layers of fat from the terrine and cut into long batons, ¼ inch wide and as straight as possible. Reserve, chilled.

For Assembling the Mosaic

Line a 16 x 1½-inch rectangular terrine mold with a sheet of acetate and trim so the long sides extend ½ inch from the rim.

Soak the gelatin sheets in ice water for 10 minutes; squeeze dry. Pour the consommé into a medium saucepan and, while cold, adjust the seasoning with salt and pepper. Bring to a simmer, remove from the heat, and stir in the gelatin until dissolved. Strain through a fine-meshed sieve into a medium bowl and cool to room temperature. The gelée should be liquid but viscous (very close to the point at which it begins to set); heat as necessary if it begins to solidify.

Place the terrine mold on a work surface aligned horizontally to you. Ladle a thin layer of gelée at the bottom of the mold. Before layering, dip the ingredients into the gelée. Starting from the farthest end and working toward you, start lining the batons horizontally to make a checkerboard pattern in this order:

Bottom: Venison, daikon, foie gras, venison, thin layer of gelée—chill to set

Second row: Daikon, foie gras, venison, daikon, thin layer of gelée—chill to set

Third row: Foie gras, venison, daikon, foie gras, thin layer of gelée—chill to set

Top row: Venison, daikon, foie gras, venison

Spoon in gelée to the rim of the terrine, chill to set, and then fold the extended acetate onto the top. Wrap the terrine in plastic wrap and refrigerate overnight.

Carefully run a small knife between the edges of the terrine and the acetate mold to loosen it, and using the acetate as an aid, remove the terrine from the mold. Peel off the acetate and wrap the terrine tightly in several layers of plastic wrap. Return to the refrigerator until well chilled, about 1 hour.

For the Plum Coulis

Combine all the ingredients in a medium saucepan and place over medium heat. Cook, stirring, for about 15 minutes, until the plums are very tender and most of the liquid in the pan has evaporated. Transfer the mixture to a blender and puree until smooth. Pass through a fine-meshed sieve, transfer to a piping bag fitted with a small tip, and reserve, chilled.

For the Daikon Radish "Tubes" and Pickles

Bring a large pot of salted water to a boil and place a bowl of ice water on the side. Slice the radish into 1-inch discs. With a ½-inch-diameter ring cutter or cannoli form, punch out at least 45 cylinders, then use a ¼-inch-diameter ring cutter to cut out the middle of the rounds to make tubes. Reserve the middle pieces in a heatproof container. Boil the tubes for about 30 seconds, until just cooked; chill in the ice water. Dry and reserve, chilled.

In a small saucepan, combine the vinegar, sugar, honey, grenadine syrup, mustard seeds, black peppercorns, and coriander and bring to a simmer. Pour over the reserved radish middles and allow to cool at room temperature. Cover and reserve, chilled.

For the Prune Paste Coins

Soak the gelatin sheets in ice water for 10 minutes; squeeze dry. Place the prunes in a food processor and process until pasty. Scrape the paste through a fine-meshed drum sieve and measure ½ cup into a medium bowl. Whisk in the almond oil, Sauternes, and then ¾ cup water until smooth. Transfer half of the mixture to a small saucepan, whisk in the agar-agar, and bring to a simmer. Remove from the heat and whisk in the gelatin until dissolved. Whisk in the remaining prune mixture, then pass everything through a fine-meshed sieve. While still hot, pour onto a rimmed plate to reach ¼-inch thickness and transfer to the refrigerator, being sure to keep it flat, for 1 hour, or until set. Use a ½-inch-diameter ring cutter to cut out at least 15 coins.

For the Compressed Red and Yellow Plums

Peel and reserve the skins from the red plums. In a small saucepan, combine the skins with 2 tablespoons of the sugar and ¼ cup water. Simmer until reduced by half. Strain the syrup through a fine-meshed sieve and chill. Cut the peeled red plums in half, remove the pits, and combine with the syrup in a sous-vide bag and vacuum-seal.

In a small saucepan, combine the 4 tablespoons remaining sugar with 2 tablespoons water and bring to a simmer until the sugar is dissolved. Chill, then add the lemon juice. Peel the yellow plums, cut in half, and remove the pits. Combine with the lemon syrup in a sous-vide bag and vacuum-seal. Chill both bags of compressed plums for at least 12 hours.

To Finish

Remove the compressed plums from their bags and cut into thin half-moon-shaped slices.

For each serving, cut two ½-inch-thick slices from the terrine and peel away the plastic wrap. Lay the slices on one side of a chilled plate, brush with almond oil, and sprinkle with fleur de sel. Arrange 3 daikon radish tubes in the center of the plate, then place a small spoonful of mostarda and a piece of pickled daikon radish next to each one. Pipe plum coulis into each daikon tube, top with micro pepper cress, and place a slice of yellow plum against it. On the other side of the plate, lay 2 slices of compressed red plum so the straight edges meet. Top with a plum paste coin, a piece of mostarda, and a leaf of micro mustard.

RABBIT PORCHETTA
FARMER LEE'S BABY VEGETABLE SALAD

SERVES 6

THIS DELICIOUS, rustic Italian and Niçoise specialty, classically made with a whole young pig stuffed with herbs, vegetables, and offal, can be found at festivals and green markets throughout the land. But I was a lucky man when, as part of the three-day bash that celebrated Craig Claiborne's seventieth birthday, I was served the best porchetta I ever tried, cooked by Alain Ducasse on the French Riviera. At Daniel, we play on the same classic dish, a roasted meat and vegetable roulade, but choose to make it with rabbit for its delicious lean meat, served with tender baby vegetables from one of our favorite purveyors, farmer Lee Jones of Chef's Garden in Huron, Ohio.

Carrot Oil

5 medium carrots, peeled

2 tablespoons grapeseed oil

Rabbit Porchetta

1 rabbit (about 2½ pounds),
with liver and kidneys, skinned

Salt

2 orange carrot batons (cut to the
length of 1 rabbit loin, ¼ inch wide)

2 yellow carrot batons (cut to the
length of 1 rabbit loin, ¼ inch wide)

4 green asparagus

¼ cup fava beans, peeled

2¼ ounces Tomato Confit (page 376),
chopped

1 ounce diced pork fatback

1 ounce diced slab bacon

2 ounces diced fresh grade A foie gras

4 teaspoons white wine

¼ teaspoon thyme leaves

⅛ teaspoon chopped rosemary

¼ teaspoon chopped savory

¼ teaspoon chopped sage

2 tablespoons canola oil

1 clove garlic, peeled and chopped

1 medium egg, whipped

4 teaspoons milk

1 tablespoon Fine White Breadcrumbs
(page 373)

Seasoning mix per pound of rabbit:

1½ teaspoons (7 grams) salt

¼ teaspoon (2 grams) ground white pepper

⅛ teaspoon (1 gram) quatre épices

2 fresh grade A foie gras batons (cut to
the length of 1 rabbit loin, 1 inch wide)

Freshly ground white pepper

2 slab bacon batons (cut to the length
of 1 rabbit loin, ¼ inch wide)

2 chorizo batons (cut to the length
of 1 rabbit loin, ¼ inch wide)

Orleans Mustard Cream

¼ cup heavy cream

1 tablespoon Orleans mustard

Freshly ground white pepper

Rabbit Jus Vinaigrette

2 tablespoons Rabbit Jus (page 370)

1 teaspoon Dijon mustard

1¼ teaspoons sherry vinegar

3 tablespoons olive oil

Salt and freshly ground white pepper

Baby Vegetable Salad

Salt

6 spring onions

7 baby purple carrots, peeled and trimmed

7 baby orange carrots, peeled and trimmed

3 baby beets, peeled and trimmed

To Finish

6 baby turnip leaves

18 baby turnips, peeled and trimmed
with a leaf still attached

¼ cup micro carrot tops

1 cup frisée lettuce, cut into bite-size
portions

Mustard Vinaigrette (page 376)

Salt and freshly ground white pepper

2 tablespoons tarragon mustard

36 tarragon leaves

*"Blending pork, rabbit, and vegetables, we revisit
the porchetta of the Riviera."*

For the Carrot Oil

Preheat the oven to 190°F. Using a mandoline, slice the carrots as thinly as possible and arrange in a single layer on an aluminum foil–lined baking sheet. Bake for 2½ hours, or until dry and crisp. Cool, then transfer to a blender or spice grinder and pulse into a powder. Shake the powder through a fine-meshed sieve into a bowl and stir in the oil. Reserve, chilled.

For the Rabbit Porchetta

On a large cutting board, lay the rabbit on its back. From inside the belly cavity, remove the kidneys and liver and pull away and discard the fat surrounding them; dice and reserve them for stuffing. Trim and reserve the tenderloins from under the rack for stuffing.

With a butcher's knife, trim away the shoulders (forelegs) by cutting flush up against the neck bone, then bend the foreleg forward to pop the bone from the joint. Carve through the joint toward the ribs to completely remove. Remove the legs by carving inward to separate the thigh from the tailbone, pop the bone from the joint, and then carve through the joint toward the tailbone to completely remove it. Debone the forelegs and legs, reserving the bones for jus. Dice the tenderloins, forelegs, and legs; reserve 11¼ ounces for grinding. Use the remaining trim for the jus.

Lay the saddle on its back and use a butcher's knife to carve off the belly flaps and loins, keeping them attached to each other by tracing along the rib cage and then backbone (from front to back). Separate the loins.

Chop all bones and meat trim into rough 1-inch pieces, rinse, dry, and reserve for the rabbit jus.

Bring a large pot of salted water to a boil and place a bowl of ice water on the side. Boil the carrots, asparagus, and fava beans in separate batches until tender, 2 to 4 minutes each, depending on their size. Allow the water to come back to a rapid boil between batches. Transfer each batch to the ice water to chill. Drain the vegetables and pat them dry.

In a medium bowl, combine the diced kidney, liver, tenderloin, shoulder, and leg meat, tomato confit, fatback, bacon, diced foie gras, wine, thyme, rosemary, savory, and sage. Heat 1 tablespoon of the oil in a small sauté pan over medium-low heat, add the garlic, and stir until cooked through. Transfer to the bowl with the meat, along with the egg, milk, and breadcrumbs, and stir to combine.

Weigh the mixture and measure the seasoning according to the seasoning ratio listed in the ingredients. Mix the seasoning into the meat and chill thoroughly. Pass the mixture through a meat grinder fit with a coarse plate into a bowl. Fold in the fava beans by hand and keep chilled.

Season the foie gras batons on all sides with salt and pepper. Freeze for 15 minutes to deeply chill. Heat a medium sauté pan over high heat. Add the foie gras batons and sear on each side until golden brown, about 2 minutes total, and chill immediately.

Lay the loins on a cutting board so that the belly flaps are spread out, facing inside up. Lightly sprinkle the loins and their belly flaps with salt and pepper.

Lightly pound the belly flaps with a flat meat tenderizer and, with a paring knife, lightly score them with a crosshatch pattern. Divide the ground meat onto the belly flaps and spread into flat layers. Line parallel rows of one of each of the seared foie gras, carrot, bacon, and chorizo batons along with 2 asparagus (tip to end) on top of each belly flap and press to nestle them into the ground meat. Roll the loins over the belly flaps, forming a log.

Rub two 12-inch sheets of aluminum foil with the remaining tablespoon of canola oil on one side. Wrap each of the logs in the foil, with the oiled side touching the meat, and twist the ends to secure into a tight log. Chill for at least 30 minutes.

Preheat the oven to 210°F. In a large sauté pan over high heat, sear all sides of the foil-wrapped logs for about 2 minutes. Transfer to a baking sheet fitted with a rack and roast until the internal temperature reaches 137°F; begin checking after 15 minutes. Rest at room temperature for 10 minutes, then chill the logs in the refrigerator overnight. When ready to serve, remove the foil and slice each log into 6 pieces.

For the Orleans Mustard Cream

Up to 1 hour in advance, whip the heavy cream to stiff peaks. With a rubber spatula, fold in the mustard and season with pepper; reserve, chilled.

For the Rabbit Jus Vinaigrette

In a small bowl, whisk the jus, mustard, and vinegar to combine. Stream in the oil while whisking and season with salt and pepper. Transfer to a small piping bag and reserve at room temperature.

For the Baby Vegetable Salad

Bring a large pot of salted water to a boil and set a bowl of ice water on the side. In separate batches, boil the spring onions, 6 purple carrots, and 6 orange carrots until tender; chill in the ice water and pat dry. Halve the spring onions and carrots lengthwise. With a mandoline, thinly shave the remaining 2 carrots and the baby beets into a bowl of ice water.

To Finish

Transfer the baby vegetable salad ingredients with the baby turnip leaves, baby turnips, micro carrot tops, and frisée to a small bowl and toss with the mustard vinaigrette; season with salt and pepper.

For each serving, dip a pastry brush into the carrot oil and paint a line through the center of a chilled appetizer plate. Place 2 slices of porchetta on opposite sides of the plate and top each one with a small spoonful of mustard cream. Arrange 2 spring onion halves, 2 purple carrot halves, 2 orange carrot halves, a few pieces of frisée, 1 turnip leaf, 3 baby turnips, 3 slices shaved carrot, 3 slices shaved beet, and 2 micro carrot tops on the carrot oil. Pipe 6 dots of tarragon mustard and rabbit jus vinaigrette onto opposite sides of the plate and top each mustard dot with a tarragon leaf.

DANIEL ON BREAD

WHAT IS IT WITH BREAD AND THE FRENCH—BREAD WITH CHEESE, of course, but also bread in soups, bread in sauces, bread and butter? Maybe our bread is just the cheapest and most convenient way to soak up the rest of our food!

When my father retired from the farm a few years ago, he built a wood-fire stone oven and started baking bread for the family. Then he transformed an old drill into the most inventive bread machine to help him knead the dough. Once a week, he bakes old-fashioned pain au levain. It's dense, heavy, delicious, and filled with tiny holes. For our cheese plate, he makes a walnut bread. Don't think I grew up on white fluffy brioche; we had crispy baguette on Sundays only.

It's fair to say that every chef dreams of making his or her bread, but until I opened my own restaurant, the bread always came from the best local bakery. Once we opened Daniel on 65th Street, I was finally able to make my dream come true, and we hired a baker. Today at our bakery kitchen on the Lower East Side, Mark Fiorentino, our wonderful baker for the last fifteen years, supervises ten bakers who produce about thirty different breads for our New York restaurants and the Épicerie.

At Daniel, besides brioche with foie gras and walnut raisin bread with cheese, we offer six varieties of bread: French mini-baguette with toasted tips, roasted garlic and Parmesan focaccia, kalamata olive and rosemary roll, whole grain loaf, three-seed roll, and rustic sourdough boule with salted butter baked inside.

Today we often forget how wonderful it can be to cook with bread, whether it is the baked pumpkin my mother made, stuffed with big croutons that absorb and support the cream, pancetta, and cheese; or a thin seaweed bread melba served with the cured fluke. At home for a gathering of friends, I recently made a daube Provençale, a beef stew full of veggies, and I sealed the pot with fresh sourdough: The bread puffs up, sealing the delicious steam. The crusty bread was served alongside the stew: dramatic and delicious at the same time. That's what you get when a French chef gets involved with dough!

"Good bread is the most fundamentally satisfying of all foods; good bread with fresh butter, the greatest of feasts!" —James Beard

CREAMY SPRING GARLIC SOUP
PETIT GRIS BEIGNETS

SERVES 8

THIS IS OUR interpretation of the ancestral garlic soup often sipped in Provence to counter the effects of a rowdy evening. We prepare it with spring garlic, the younger relative of the heady bulb, which provides grassy sweetness, a taste the small petits gris escargots relish in the countryside. If you have the time, and live escargots are available to you, do follow our process for a rewarding gustatory experience. You can also easily find them already cooked in a jar.

On the rim of the plate, crispy snails in tempura batter balance tender sautéed snails and spiraling fiddlehead ferns placed delicately on the soup. Keeping the traditional parsley, garlic, and snail combination evokes the escargots persillade of the popular lyonnais bouchons of my youth.

CREAMY SPRING GARLIC SOUP
PETIT GRIS BEIGNETS

Escargots

48 live petit gris snails (live snails take 3 days to prepare), or substitute canned Burgundy snails (we recommend Sarl Henri Maire, very large)

If using live snails:

2 tablespoons buckwheat flour

Salt

1 cup dry white wine

1 small onion, sliced

½ stalk celery, sliced

½ medium carrot, peeled and sliced

1 small leek, white part only, sliced and rinsed well

1 bay leaf

2 sprigs sage

4 sprigs thyme

1 sachet (1 teaspoon each black peppercorns and coriander seeds wrapped in cheesecloth and secured with butcher's twine)

Purple Potato Discs

4 large purple potatoes (4 ounces each)

2 cloves garlic, peeled

2 sprigs thyme

Salt and freshly ground white pepper

Spring Garlic Confit

16 spring garlic stalks (about 1 pound)

Salt and freshly ground white pepper

1 cup olive oil

Creamy Spring Garlic Soup (makes approximately 2 quarts/ 1 cup soup per portion)

Salt

24 fiddlehead ferns

6 ounces (about 3 bunches) parsley leaves

1 cup (2 sticks) butter

2 pounds spring garlic, trimmed and thinly sliced

½ Vidalia onion, thinly sliced

1 sachet (1 teaspoon each black peppercorns and coriander seeds, 6 sprigs thyme, and 1 bay leaf wrapped in cheesecloth and secured with butcher's twine)

1 medium Yukon gold potato, peeled and diced

2 quarts Chicken Stock (page 368)

2 cups heavy cream

Freshly ground white pepper

To Finish

Canola oil for frying

Tempura Batter (page 374)

Salt and freshly ground white pepper

½ cup small miner's lettuce leaves

For the Escargots

If you are using live snails, place them in a ventilated, covered container in the refrigerator for 1 day. Sprinkle the flour into the container, over the snails, on the second day. On the third day, fill a large vessel with 3 quarts of heavily salted water and submerge the snails inside. Soak the snails for 1 hour, allowing them to disgorge (they will produce a lot of foam and the water will turn milky). Drain off the salt water and rinse. In a large Dutch oven or heavy-bottomed saucepan, combine 2 quarts water, the white wine, onion, celery, carrot, leek, bay leaf, sage, thyme, sachet, and snails. Simmer for 1½ hours, or until the snail flesh is tender, skimming any foam that rises to the surface as needed. Strain the snails, reserving 2 cups of the liquid and discarding the rest. Once they are cool enough to handle, use a toothpick to remove the snails from their shells. Cut off and discard the entrails (tortillon). Submerge the snails in the reserved liquid, cover, and reserve, chilled.

If using canned snails, rinse with cold water until it runs clear. Cut off and discard the entrails (tortillon).

For the Purple Potato Discs

Cut the potatoes lengthwise into ¼-inch-thick slices. Use a 1-inch-diameter ring cutter to punch out 24 discs. In a small saucepan, combine the discs, garlic, and thyme and cover with water. Season with salt and pepper and bring to a light simmer. Cook for 5 minutes, or until the potatoes are tender when pierced with a cake tester. Remove from the heat to cool at room temperature in the liquid. Reserve in the liquid, chilled.

For the Spring Garlic Confit

Cut the stems from the spring garlic, peel away any damaged outer layers, and cut them on a bias to make twenty-four 1-inch batons. Trim the 16 bulbs into ½-inch lengths and season them with salt and pepper. In a small saucepan over medium heat, submerge the batons and bulbs in the olive oil. Cook at 185°F for 1 hour, or until tender. Keep warm.

For the Creamy Spring Garlic Soup

Bring a large pot of salted water to a boil and place a bowl of ice water on the side. Add the fiddlehead ferns and boil for 3 minutes, or until tender, and chill in the ice water; pat dry and reserve for finishing. Add the parsley leaves and boil for 45 seconds, then chill in the ice water; squeeze dry and reserve. Brown the butter in a large Dutch oven over medium heat. Add the spring garlic, onion, and sachet and cook, stirring, for 10 minutes, or until tender. Add the potato, chicken stock, and a pinch of salt and bring to a boil. Reduce the heat to a light simmer and cook for 15 minutes, or until the potatoes are soft. Remove the sachet and add the cream. Transfer the mixture to a blender, add the parsley, and puree until smooth (you may need to do this in batches). Adjust the seasoning with salt and pepper and serve immediately or transfer to a bowl set over ice; stir to chill. When ready to serve, reheat the soup.

To Finish

Fill one-third of a medium saucepan with canola oil and heat to 350°F. Transfer the purple potatoes with their liquid to a saucepan, place over medium heat, and stir until heated through. Strain the snails and pat dry. Dip 24 of the snails into the tempura batter to coat, transfer to the oil with a fork, and fry until golden brown (you will need to do this in batches). Transfer to a paper towel–lined tray and sprinkle with salt. Spoon 2 tablespoons of the spring garlic confit oil into a small sauté pan and warm over medium heat. Toss in the reserved fiddlehead ferns and remaining snails to heat through; season with salt and pepper.

For each serving, ladle some of the soup into a bowl with a flat, wide rim. Float 3 batons of spring garlic stem confit, 3 fiddlehead ferns, and 3 sautéed snails on the soup. Arrange 3 purple potato discs in a line on the rim of the bowl and top each with a tempura escargot. Place two spring garlic confit bulbs in between the potatoes. Garnish with 2 miner's lettuce leaves.

PEA AND LETTUCE VELOUTÉ
HICKORY SMOKED SQUAB BREAST

SERVES 4

THE INSPIRATION for this soup came from one of our landmark recipes, the chilled pea soup. In the spring of 1993, as we prepared the opening of the original Restaurant Daniel, we searched for a dish that would come to symbolize the new, the spring, and the greenmarket's best produce. An intense bright green pea soup was born. It truly marked the beginning of each spring season.

We started with the idea of peas mixed with an onion fondue and rosemary. And we kept playing with it, adding different kinds of peas, some more sugary, sweet, waxy, and starchy. Today the evolution of the recipe has led us to replace the original bacon flavor with a smoked breast of squab. This intensely green pea soup is served, in the same spirit as in the original, with rosemary cream and a crispy golden crouton.

Smoked Squab Breast

1 cup hickory wood chips

4 squab breasts

¾ teaspoon salt

⅛ teaspoon freshly ground white pepper

**Chilled Pea Soup
(makes approximately 1½ quarts)**

Salt

¼ head romaine lettuce, green
outer leaves only

2½ pounds fresh shelled English peas

4 ounces snow peas

4 ounces snap peas

2 ounces pea greens

2 large mint leaves

2 tablespoons olive oil

1 medium shallot, sliced

1½ quarts Chicken Stock (page 368)

¾ cup crème fraîche

Freshly ground white pepper

Rosemary Cream

1 cup heavy cream

2 (3-inch) rosemary stems

Pea Puree and Powder

½ cup rosemary cream, reserved
from above

2 cups English peas, reserved
from above

Salt and freshly ground white pepper

½ cup dehydrated peas
(we recommend Just Peas)

To Finish

3 tablespoons olive oil

1 small carrot, peeled, thinly sliced, and
trimmed into at least twelve ¼-inch-wide
diamonds

½ cup split English peas, reserved
from above

Salt and freshly ground white pepper

4 green pea shoots

4 yellow pea shoots

8 Crispy Shallot Rings (page 372)

4 (½-inch-diameter) round Melba Croutons
(page 372)

8 micro pea flowers

For the Smoked Squab Breast

Sprinkle the wood chips in the bottom of a stovetop smoker or roasting pan fitted with a rack. Ignite the wood chips and cover with a lid until the flames are extinguished. Place the breasts on the rack inside and cover. Smoke for 5 minutes, then remove from the smoker and season the breasts on both sides with the salt and pepper. Transfer the breasts to a sous-vide bag and vacuum-seal; reserve, chilled.

For the Chilled Pea Soup

Bring a large pot of salted water to a boil and place a bowl of ice water on the side. Boil the lettuce, peas, pea greens, and mint in separate batches until tender, 2 to 5 minutes each, depending on their size. Allow the water to come back to a rapid boil between batches. Once tender, transfer each batch to the ice water to chill. Drain the greens and peas and pat dry. Set aside 2 cups of the shelled English peas for the puree. Peel and split ½ cup of the shelled English peas for finishing.

Heat the olive oil in a large saucepan over medium heat. Add the shallot and cook, stirring, for 2 minutes, or until translucent. Add the chicken stock and bring to a simmer. Combine the hot stock with the boiled greens and peas and the crème fraîche in a blender and puree until smooth (you will need to do this in batches). Pass through a fine-meshed sieve into a bowl set over ice. Stir until chilled and adjust the seasoning with salt and pepper. Transfer to a pitcher and reserve, chilled.

For the Rosemary Cream

Pour the heavy cream into a small saucepan and bring to a simmer. Remove from the heat, add the rosemary, cover, and infuse for 20 minutes. Strain through a fine-meshed sieve and chill. Set aside ½ cup for the pea puree. Up to 30 minutes before serving, whip the remaining cream to stiff peaks and reserve, chilled.

For the Pea Puree and Powder

For the puree, in a small saucepan, bring the reserved ½ cup rosemary cream to a simmer, then transfer to a blender; add the peas and puree until smooth. Pass through a fine-meshed sieve into a bowl placed over ice. Stir until chilled and season with salt and pepper. Reserve, chilled.

For the powder, transfer the dehydrated peas to a clean, dry blender or spice grinder and pulse to make a fine powder. Shake through a fine-meshed sieve and reserve.

To Finish

Using an immersion circulator, heat a water bath to 145°F. Submerge the bag of squab breasts in the water bath and cook for 30 minutes, or until the internal temperature reaches 130°F. In a medium sauté pan, warm 2 tablespoons of the olive oil over medium-high heat. Remove the squab breasts from the bag, pat them dry, and add to the pan skin side down. Sear for 1 minute, or until the skin is golden brown.

In a small sauté pan, warm the remaining 1 tablespoon olive oil over medium heat. Add the carrot and cook for 2 minutes, or until just tender. Add the peas and toss to heat through. Season with salt and pepper.

For each serving, place 1 squab breast at one side of a plate and spoon a line of pea puree next to it. Garnish the line of puree with a few peas, 3 carrot diamonds, 1 green pea shoot, 1 yellow pea shoot, and 2 crispy shallots. Sprinkle a line of pea powder above the puree and arrange a few peas on top. Set a small soup cup on the other side of the plate and fill with the pea soup. Float a crouton on top, and top the crouton with a spoonful of the whipped rosemary cream. Place 1 pea flower on the cream and 1 on the puree.

WARM WHITE ASPARAGUS SALAD
POACHED EGG DRESSING

SERVES 4

THE KEY to the white asparagus, the sprouting symbol of spring, is to ensure that it is completely peeled. Its refined grassy flavor doesn't need much flourish to shine. After we cut the stems for our soup on page 52, we boil the delicate tips until just right and serve them with lovage dressing. I love this wild herb for its celery-like taste.

White Asparagus

20 jumbo Provence white asparagus (3¾ pounds) (each about 9 inches long and 1 inch thick)

Herb Salad

¼ cup chervil leaves

¼ cup yellow celery leaves

¼ cup ½-inch chive batons

¼ cup tarragon leaves

¼ cup small parsley leaves

2 cups frisée lettuce trimmed into bite-size pieces

Almond Egg Yolk Sauce

4 egg yolks

1 teaspoon almond oil

Freshly ground white pepper

Lovage Dressing

Salt

12 ounces lovage leaves

½ cup grapeseed oil

1 egg white

½ teaspoon lemon juice

1 splash of Tabasco sauce

Poached Egg Dressing

Salt

1 egg, in the shell

1 tablespoon Orleans mustard

2 teaspoons Dijon mustard

1 splash of sherry vinegar

1 splash of Tabasco sauce

¾ cup grapeseed oil

1½ tablespoons olive oil

To Finish

1 tablespoon sugar

Salt

Olive oil

Freshly ground white pepper

¼ cup sliced blanched almonds

1 hard-boiled egg yolk, passed through a drum sieve

4 (4 x 1-inch) rectangular Melba Croutons (page 372)

For the White Asparagus

Prepare each asparagus spear by laying it flat on a cutting board and lightly peeling from just below its tips to the end, rolling it clockwise as you work. Trim and discard the bottom fibrous 1 inch, and then trim the next 3 inches for soup, forming 4-inch long spears (see page 52). Repeat with the remaining asparagus. Use butcher's twine to secure bunches made of 5 spears. Reserve, chilled.

For the Herb Salad

Soak the herbs and frisée for 20 minutes in a bowl of ice water to crisp. Transfer to a salad spinner to dry. Reserve in the refrigerator covered with wet paper towels.

For the Almond Egg Yolk Sauce

Using an immersion circulator, preheat a water bath to 145°F. Transfer the egg yolks to a sous-vide bag and vacuum-seal. Transfer to the water bath and cook for 1 hour. Fill a bowl with ice water and submerge the bag in the water until completely chilled. Transfer the yolks to a small bowl and slowly whisk in the almond oil. Season with pepper, but do not salt, as it will make the sauce discolor. Cover and reserve, kept warm.

For the Lovage Dressing

Bring a medium pot of salted water to a boil and place a bowl of ice water on the side. Boil the lovage for 1 minute, or until tender, then transfer to the ice water to chill. Squeeze dry and transfer to a blender with the oil and puree until smooth. Pass the lovage oil through a fine-meshed sieve lined with a coffee filter.

In a medium bowl, whip the egg white until it forms soft peaks. Slowly stream in the lovage oil while whisking. Add the lemon juice and season with the Tabasco and salt.

For the Poached Egg Dressing

Bring a medium pot of salted water to a boil. Add the egg and boil for 3 minutes. Scoop the egg from the water and crack it over a small bowl, scooping all of the white and yolk out with a spoon. Transfer to a blender with ½ teaspoon salt, the mustards, vinegar, and Tabasco. Puree on low speed, slowly streaming in the oils until emulsified. Transfer to a squeeze bottle with a large tip or a piping bag, and reserve, kept warm.

To Finish

Fill a large pot with 2 gallons of water; add the sugar and season with salt. Bring to a boil, add the asparagus bunches, and boil for 9 minutes, or until easily pierced with a cake tester. Strain onto paper towels and cut away the twine. Transfer to a large bowl and gently toss with olive oil and season with salt and pepper. Transfer the herb salad and almonds to a small bowl and season with olive oil, salt, and pepper.

For each serving, pipe a large dollop of poached egg dressing onto a warm plate. Spoon a dot of almond egg yolk sauce in the center and sprinkle with hard-boiled egg yolk. Scoop a spoonful of lovage dressing to the side. Arrange 5 warm asparagus spears on the opposite side of the plate and top with a crouton and herb salad.

CHILLED WHITE ASPARAGUS SOUP
WILD CHERVIL, CHIVE BLOSSOMS

SERVES 4

AT THE RESTAURANT, we extract the full flavor of the denser white asparagus stems for this thick nutty velouté. The blended potato creates a smoother, creamier consistency that supports in the center a quenelle of chervil whipped cream awaiting the spoon.

White Asparagus Soup

1 tablespoon sugar

Salt

1 pound white asparagus stems (reserved from Warm White Asparagus Salad, page 51), peeled and cut into 1-inch pieces

3 white asparagus tips

2 tablespoons grapeseed oil

¼ large onion, thinly sliced

⅓ leek, white part only, thinly sliced and rinsed well

1 stalk celery, thinly sliced

½ clove garlic

½ russet potato, cut into small dice

1 quart Chicken Stock (page 368)

½ cup heavy cream

Freshly ground white pepper

Juice of 1 lemon

Wild Chervil Cream

6 tablespoons heavy cream

6 ounces wild chervil leaves

To Finish

4 nasturtium leaves

Wild Chervil Oil
(see Green Herb Oil, page 376)

12 wild chervil leaves

12 chive blossoms

For the White Asparagus Soup

Fill a large saucepan with 2 gallons of water. Add the sugar and season with salt. Bring to a boil, add the asparagus stems and tips, and boil for 9 minutes, or until easily pierced with a cake tester. Strain and cut ¼ cup of brunoise from the stems and reserve. Slice the tips in quarters lengthwise; reserve, chilled.

Heat the grapeseed oil in a large saucepan over medium heat. Add the onion, leek, celery, garlic, and 1 teaspoon salt. Cook, stirring, for 6 minutes, until tender but not colored. Add the potato, the remaining asparagus stems, and the chicken stock. Simmer for 8 minutes, or until the potatoes are tender. Add the cream and simmer for an additional 5 minutes. Transfer the mixture to a blender and puree until smooth. Pass through a fine-meshed sieve into a bowl set over ice. Chill, then season with salt, pepper, and the lemon juice. Reserve, chilled.

For the Wild Chervil Cream

Pour 4 tablespoons of the cream into a small saucepan and bring to a simmer. Transfer to a blender with the chervil leaves and puree until smooth. Pass through a fine-meshed sieve into a bowl placed over ice. Chill well, then add the remaining 2 tablespoons cream. Whip the cream to stiff peaks and reserve, chilled.

To Finish

For each serving, place a spoonful of the reserved brunoised asparagus stems in the center of a chilled bowl. Arrange 3 asparagus tip quarters around the brunoise, standing them upright. Gently pour the soup into the bowl. Top the brunoise with a nasturtium leaf and a spoonful of the wild chervil cream. Garnish the soup with 3 drops of the wild chervil oil, 3 wild chervil leaves, and 3 chive blossoms.

CRAYFISH TIMBALE
COCKSCOMBS, WATERCRESS VELOUTÉ

SERVES 4

THIS THOROUGHLY modern dish in fact revisits a legendary Bresse classic, Alain Chapel's gâteau de foies blonds aux écrevisses. When the garnish plays as important a role as the soup, I feel that we have elevated the dish into a complete experience. Each crayfish tail sits atop a chicken ballotine, made with deboned chicken wings filled with crayfish-chicken mousse, while crispy cockscombs add a contrast in texture. The brightly colored watercress soup is just bitter enough to counter the sweetness of the crayfish and black garlic.

CRAYFISH TIMBALE
COCKSCOMBS, WATERCRESS VELOUTÉ

Cockscomb Tempura

12 cockscombs (about 6 ounces), submerged in ice water for 24 hours

1 quart Chicken Stock (page 368)

¼ large onion, sliced

½ medium carrot, peeled and sliced

2 cloves garlic, peeled

1 sachet (½ teaspoon each black peppercorns and coriander seeds, 2 sprigs thyme, 2 sprigs parsley, and 1 fresh bay leaf wrapped in cheesecloth and secured with butcher's twine)

1 cup dry white wine

1 teaspoon salt, plus more for sprinkling

Crayfish Timbales

36 pieces (4½ pounds) live large crayfish

1 gallon Court Bouillon (page 369)

1 cup (2 sticks) butter, softened

5 ounces chicken breast

1 ounce chicken liver

½ teaspoon salt

¼ teaspoon freshly ground white pepper

1 pinch of piment d'Espelette

1 egg white

½ cup plus 3 tablespoons heavy cream

1 teaspoon dry sherry (we recommend Tio Pepe Fino)

Chicken Wing Ballotine

4 middle sections of a chicken wing

Salt and freshly ground white pepper

Watercress Velouté (makes 1½ quarts)

Salt

3 bunches (approximately 12 ounces) watercress, leaves picked

4 ounces parsley leaves

1 cup heavy cream

Freshly ground white pepper

2 tablespoons olive oil

½ large onion, chopped

1 medium leek, white and light green parts only, sliced and rinsed well (save the green top)

1 bouquet garni (1 bay leaf, 1 parsley sprig, and 1 thyme sprig, sandwiched in a 2-inch green leek top, secured with butcher's twine)

2 cloves garlic, peeled and chopped

1 Yukon gold potato (4 ounces), peeled and diced

2 quarts Chicken Stock (page 368)

¼ cup crème fraîche

Morels and Fava Beans

Salt

12 fava beans

4 small morel mushrooms

1 tablespoon butter

3 tablespoons Chicken Stock (page 368)

Freshly ground white pepper

To Finish

Canola oil for frying

Tempura Batter (page 374)

Salt

12 slices black garlic

¼ cup wild chervil

For the Cockscomb Tempura
Drain the cockscombs and place them in a large saucepan with the chicken stock, onion, carrot, garlic, sachet, wine, and salt and bring to a light simmer. Cook, stirring occasionally, for 2 hours, or until the cockscombs are tender. Remove from the heat and cool in the liquid. Store in the liquid, chilled.

For the Crayfish Timbales
Preheat the oven to 325°F.

Rinse the crayfish very well under cold water. Pour 2 cups of the court bouillon into a bowl placed over ice. Transfer the remaining court bouillon to a large pot and bring to a boil. Boil the crayfish in 5 separate batches for 30 seconds each, allowing the court

bouillon to return to a full boil between batches. While the crayfish are still hot, twist the tails from the bodies. Crack open the back of the tails and pull out the meat with one hand, while pinching the middle section of the fin with the other hand to devein them (the vein should slide out and remain attached to the fin). Reserve the shells. Transfer the tail meat to the chilled court bouillon and stir until cold. Use a paring knife to neatly trim the thick ends of 24 of the tails and reserve them, chilled. Chop the trim and remaining 12 tails for the mousse (below); reserve, chilled.

In the bowl of an electric mixer fitted with a paddle attachment, combine the crayfish shells, heads, claws, and butter and mix on medium speed for 5 minutes, or until broken down into a mash. Transfer to a medium saucepan and bring to a simmer, stirring occasionally. Cover and transfer to the oven. Bake for 30 minutes, or until deep red and aromatic and the butter stops forming bubbles. Carefully strain the butter through a fine-meshed sieve into a heatproof container. Refrigerate undisturbed for at least 4 hours, or until the butter separates from the liquid and solidifies on top. Scrape the butter from the top into a medium saucepan; discard the liquid from the bottom. Melt the butter over medium heat, then pass through a fine-meshed sieve lined with cheesecloth and keep warm.

Chill the bowl and blade of a food processor. Add the chicken breast, chicken liver, and salt, and pulse until pasty. Add the pepper, piment d'Espelette, and egg white and combine well. With the machine running, stream in ½ cup of the heavy cream and sherry to form a smooth mousse. Pass the mousse through a drum sieve and fold in the reserved chopped crayfish. Refrigerate, covered, for at least 5 hours, or overnight. In a small bowl, whip the remaining 3 tablespoons heavy cream to medium peaks. Fold into the mousse and chill again for at least another 20 minutes or up to 2 hours. Transfer the mousse to piping bags.

To form the timbales, place 2 crayfish tails in the bottom of each of twelve metal 1-inch-tall mini timbale molds with a ¾-inch-diameter rim. Pipe approximately 1 tablespoon of the mousse in each mold; reserve the remaining mousse for the chicken wing ballotine. Add ½ teaspoon of warm crayfish butter to each mold. Reserve the timbales and the remaining butter, chilled.

For the Chicken Wing Ballotine

With an immersion circulator, preheat a water bath to 144°F. Chop the tips off the bones on both ends of the chicken wings. Carefully push out the bones and discard them. Pipe about ½ tablespoon reserved mousse into the center of each wing. Season the wings with salt and pepper. With plastic wrap, roll each wing tightly into a ¾-inch-diameter log and tie the ends to seal. Submerge the logs in the prepared water bath and cook for 1 hour. Transfer to the refrigerator until chilled, then trim each chicken wing into 3 equal discs. Reserve, chilled.

For the Watercress Velouté

Bring a large pot of salted water to a boil and place a bowl of ice water on the side. Add the watercress and parsley leaves and boil for 45 seconds. Transfer to the ice water to chill; squeeze dry. Pour the cream into a small saucepan and bring to a simmer. Combine the watercress, parsley, and hot cream in a blender and puree until smooth; season with salt and pepper. Pass the watercress cream through a fine-meshed sieve into a bowl set over ice and stir until chilled.

Heat the olive oil in a large Dutch oven or heavy-bottomed pot over medium heat. Add the onion, leek, bouquet garni, and garlic. Cook, stirring, until the onion is translucent, about 2 minutes. Add the potato and chicken stock and bring to a boil. Reduce the heat and simmer until the potatoes are tender, about 20 minutes. Stir in the crème fraîche. Carefully transfer the mixture to a blender (you may need to do this in batches) and puree until smooth; season with salt and pepper. Pass through a fine-meshed sieve and reserve, chilled.

Just before serving, reheat the soup and whisk the watercress cream. Adjust the seasoning with salt and pepper if needed.

For the Morels and Fava Beans

Bring a medium saucepan of salted water to a boil and set a bowl of ice water on the side. Boil the fava beans for 2 minutes, or until tender, and then chill in the ice water. Peel the beans.

To clean the morels, submerge them in a bowl of cold water, leave for 2 minutes, strain from the top, and repeat until the water that settles at the bottom is clear. Strain and pat dry with a towel. Melt the butter in a medium sauté pan over medium heat. Add the morels, sprinkle with salt, and cook, stirring occasionally, for 5 minutes. Add the chicken stock and simmer until the morels are cooked and the liquid has reduced to a glaze, about 5 minutes. Slice each morel into 3 rings and return to the pan. Add the fava beans and toss to heat through. Check the seasoning and reserve, kept warm.

To Finish

Fill one-third of a medium saucepan with canola oil and heat to 350°F. Melt the reserved crayfish butter.

Place a slice of chicken wing ballotine inside each crayfish timbale to top it off. Pour ½ inch of water in a large medium saucepan and bring to a simmer. Reduce the heat, stand the timbales inside, cover with aluminum foil, and cook for 15 minutes at just under a simmer.

Strain and pat dry the cockscombs; individually dip them into the tempura batter. Fry for 1 minute, or until golden brown. Transfer to a paper towel–lined tray and sprinkle with salt.

For each serving, unmold 3 timbales and arrange crayfish side up in the bottom of a soup bowl. Top each timbale with a slice of black garlic and place a piece of fried cockscomb on top. Alternate 3 morel rings topped with a fava bean between the timbales. Pour in the soup and garnish with a few dots of crayfish butter. Arrange 3 leaves of wild chervil against the timbales.

VENISON CONSOMMÉ
WITH BLACK TRUFFLE

SERVES 6 (WITH 1¼ CUPS CONSOMMÉ PER SERVING)

JUST AS THE Japanese dashi broth with its bonito flakes can be seen as the essence of Japanese cuisine, the French consommé is the purest and clearest form of broth, infused with nature. A perfect consommé shines a golden hue and beats with the essence of its components, whether meat or shellfish or vegetables and herbs.

In this recipe, the consommé is fortified with venison and root vegetables. And to expand the flavor, we add a delicate truffle cream that melts over the liquid in a frothy blanket of richness.

Black Truffle Cream

1 small black winter truffle

½ cup heavy cream

1 tablespoon finely chopped black winter truffle

Salt and finely ground white pepper

Vegetable Medley

1 small turnip, peeled

1 stalk celery

1 small celery root, peeled

1 small rutabaga, peeled

1 small purple potato, peeled

1 large porcini mushroom, stem peeled and cap wiped clean

Truffle-Encrusted Venison Loin

2 cups Venison Consommé (page 368)

12 ounces venison loin, trimmed of any sinew and fat

1 pinch of ground juniper berries

Salt and freshly ground white pepper

Veal stock, if needed

Chopped black truffle, reserved from above

To Finish

2 quarts Venison Consommé (page 368)

4 ounces Hon-shimeji mushrooms, trimmed and rinsed

1 small black winter truffle

6 small spinach leaves

¼ cup fresh chervil leaves

For the Black Truffle Cream

Chop the truffle finely and set aside three-quarters of it for the truffle-encrusted loin. Up to 1 hour in advance, whip the heavy cream to stiff peaks and fold in the remaining chopped black truffle. Season with salt and pepper and reserve, chilled.

For the Vegetable Medley

With a mandoline, cut the turnip, celery, celery root, rutabaga, and potato into approximately ¼-inch slices. Cut the slices into various shapes, no larger than ½ inch in width. Cut the porcini into small pieces no larger than ½ inch wide. Set the vegetables aside.

For the Truffle-Encrusted Venison Loin

Pour 2 cups consommé into a medium saucepan and bring to a light simmer. Season the loin on all sides with the juniper, salt, and pepper, and tie with butcher's twine in 1-inch intervals. Submerge the loin in the consommé (cut the loin in half if needed to fit the pan and top with veal stock if needed) and poach until the internal temperature reaches 130°F, about 20 minutes.

Remove the venison and reserve the consommé to heat the vegetables. Cut away the twine and pat dry. Spread the reserved chopped black truffle on a tray and roll the venison on it to coat. Top with a sheet of aluminum foil and reserve, kept warm.

To Finish

Pour the 2 quarts consommé into a large saucepan and bring to a simmer. Add the vegetables and the porcini and Hon-shimeji mushrooms to the reserved venison poaching liquid and simmer for 3 minutes, or until just cooked through. Thinly slice the truffle on a truffle shaver or mandoline, cut 2 shavings into julienne, and divide the rest among 6 hot soup bowls, lining the bottoms. Slice the venison loin into 6 portions.

For each serving, set 1 spinach leaf in the center of the truffles and place a slice of venison on top. With a slotted spoon, scoop a spoonful of vegetables and arrange them around the venison. Top the venison loin slice with a spoonful of truffle cream and a few julienned truffles. Place a couple of chervil leaves on the vegetables.

Pour or ladle the 2 quarts of hot consommé into the bowls at the table.

FROG LEG
SOUPE EN CROÛTE VGE

MAKES 2 QUARTS, OR 8 (10-OUNCE, 2.5-INCH-DEEP
X 3.75-INCH-DIAMETER RIM) SOUP CUPS

IN 1974, as he was about to receive the French Légion d'honneur, my friend and mentor Paul Bocuse first served a wonderful truffle, sweetbreads, and foie gras consommé hidden under a golden puff pastry crust to President Valéry Giscard d'Estaing. This soup would soon become a legendary staple on Bocuse's menu and was named Soup VGE. A myth within a golden crust was born.

At Daniel, we honor Monsieur Paul by giving the "VGE" treatment to a number of different soups. This frog leg velouté with potatoes and a touch of cream revisits the classic garlic and parsley accompaniments and complements the crusty bubble perfectly.

Frog Leg Velouté

3 pounds fresh frog hindquarters

2 medium onions, 1 chopped and
1 thinly sliced

1 medium leek, white and light green
parts sliced and rinsed (save
the green top)

1 bouquet garni (1 bay leaf, 1 parsley
sprig, and 1 thyme sprig, sandwiched
in a 2-inch green leek top, secured
with butcher's twine)

2 cups dry white wine

1½ quarts Chicken Stock (page 368)

2 tablespoons olive oil

7 cloves garlic, peeled, 5 halved and
2 chopped

2 Yukon gold potatoes (8 ounces),
peeled and cut into small dice

¼ cup crème fraîche

Salt and freshly ground white pepper

3 tablespoons butter

½ cup (about 2½ ounces) Hon-shimeji
mushroom caps

2 egg yolks, whipped with 1 tablespoon
water

8 discs frozen puff pastry sheets,
cut ¼ inch wider than the soup
cup diameter

Parsley Whipped Cream

Salt

8 ounces parsley leaves

1 cup heavy cream

Freshly ground white pepper

For the Frog Leg Velouté

With a chef's knife, separate the legs of
the frog hindquarters and remove the feet.
Separate the drumsticks from the thighs.
With a paring knife, carve the meat off the
bones. Rinse and reserve the bones. Cut
the meat into small morsels.

In a 5-quart Dutch oven or heavy-bottomed
pot, combine the bones, chopped onion,
sliced leek, bouquet garni, white wine, and
chicken stock and bring to a boil. Reduce the
heat and simmer for 30 minutes, skimming off
any foam that rises to the surface. Strain the
broth through a sieve set over a bowl and
discard the solids.

Rinse and dry the Dutch oven and return
to medium-high heat. Add the olive oil, the
sliced onion, and the halved garlic and cook,
stirring, for 5 minutes, without coloring. Add
three-quarters of the diced potato and cook,
stirring, for another 2 minutes. Add the
reserved frog leg broth and bring to a boil.
Reduce the heat and simmer until the
potatoes are tender, about 15 minutes. Stir
in the crème fraîche. Carefully transfer the
mixture to a blender (you may need to do this
in batches) and puree until smooth. Season
with salt and pepper. Pass the soup through
a fine-meshed sieve into a bowl set over ice
and stir until chilled.

Heat 2 tablespoons of the butter in a
large sauté pan over medium-low heat.
Season the frog morsels with salt and pepper,
add them to the pan, and cook, stirring
without browning, until firm, 3 to 4 minutes.
Transfer the meat to a plate. Add the
remaining 1 tablespoon butter to the pan
with the chopped garlic and cook, stirring,
for 2 to 3 minutes, or until tender. Add the
mushrooms and the remaining potato and
cook, stirring, for 5 more minutes, or until
the potato is cooked but not mushy. Return
the frog meat to the pan and stir to combine.
Season with salt and pepper and remove
from the heat.

Lightly brush a ring of egg yolk on the outside rims of eight 10-ounce heatproof, 2½-inch-deep x 3¼-inch-diameter rim soup cups or tête de lion cups. Divide the frog meat mixture into the cups and pour in enough chilled soup to reach ½ inch from the rim. Working in batches of 2, remove frozen puff pastry discs and allow them to thaw at room temperature for 3 minutes so they are slightly flexible but not soft. Working quickly so that the dough stays firm, place the pastry on the soup cup and use your thumbs to press the overhanging dough firmly onto the cup's sides. Lightly brush the pastry with the egg mixture. With a paring knife, being careful not to pierce the pastry, very lightly score a crosshatch pattern on top. Transfer to the refrigerator and continue to make 8 cups. Keep, refrigerated, for up to 6 hours.

For the Parsley Whipped Cream

Bring a medium pot of salted water to a boil and place a bowl of ice water on the side. Add the parsley leaves and boil for 2 minutes, or until tender. Transfer to the ice water to chill, squeeze dry, and transfer to a blender. Pour the cream into a small saucepan and bring to a simmer. Pour the hot cream into the blender and puree with the parsley until smooth. Pass the mixture through a fine-meshed sieve into a bowl set over ice. Stir to chill, and when ready to serve, whip the cream to form stiff peaks. Season with salt and pepper.

To Finish

Preheat a convection oven to 410°F (for a regular oven, 420°F). Transfer the soups to a baking sheet and bake for 8 to 10 minutes (for a regular oven, 10 to 15 minutes), until the pastry puffs up and is browned on top. At the table, poke a hole in the crust and insert a spoonful of parsley cream.

FLAKED NEW ENGLAND COD
TARBAIS BEANS, CHORIZO, ALMOND CLOUD

SERVES 6

RISING ELOQUENTLY over a round hill surrounded by a cloud of Marcona almond foam, the ubiquitous cod is elevated to new heights. Though the Tarbais bean, whole and pureed, constitutes the lower layer of the dish, it doesn't play the supporting role. In fact, the Tarbais bean is our star.

First brought back to Europe from the New World by Christopher Columbus, the bean quickly became a reliable staple for the waves of frequently famished populations. It was during the eighteenth century that it flourished in the foothills of the Pyrénées in southwest France, winding along the corn stalks near the city of Tarbes. Imagine, in 1881 the region produced more than six million pounds of Tarbais beans!

With the introduction of more intensive mechanical agriculture in the 1950s, the cultivation of the bean, which has to be picked by hand, diminished greatly, but gourmand farmers always kept a few furrows for their own use. We had to wait until 1986, when a group of farmers met in Tarbes with a local agricultural adviser. Brainstorming about their difficulties, they decided to reintroduce their beloved Tarbais bean to the world, positioning it as an artisanal and cultural delicacy.

FLAKED NEW ENGLAND COD
TARBAIS BEANS, CHORIZO,
ALMOND CLOUD

Tarbais Bean Puree

2 cups dried Tarbais beans

3 quarts Chicken Stock (page 368)

1 small onion

2 cloves

1 medium carrot, peeled and
cut into 4 pieces

1 stalk celery, cut into 4 pieces

2 cloves garlic, peeled and smashed

1 bouquet garni (one 3-inch piece
leek, 2 sprigs fresh thyme, and 1 bay leaf,
bundled together and secured with
butcher's twine)

Salt

¼ cup olive oil

1 tablespoon sherry vinegar

Freshly ground white pepper

Cod Confit

2 cups kosher salt

1 cup sugar

Finely grated zest of 4 lemons

Finely grated zest of 4 limes

1 (2-pound) skinless, boneless cod fillet
preferably from the thicker end

3 cups olive oil

1 sachet (1 clove garlic, peeled, 2 sprigs
thyme, 1 bay leaf, 1 teaspoon each white
peppercorns and coriander seeds, and a
pinch of chili flakes wrapped in cheesecloth
and secured with butcher's twine)

Almond Cloud

½ cup finely chopped Marcona almonds

1 tablespoon butter

½ cup heavy cream

1 teaspoon sherry vinegar

1 tablespoon soy lecithin powder

To Finish

1 tablespoon Chicken Stock (page 368)

¼ cup small-diced manouri cheese

¼ cup brunoised chorizo

4 petals Tomato Confit (page 376),
julienned

4 teaspoons lilliput capers, drained

24 small flat-leaf parsley leaves

1 pinch of Korean dried chili threads

2 teaspoons finely chopped Marcona
almonds

1 pinch of piment d'Espelette

For the Tarbais Bean Puree

Rinse the Tarbais beans with cold water until
it runs clear. Cover the beans with the chicken
stock and refrigerate overnight. Stud the
onion with the cloves. Transfer the beans and
stock to a medium heavy-bottomed saucepan; add the onion, carrot, celery, garlic, and
bouquet garni. Place over medium-high heat
and bring to a low, steady simmer; cover.
Cook, occasionally stirring and skimming the
foam that rises to the surface, until the beans
are tender, about 4 hours. Season with salt in
the final 15 minutes of cooking. Scoop and
reserve ½ cup of the cooked beans for garnish.
Continue cooking the remaining beans for
another 45 to 60 minutes, until very soft.
Pick and discard the vegetables and bouquet
garni. With a slotted spoon, transfer the beans
to a blender and mix with enough stock to
form a thick puree. Stream in the olive oil
and vinegar. Pass through a fine-meshed
sieve, season with salt and pepper, and
reserve, chilled.

For the Cod Confit

In a nonreactive container, mix the salt, sugar,
and zests. Add the cod and pack the salt
mixture around to coat completely. Cover
and refrigerate for 30 minutes. Remove the
cod; rinse off and discard the salt mixture,
then pat dry. Reserve, chilled.

In a 3-quart saucepan, combine the olive
oil and sachet, cover, and warm over low heat
for 30 minutes. Remove and discard the sachet;
set aside.

For the Almond Cloud

In a medium saucepan, combine the almonds, butter, cream, and vinegar with 1 cup water and place over medium heat. Bring to a simmer, cover, and set aside to infuse for 10 minutes. Strain off the almonds through a fine-meshed sieve and return the liquid to the pan. Using a hand blender, dissolve in the soy lecithin.

To Finish

Rest the cod at room temperature for 10 minutes and heat the prepared confit oil to 165°F. Submerge the cod in the oil and begin checking for doneness after 8 minutes by piercing the flesh with a cake tester. When the fish is easily pierced and the fillet shows signs of separating, remove it from the oil (the internal temperature should reach 135°F) and keep warm.

Heat the almond cloud liquid to 170°F. Position the head of a hand blender just below the surface of the liquid and mix to produce a light foam.

In a medium saucepan over medium heat, warm the bean puree. In a small sauté pan, bring the chicken stock to a simmer, add the reserved beans, and toss to warm.

For each serving, spread a spoonful of the puree into the center of a warm bowl or plate. Gently break the warm cod into large flakes and place 4 to 5 flakes on top of the puree. Arrange some of the whole beans with a few pieces of manouri cheese around the perimeter. Sprinkle the chorizo, tomato confit, capers, parsley, dried chili threads, and chopped almonds on top of the fish. Sprinkle with piment d'Espelette and spoon the almond foam on top to encircle the cod.

JADE TIGER ABALONE
CAULIFLOWER CONCASSÉ, CAVIAR

SERVES 4

I ALWAYS LOVE cauliflower with caviar, a combination perfected by Joël Robuchon in the 1980s. The Jade Tiger Abalone, maybe the most interesting mollusk, arrives from the fishmonger still in its turquoise iridescent single shell. Before you cure them in salt, let your abalone rest in the refrigerator for two days, covered in a damp cloth—it makes for a more tender result.

Back in its vessel, cooked and mixed with cauliflower puree, the mollusk now reads both briny and rich. Under a sprinkling of caviar, another briny salty touch, and hard-boiled eggs, a vodka beurre blanc finishes this Russian-themed appetizer.

Alongside the abalone on the plate are different cauliflower preparations: pureed, pickled, in florets, and in crispy tempura. Mixed lettuce planted throughout the dish mirror delicate seaweed moving with the tide—a delicious underwater landscape.

JADE TIGER ABALONE
CAULIFLOWER CONCASSÉ, CAVIAR

Jade Tiger Abalone

8 Jade Tiger Abalone, in their shells

½ cup kosher salt

1 quart Chicken Stock (page 368)

1 cup heavy cream

3 tablespoons Dijon mustard

Cauliflower Puree and Concassé

1 head (1½ pounds) cauliflower

1 cup milk

½ cup Chicken Stock (page 368)

Salt

1 tablespoon crème fraîche

1 teaspoon lemon juice

1 splash of Tabasco sauce

Freshly ground white pepper

Cauliflower and Romanesco Florets

Salt

1 head (1 pound) romanesco

16 small cauliflower florets, reserved from above

½ cup Pickling Liquid (page 377)

10 white peppercorns

Cauliflower Tempura

Canola oil for frying

3 large cauliflower florets, reserved from above

Tempura Batter (page 374)

Salt

Vodka Beurre Blanc

1 tablespoon finely minced shallot

4 tablespoons vodka

2 tablespoons heavy cream

4 tablespoons (½ stick) chilled butter, diced

Salt

To Finish

1½ tablespoons butter

2 tablespoons Chicken Stock (page 368)

8 small boiled cauliflower florets, reserved from above

8 small boiled romanesco florets, reserved from above

Salt and freshly ground white pepper

1 tablespoon crushed black peppercorns

1 tablespoon thinly sliced chives

2 hard-boiled eggs, peeled and passed through a drum sieve

¼ cup golden osetra caviar

12 leaves baby mixed lettuce

For the Jade Tiger Abalone

Scrub the abalone with a stiff brush while rinsing with cold water to remove the black skin from the flesh. Using a spoon, remove the abalone from their shells. Trim and discard the entrails. Place in a nonreactive container with the salt, toss to coat, and cover. Refrigerate, covered, for 12 hours.

Meanwhile, bring a large pot of water to a boil and add the shells. Boil for 30 minutes, strain, wipe the shells clean, and reserve.

Combine the chicken stock, heavy cream, and mustard in a large saucepan and bring to a light simmer. Rinse the salt from the abalone, pat dry, and add to the liquid. Cover and cook at a low simmer for 2 hours. Remove from the heat and cool the abalone in the liquid; strain. Slice the abalone crosswise into ⅛-inch-thick diagonal slices and arrange them back into their original shape. Reserve, chilled.

For the Cauliflower Puree and Concassé

Trim and reserve 16 small florets and 3 large florets from the head of the cauliflower. Roughly chop the remaining cauliflower and combine with the milk and chicken stock in a medium saucepan with a pinch of salt. Bring to a simmer and cook, stirring occasionally, until tender, about 20 minutes.

Strain the cauliflower and transfer three-quarters to a blender with the crème fraîche and lemon juice. Puree until smooth and season with the Tabasco and salt and pepper. Coarsely chop the remaining cooked cauliflower into concassé, transfer to a small bowl, and season with salt and pepper. Reserve the puree and concassé, chilled.

For the Cauliflower and Romanesco Florets

Bring a large pot of salted water to a boil and place a bowl of ice water on the side. Trim the romanesco into at least 16 small florets. Boil the romanesco florets and the reserved 16 small cauliflower florets for about 2 minutes, until tender, then chill in the ice water. Strain and pat dry.

Transfer the pickling liquid and peppercorns to a small saucepan and bring to a simmer. Remove from the heat, cover, and

infuse for 10 minutes. Add half of the boiled cauliflower and romanesco florets and chill in the liquid.

For the Cauliflower Tempura

Fill one-third of a medium saucepan with canola oil and heat to 350°F. Using a mandoline, slice the large cauliflower florets into at least eight ¹⁄₁₆-inch slices. When ready to serve, dip the cauliflower slices into the tempura batter to coat; fry in batches until crisp and golden. Strain onto a paper towel–lined plate and sprinkle with salt.

For the Vodka Beurre Blanc

When ready to serve, in a small saucepan, combine the shallot and 3 tablespoons of the vodka. Simmer until almost dry. Over low heat, stir in the cream and whisk in the butter piece by piece (the sauce will thicken). Do not boil or it will separate. Add the remaining tablespoon of vodka and season with salt. Reserve, kept warm.

To Finish

Arrange a rack on the top shelf of the oven and preheat the oven to 350°F.

Transfer the cauliflower puree to a small saucepan over medium heat and stir until heated through. In another small pan, bring the butter, chicken stock, and remaining boiled cauliflower and romanesco florets to a simmer, stirring, until heated through and the liquid is reduced to a glaze. Season with salt and pepper.

Place the abalone shells face up on a baking sheet and divide the cauliflower concassé into the bottoms. Top each with an abalone, slightly fanning the slices. Cover with foil and bake for 5 minutes, or until the abalone is heated through; remove from the oven and spoon the vodka beurre blanc onto the tops of the abalone to coat. Bake until the sauce is shiny, 2 to 4 minutes. Sprinkle the abalone with crushed black peppercorns, chives, and hard-boiled eggs.

For each serving, place 2 abalone on opposite sides of the plate and top each with ½ tablespoon of caviar. Place a few spoonfuls of cauliflower puree in the center and arrange 2 glazed romanesco, 2 glazed cauliflower, 2 cauliflower pickles, 2 romanesco pickles, and 2 tempura-fried cauliflower slices around. Garnish with 3 pieces of baby lettuce.

FROG LEG FRICASSÉE
KAMUT BERRIES, SPINACH PUREE

SERVES 6

I NO LONGER run after the frogs at dusk the way I used to do at the farm, but I still get excited when we put frog legs on the menu! Frog legs were very popular when I was growing up, and as the seventeen-year-old chef de partie at Georges Blanc in Vonnas, I cooked about fifty portions of cuisses de grenouilles persillade every day. The guests would wear a bib and eat with their fingers. When I first moved to New York, we imported them from France, but now we can get them from the Everglades in Florida.

To keep the connection with the frog legs eaten on the bone, we have breaded our own frog "lollipops" lightly and set them so they frame a frog fricassée persillade, topped with fried shallot rings and black garlic. The kamut "berries," ancient wheat kernels, take on a risotto consistency.

Kamut Berries

½ cup kamut berries

2 cups Chicken Stock (page 368), plus extra as needed

1 sachet (2 sprigs thyme, 1 teaspoon black peppercorns, 1 clove garlic, peeled, and 1 bay leaf wrapped in cheesecloth and tied with butcher's twine)

1 teaspoon salt

¼ cup heavy cream

¼ cup Garlic Paste (page 371)

Frog Leg Lollipops

18 fresh frog hindquarters, skinned and cleaned

3 eggs, beaten with ¼ cup milk

⅓ cup flour

⅓ cup Fine White Breadcrumbs (page 373)

Salt and freshly ground white pepper

Frog Leg Fricassée

4 tablespoons olive oil

12 medium white button mushrooms, cleaned, trimmed, and quartered

Salt and freshly ground white pepper

Frog drumstick and thigh morsels, reserved from above

Flour, as needed, for dusting the legs

2 sprigs thyme

1 clove garlic, peeled and smashed

1 tablespoon butter

1 cup baby spinach leaves

1 clove black garlic, peeled and minced

2 teaspoons cracked black pepper

2 tablespoons sherry vinegar

¼ cup Chicken Jus (page 369)

2 tablespoons chopped parsley

To Finish

Canola oil for frying

1½ cups Spinach Puree (page 371)

Salt

24 Crispy Shallot Rings (page 372)

3 cloves black garlic, peeled and sliced

¼ cup baby spinach leaves

For the Kamut Berries

Rinse the kamut berries with cold water until the water runs clear. Place in a bowl, combine with the chicken stock and sachet, and soak in the refrigerator overnight. The next day, transfer to a large saucepan, add the salt, and bring to a simmer. Simmer lightly for approximately 3 hours, stirring occasionally, until the kamut berries are tender. If the liquid reduces before the kamut is tender, add more chicken stock as necessary. Remove the sachet and, when ready to serve, add the heavy cream and garlic paste and simmer for 3 minutes, or until thickened; check the seasoning and reserve, kept warm.

For the Frog Leg Lollipops

Using a sharp knife, separate the legs of the hindquarters and remove the feet. Separate the drumsticks from the thighs. With a paring knife, scrape the meat down from 12 of the drumsticks, starting from the joint end of the bone, to form a ball of meat at the foot end to resemble a lollipop. Trim the meat away from the remaining frog drumsticks and thighs and cut into small morsels for the fricassée. Place the beaten egg, flour, and white breadcrumbs in separate shallow dishes and season each with a pinch of salt and pepper. While holding the bone, dip the frog leg lollipops one by one into the flour, eggs, and then breadcrumbs to evenly coat the meat. Reserve, chilled.

For the Frog Leg Fricassée

In a large sauté pan, heat 1 tablespoon of the olive oil over medium-high heat. Add the mushrooms and sauté until browned, about 4 minutes, season with salt and pepper, then transfer to a paper towel–lined plate.

When ready to serve, season the frog morsels with salt and pepper. Dust with flour and pat away the excess. In the same pan, heat the remaining 3 tablespoons olive oil over high heat. Add the frog morsels and brown on all sides, adding the thyme and garlic halfway through cooking. Strain onto a paper towel–lined plate; discard the thyme and garlic. Add the butter to the same pan and reduce the heat to medium-high. Add the spinach and black garlic and sauté until wilted. Return the mushrooms and frog legs to the pan along with the cracked black pepper. Toss to combine, then deglaze with the vinegar. Stir in the chicken jus and chopped parsley; check the seasoning and keep warm.

To Finish

Fill one-third of a medium saucepan with canola oil and heat to 350°F. Transfer the spinach puree to a small saucepan over medium heat and stir to heat through. Transfer to a piping bag and keep warm. Fry the frog leg lollipops until golden brown and cooked through, about 2 minutes. Drain onto a paper towel–lined tray, sprinkle with salt, and keep warm.

For each serving, set a 6-inch square mold on a warm plate and pipe spinach puree around the inside perimeter. Fill the middle with a spoonful of kamut berries. Top with a large spoonful of fricassée and place 2 fried lollipops around the perimeter. Remove the mold and garnish with 4 crispy shallot rings, some sliced black garlic, and a few baby spinach leaves.

SOFT-SHELL CRAB TEMPURA
LEMON GREMOLATA, PICKLED FRESNO PEPPERS

SERVES 6

IT'S A LONG AND PASSIONATE affair between the Maryland soft-shell crab and me. Since they are indigenous to the New World, I'd never seen any until I came to the United States, but it was love at first bite. Then, every year in late spring, I would hop a plane to see my parents in Lyon and surreptitiously smuggle on board a bag of five or six dozen of the live creatures, ever so carefully packed. They traveled well and the next day, I would cook them for my whole family. What a rare feast!

I often like them very crunchy, as in this recipe, wrapped in tempura batter but still tender and juicy at the core, with a peppery gremolata dressing and adorned with wild foraged Golden Alexander flowers.

Pickled Fresno Peppers

2 Fresno peppers

Pickling Liquid (page 377)

1 teaspoon chili flakes

Broccoli Marmalade, Puree, and Broccolini

Salt

½ bunch broccolini

2 heads broccoli

3 tablespoons olive oil

Freshly ground white pepper

Lemon Gremolata

1 lemon, finely grated zest and small-diced supremes

1 teaspoon olive oil

½ teaspoon cracked black pepper

1 pinch of fleur de sel

1 tablespoon wild lumpfish caviar (we recommend Société-Orignal)

1 teaspoon thinly sliced chives

Soft-Shell Crabs

Canola oil for frying

6 live hotel-size soft-shell crabs (4 to 4½ inches wide)

Tempura Batter (page 374)

Salt and freshly ground white pepper

To Finish

2 teaspoons butter

Salt and freshly ground white pepper

1 head baby lettuce

¼ cup golden Alexander flowers

For the Pickled Fresno Peppers

Slice the peppers into thin rounds and transfer to a heatproof container. In a small saucepan, combine the pickling liquid with the chili flakes and bring to a simmer. Pour over the top of the peppers and refrigerate overnight or up to 2 weeks.

For the Broccoli Marmalade, Puree, and Broccolini

Bring a large pot of salted water to a boil and place a bowl of ice water on the side. Trim away any woody stalks from the broccolini and cut them into 1-inch florets. Cut ½-inch florets from the broccoli heads and set aside. Using a vegetable peeler, remove the skin from the stalks, then cut them into rough 1-inch pieces.

Boil the broccolini florets until tender, about 2 minutes, then chill in the ice water. Pat dry and reserve. Boil the broccoli florets until tender, about 2 minutes, then chill in the ice water. Remove, pat dry, and transfer to a cutting board. Finely chop the florets and transfer one-third to a blender. Boil the broccoli stalks until tender, about 3 minutes, then transfer to the blender with the florets.

Add the olive oil and puree until smooth; season with salt and pepper. Pass the puree through a fine-meshed sieve into a bowl set over ice and stir until chilled. Reserve the remaining chopped florets, chilled.

For the Lemon Gremolata

In a small bowl, combine the lemon zest, supremes, olive oil, black pepper, and fleur de sel. Just before serving, stir in the lumpfish caviar and the chives.

For the Soft-Shell Crabs

Fill one-third of a medium saucepan with canola oil and heat to 350°F. Use kitchen shears to cut off the face of a crab, about ½ inch behind the eyes and mouth; squeeze out the small sac located directly behind the eyes and mouth. Lift the pointed ends of the crab's outer shell to cut away the gills. Turn the crab over and snip off the small flap (apron). Rinse the crab well and pat dry. Repeat with the remaining crabs. With long tweezers or a fork, dip the crabs individually into the tempura batter to coat and fry until golden brown. Transfer to a paper towel–lined tray and sprinkle with salt and pepper. With a sharp knife, cut the crabs in half crosswise.

To Finish

Melt the butter in a small sauté pan over medium heat and add the broccolini. Toss to heat through and adjust the seasoning with salt and pepper. Transfer the puree to a medium saucepan over medium heat and stir to heat through. Scoop half of the hot puree into a squeeze bottle or piping bag; keep warm. Stir the reserved chopped florets into the remaining puree to heat through; adjust the seasoning if needed.

For each serving, pipe 2 parallel lines of puree about 3 inches apart onto a warm plate. Spoon marmalade into the center and top with 2 crab halves, claws facing upward. Garnish with a few pieces of broccolini, pickled peppers, and baby lettuce leaves. Sprinkle the lemon gremolata and Golden Alexander flowers over the top.

HAZELNUT-CRUSTED MAINE SEA SCALLOPS
NETTLES, SWISS CHARD

SERVES 4

FEW CREATURES of the sea offer as much versatility, texture, and taste as our Maine sea scallops. We love to serve them raw, barely cooked, or, as in this dish, encrusted with a morel and hazelnut mélange to concentrate more of a toasty flavor onto the sweet mollusk. With Swiss chard, grassy nettle foam, and peppery paper-thin nettle chips, we balance the marine foundation with fresh woodsy flavors.

Sautéed Morels

20 medium morel mushrooms
(about 8 ounces)

2 tablespoons butter

1 large shallot, minced

Salt and freshly ground white pepper

¼ cup vermouth

⅓ cup Chicken Stock (page 368)

3 tablespoons Chicken Jus
(page 369)

Hazelnut and Morel Crust (makes extra)

3 ounces (about 8) sautéed morels,
reserved from above

2 ounces toasted hazelnuts

½ cup (1 stick) butter, at room temperature

5 ounces Fine White Breadcrumbs
(page 373)

1 tablespoon Dijon mustard

Nettle Foam

2 cups Chicken Stock (page 368)

1 tablespoon butter

1 medium shallot, diced

2 ounces nettle leaves

¼ cup heavy cream

1 tablespoon soy lecithin powder

Salt and freshly ground white pepper

Swiss Chard

1 bunch Swiss chard

1 tablespoon butter

¼ cup Chicken Stock (page 368)

1 clove garlic, peeled

2 sprigs thyme

Salt and freshly ground white pepper

To Finish

½ cup Chicken Jus (page 369)

8 large sea scallops

Salt and freshly ground white pepper

1 tablespoon olive oil

12 Nettle Chips
(see Herb Chips, page 373)

12 leaves miner's lettuce

For the Sautéed Morels

To clean the morels, submerge them in a bowl of cold water, leave for 2 minutes, strain from the top, and repeat until the water that settles at the bottom is clear. Strain and pat dry with a towel. Melt the butter in a medium sauté pan over medium heat and add the shallot. Cook, stirring, until translucent, about 2 minutes. Add the morels, season with salt and pepper, and cook, stirring occasionally, for 5 minutes. Add the vermouth and reduce until almost dry. Add the chicken stock and simmer until the morels are cooked and the liquid has reduced to a glaze, about 12 minutes. Add the chicken jus and toss. Check the seasoning and set aside 12 pieces for garnish; use the rest for the crust. Reserve, chilled.

For the Hazelnut and Morel Crust

In the bowl of a food processor fitted with a blade, pulse the sautéed morels and hazelnuts until coarse. Add the butter, breadcrumbs, and mustard and pulse until combined. Scoop the mixture onto a sheet of parchment paper. Using the paper as an aid, roll the mixture into a log the diameter of the scallops and freeze until hardened.

For the Nettle Foam

Pour the chicken stock into a small saucepan and bring to a simmer. In a medium sauté pan over medium heat, melt the butter and add the shallot. Cook, stirring, until translucent, about 2 minutes. Add the nettle leaves and stir until wilted. Transfer the nettles to a blender with the hot stock, the heavy cream,

and the soy lecithin, and puree until smooth. Pass through a fine-meshed sieve into a bowl set over ice. Season with salt and pepper. Stir to chill.

For the Swiss Chard

Separate the leaves from the stems of the Swiss chard and roughly chop the leaves. Peel the tough skin from the thicker ends of the stems and cut them on a bias into at least twelve ½-inch diamonds.

Place the stems in a small sauté pan with the butter, chicken stock, garlic, and thyme. Cook over medium heat until the stock and butter have reduced to a glaze and the stems are tender. Add the leaves and toss until wilted, about 1 minute. Season with salt and pepper; discard the garlic and thyme and keep warm.

To Finish

Preheat the broiler to medium-high. Transfer the chicken jus to a small saucepan and bring to a simmer.

Pat the scallops dry and season with salt and pepper. Heat the olive oil in a large sauté pan over medium-high heat. Sear both sides of the scallops, about 20 seconds each, and transfer them to an aluminum foil–lined baking sheet. Cut ¹⁄₁₆-inch slices from the hazelnut and morel crust and place them on top of the scallops. Broil the scallops until the crust is lightly browned and the scallops are cooked.

Transfer the foam to a small saucepan and heat to 170°F. Position a hand blender head just below the surface of the liquid and blend to produce a light foam.

For each serving, place a spoonful of Swiss chard greens with 3 pieces of stem on the bottom of a warm appetizer plate. Top with 2 scallops and spoon a dollop of foam around them. Arrange 3 morels, 3 nettle chips, and 3 miner's lettuce leaves around the scallops. Drizzle a spoonful of chicken jus on the plate.

SPOT PRAWN CROUSTILLANT
HEARTS OF PALM TANDOORI, KUMQUAT

SERVES 6

IN THE 1970S, Chef Louis Outhier, my friend Jean-Georges Vongerichten's mentor, whose main restaurant was L'Oasis on the French Riviera, created a dish I still remember fondly: langoustines paired with Thai curry. What struck me the most then was the perfect contrast he achieved between spicy and sweet, and this is what I have tried to reenact, but with prawns, given here the Indian spice treatment.

Over a bed of fresh Hawaiian hearts of palm, the spot prawns are crisped within a nest of spring roll pastry sheets. Pickled kumquats lend their tart citrusy dab to a dish we wish to be fragrant but not spicy.

Pickled Kumquats

4 kumquats, cut into ¼-inch slices

½ cup Pickling Liquid (page 377)

1 pinch of chili flakes

Tandoori Kumquat Sauce

Finely grated zest and juice of 10 kumquats

3 tablespoons olive oil

2 teaspoons tandoori paste (we recommend Kalustyan's)

1 teaspoon lime juice

½ teaspoon crushed black pepper

Salt

Spot Prawn Croustillant

1 egg yolk

1 tablespoon tandoori paste

1 pinch of piment d'Espelette

1 teaspoon salt

Freshly ground white pepper

12 large spot prawns, peeled and deveined

10 spring roll pastry sheets, finely julienned

Hearts of Palm Brunoise and Puree

1 pound (an approximately 6-inch-long section) fresh hearts of palm, preferably from the thick base

1 cup Chicken Stock (page 368)

1 cup heavy cream

Salt

1 tablespoon coconut oil

1 tablespoon tandoori paste

Freshly ground white pepper

To Finish

Canola oil for frying

Salt

¼ cup lemon balm

For the Pickled Kumquats

Place the kumquats in a heatproof container. In a small saucepan, combine the pickling liquid and chili flakes, bring to a boil, then pour over the kumquats. Cover and refrigerate for at least 1 day or up to 2 weeks.

For the Tandoori Kumquat Sauce

In a small bowl, mix all of the ingredients together and season with salt. Reserve, chilled.

For the Spot Prawn Croustillant

In a small bowl, whisk the egg yolk with the tandoori paste, piment d'Espelette, salt, and pepper. Curl each prawn into a disc shape and secure with a toothpick. Evenly coat the prawns in the egg mixture. Lay the spring roll julienne on a cutting board, place the prawns on top, and wrap the dough around to coat. Transfer to a tray, cover, and reserve, chilled.

For the Hearts of Palm Brunoise and Puree

Cut 24 matchsticks from the hearts of palm and reserve for garnish. Cut 1 cup of brunoise from the remainder and set aside.

In a small saucepan, combine all the remaining hearts of palm trim with ½ cup of the chicken stock, ½ cup of the cream, and ½ teaspoon salt. Simmer over medium heat until very tender, about 15 minutes. Scoop the hearts of palm into a blender and puree with enough of the cooking liquid to make a smooth, thick puree. Pass through a fine-meshed sieve and reserve, kept warm.

In a medium sauté pan over medium heat, combine the coconut oil and tandoori paste and cook, stirring, for 2 minutes, or until fragrant. Add the brunoised hearts of palm and sauté for 2 minutes, or until tender but not browned. Add the remaining ½ cup chicken stock and ½ cup heavy cream and simmer until reduced to a thick sauce. Season with salt and pepper. Reserve, kept warm.

To Finish

Fill one-third of a medium saucepan with canola oil and heat to 350°F. Fry the prawns in batches until golden brown, 1 to 2 minutes, then strain onto a paper towel–lined tray. Pull out the toothpicks and sprinkle with salt.

For each serving, place 2 spoonfuls of brunoised hearts of palm on a warm plate and top each with a prawn. Top each prawn with 2 matchsticks of hearts of palm, 2 slices of pickled kumquat, and 2 leaves of lemon balm. Spoon dots of puree around the prawns, and drizzle tandoori kumquat sauce on the plate.

LOBSTER BIRYANI MASALA
FRESH COCONUT CHUTNEY, SPICED SHEEP'S YOGURT

SERVES 8

SINCE THE BEGINNING of time, globe-trotter chefs have been inspired by travel around the world and their culinary discoveries. This dish is an invitation to explore, inspired by India and its complex spice combinations (*masala* means mélange of spices ground into a paste). Cardamom, coriander, cumin, cinnamon, and red chiles blend with the perfectly light coconut oil and round up the different ingredients: a crispy samosa filled with spiced lobster and hearts of palm, lightly poached and glazed lobster tail, and tangy Old Chatham sheep's yogurt.

LOBSTER BIRYANI MASALA
FRESH COCONUT CHUTNEY,
SPICED SHEEP'S YOGURT

Biryani Masala Oil

1 tablespoon Biryani Masala
Spice Mix (page 372)

1½ tablespoons grapeseed oil

1½ tablespoons coconut oil

Lobster

2 quarts Court Bouillon (page 369)

4 live lobsters, 1½ pounds each

Coconut Chutney

1 mature coconut

1 young Thai coconut

⅓ cup heavy cream

Juice from ½ lime

1 teaspoon mustard seeds, soaked
in water overnight and strained

Salt and freshly ground white pepper

Grilled Hearts of Palm

1 pound (an approximately 6-inch-long
section) fresh heart of palm, preferably
from the thick base

2 tablespoons Biryani Masala Oil
(see above)

Salt and freshly ground white pepper

Lobster Samosa

2 tablespoons coconut oil

¼ cup brunoised hearts of palm, reserved
from above

¼ cup brunoised yellow bell pepper

¼ cup brunoised red bell pepper

2 teaspoons Biryani Masala Spice Mix
(page 372)

Salt and freshly ground white pepper

1 tablespoon lime juice

1 tablespoon Mayonnaise (page 370)

2 tablespoons Coconut Chutney
(see above)

8 (2 x 7-inch) strips of Japanese
spring roll dough

1 egg yolk, beaten

Romaine Lettuce Salad

4 small heads romaine lettuce

3 tablespoons coconut oil

1 tablespoon lime juice

½ teaspoon salt

To Finish

Canola oil for frying

Salt

1 tablespoon coconut oil

Freshly ground white pepper

1 cup sheep's milk yogurt
(we recommend Old Chatham
Sheepherding Company)

2 teaspoons Biryani Masala
Spice Mix (page 372)

Finely grated zest of 1 lime, plus
the lime segments, chopped

¼ cup purple shiso leaves

*"Tart and creamy, yogurt boosts
spices and herbs, letting the complex
flavor linger."*

For the Biryani Masala Oil

In a small saucepan, combine all the ingredients over medium heat. Cook, stirring, for 2 minutes, or until very fragrant but not burned. Remove from the heat, cover, and rest for 15 minutes. Strain the oil through a fine-meshed sieve lined with a coffee filter and reserve.

For the Lobster

Pour the court bouillon into a large stockpot, bring to a boil, and place a bowl of ice water on the side. Boil the lobsters for 1 minute, then remove them with tongs and rinse under cold water. Twist the arms and tails from the lobsters. Grasp the middle fin of the tails and gently twist and pull out the veins. Boil the tails for 3½ minutes more, then remove and chill in the ice water. Boil the arms for 6 minutes more; remove and chill in the ice water. Crack the tails and arms and extract the meat. Pick and discard any cartilage from the claws and knuckles. Slice the tails in half lengthwise. Chop the claws into ⅛-inch dice. Reserve the lobster, chilled.

For the Coconut Chutney

To open the mature coconut, puncture one of the eyes on the top of the coconut (of the three, one will always be soft enough). Pour out the water from the inside through a strainer set over a medium saucepan. Wrap the coconut in a towel and use a hammer to crack the shell into large pieces. Using a butter knife, pry the meat from the shell. With a mandoline, thinly shave 1 large piece into ribbons for the garnish.

To open the young Thai coconut, use a sharp, heavy knife to carefully chop a 2-inch cap from the pointed tip. Pour out the water through the strainer into the pan. Use a spoon to scrape the meat from the shell.

Chop both coconut meats into ½-inch chunks and transfer to the saucepan with the juice. Add the heavy cream. Simmer for 45 minutes, or until the liquid has reduced by half and the coconut is tender. Transfer the mixture to a blender and puree until smooth but small chunks remain. Stir in the lime juice and mustard seeds and season with salt and pepper. Reserve, chilled.

For the Grilled Hearts of Palm

Heat a grill or cast-iron grill pan over high heat. Cut sixteen 6-inch-long by ½-inch-thick planks from the hearts of palm. With the remaining hearts of palm, use a mandoline to slice 16 long, thin shavings for the garnish. Cut all the remaining hearts of palm into brunoise and reserve for the samosa and romaine lettuce salad. Rub the planks with the biryani masala oil and season with salt and pepper. Grill on both sides until well marked. Set aside.

For the Lobster Samosa

Heat the coconut oil in a small saucepan over medium heat and add the brunoised hearts of palm and bell pepper. Cook, stirring, until tender, about 3 minutes. Add the biryani masala spice mix, season with salt and pepper, and stir to coat. Transfer to a bowl and stir in the reserved chopped lobster claws, the lime juice, the mayonnaise, and the coconut chutney. Adjust the seasoning as necessary with salt and pepper.

Lay the spring roll strips vertically on a cutting board and use a brush to lightly coat each with the beaten yolk. Use a spoon to equally distribute the mixture in a mound on the end of each strip. Fold the bottom right corner up to the left side to form a triangle shape, then fold the triangle forward. Continue folding in this manner to form triangular packets. Transfer to a covered container and store, chilled.

For the Romaine Lettuce Salad

Pull away and discard any damaged outer leaves from the heads of lettuce, then rinse them with cold water. Cut each head lengthwise to form 2 flat ½-inch-thick slices. Set the slices on a cutting board and trim away as much core as possible without breaking them apart.

In a small bowl, stir together the remaining hearts of palm brunoise, the coconut oil, the lime juice, and the salt. Reserve, chilled, for dressing the lettuce.

To Finish

Preheat the oven to 350°F. Fill one-third of a medium saucepan with canola oil and heat to 350°F. Fry the samosas until golden brown and transfer them to a paper towel–lined tray. Sprinkle with salt.

Heat the coconut oil in a heatproof sauté pan over medium heat and add the lobster tails and knuckles; season with salt and pepper. Warm the lobster for 1 minute on each side without browning. Arrange the tails cut side down and coat them with the yogurt. Transfer the pan to the oven for 5 minutes. Remove and sprinkle the biryani masala spice on top of the yogurt.

For each serving, set 1 slice of lettuce on an appetizer plate and sprinkle with the dressing, lime zest, and lime segments. Arrange ½ lobster tail, 2 knuckles, and 1 samosa on top of the lettuce. Spoon a line of biryani masala oil on the plate. Garnish around the lobster with 2 hearts of palm shavings, 2 coconut shavings, 2 grilled hearts of palm, and a few purple shiso leaves. Spoon a few dots of coconut chutney on the plate.

MISO-GLAZED SEA SCALLOP ROSACE
BRUSSELS SPROUTS, CRISPY RICE

SERVES 4

WHEN I ARRIVED in New York, I discovered that Maine sea scallops, which come to us live in the shell, were much sweeter than the ones I had been cooking in Europe. If sliced and overlapped in a rosace (rose pattern), they naturally stick together when cooked. Early on, I would sear the rosace only on one side, so that it would caramelize rapidly and remain barely cooked. Here the layering technique is the same, but the cuisson is achieved through gentle heat rather than a searing in a pan. The delicate mollusks, glazed with miso and black garlic jus, are sprinkled with crispy rice and chive blossoms, and are presented over stewed Brussels sprouts.

Crispy Rice (makes extra)

¼ cup short-grain sushi rice

Salt

About 3 tablespoons rice flour, as needed

Canola oil for frying

Sea Scallop Rosace

8 large sea scallops

Olive oil, as needed

Shallot Confit

6 medium shallots, halved lengthwise

1 cup olive oil

⅛ teaspoon chili flakes

1 teaspoon white balsamic vinegar

Salt and freshly ground white pepper

1 tablespoon thinly sliced chives

Black Miso Sauce

1 teaspoon olive oil

Scallop mussels and scraps, reserved from above

1 teaspoon brunoised onion

1 teaspoon brunoised carrot

1 teaspoon brunoised celery

⅓ cup rice vinegar

⅓ cup mirin

1 tablespoon black miso

½ tablespoon chopped black garlic

1 cup Chicken Jus (page 369)

Salt and freshly ground white pepper

Stewed Brussels Sprouts

Salt

16 Brussels sprouts

1 tablespoon butter

1 tablespoon brunoised carrot

1 tablespoon brunoised onion

1 tablespoon brunoised celery

1 cup Chicken Stock (page 368)

Freshly ground white pepper

To Finish

Crushed black pepper

Salt and freshly ground white pepper

3 cloves black garlic, peeled and thinly sliced

¼ cup purple shiso leaves

¼ cup chive blossoms

For the Crispy Rice

Rinse the rice with cold water until it runs clear. Bring a large pot of salted water to a boil. Add the rice and boil, stirring occasionally, until very soft, 10 to 15 minutes. Strain the rice and pat it dry with a paper towel. Transfer to a parchment-lined baking sheet, sprinkle rice flour over the top, and toss to lightly coat. Spread the rice flat and rest, uncovered, in a warm place for 6 hours, or until dry. Fill one-third of a large saucepan with canola oil and heat to 375°F. Fry the rice in 3 batches until puffed. Strain onto a paper towel–lined plate.

For the Sea Scallop Rosace

Remove the side muscle from the scallops and reserve. Using a 2-inch-diameter ring cutter, cut the scallops into straight cylinders; reserve the trim. Slice each scallop into ⅛-inch-thick discs. Trace 5-inch circles onto four 6-inch squares of parchment paper, turn them over, and lightly brush the papers with oil. Layer the slices from 2 scallops on the oiled side of each paper, inside the circles in a slightly overlapping pattern. Top the scallops with another piece of oiled parchment, oiled side down. Repeat to make 4 "rosaces." Reserve, chilled.

For the Shallot Confit

Combine the shallots, olive oil, chili flakes, and vinegar in a small saucepan, making sure the shallots are submerged, and season with salt and pepper. Bring to a simmer, then reduce the heat to just below a simmer and cook until the shallots are very tender, about 20 minutes. Strain and reserve the oil and keep warm. Just before serving, toss in the chives.

For the Black Miso Sauce

Heat the olive oil in a large sauté pan over medium-high heat. Add the reserved scallop muscles and scraps and cook, stirring often, until cooked through. Add the onion, carrot, and celery and cook, stirring, until tender, about 2 minutes. Add the vinegar and mirin and simmer until almost dry. Add the miso, black garlic, and jus. Simmer until reduced enough to coat the back of a spoon. Transfer to a blender and puree until smooth. Pass through a fine-meshed sieve, season with salt and pepper, and reserve, chilled.

For the Stewed Brussels Sprouts

Bring a medium pot of salted water to a boil and place a bowl of ice water to the side. Peel at least 12 green outer leaves from the Brussels sprouts and boil them until tender, about 30 seconds. Chill them in the ice water, strain, pat dry, and reserve for the garnish.

Shave the remaining Brussels sprouts on a mandoline, avoiding the core. Melt the butter in a large sauté pan over medium heat. Add the carrot, onion, and celery; cook, stirring, until tender, about 3 minutes. Add the shaved Brussels sprouts and stock and bring to a simmer, stirring, until the Brussels sprouts are cooked through, about 10 minutes. Season with salt and pepper and keep warm.

To Finish

Preheat the oven to 300°F. Put the miso sauce in a small saucepan, place over low heat, and stir to heat through; season with crushed black pepper to taste. Remove the top parchment from the scallops, sprinkle with salt and white pepper, and cover again. Transfer to a baking sheet in a single layer and bake for 5 to 6 minutes, until just cooked through.

For each serving, place a 5-inch ring mold in the center of a warm appetizer plate and spoon a layer of stewed Brussels sprouts onto the bottom. Remove the ring from the plate and remove the top layer of parchment from the rosace of cooked scallop. Flip onto the Brussels sprouts and remove the parchment from the top. Glaze with black miso sauce and arrange 3 shallot confit halves, 3 pieces shaved black garlic, a few pieces of purple shiso leaves, and a few Brussels sprout leaves on top. Sprinkle with crispy rice and chive blossoms.

"An herb is the friend of physicians and the praise of cooks." —Charlemagne

DANIEL ON SEASONING AND SPICING

SEASONING AND SPICING IS THE FIRST THING A YOUNG COOK needs to learn, and it's the hardest thing to teach. There's no miracle recipe to follow. Is the fish fillet sliced thin or is it thick and meaty? Are we planning to finish the dish with fleur de sel? Does the steak get a pepper rub before or after cooking?

Great chefs are maniacs about seasoning. While there's no single rule one can follow, you can gauge a confident and precise chef from the way he or she seasons. A perfectly seasoned piece of meat will literally resonate with flavor.

French cuisine lies at the crossroads of what I see as the right balance between seasoning and spicing. At Daniel, we use a vast array of spices and many different techniques for seasoning. Every family of ingredients requires specific seasoning. Sometimes, as in the case of charcuterie, the seasoning must mature before the preparation is ready. A terrine always tastes better a few days after it was made, when the spices have reached the inner boroughs of the meat. But when we work with raw fish for a ceviche or sashimi, for example, we apply a short curing, imparting external flavoring and firmness as quickly as possible.

Let's turn to salt: My favorite way to measure and control salt is to use two, three, or four fingers to pinch, and with each combination, you dose: small, medium, or large. When a young cook puts a hand in the salt, I know instantly if this is someone who knows what he or she is doing! A golden rule: Never change the kind of salt that is being used in a kitchen or you will create terrible chaos. At Daniel, we prefer classic sel de mer from La Baleine, and we never, never change the brand or the grain size; but beware, the degree of strength of that sea salt is very different from the kosher salt many chefs work with in the United States.

Do you know that pepper was the first spice to be introduced to Europe through India? For the peppered rib eye at Daniel, we favor Pierre Poivre, a blend of eight different peppers named for an eighteenth-century French horticulturist and spice trader. The blend was created by our favorite spice master, Lior Lev Sercarz, a young Israeli chef who worked at Restaurant Daniel for four years, and whose passion for spices led him to create his own business in New York, La Boîte à Epice.

I am also particularly fond of piment d' Espelette, a pepper from the French Basque area. As opposed to many other strong spices, its intensity of heat ends in a plateau. It doesn't carry on and burn your palate; it exudes a delicate, pleasant, and almost perfumed heat, very different from more scorching chiles. I find that it is exactly the kind of heat that protects and even enhances the taste of a great wine. With Lior, we have developed many spice blends for several of our restaurants, and here at Daniel, we create spice blends for fish, for meats, and even for desserts and cocktails. We use Vadouvan curry in the yogurt dressing that accompanies the squab pastilla and smoked paprika in our shrimp-coated halibut. The range of exotic tastes is endless, but we constantly strive for the ideal equilibrium that defines my idea of French cuisine.

As far as herbs are concerned, you may be surprised to hear that I often favor our own dried herbs rather than fresh ones to create an intense powder that can flavor a salt for a particular dish such as the Provençal loup de mer. Take a blend such as herbes de Provence. Just as with tea, you need to dry the leaves to get the full length of flavor. I would not dry parsley or dill, for example, but I love to dry rosemary, sage, savory, and thyme.

My French cuisine can be perceived to be as global as New York's tasty mosaic of cultures, but its refined equilibrium of flavors makes it, in my mind, completely French.

DANIEL ON TRUFFLES

TRUFFLES ARE WONDERS OF NATURE, THE TRUE DIAMONDS OF the food chain. Seasonally, the white truffle, or *Tuber magnatum*, precedes the black, making its appearance in our kitchen from October to January. Most often, our suppliers let us have first pick of the shipment, or perhaps they let us think we do, because every chef in New York hopes to be the first.

As soon as we open the insulated boxes, the magical aroma wafts through the whole restaurant. In 2007, we bought the biggest white truffle we had ever seen, coming in at nearly two pounds. It looked like a prehistoric rock the size of a child's head and came from Alba, the capital of white truffles in Piedmont. We shaved it over fresh pasta, risotto, eggs, and veal trio for an entire week.

At Daniel, we are always interested in buying the biggest white truffle of the season, even if it costs the price of a small car. It's about the power of nature, the smell, the taste, and the umami. The white truffle calls for simplicity, but always with a touch of fat: cream, butter, mascarpone, or aged cheeses.

Perhaps my most successful marriage with this ingredient took place at Le Cirque, where I cooked a basic baked potato on a bed of salt, crushed the inside with truffle pieces and butter, and covered it with a mountain of paper-thin sliced truffles. To me it is a peasant dish for royalty!

That year, my parents came to see me for Christmas and we sat together for a candlelit dinner. I made the baked potato recipe, but my father didn't see me shave the truffles. At the end of the meal, I looked at my father's plate and realized that his was covered with

"They can, on certain occasion, make women more tender and men more lovable."
—Referring to truffles, Alexandre Dumas

truffle shavings. Because of the dim light, he had thought they were potato peels and just pushed them aside. It remains a classic Boulud family joke.

While it belongs to the same family, the black truffle, or *Tuber melanosporum*, is completely different from its white cousin. In the summer, we now receive Australian "Périgord-style" black truffles cultivated there during their winter, but for us in New York, the fresh black truffle is at its peak from December to March. It's during the holidays, when black and white truffles are both available at the same time, that our level of truffle testosterone is at its highest. Around these pristine gems, we create many dishes and tasting menus. And every year, I invite friends to come to my home and celebrate black and white feasts.

I often shave black truffles over eggs or bake a whole black truffle the size of a golf ball wrapped in pancetta, and braised on a "salpicon" of root vegetables with touches of port wine, duck jus, and foie gras. I favor the purest and simplest manners of preparing them: truffe en croûte, a whole truffle encased in fresh sourdough, just baked in the oven, split in half, spread with shavings of salted butter. Then just take a crusty and scrumptious bite!

Black truffles are all about the struggle for fragile domination on the plate. And there are basically two possible routes: either a subtle and delicate support like a poularde, or a powerful, earthy combination, as in our venison consommé or in truffle and beef, a classic. In the seventeenth century, many recipes were created for royalty or the celebrities of the era featuring black truffle, such as the tournedos Rossini, created in honor of the Italian composer.

There isn't a single French chef who is not associated with a truffle dish: Michel Rostang and his world-famous warm truffle sandwich; Paul Bocuse's soupe VGE; Guy Savoy's soupe d'artichauts aux truffes noires; Roger Vergé's bouquet de salade de truffes fraîches; or Michel Guérard's salade gourmande. In the old days, those were the dishes that differentiated haute cuisine from bistro food. In order to eat truffles, you needed to go to a gastronomic restaurant, and of course that was an expensive and slippery slope, because with great truffles, chances are you will crave a great Châteauneuf-du-Pape, an Hermitage, or a Barolo.

When you buy your truffles, keep them for the first twenty-four hours, if you can, in a sealed jar or box filled with rice or eggs so the aroma will infuse and linger in your next meal.

WHITE TRUFFLE SCRAMBLED EGGS

SERVES 4

Grilled Brioche Crouton

4 (6-inch-long x ¼-inch-wide) rectangular batons of brioche

3 tablespoons butter, melted

Spinach-Lined Bowls

2 cups New Zealand baby spinach

To Finish

1½ cups Spinach Puree (page 371)

½ cup Chanterelle Duxelle (page 377)

2 tablespoons diced Fontina cheese

3 tablespoons butter, softened

8 small chanterelles, cleaned, trimmed, and halved

Salt and freshly ground white pepper

4 medium organic eggs, at room temperature

2 tablespoons crème fraîche

¼ cup New Zealand baby spinach leaves

Fresh white truffle for shaving

For the Grilled Brioche Crouton

Heat a grill or cast-iron grill pan over medium heat. Lightly brush all sides of the brioche batons with melted butter. Grill each side of bread until marks form; set aside.

For the Spinach-Lined Bowls

Preheat a steam oven or stovetop steamer. Line the inset rim of 4 small bowls (with bottoms approximately 5 inches in diameter) with a ring of spinach leaves with tips facing outward. Cover each bowl with plastic wrap and steam 3 minutes, to slightly wilt the leaves. Keep warm.

To Finish

Transfer the spinach puree to a small saucepan over medium heat and stir to heat through.

Transfer the chanterelle duxelle to a small sauté pan over medium heat and stir until heated through; stir in the diced Fontina and keep warm.

Melt 2 tablespoons of the butter in a small sauté pan over high heat. Add the halved chanterelles and sauté for 2 minutes, or until lightly browned and tender. Season with salt and pepper.

Add 2 inches of water to the bottom of a medium saucepan (about 8 inches in diameter) and bring to a simmer. Crack the eggs into a medium heatproof bowl (about 10 inches in diameter) and beat with a whisk until smooth. Season generously with salt and pepper and place the bowl on top of the pan, making sure that the bottom of the bowl does not touch the water.

Using a small heatproof rubber spatula, stir the eggs in a zigzag pattern from left to right, then up and down. If the eggs begin to coagulate too fast, lower the heat. It should take about 5 minutes for a light film to form on the bottom and sides of the bowl. Keep stirring the eggs. When small curds appear, switch to a whisk to stir the eggs, making sure to scrape the bottom of the bowl as much as possible. When the eggs take on a porridge-like texture (they should be soft but not soupy or runny), remove the bowl from the heat and whisk in the remaining 1 tablespoon butter and the crème fraîche. Check the seasoning and adjust if necessary.

For each serving, remove the plastic wrap from a spinach-lined bowl and set a 4-inch ring mold inside. Spoon in a layer of chanterelle duxelle, and then top with an even layer of spinach puree. Spoon the scrambled eggs on top. Arrange 4 roasted chanterelle halves and 3 leaves of spinach around the rim. Lift the ring from the plate and shave fresh white truffle over the top. Set a brioche crouton on the rim of the bowl.

BLACK TRUFFLE OEUF EN COCOTTE

SERVES 4

Brioche Crouton

4 thin slices brioche

2 tablespoons butter, melted

Salt

Sliced Chanterelles

20 small chanterelles, cleaned and trimmed

1 tablespoon butter

Salt and freshly ground white pepper

Oeuf en Cocotte

Fresh black truffle for shaving

½ cup Chanterelle Duxelle (page 377)

4 medium organic eggs, at room temperature

1 tablespoon thinly sliced chives

Fleur de sel

For the Brioche Crouton

Preheat the oven to 225°F. Use a fluted ring cutter to cut the brioche in half circles slightly larger than the rim of the dishes you will cook the eggs in. Line a baking sheet with parchment paper and lay the slices on top in a single layer. Brush the bread with the butter and top with another sheet of parchment. Top with another baking sheet and bake for 20 minutes, or until golden and crispy. Sprinkle with salt, cool, and reserve in an airtight container.

For the Sliced Chanterelles

Use a mandoline to cut the chanterelles lengthwise into thin slices. Melt the butter in a medium sauté pan over medium heat. Add the mushrooms and cook, stirring, for 2 minutes, or until tender. Season with salt and pepper and set aside.

For the Oeuf en Cocotte

Thinly slice the black truffle and line the slices along the inside walls of four 3-ounce cocotte dishes or ramekins. Line the sliced chanterelles onto the truffles, with their tops facing upward. Divide the chanterelle duxelle into the bottom of the cocottes and form a well in their centers. Top each with a cracked egg.

Transfer the cocottes to a large saucepan or roasting dish. Fill the saucepan with enough water to reach halfway up the sides of the cocottes. Place over high heat, bring the water to a simmer, and cover the pan tightly with a lid or aluminum foil. Reduce the heat to its lowest setting and cook just until the whites are set, about 5 minutes. Carefully remove the cocottes from the water and use a towel to wipe off any water. Sprinkle the eggs with chives and fleur de sel and shave more black truffle over the top. Set a crouton on the side of the bowl.

BEAUFORT AND RIESLING FONDUE RAVIOLI
GREEN PEPPERCORNS, SUNCHOKES

SERVES 6

ONCE IN MY New York apartment on a cold February night, I decided to invite Jean-Georges Vongerichten, Alfred Portale, and Gray Kunz, among many famous toques, for a fondue party. Each chef headed his own pot and made his own fondue recipe, convinced his was the best. Late into the night, we stirred our bread croutons into the gooey cheese, eating cured ham and viande des grisons and downing plenty of Kirshwasser shooters!

Why not fill a ravioli with fondue? As a French cook, I love pasta, but I'll make it my way! With it, I capture the memories of that moment of friendship and fun. Under soft domes, we uncover the rich complexity of a blend of Fontina, Comté, and tart Beaufort cheese from the Alps, mixed with béchamel, rich riesling, and nutmeg, the often-hidden ingredient of the fondue.

Beaufort Ravioli

2 tablespoons butter

1 clove garlic, peeled and chopped

3 tablespoons flour

2 tablespoons riesling wine

¾ cup milk

1 tablespoon heavy cream

2½ ounces Fontina cheese,
cut into small dice

2½ ounces Comté cheese,
cut into small dice

2½ ounces Beaufort cheese,
cut into small dice

Freshly grated nutmeg

Salt and freshly ground white pepper

2 tablespoons green peppercorns
in brine

1 pound Pasta Dough (page 374)

Flour, for dusting

Sunchokes

8 ounces sunchokes, peeled

1 tablespoon butter

¼ cup Chicken Stock (page 368)

Salt and freshly ground white pepper

Wild Mushroom Sauce

12 ounces hen of the woods
mushrooms, cleaned

2 tablespoons butter

2 tablespoons chopped
speck ham

1 shallot, minced

1 teaspoon green peppercorns
in brine

1 splash of riesling wine

1 cup Chicken Stock (page 368)

½ cup heavy cream

Salt and freshly ground
white pepper

To Finish

Salt

1 tablespoon butter

1 tablespoon olive oil

3 tablespoons diced speck ham

8 ounces hen of the woods
mushrooms, reserved from above

2 tablespoons green peppercorns
in brine

12 thin slices speck ham

½ cup red watercress leaves

½ cup frilly red mustard leaves

½ cup Candied Walnuts (page 373)

For the Beaufort Ravioli

Melt the butter in a medium saucepan over low heat. Add the garlic and cook, stirring, until it is cooked but not colored. Add the flour and continue stirring for 3 minutes without browning. Whisk in the wine and simmer until reduced by one-third. Whisk in the milk and heavy cream and return to a simmer. Cook over low heat, whisking occasionally, until thickened, about 15 minutes. Remove from the heat and whisk in the cheeses until melted. Season with nutmeg, salt, and pepper. While still warm, transfer the fondue to a piping bag.

Place a spherical Flexipan mold (we use a 96-form Flexipan Pomponettes Mold) on a flat surface and fill each of at least 36 cups with 1 green peppercorn and then the fondue. Spread with a small offset metal spatula to level off the tops. Freeze until solid.

Remove the pasta dough from the refrigerator to rest at room temperature for 1 hour. Sprinkle the counter with flour, unwrap the dough, and divide it into 4 equal pieces. Roll the pieces of dough through a pasta machine until about 12 inches by 5 inches and thin enough to see your hand through. While working, cover the dough with sheets of plastic wrap to keep it from drying.

Place half of the frozen domes at 1-inch intervals on top of one sheet of pasta, and using a pastry brush, lightly moisten the dough with water. Top with a second sheet and gently press around each dome to seal the dough together and release air pockets. Using a 1½-inch fluted ring cutter, cut out the raviolis and transfer to a tray lined with flour. Repeat the process with the remaining fondue and dough, and chill the raviolis until needed.

For the Sunchokes

Using a mandoline, cut 18 thin slices from a sunchoke, and using a ½-inch ring cutter, cut them into discs. Set aside. Cut the remaining sunchokes into at least 18 approximately ¾-inch-long tournés. In a small sauté pan over medium heat, brown the butter and add the tournéed sunchokes. Sauté for 2 minutes, or until golden, then add the chicken stock, bring to a simmer, and season with salt and pepper. Cook, stirring, until the liquid is reduced to a glaze and the sunchokes are tender, about 4 minutes. Keep warm.

For the Wild Mushroom Sauce

Trim the mushrooms from their stems into bite-size pieces. Dunk in cold water; scoop and pat dry. Set aside 8 ounces of the mushrooms for finishing. Melt the butter in a medium saucepan over medium heat. Add the diced ham, shallot, and green pepper-corns and cook, stirring, for 2 minutes. Add the remaining mushrooms and sauté for 3 minutes, or until golden. Add the wine and simmer until almost dry. Add the chicken stock and heavy cream and reduce by half. Season with salt and pepper. Strain through a fine-meshed sieve and reserve for finishing.

To Finish

Bring a large pot of salted water to a boil. In a medium sauté pan, heat the butter and oil over medium heat. Add the diced ham and reserved mushrooms and sauté for 4 minutes. Add the reserved mushroom sauce and green peppercorns and bring to a simmer. Boil the raviolis until tender, 3 to 4 minutes. Drain the pasta and transfer to the mushroom sauce and gently swirl to coat.

For each serving, arrange 6 raviolis in a pasta bowl. Add 3 pieces of sunchoke, a spoonful of mushrooms, and enough sauce to reach halfway up the pasta. Garnish with 2 slices of shaved ham, 3 red watercress leaves, 3 frilly red mustard leaves, and 3 reserved sunchoke shavings. Crumble 1 to 2 walnuts over the top.

FORAGED HERB PYRAMID AGNOLOTTI
PATA NEGRA, NETTLESOME CHEESE

SERVES 8

WHEN TAMA MATSUOKA WONG asked our receptionist if we could use the herbs she'd found in her New Jersey backyard in the menu we would serve her and her husband that night, she didn't realize that we would never want to cook without them again. Little by little, she started bringing different and unusual herbs, coaxing our chef de cuisine, Eddy Leroux, to continuously create new recipes around these wild edibles. And she couldn't have known that, with Eddy, she would end up writing a book: *Foraged Flavors*. Bursting with deep flavors—bitter, peppery, and tangy—the small packets complete a forest-style landscape with morels, baby turnips, and cheese studded with nettles. Paper-thin curls of pata negra (Spanish jamón serrano from Iberian pigs) provide a smoky touch, lighting up the cream and white wine liaison.

FORAGED HERB PYRAMID AGNOLOTTI
PATA NEGRA, NETTLESOME CHEESE

Foraged Herb Pyramids

6 ounces green watercress, stems trimmed

4 ounces spinach leaves, stems trimmed

4 ounces dandelion greens, stems trimmed

4 ounces arugula leaves, stems trimmed

4 ounces mixed foraged herbs (such as cardamine, garlic chives, garlic mustard, stinging nettles, chickweed, and ground ivy)

1 ounce chives

Salt

1 tablespoon butter

½ cup chopped onion

2 cloves garlic, peeled and chopped

4 ounces ricotta cheese

2 ounces mascarpone cheese

2 ounces grated Parmesan cheese

Salt and freshly ground white pepper

Pasta Dough (page 374)

Flour

Soft-Poached Quail Eggs

Salt

16 quail eggs

Mushroom and Pata Negra Sauce

1 ounce diced fat from pata negra ham (we recommend Cinco Jotas brand)

2 medium shallots, minced

2 cups wild mushroom stems or button mushrooms, cleaned and chopped

1 tablespoon riesling wine

1 cup Chicken Stock (page 368)

¼ cup heavy cream

¼ cup shredded Valley Shepherd Creamery Nettlesome cheese

1 splash of sherry vinegar

Salt and freshly ground white pepper

Wild Mushroom Fricassée

6 ounces black trumpet mushrooms, stems trimmed

6 ounces yellowfoot mushrooms, stems trimmed

6 ounces morel mushrooms, stems trimmed

2 tablespoons olive oil

1 tablespoon butter

2 tablespoons Mushroom and Pata Negra Sauce (see above)

1 clove garlic, peeled

1 sprig thyme

Salt and freshly ground white pepper

To Finish

Salt

32 fiddlehead ferns, trimmed

16 baby turnips, peeled and trimmed

4 ounces Valley Shepherd Creamery Nettlesome cheese shavings

4 ounces sliced pata negra, torn into bite-size pieces

¼ cup micro wood sorrel leaves

For the Foraged Herb Pyramids

If using nettles, wear gloves to guard your skin from irritants. Separately rinse all of the greens with cold water to remove any dirt. Bring a large pot of heavily salted water to a boil and set a large bowl of ice water on the side. Boil the greens in separate batches until tender, 1 to 2 minutes each, depending on their size, and transfer them to the ice water. Once chilled, transfer the greens to a colander lined with cheesecloth. Press the greens and squeeze the cheesecloth to remove any excess water. Transfer to a cutting board and roughly chop. In a small sauté pan, melt the butter over medium heat and add the onion and garlic. Cook, stirring, until translucent, about 2 minutes. Transfer to a food processor with the chopped greens, cheeses, and salt and pepper to taste. Pulse until well combined but still coarse. Transfer the filling to piping bags and store, chilled.

Remove the pasta dough from the refrigerator to rest at room temperature for 1 hour. Sprinkle the counter with flour, unwrap the dough, and divide it into 4 equal pieces. Roll the pieces of dough through a pasta machine to make sheets thin enough to see your hand through. While working, cover the dough with sheets of plastic wrap to keep it from drying.

Cut each sheet into at least eight 1½-inch squares. While working, cover the dough with sheets of plastic wrap to keep it from drying. Pipe 1 tablespoon of the filling into the center of each square and brush the outside edges of the dough with water. Using your fingertips, pinch two opposite corners of the square and pull them up toward each other to meet above the filling; press lightly so they stick. Repeat with the remaining two corners. Seal the edges by pinching from the bottom four corners upward to the tip, forming a pyramid. Pinch the top to seal. Transfer to a baking sheet dusted with flour. Repeat the process to make at least 32 pyramids and chill until ready to use. (At this point you can freeze the pyramids for up to 3 weeks.)

chickweed

ground ivy

For the Soft-Poached Quail Eggs

Bring a medium saucepan of salted water to a boil. Boil the eggs for 2 minutes, then strain and peel under cold running water; reserve on the side.

For the Mushroom and Pata Negra Sauce

In a medium sauté pan over medium heat, cook the ham fat for 10 minutes, or until well rendered but not colored. Add the shallots and mushroom stems and cook, stirring, until the shallots are translucent, about 3 minutes. Add the wine and simmer until almost dry. Add the chicken stock and simmer to reduce by half. Transfer the mixture to a blender, add the heavy cream and cheese, and puree. Season with the sherry vinegar and salt and pepper. Pass through a fine-meshed sieve; reserve chilled.

For the Wild Mushroom Fricassée

To clean the mushrooms, dunk them in a bowl of cold water, leave for 2 minutes, scoop them up, and repeat until the water that settles at the bottom is clear. Strain and pat dry with a towel.

Heat the olive oil in a large sauté pan over medium-high heat. Add the mushrooms and sauté for 2 minutes. Add the butter, sauce, garlic, and thyme. Cook, stirring, for 5 minutes, or until the mushrooms are cooked. Adjust the seasoning with salt and pepper and keep warm.

To Finish

Bring a large pot of salted water to a boil. Transfer the remaining sauce to a large sauté pan over medium heat and stir to heat through. Add the fiddlehead ferns and turnips to the boiling water and boil until tender, about 2 minutes. With a slotted spoon, scoop them into the wild mushroom fricassée and toss to combine. In 4 separate batches, boil the pyramids for 2 minutes. With a strainer, scoop them into the pan with the sauce. Swirl the pyramids in the sauce to coat.

For each serving, scoop 4 pyramids into a warm pasta bowl. Spoon the mushroom fricassée with 2 turnips and 4 fiddlehead ferns around the pyramids. Garnish with 2 quail eggs, several shavings of Nettlesome cheese, 4 pieces of ham, and 4 micro wood sorrel leaves.

FISH

DOVER SOLE BALLOTINE
À LA POLONAISE

SERVES 4

HERE AGAIN we are inspired to explore a classic French recipe and add our own twist. The concept of cauliflower à la Polonaise, a simple recipe involving a sprinkle of hard-boiled eggs, is reinvented as the accompaniment for an elegant sole cylinder stuffed with a delicate fish mousse and topped with a caper and Marcona almond gremolata, a chopped herb condiment. The saltiness of the capers nicely offsets the subtlety of the fish.

DOVER SOLE BALLOTINE
À LA POLONAISE

Dover Sole

12 fillets Dover sole from three
22- to 24-ounce fish

1 egg

Salt and freshly ground white pepper

Piment d'Espelette

1⅓ cups plus 1 tablespoon heavy cream

Cauliflower Puree and Gratin

1 head (about 1½ pounds) cauliflower

2 cups milk

Salt and freshly ground white pepper

Tabasco sauce

2 egg yolks

2 tablespoons lemon juice

2 cups (4 sticks) warm melted butter

Caper-Almond Gremolata

2 tablespoons tiny cauliflower
florets, reserved from above

2 tablespoons chopped
Marcona almonds

2 tablespoons chopped capers

1 tablespoon brunoised shallots

1 tablespoon chopped parsley

1 tablespoon white balsamic vinegar

2 tablespoons olive oil

Salt and freshly ground white pepper

1 hard-boiled egg, peeled

Potato Tempura

1 cup Clarified Butter (page 377)

1 large russet potato, peeled

Salt and freshly ground white pepper

Canola oil for frying

Tempura Batter (page 374)

Glazed Romanesco

Salt

1 head (about 1½ pounds) romanesco

2 tablespoons butter

¼ cup Chicken Stock (page 368)

Freshly ground white pepper

To Finish

Salt and freshly ground white pepper

1 tablespoon butter, melted

For the Dover Sole

Chill the bowl and blade of a food processor. Trim the ends and sides of 8 sole fillets to square them off and lightly score the skin side of each fillet (this will help prevent them from curling while cooking). Dice the trim and remaining 4 fillets and transfer to the chilled food processor with the egg, 1¼ teaspoons salt, ¼ teaspoon pepper, and ½ teaspoon piment d'Espelette, and pulse until well combined. Scrape the sides of the bowl with a spatula, and with the machine running, stream in the heavy cream to make a smooth mousse. Pass the mousse through a fine-meshed drum sieve, transfer to a piping bag with a ½-inch-diameter tip, and reserve, chilled.

Season the scored sides of the sole fillets lightly with salt, pepper, and piment d'Espelette. Horizontally lay 1 fillet, seasoned side up, on a 12-inch sheet of plastic wrap. Pipe a line of mousse across the top. Lay a second fillet, seasoned side down, on top, with its thicker end meeting the bottom fillet's thinner end. Tightly roll the fish in the plastic to form a cylinder and tie off the ends. Repeat with the remaining fish to make 4 rolls; reserve, chilled.

For the Cauliflower Puree and Gratin

Cut at least eight 1-inch cubes from the cauliflower head so that the cubes can stand with the florets facing upward. Preheat a steam oven or stovetop steamer, add the cubes, and steam for 6 to 8 minutes, until easily pierced with a cake tester. Reserve, chilled.

Trim 2 tablespoons tiny cauliflower florets from the remaining cauliflower and reserve for the gremolata. Chop the rest of the cauliflower with the stem into small dice and transfer to a small saucepan. Add the milk and 1 teaspoon salt and bring to a simmer. Cover and cook, stirring occasionally, for 15 minutes, or until the cauliflower is very tender. With a slotted spoon, scoop the cauliflower into a blender and puree with just enough of its cooking liquid to form a thick puree. Season with salt, pepper, and Tabasco sauce and pass through a fine-meshed sieve; reserve, chilled.

Up to 1 hour before serving, season the cauliflower cubes with salt and pepper and stand upright on a foil-lined baking sheet. In a heatproof bowl, whisk together the yolks, lemon juice, and 2 tablespoons water. Bring a small pot of water to a simmer and place the bowl on top. Heat the mixture, whisking continuously, until thickened and pale but not curdled (155°F). Remove from the heat and slowly whisk in the 2 cups warm melted butter until well emulsified, to make a hollandaise sauce. Season to taste with salt and pepper. Keep in a warm place, covered.

For the Caper-Almond Gremolata

In a small bowl, combine all the ingredients except the egg and season with salt and pepper. Separate the egg yolk from the white, press both through a fine-meshed drum sieve, and reserve, chilled.

For the Potato Tempura

Melt the clarified butter in a medium sauce-pan. With a mandoline, slice the potato length-wise into ⅛-inch slices. Cut at least eight 1-inch triangles from the slices. Season the triangles with salt and pepper and submerge them in the butter. Cook at just below a simmer for 15 to 20 minutes, until tender. Strain the potatoes onto a paper towel–lined plate and pat dry. When ready to serve, fill one-third of a medium saucepan with canola oil and heat to 350°F. Individually coat the potatoes in the tempura batter and fry until golden brown (you may need to do this in batches). Transfer to a paper towel–lined tray and sprinkle with salt.

For the Glazed Romanesco

Bring a large pot of salted water to a boil and place a bowl of ice water on the side. Cut at least twelve 1-inch-tall florets from the romanesco, trimming the stems so that they can stand. Trim 2 tablespoons of ¼-inch florets from the remaining romanesco. Boil the large florets for 3 minutes, or until tender, then chill in the ice water; strain and pat dry. Boil the ¼-inch florets for 15 seconds, then chill in the ice water; strain and pat dry. When ready to serve, in a small sauté pan, melt the butter with the chicken stock. Add the large

romanesco florets and cook, stirring, until heated through and glazed; toss in the ¼-inch florets. Adjust the seasoning with salt and pepper if needed and keep warm.

To Finish

Preheat the broiler. Using an immersion circulator, preheat a water bath to 145°F. *Alternately, preheat a large saucepan filled halfway with water to 145°F, and maintain the temperature as best as possible using a stem thermometer.* Transfer the cauliflower puree to a medium saucepan over medium heat and stir to heat through. Spoon the hollandaise sauce onto the cubed cauliflower to coat and broil until the sauce is browned.

Submerge the fish in the prepared water bath and cook for 9 minutes, or until just cooked (you can check with a cake tester or stem thermometer; it should reach 140°F internally). Remove the fish, trim the ends, remove from the plastic, season with salt and pepper, and brush with the melted butter. Evenly divide the gremolata, a sprinkle of egg, and a few tiny romanesco florets into a neat layer on top of each fish portion.

For each serving, spread a spoonful of cauliflower puree in a rectangular shape the length of the fish onto the bottom of a warm dinner plate. Place the fish on top. Alternate 3 glazed romanesco, 2 cauliflower gratin cubes, and 2 pieces of potato tempura in a line parallel to the fish.

RED SNAPPER "EN CROÛTE DE SEL"
HARISSA, PISTACHIO BUTTER

SERVES 4

RESTAURANT TRENDS come and go, and so do service styles. I take pleasure in going back in time and believing in the charm of tableside service, in the drama that flows from the kitchen to the dining room. This red snapper, encased in a salt crust over smoking and fragrant dry fennel stems— a whiff of Provence—seems to emerge from a baker's oven. Finally, our skilled maître d' removes the crust to reveal the moist and delicate fish, infused with harissa and piment d'Espelette for an unexpected kick.

RED SNAPPER "EN CROÛTE DE SEL"
HARISSA, PISTACHIO BUTTER

Artichoke Confit and Artichoke Vinaigrette

2 lemons

12 baby artichokes

Salt

1¾ cups olive oil

2 tablespoons white balsamic vinegar

1 tablespoon Dijon mustard

Freshly ground white pepper

Harissa Sauce

15 canned piquillo peppers, rinsed and seeded

6 tablespoons olive oil

¼ cup sliced shallots

2 tablespoons chopped garlic

1 teaspoon ground cumin

½ teaspoon ground coriander

½ teaspoon piment d'Espelette

1 tablespoon honey

2 tablespoons sherry vinegar

2 tablespoons tomato puree

Salt

Couscous Croquettes

2 cups cooked couscous

1 egg

1 tablespoon za'atar

1 teaspoon salt

¼ teaspoon piment d'Espelette

Salt-Crusted Snappers

3 cups flour

2⅔ cups coarse sea salt (we recommend la Baleine), plus extra for garnish

6 eggs

7 egg yolks

1 teaspoon piment d'Espelette

¼ cup harissa sauce, reserved from above

4 teaspoons fennel pollen

1 teaspoon freshly ground white pepper

10 (4-inch) dried fennel stems

2 red snappers (3 pounds each), scaled, fins and gills removed

2 tablespoons milk

Pistachio Butter

½ cup cultured farm butter, softened (we recommend Vermont Creamery)

3 tablespoons finely chopped pistachios

1 tablespoon pistachio oil

½ teaspoon salt

¼ teaspoon piment d'Espelette

To Finish

Canola oil for frying

2 heads gem lettuce

Salt and freshly ground white pepper

1 tablespoon olive oil

Artichoke Chips (page 372)

For the Artichoke Confit and Artichoke Vinaigrette

Make the confit: Juice the lemons, reserving 2 tablespoons for vinaigrette, and combine the rest in a large bowl with ice water. To clean each artichoke, trim the end of the stem and ½ inch from the tip. Peel away the rough outer leaves, leaving the pale yellow tender leaves intact. Using a vegetable peeler, remove the skin from the stem and any tough leaf remnants from the base. Submerge the artichokes in the ice water immediately after cleaning them.

Reserve 6 artichokes: 3 for artichoke chips and 3 for finishing. Transfer the remaining artichokes to a medium saucepan with 1 teaspoon salt and cover with the olive oil and vinegar. Place over medium-low heat and cook, stirring occasionally, at just below a simmer, for 45 minutes, or until the artichokes are easily pierced with a cake tester. Cool the artichokes in their liquid.

Make the vinaigrette: In a small bowl, whisk the mustard with the reserved 2 tablespoons lemon juice. Slowly stream in ¾ cup of the artichoke confit liquid, while whisking, until emulsified. Adjust the seasoning with salt and pepper. Reserve the confit artichokes and vinaigrette, chilled.

For the Harissa Sauce

Cut twelve 1-inch triangles from the peppers, line on a baking sheet, and reserve for the garnish, saving the trim.

Heat 2 tablespoons of the olive oil in a medium saucepan over medium-high heat. Add the shallots and garlic and cook, stirring occasionally, until they begin to soften and caramelize, about 3 minutes. Add the remaining peppers, pepper trim, cumin, coriander, and piment d'Espelette, and cook, stirring, until tender, about 5 minutes. Add the honey, vinegar, and tomato puree and bring to a simmer. Transfer the mixture to a blender and puree, streaming in the remaining 4 tablespoons olive oil, until emulsified. Pass through a fine-meshed sieve and season with salt; reserve, chilled.

For the Couscous Croquettes

In a medium bowl, combine the couscous, egg, za'atar, salt, and piment d'Espelette. Line a flat surface with a 12-inch-square double layer of plastic wrap. Arrange half of the couscous in the center in a horizontal 8-inch-long line. Fold the bottom corners of the plastic wrap to meet the top corners and press to seal tightly around the couscous. Roll the couscous forward in the plastic to form a ½-inch-diameter log, then tie off the ends of the plastic. Repeat with the remaining couscous. Chill well, then cut the logs into at least twelve ¾-inch-long cylinders. Gently peel away the plastic wrap and reserve them, chilled.

For the Salt-Crusted Snappers

In the bowl of an electric mixer fitted with a paddle, combine 1½ cups of the flour, 1⅓ cups of the coarse salt, 3 of the eggs, and 2 of the egg yolks on low speed. While mixing, stream in 1⅔ cups water until a pliable dough forms. Remove the dough and split it into 2 discs; wrap tightly in plastic wrap. Repeat the process to make 2 more discs of dough. Rest the 4 discs at room temperature for 30 minutes. Unwrap 1 disc and place between 2 sheets of parchment paper. Using a rolling pin, roll the dough into a ⅓-inch-thick oval sheet with edges 3 inches larger than the fish. Repeat

with the remaining discs of dough and set aside; keep covered

Divide the piment d'Espelette, harissa sauce, fennel pollen, pepper, and fennel stems into the 2 belly cavities of the fish. Whip the remaining 3 egg yolks with the milk.

Remove the parchment paper from the salt dough sheets. Center a fish on top of 1 sheet and brush the egg mix onto the dough to outline the fish. Top with a second sheet of dough and press to seal the edges tightly. With a sharp knife, score into the dough a shallow outline of the top fillet (to aid in carving once cooked). Trim the dough around the fish, forming a faux top and bottom fin and leaving a 1-inch outline. Cut away pieces of the dough to expose each fish's head and tail. Using a small ring cutter or the tip of a spoon, press into the top of the dough in a pattern to mimic scales. Brush the tops of the dough with the egg mixture. Repeat with remaining dough and fish. Sprinkle some coarse sea salt on the dough for garnish. Refrigerate the fish for at least 30 minutes, but no longer than 6 hours.

For the Pistachio Butter

In a medium bowl, whisk all the ingredients until well combined. Reserve at room temperature.

To Finish

Preheat the oven to 410°F. Fill one-third of a medium saucepan with canola oil and heat to 300°F. Remove the fish from the refrigerator to rest at room temperature for 15 minutes.

Peel any damaged outer leaves from the lettuce; rinse well and pat dry. Cut each head lengthwise into four ½-inch flat slices. Using a mandoline, thinly shave the 3 reserved artichokes lengthwise into a small bowl. Season the lettuce slices and shaved artichokes with the artichoke vinaigrette and salt and pepper.

Transfer the fish to a parchment-lined baking sheet and bake for 20 minutes (the thickest part of the fillet should reach 117°F). Remove from the oven and rest in a warm place for 10 minutes. Reduce the oven temperature to 300°F. Drizzle the reserved tray of piquillo peppers with the olive oil, sprinkle with salt, and heat in the oven for 5 to 8 minutes.

Meanwhile, fry the couscous croquettes until golden brown and crispy (you may need to do this in batches). Drain onto a paper towel–lined tray, sprinkle with salt, and keep warm.

To remove the salt crust from the fish, use a sharp knife to loosen the top crust by tracing the scored line around the top fillet in the crust. Lift the crust off (the skin should come off with it) and trim away any dark belly meat from the fillet. Starting from the spine, gently run a dinner knife underneath the fillet to loosen from the bones. Remove the fillet onto a plate. Using the dinner knife, peel away the bones to reveal the bottom fillet. Run the knife underneath the fillet to remove.

For each serving, arrange 3 couscous croquettes, 2 pieces of gem lettuce, 3 triangles of piquillo pepper, a few chips and shavings of artichoke, and a few dollops of harissa sauce on the side of a warm dinner plate. Transfer a fillet to the other side of the plate and spoon some pistachio butter on top.

SLOW-BAKED SEA BASS
POMMES LYONNAISE, LEEK ROYALE

SERVES 6

SOME WORKS of art stay with you forever. I often think of my mentors' classic recipes as true works of art. In the mid-1980s, I visited Frédy Girardet in Switzerland, where I savored a fillet of red mullet covered with tiny discs of zucchini to mirror the scales of the fish. Paul Bocuse then made his own version by switching to the more versatile potato "scales," creating a crispy skin. Once at Le Cirque in New York, I developed my own take with the local black sea bass on a bed of leeks and doused with a rich red wine sauce. It instantly became the most popular dish on the menu and a new classic was born! In the kitchen, the trick is to roast the potatoes to a golden crisp while the fish cooks gently inside the shell. In *Cooking with Daniel Boulud*, my first cookbook, I introduced the original recipe.

After more than twenty years on my menu, it took Eddy Leroux, our chef de cuisine, three years to convince me to take the sea bass en paupiette off, and then only under the condition that we were going to keep the combination of black sea bass, potato, leeks, thyme, and red wine sauce because I couldn't part with the elements that made that dish a success.

In fact, Leroux kept the exact same ingredients but played with them in completely different ways. For example, thyme, which found itself sprinkled on the fish in my original version, now infuses the potatoes, mixed with garlic and onions. The texture of the fish, which cooks in its own steam while encased in the potato scales, is similar in this new version, something we achieve by baking it wrapped in parchment paper.

SLOW-BAKED SEA BASS
POMMES LYONNAISE, LEEK ROYALE

Leek Royale (makes extra)

Salt

3 cups (10 ounces) diced and rinsed leek, green part only, from 2 medium leeks (reserve the bottom white ends for crispy leeks, below)

½ cup parsley leaves

1¾ cups heavy cream

3 eggs

Freshly ground white pepper

1 tablespoon butter, softened

Pommes Lyonnaise (makes extra)

3 tablespoons butter

2 Vidalia onions, thinly sliced

Salt

2 teaspoons chopped thyme

2 large russet potatoes (at least 5 inches long)

Freshly ground white pepper

½ cup Garlic Paste (page 371)

2 tablespoons chopped parsley

2 cups Clarified Butter (page 377), plus extra as needed

Crispy Leeks and Potato Gaufrettes

Canola oil for frying

2 (3-inch) pieces of white leek, reserved from above

3 tablespoons rice flour

Salt

1 large russet potato, peeled

Sea Bass

6 (7-ounce) boneless black sea bass fillets, skin on

Salt and freshly ground white pepper

2 tablespoons butter, melted

⅓ cup Syrah Reduction (page 371)

1 tablespoon heavy cream

2 cups (4 sticks) cold butter, cubed

To Finish

Fleur de sel

Cracked black pepper

¼ cup parsley leaves

For the Leek Royale

Preheat the oven to 275°F. Bring a large pot of salted water to a boil and set a bowl of ice water on the side. Add the diced leeks and parsley and boil until very tender, 3 to 4 minutes. Transfer to the ice water to chill; strain and squeeze dry. In a medium saucepan, combine the boiled leeks, parsley, ¾ cup of the heavy cream, and ¾ teaspoon salt and bring to a simmer. Transfer the mixture to a blender and puree until smooth. Pass through a fine-meshed sieve and chill over ice.

In a medium bowl, whisk to combine 1½ cups of the puree with the remaining 1 cup heavy cream, ¾ teaspoon salt, and the eggs; season with pepper. Butter an 8½ x 4½-inch loaf pan and line with parchment paper on the bottom and sides. Pour in the mixture and wrap the pan with plastic wrap; poke 3 small holes in the top of the plastic wrap. Transfer the loaf pan to a roasting pan and fill the roasting pan with enough hot water to reach the level of the leek mixture. Transfer to the oven and bake for 40 minutes, or until set. Cool at room temperature for 10 minutes, remove the pan from the water, then chill in the refrigerator.

Run a knife around the inside edges of the pan and flip the royale onto a cutting board. Peel off the parchment paper and cut into at least twelve 1-inch cubes. Transfer the cubes to a parchment paper–lined baking sheet and reserve, chilled.

For the Pommes Lyonnaise

In a large saucepan over medium-low heat, melt the butter and stir in the onions with 1 teaspoon salt. Cook, undisturbed, for about 5 minutes, until the onions begin to lightly brown on the bottom. Continue to cook, allowing the onions to lightly brown between stirs, for 15 minutes. If the onions stick to the pan, add a small amount of water. Add half of the thyme and continue the process for another 15 minutes, or until the onions are caramelized and tender. Transfer to a cutting board and finely chop.

Peel the potatoes, and using a Japanese Chiba Peel S turning slicer, cut into long, wide sheets, working quickly to prevent oxidizing.

Trim the sheets into two 4-foot lengths and lay them flat. Pat excess water dry with a paper towel. Sprinkle the potato sheets with salt and pepper and spread the surface with a fine layer of garlic paste, followed by the caramelized onion and chopped parsley. Roll the potatoes up from end to end to form tight logs. Tightly roll each log in 2 layers of plastic wrap, then tie off the ends. Using a sharp paring knife, lightly pierce the plastic wrap in several places.

In a medium saucepan, melt the clarified butter with the remaining thyme and heat to 190°F. Submerge the potato logs. Cook until a cake tester easily passes through the potatoes, about 1½ hours. Cool to room temperature, then remove the potatoes from the butter and the plastic. Reserve the butter, chilled. Slice each log into at least three 1-inch discs. Reserve, chilled.

For the Crispy Leeks and Potato Gaufrettes
Fill one-third of a medium saucepan with canola oil and heat to 325°F. Halve the white leek ends lengthwise and julienne into 1-inch strips. Rinse the leeks with cold water and pat dry with paper towels. Lightly dust with the rice flour. Fry the leeks, in 3 batches, until lightly colored and crispy. Drain onto a paper towel–lined tray and sprinkle with salt.

Slice the potato about ¹⁄₁₆-inch thick on a mandoline fitted with a waffle blade, turning the potato a quarter turn after each cut. Using a 1¼-inch ring cutter, punch the slices into at least 6 discs. Increase the oil temperature to 350°F and fry, in batches, until golden brown and crisp. Drain onto a paper towel–lined tray, and sprinkle with salt.

For the Sea Bass
Cut six 8 x 11-inch sheets of parchment paper and set aside.

Square off the ends and sides of the fillets to form a 7 x 2½-inch rectangle. Lay the fillets skin side up and score a deep cut down the center of the length of the fillet, leaving about ⅓ inch of flesh intact. Fold in the fillets along the score, so the skin is facing outward. Keep chilled.

When ready to serve, season the fish with salt and pepper on all sides. Brush one side of a prepared sheet of parchment paper with butter and wrap, buttered side in, snugly around a piece of fish. Repeat until all the fish is wrapped and place on a baking sheet.

To Finish
Preheat the oven to 350°F.

In a small saucepan, bring the syrah reduction and heavy cream to a boil. Remove from the heat. Whisk in the butter, a few pieces at a time, just until melted. Season with salt and white pepper and pass through a fine-meshed sieve. Keep warm but do not simmer.

In a medium sauté pan, melt a thin layer of reserved clarified butter and sear the pommes lyonnaise discs on all sides until browned and crispy.

Transfer the fish to the oven and bake for 8 to 10 minutes, until just cooked through. Transfer the leek royale to the oven and bake for 5 minutes. Remove the fish from the parchment paper and sprinkle with fleur de sel and cracked black pepper.

For each serving, place a bass on one side of a warm dinner plate and set 2 discs of pommes lyonnaise and 2 cubes of leek royale on the side. Top the pommes lyonnaise with a gaufrette chip and a leaf of parsley and top each leek royale with crispy leeks. Spoon a line of sauce near the fish.

BACON-WRAPPED MONKFISH WITH LOBSTER
FALL SQUASH, TELLICHERRY PEPPER JUS

SERVES 6

SLICED TO RESEMBLE a maritime tournedos, the monkfish, often called the poor man's lobster for its similarity of texture, hides real lobster tail inside. To get to the essential fillets, we trim them from the ferocious monkfish tails, then carefully wrap them in the thinnest sheet of double-smoked bacon for a shot of intensity and complexity. As we slowly rotate the fillets while roasting the bacon to crispiness, the delicate fish cooks gently, warming the opaque lobster at its core. A variety of sweet fall squash, glazed, roasted, pureed, and pickled, counterbalances the brininess and smokiness of the dish.

BACON-WRAPPED MONKFISH WITH LOBSTER
FALL SQUASH, TELLICHERRY PEPPER JUS

Monkfish

2 quarts Court Bouillon (page 369)

2 raw lobster tails (from 2-pound lobsters), in their shells

2 (3-pound) monkfish tail fillets

2 pounds double-smoked slab bacon, cut into approximately 9-inch-long paper-thin slices

Salt and freshly ground white pepper

Glazed Squash

2 small butternut squash

6 tablespoons butter

1½ cups Chicken Stock (page 368)

¼ pound delicata squash, cut into at least eighteen 1½ x ¼-inch batons

Salt and freshly ground white pepper

Pickled Squash Ribbons

12 (1-inch-wide by 3-inch-long) butternut squash ribbons, reserved from above

1 cup rice vinegar

3 tablespoons plus 1 teaspoon sugar

Roasted Spaghetti Squash

1 spaghetti squash (about 2 pounds)

2 tablespoons olive oil

Salt and freshly ground white pepper

Butternut Squash Puree

3 tablespoons butter

1 pound butternut squash, cut into small dice, reserved from above

1 sprig sage

Salt and freshly ground white pepper

1 cup Chicken Stock (page 368)

Tellicherry Pepper and Bacon Jus

½ cup diced bacon trim, reserved from above

1 tablespoon crushed Tellicherry peppercorns

1 sprig sage

2 tablespoons sherry vinegar

1 cup Chicken Jus (page 369)

3 tablespoons Chicken Stock (page 368)

To Finish

3 tablespoons Clarified Butter (page 377)

2 cloves garlic, peeled and smashed

2 sprigs sage

Cracked black pepper

Fleur de sel

¼ cup baby purple shiso

For the Monkfish

In a large saucepan, bring the court bouillon to a boil and place a large bowl of ice water on the side. Devein the lobster tails by gently twisting and pulling away the center tail fin; the vein should slide out. If needed, use fish tweezers and rinse with cold water. Insert a skewer through the tails lengthwise to straighten them. Boil the tails for 1 minute, then submerge them in the ice water to chill. Remove the tails from their shells and slice them in half lengthwise.

Cut the dark translucent membrane away from the monkfish fillets. With a small knife, score a line halfway into the flesh down the center length of each fillet to create a channel that will later hold the lobster tails.

Place a sheet of parchment paper a few inches longer than a fillet on a flat work surface. Arrange the bacon by laying 2 slices vertically on one side of the paper, with the ends overlapping by ½ inch. Working horizontally toward the other end of the paper, continue layering bacon slices in vertical pairs, with each pair overlapping the last by ¼ inch. Continue building to form a rectangle with a length that is 1 inch longer than a monkfish fillet. Trim the edges of the rectangle into straight lines and reserve ½ cup of the scraps for the Tellicherry pepper and bacon jus.

Season the monkfish fillets and lobster tails with salt and pepper on all sides. Lay 1 fillet horizontally with the channel facing up on the bacon 4 inches from the bottom edge. Nestle the lobster tail halves into the channel; be sure to slightly overlap the ends for a uniform thickness. Place the second monkfish fillet on top, channel side down, with its thicker end meeting the thinner end of the bottom fillet, covering the lobster.

Using the parchment paper as an aid, wrap the bacon up and around the top of the monkfish, and then roll forward to completely enrobe the monkfish with the bacon. Cut several 10-inch lengths of butcher's twine and snugly tie them around the monkfish at 1-inch intervals to secure the bacon. Reserve, chilled, until ready to serve.

For the Glazed Squash

Peel the butternut squash and separate the neck from the base. With a sharp mandoline, make 12 paper-thin lengthwise slices from the neck and trim into 1-inch-wide x 3-inch-long ribbons; reserve for pickling. Cut the rest of the neck into at least eighteen ½-inch cubes, reserving the trim and base for the puree.

When ready to serve, place the butternut squash cubes in a pan large enough to fit them in a single layer and add 3 tablespoons of the butter and 1 cup of the chicken stock. In a small sauté pan, combine the delicata squash batons with the remaining 3 tablespoons butter and ½ cup chicken stock. Season both pans with salt and pepper and cook at a light simmer for about 8 minutes, until the squash is tender but not colored and the liquid is reduced to a glaze. Be careful not to over-cook the squash, which could mash the edges.

For the Pickled Squash Ribbons

Place the squash ribbons in a heatproof container. In a small saucepan, combine the vinegar and sugar and bring to a simmer; pour over the ribbons and reserve, chilled, for at least 1 hour and up to 1 week.

For the Roasted Spaghetti Squash

Preheat the oven to 350°F. Fit a baking sheet with a wire rack. Halve the squash lengthwise and remove the seeds. Season the flesh with the olive oil and salt and pepper, wrap with foil, and place on the prepared baking sheet. Bake until just cooked, about 45 minutes (be careful not to overcook, or the squash will lose the spaghetti strand texture). Remove from the foil and invert onto the rack to cool and strain off excess liquid, about 10 minutes. Using a fork, scoop the strands from the shell.

For the Butternut Squash Puree

Preheat the oven to 350°F. In a large heatproof saucepan over medium heat, lightly brown the butter and add the squash, sage, and a sprink-ling of salt and pepper. Stir, cover, and transfer to the oven. Bake until tender, about 35 minutes. Discard the sage, transfer the squash to a blen-der, and puree, streaming in enough chicken stock to form a thick puree. Adjust the seasoning with salt and pepper and keep warm.

For the Tellicherry Pepper and Bacon Jus

Heat a medium sauté pan over medium heat and add the bacon trim. Cook, stirring occa-sionally, until crispy. Strain and discard the fat from the pan and add the peppercorns, sage, and vinegar. Reduce until almost dry, then add the chicken jus and stock. Simmer for 10 minutes, strain through a fine-meshed sieve, and reserve, kept warm.

To Finish

Preheat the oven to 350°F.

In a sauté pan or roasting pan large enough to fit the monkfish (if needed, cut the fish into 2 pieces), melt the clarified butter over medium-high heat. Add the monkfish and sear on all sides, turning about every 30 sec-onds, until the bacon is evenly browned. Add the garlic and sage; reduce to medium heat and baste the bacon fat over the fish. Place the pan in the oven for 8 to 12 minutes, or until the fish is just cooked through, turning and basting the fish every 2 minutes. Remove the fish from the pan and let rest for 5 minutes in a warm place. Remove the twine and slice into 6 portions. Transfer the spaghetti squash to a small sauté pan over medium heat and toss to heat through; adjust the seasoning if needed.

For each serving, place a spoonful of hot spaghetti squash at the center of a plate and arrange 3 cubes of butternut squash around the rim; top each one with a baton of delicata squash. Place 2 large spoonfuls of butternut squash puree between the dice and surround them with 2 pickled squash ribbons. Sprinkle cracked black pepper and fleur de sel onto a slice of monkfish and place on top of the spaghetti squash. Dot the jus on the plate and garnish with 4 pieces of baby purple shiso.

SWEET MAINE SHRIMP–COATED HALIBUT
CHORIZO, CRUSHED GARBANZO BEANS

SERVES 4

DURING THE HEIGHT of the halibut season, the kitchen at Daniel sees some of the most amazing fish from the East and West Coasts. I even remember a halibut that weighed 90 pounds, with thick fillets and pristine white flesh. We have served a combination of halibut and sweet shrimp many different ways, but I particularly relish this delicate cooking method: The mousse covers the fillet, creating two layers of taste and texture, to which we add a dab of smokiness with a cream of paprika and chorizo. Whole shrimp and shrimp crackers offer depth and crunch.

SWEET MAINE SHRIMP–
COATED HALIBUT
CHORIZO, CRUSHED GARBANZO BEANS

Shrimp Cracker (Makes extra)

1¾ ounces peeled sweet Maine shrimp

6 tablespoons tapioca flour

⅓ teaspoon salt

1 pinch of white pepper

1 pinch of smoked paprika

Canola oil for frying

Chorizo Cream Sauce

4 ounces chorizo sausage, thinly sliced

¼ cup sliced onion

1 clove garlic, peeled and chopped

1 sachet (¼ teaspoon each ground star anise, coriander seeds, fennel seeds, smoked paprika, black peppercorns, and Szechuan peppercorns wrapped in cheesecloth and secured with butcher's twine)

¼ cup dry white wine

2 teaspoons sherry vinegar

¾ cup heavy cream

½ cup Chicken Stock (page 368), plus extra if needed

Shrimp-Coated Halibut

1 pound halibut fillet, preferably a thick piece from the head side

1⅓ teaspoons coarse sea salt

⅔ teaspoon sugar

10 ounces peeled sweet Maine shrimp

⅓ teaspoon salt

1 egg white

1 tablespoon heavy cream

Freshly ground white pepper

1 tablespoon butter, softened

Cippolini Onion Confit

6 cippolini onions, peeled

Salt and freshly ground white pepper

1 bay leaf

1 sprig thyme

1 clove garlic, peeled

Olive oil

Saffron Potatoes

4 (3-inch-long) fingerling potatoes

Salt and freshly ground white pepper

1 cup Chicken Stock (page 368)

1 clove garlic, peeled

2 sprigs thyme

1 bay leaf

1 small pinch of saffron threads

Garbanzo Bean Fricassée

Salt

3 cups (about 6 ounces) fresh garbanzo beans

12 Thai basil leaves

Salt and freshly ground white pepper

To Finish

12 Thai basil leaf sprigs

1 pinch of Korean dried chili threads

For the Shrimp Cracker

Preheat a steam oven or stovetop steamer. In a chilled food processor fitted with a blade, combine the shrimp, flour, salt, pepper, and paprika and pulse until smooth. Line a flat surface with a 2-foot-square double layer of plastic wrap. Scrape the mixture into a 1-foot-long horizontal line in the center of the plastic wrap. Tightly roll the mixture in the plastic to form a 1-inch-diameter cylinder and tie off the ends. Steam for 1 hour, and then chill.

Fill one-third of a medium saucepan with canola oil and heat to 350°F. Remove the cylinder from the plastic and slice into at least twelve ¹⁄₁₆-inch-thick discs.

Fry the discs in a few batches, until lightly colored and crispy. Drain onto a paper towel–lined tray. Cool and store at room temperature in an airtight container.

For the Chorizo Cream Sauce

Place the chorizo in a medium sauté pan over medium-low heat and cook, stirring until its oil releases, about 4 minutes. Add the onion and garlic and cook, stirring, until softened and caramelized. Add the sachet, white wine, and vinegar and simmer until almost dry. Add the heavy cream and stock and simmer lightly for 20 minutes. Remove the sachet and transfer to a blender; puree until smooth. Pass through a fine-meshed sieve into a small bowl and, if needed, add extra chicken stock to adjust to a consistency that will lightly coat a spoon. Store, chilled.

For the Shrimp-Coated Halibut

Cut the halibut into four 4-ounce rectangular portions (approximately 6 x 1½ inches) and transfer to a shallow nonreactive dish. Evenly sprinkle the coarse salt and sugar over the fish on all sides and refrigerate for 15 minutes. Rinse the fish with cold water and pat dry with paper towels.

Pick and reserve 16 perfect pieces of shrimp (2 ounces, total), leaving 8 ounces for mousse. Combine the remaining 8 ounces shrimp with the salt, egg white, and heavy cream in a food processor. Pulse until smooth to make a mousse. Pass the mousse through a fine-meshed drum sieve into a bowl set over ice. Divide the mousse onto the tops of the

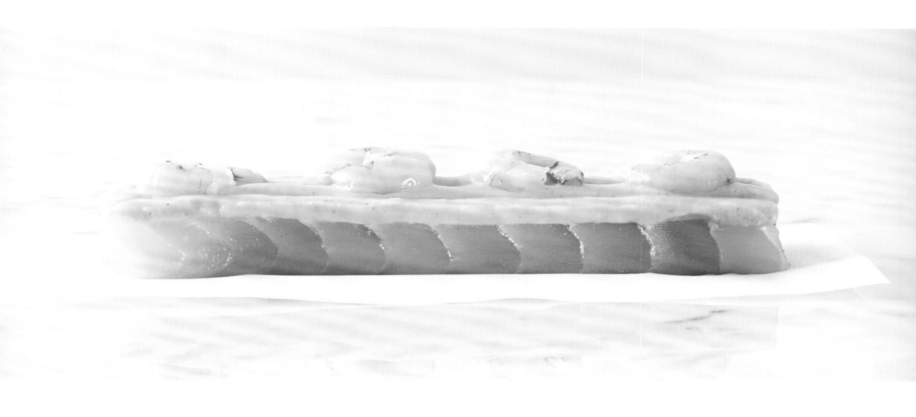

fish and spread with an offset spatula to make an even layer. Top each with 4 shrimp and gently press them so they settle into the mousse. Sprinkle with pepper. Cut four 7-inch squares of parchment paper and brush one side with butter. Wrap 1 square of paper, buttered side in, snugly around each portion of fish and transfer them to a baking sheet. Reserve, chilled.

For the Cippolini Onion Confit

Season the onions on both sides with salt and pepper. Transfer to a small saucepan with the bay leaf, thyme, and garlic and add enough oil to cover. Place over medium heat and heat until bubbles begin to surface. Reduce the heat to low and cook for 45 minutes, or until the onions are tender. Halve the onions through their centers, return to the oil, and reserve, kept warm.

For the Saffron Potatoes

In a small saucepan, submerge the potatoes in cold water and season with salt and pepper. Bring to a simmer and cook until tender, about 15 minutes. Remove the pan from the heat, and when cool enough to handle, peel the skin from the potatoes.

Cut the potatoes into at least eight ½-inch-thick slices or geometric shapes such as triangles or teardrops. Pour the chicken stock into a small saucepan with the garlic, thyme, bay leaf, saffron, and a sprinkle of salt and pepper and bring to a simmer. Add the potatoes, cover, remove from the heat, and set aside to infuse for 20 minutes. Keep warm.

For the Garbanzo Bean Fricassée

Bring a large pot of salted water to a boil and place a bowl of ice water on the side. Add the beans and boil for 30 seconds, then transfer to the ice water to chill. Peel the beans and transfer them to a cutting board. Roughly chop and transfer to a small sauté pan with a spoonful of the cippolini onion oil and the Thai basil leaves. Place over medium heat and toss until heated through. Season with salt and pepper and keep warm.

To Finish

Preheat the oven to 225°F. Transfer the fish to the oven and bake for 12 to 14 minutes, or until the temperature reaches 130°F in the center. Transfer the chorizo sauce to a small saucepan and stir over medium heat until heated through. Carefully unwrap the fish from the paper and spoon chorizo sauce on top.

For each serving, place 1 portion of fish on the side of a warm dinner plate and spoon some garbanzo bean fricassée in a similar rectangular shape adjacent. Top the fricassée with 3 cippolini onion halves, 2 saffron potato slices, and 3 Thai basil leaf sprigs. Top the fish with 3 shrimp crackers and a few chili threads.

SEARED PACIFIC SABLE
GOURGANE PANISSE, PICKLED RAMPS

SERVES 4

THE COMBINATION of cured and traditionally smoked sable is a prized item in the Jewish delis of New York. Here, we combine it with fresh sable (you may know it as black cod) dusted with fine gourgane flour. This gluten-free flour comes from a broad bean cultivated in Quebec. With it, the firm and flaky fish takes on a golden tint, matching the square gourgane flour cakes. Similar to the French panisses or the Italian panelle, usually made with chickpea flour, the cakes feel crispy on the outside and taste creamy on the inside. Traces of savory cream add pungent and lemony fizz, while fava bean puree and pickled ramps remind us that spring has arrived, in all its glory.

Pickled Ramps (makes extra)

Salt

1 bunch (about 12 pieces) wild ramps, leaves trimmed

Pickling Liquid (page 377)

1 sachet (½ teaspoon each black peppercorns, coriander seeds, and fennel seeds wrapped in cheesecloth and secured with butcher's twine)

Crispy Gourgane Cakes

1 cup gourgane flour (we recommend Société-Orignal)

¼ teaspoon salt

1 tablespoon lemon oil

1 tablespoon olive oil

1 splash of Tabasco sauce

Freshly ground white pepper

Savory Cream

2 sprigs savory

1 clove garlic, peeled

1¼ cups heavy cream

Salt and freshly ground white pepper

Savory Jus

¾ cup Chicken Jus (page 369)

2 sprigs savory

Fava Bean Puree and Fricassée

Salt

4 cups fresh fava beans, peeled

1 cup savory cream, reserved from above

Freshly ground white pepper

1 tablespoon butter

1 tablespoon Chicken Stock (page 368)

15 fresh savory leaves, chopped

To Finish

Canola oil for frying

Salt

2 spring onions, trimmed and halved lengthwise

3 tablespoons olive oil

Freshly ground white pepper

3 tablespoons sheep's milk yogurt (we recommend Old Chatham Sheepherding Company)

6 ounces smoked sablefish, cut into 2-inch-long x ¼-inch-wide batons

1½ pounds fresh black cod (sablefish) fillet, cut into 8 approximately 2½ x ½-inch portions

½ cup gourgane flour

2 sprigs thyme

1 clove garlic, peeled and smashed

1 tablespoon butter

2 teaspoons thinly sliced chives

1 teaspoon cracked black pepper

¼ cup green pea shoots

¼ cup micro savory leaves

For the Pickled Ramps

Bring a large pot of salted water to a boil and place a bowl of ice water on the side. Prepare the ramps by trimming the roots and cutting them from the stem end into 4-inch lengths; rinse with cold water. Boil the ramps for 30 seconds, then chill in the ice water, strain, and pat dry. Place in a heatproof container. Pour the pickling liquid into a small saucepan, add the sachet, and bring to a simmer. Pour over the top of the ramps; cover and store, chilled.

For the Crispy Gourgane Cakes

Combine 1¼ cups of water with the gourgane flour and salt in a blender and puree until smooth. Pour 1½ cups of water into a medium saucepan, bring to a simmer, and slowly whisk in the gourgane mixture. Cook over low heat for 1 hour, covered, stirring often, making sure not to brown the bottom of the pan. Transfer the mixture to a food processor and pulse with the lemon oil, olive oil, and Tabasco sauce; season with pepper. While still hot, pour into an 8½ x 4½-inch loaf pan and using a small offset spatula, spread the top into an even layer. Refrigerate for 2 hours, or until firm. Turn the mixture onto a cutting board and cut into 1-inch squares; store, chilled.

For the Savory Cream

In a small saucepan, combine the savory, garlic, and cream and bring to a simmer. Remove from the heat, cover, and infuse for 20 minutes. Remove the savory and garlic, season with salt and pepper, and chill. Reserve 1 cup for the fava bean puree. Up to 30 minutes before serving, whip the remaining ¼ cup cream to stiff peaks.

For the Savory Jus

Transfer the chicken jus to a small saucepan and bring to a simmer. Add the savory, cover, and infuse for 20 minutes. Pick and discard the savory and keep warm.

For the Fava Bean Puree and Fricassée

Bring a large pot of salted water to a boil and place a bowl of ice water on the side. Add the fava beans and boil until tender, about 2 minutes, then chill in the ice water. Pour the reserved 1 cup of savory cream into a small saucepan and bring to a simmer. Transfer to a blender with 3 cups of the fava beans and puree until smooth. Season with salt and pepper. Pass through a fine-meshed sieve into a small saucepan and keep warm.

In a small sauté pan, bring the butter and chicken stock to a simmer. Add the remaining 1 cup fava beans and the savory and toss until heated through and glazed. Season with salt and pepper and keep warm.

To Finish

Fill one-third of a medium saucepan with canola oil and heat to 350°F. Heat a grill or cast-iron grill pan over high heat.

Deep-fry the gourgane cakes until crispy. Drain on a paper towel–lined plate and sprinkle with salt.

Brush the halved spring onions with 1 tablespoon of the olive oil and sprinkle with salt and pepper. Grill them on the cut sides until well-marked, turn over, and continue cooking until tender, about 1 more minute.

In a small bowl, season the yogurt with salt and pepper, add the smoked sablefish, and roll in the yogurt to coat.

Heat the remaining 2 tablespoons olive oil in a large sauté pan over medium heat. Season the cod on all sides with salt and pepper and sprinkle with gourgane flour to coat. Sear the cod on all sides, about 30 seconds each, until golden brown. Add the thyme, garlic, and butter. Baste the butter over the fish, turning it occasionally until it is cooked, 3 to 4 minutes more. Strain onto a paper towel–lined plate.

For each serving, place a spoonful of fava bean puree into the center of a warm dinner plate and top with a spoonful of fava bean fricassée. Place 2 pieces of cod on opposite sides of the plate and top each with a smoked sablefish baton; sprinkle the baton with chives and cracked black pepper. Rest 2 pickled ramps against the fish and place a grilled spring onion in between them. Garnish the plate with a few pea shoots and micro savory leaves. Swirl the whipped savory cream into the jus and spoon onto the plate.

LOUP DE MER
TENDER LEEKS, OVOLI MUSHROOMS À LA CRÈME

SERVES 6

ONE OF MY FAVORITE wild mushrooms, the Amanita Caesarea, also called ovoli, or *oronge* in French, has been revered since Roman times. To me, the ovoli bear a mythical aura, perhaps because they have become so rare. They can be eaten roasted or raw. Raw, they remind me of hazelnut; cooked, they taste of earthy forest. So why choose? At Daniel, we present them both ways: Paired with the pristine flesh of the loup de mer, we concentrate their roasted flavor with cream, shallots, and vermouth. Raw slices, silky and fresh, are drizzled with olive oil and counterbalance the richness of the fish.

LOUP DE MER
TENDER LEEKS, OVOLI MUSHROOMS À LA CRÈME

Loup de Mer

Salt

2 (12-ounce) boneless, skin-on loup de mer fillets

Olive oil

Freshly ground white pepper

4 (2½-ounce) ovoli mushrooms

Ovoli and Yukon Gold Potato Ragout

2 tablespoons butter

1 medium shallot, minced

1 clove garlic, peeled and chopped

1½ cups small-diced ovoli mushroom stems, reserved from above

3 tablespoons dry vermouth

1 medium Yukon gold potato

½ cup heavy cream

2 tablespoons Chicken Jus (page 369)

½ teaspoon salt

Lemon juice

Freshly ground white pepper

2 teaspoons thinly sliced chives

Roasted Ovoli Mushrooms

2 tablespoons butter

1 medium shallot, minced

3 (2½-ounce) ovoli mushrooms, peeled, cleaned, and quartered

Salt and freshly ground white pepper

1 splash of dry vermouth

Steamed Leek

1 small, slender leek

Olive oil

Salt and freshly ground white pepper

To Finish

Olive oil

Salt

Lemon juice

18 (2-inch) chive tips

30 chive blossoms

For the Loup de Mer

Preheat the oven to 315°F.

Bring a medium pot of salted water to a boil. Remove the skin from the loup de mer fillets and boil it for 30 seconds. Strain, rinse with cold water, and pat dry. Line a baking sheet with parchment paper and brush with a thin coating of olive oil. Line the skin on top in a flat layer. Brush another sheet of parchment with oil and set on top of the skin, oiled side down. Set another baking sheet on top to keep the skin flat and bake for 45 minutes, or until the skin is crispy. While still hot, transfer the skin to a cutting board and cut each into three ½-inch-wide strips. Cool to room temperature and store in an airtight container.

Divide each fillet into 3 equal portions and season on both sides with salt and pepper. Cut six 6 x 10-inch rectangles of parchment paper and brush them on one side with olive oil. Cut away the white outer skin from the mushrooms and gently wipe away any dirt from the stems and caps with a damp cloth. Separate the caps from the mushrooms and reserve the stems for the ragout. With a sharp mandoline, cut the caps widthwise into thin slices. Set 18 slices onto a plate, wrap with plastic wrap, and reserve, chilled, for garnishing. Divide the remaining slices lengthwise in an overlapping line on each portion of fish, slightly off-center. Individually wrap each portion of fish in the parchment rectangles, oiled side in. Transfer to a baking sheet and reserve, chilled.

For the Ovoli and Yukon Gold Potato Ragout

Brown the butter in a medium saucepan over medium heat. Add the shallot and garlic. Cook, stirring, for 1 minute. Add the mushrooms and continue to cook, stirring, until golden. Add the vermouth and simmer until reduced by half. Remove from the heat.

Peel the potato, cut it into ¼-inch dice, and add to the pan. Add the cream, chicken jus, and salt and simmer over low heat until the potatoes are cooked but not mushy. Season with lemon juice and pepper. Keep warm and stir in the chives just before serving.

For the Roasted Ovoli Mushrooms

In a medium sauté pan, brown the butter over medium heat. Add the shallot and cook, stirring, until soft. Add the ovoli mushrooms and season with salt and pepper. Sauté for 3 minutes over medium heat. Add the vermouth and simmer until almost dry. Keep warm.

For the Steamed Leek

Preheat a stovetop steamer. Peel any tough outer skins from the leek and rinse it well with cold water. Cut on a bias into at least eighteen ¼-inch rounds. Drizzle with the olive oil and season with salt and pepper. Transfer to the steamer and cook for 5 minutes, or until tender.

To Finish

Preheat the oven to 200°F. Remove the fish from the refrigerator and allow to rest at room temperature for 15 minutes. Season the reserved slices of ovoli caps with olive oil, salt, and lemon juice.

Bake the fish for 12 minutes, or until a cake tester passes easily through the fillet with little resistance. Unwrap the loup de mer from the parchment paper and sprinkle with a bit of lemon juice.

For each serving, spoon ragout onto one side of a warm dinner plate and rest a portion of loup de mer on top, mushroom side up. Spoon some of the sauce from the ragout over the fish to glaze. Place a piece of crispy skin on the fish opposite the sliced ovoli. On the other side of the plate, arrange 3 leek pieces, 2 pieces roasted ovoli, 3 ovoli cap slices, and 3 chive tips in a line. Garnish the plate with 5 chive blossoms.

CLAY-BAKED KING SALMON
FENNEL ROYALE, CARAMELIZED FIGS

SERVES 6

THIS ANCIENT COOKING method was imagined centuries ago and can be found in numerous cultures. Tightly wrapped in the fragrant fig leaf and encased within the clay, the salmon literally drinks up the seasoning, in this case the lemony sumac and piquant piment d'Espelette. As the heating vessel hardens, the fish cooks slowly and consistently, producing tender, luscious flesh.

Every year during fig season (usually between July and October), when Alaskan wild king salmon makes its way to our kitchen, we offer this wonderful preparation as a special. Several years ago, I was invited to cook for a birthday bash on Lake Tahoe, and I decided to bake a whole fish in a similar fashion. The combination of flavors was a hit!

CLAY-BAKED KING SALMON
FENNEL ROYALE, CARAMELIZED FIGS

Fennel Royale (makes extra)

Salt

2 heads (1¾ pounds) fennel, with stalks

2 cups heavy cream

4 eggs

1 teaspoon fennel pollen

Freshly ground white pepper

1 tablespoon butter, softened

Salmon Wrapped in Clay

1 (5-pound) block red self-hardening clay

4 pounds center-cut, boneless and skinless king salmon fillet

2 teaspoons fennel pollen

1 tablespoon ground sumac

2 teaspoons piment d'Espelette

Fleur de sel

Freshly ground white pepper

12 fresh fig leaves

Baby Fennel Salad and Confit

8 baby fennel bulbs, with stalks

1 cup olive oil

1 teaspoon fennel pollen

2 teaspoons salt

Red Wine and Fig Sauce

⅓ cup Syrah Reduction (page 371)

1 tablespoon heavy cream

12 tablespoons cold butter, cut into small dice

2 tablespoons fig balsamic vinegar (we recommend Restaurant LuLu)

2 ripe figs, cut into brunoise

Salt and freshly ground white pepper

To Finish

2 tablespoons butter

6 figs, halved lengthwise

1 tablespoon fig balsamic vinegar

Salt and freshly ground white pepper

For the Fennel Royale

Preheat the oven to 275°F. Bring a large pot of salted water to a boil and set a bowl of ice water on the side. Trim and weigh 4 ounces of the fennel stalks with their leaves. Boil the stalks and leaves until very tender, about 3 minutes, and chill in the ice water. Strain and squeeze dry.

Cut the bulbs into thin slices and place in a medium saucepan. Add 1 cup of the cream with 1 teaspoon salt and bring to a simmer. Cook, stirring occasionally, for 15 minutes, or until the fennel is tender. Scoop the fennel with a slotted spoon into a blender; reserve the cream. Add the boiled fennel stalks and leaves and puree with enough of the hot cream to form a smooth, thick puree. Measure 2 cups into a bowl. Whisk in the remaining 1 cup cream, the eggs, fennel pollen, 1 teaspoon salt, and a pinch of pepper until well combined.

Spread the butter on the inside of an 8½ x 4½-inch loaf pan and line with parchment paper on the bottom and sides. Pour in the mixture and wrap with plastic wrap; poke 3 small holes in the plastic wrap. Transfer the loaf pan to a roasting pan and fill the roasting pan with enough hot water to reach the level of the fennel mixture. Transfer to the oven and bake for 40 minutes, or until set. Cool at room temperature for 10 minutes, remove the pan from the water, then chill in the refrigerator. Run a knife around the inside edges of the pan and flip the royale onto a cutting board. Peel off the parchment paper and cut with a 1-inch-diameter ring mold into at least 12 cylinders or other desired shapes. Transfer to a parchment paper–lined baking sheet and reserve, chilled.

For the Salmon Wrapped in Clay

With a large knife, cut the clay in half. Place each piece on a flat surface between two 2-foot-long pieces of parchment or wax paper. Roll the clay between the papers to form ¼-inch-thick sheets. Set aside.

Season the salmon on both sides with the fennel pollen, sumac, piment d'Espelette, fleur de sel, and pepper.

Remove the paper from the surface of 1 clay sheet. Arrange the fig leaves on top, with their ribbed sides facing up, in a slightly overlapping layer large enough to wrap around the fish. Place the salmon in the center of the leaves and wrap the leaves around it to fully enclose. Lightly brush the edges of the clay with water.

Remove the paper from the surface of the second sheet of clay and flip it over onto the fish to cover. Peel off the remaining paper and press the clay around the fish to seal. Trim the edges to form a 1-inch border.

With a paring knife, score the clay around the perimeter of the salmon fillet to aid in lifting the top once baked. Decorate the surface of the clay as desired. Transfer to a foil-lined baking sheet and store, chilled.

For the Baby Fennel Salad and Confit

Pick the baby fennel fronds, wrap in wet paper towels, and reserve, chilled, for the salad. Trim the remaining stalks from the bulbs. Using a mandoline, shave 2 of the fennel bulbs lengthwise into ice water and set aside.

Slice the remaining fennel in half lengthwise; combine with the olive oil, fennel pollen, and salt in a small saucepan and warm to 185°F over medium heat. Cook, stirring occasionally, for 20 minutes, or until the fennel is tender. Keep warm.

For the Red Wine and Fig Sauce

When ready to serve, in a small saucepan, bring the syrah reduction and heavy cream to a boil. Remove from the heat and whisk in the butter a few pieces at a time until melted. Add the vinegar and figs and season with salt and pepper. Keep warm but do not simmer.

To Finish

Preheat the oven to 390°F. Rest the salmon at room temperature for 30 minutes. Bake the salmon for 12 minutes, or until the center of the fillet reaches 120°F. Turn off the oven, remove the fish, and rest for 10 minutes. Place the fennel royale in the oven for 3 minutes, or until just heated through.

Brown the butter in a small sauté pan over low heat. Add the figs cut side down and cook undisturbed until caramelized, about 3 minutes. Add the vinegar, turn the figs over, season with salt and pepper, and swirl to coat.

Cut the clay along the scored line and lift off the top. Peel away the top layer of leaves from the fish and, with a sharp slicing knife, carve it into 6 portions.

For each serving, transfer a portion of salmon to a warm dinner plate and arrange 2 pieces of fennel royale, 2 pieces of confit fennel, 2 roasted fig halves, and a few pieces of shaved fennel and fennel fronds around the fish. Spoon the sauce around the salmon.

STRIPED BASS IN A CILANTRO-TAPIOCA PISTOU
ARTICHOKES, LEMON CROQUETTES

SERVES 4

IN SEASON from mid-April to late October, I find the striped bass—equally at ease in rivers and in the ocean—to be the most fascinating, delicious fish of the East Coast. Pesto, or pistou, is usually made with basil, but here we've used the refreshing, vibrant taste of cilantro to match the lemony croquettes, our own take on the classic arancini. At the bottom of the plate, a cilantro tapioca nage surrounds the artichoke and fava bean medley.

Cilantro Pistou

4 ounces cilantro leaves, roughly chopped

2 tablespoons toasted pine nuts

¼ cup olive oil

¾ teaspoon salt

Freshly ground white pepper to taste

Artichokes and Fava Beans

Salt

4 ounces peeled fava beans

1 sachet (1 teaspoon coriander seeds and ½ teaspoon chili flakes wrapped in cheesecloth and secured with butcher's twine)

1 fresh bay leaf

2 sprigs thyme

2 cups Chicken Stock (page 368)

2 tablespoons lemon juice

4 large artichokes

Salt and freshly ground white pepper

Lemon Croquettes (makes extra)

7 cups Chicken Stock (page 368)

½ cup (1 stick) butter

1 small onion, small-diced

2 cups Arborio rice

½ cup grated Parmesan cheese

1 tablespoon mascarpone cheese

Finely grated zest of 1 lemon

½ cup lemon juice

Salt and freshly ground white pepper

Dijon Tapioca Sauce

2 tablespoons large tapioca pearls

2 tablespoons Dijon mustard

½ cup olive oil

3 tablespoons Cilantro Pistou (see above)

2 cilantro leaves, sliced

To Finish

Canola oil for frying

4 (5-ounce) boneless and skinless striped bass fillets

4 tablespoons olive oil, plus extra for salad

Salt and freshly ground white pepper

Lemon juice

Cilantro Pistou (see above)

½ cup cornstarch

¼ cup micro cilantro

For the Cilantro Pistou

Combine all the ingredients in a blender and puree until smooth. Reserve, chilled.

For the Artichokes and Fava Beans

Bring a large pot of salted water to a boil and place a bowl of ice water on the side. Add the fava beans and boil until tender, about 1 minute. Chill in the ice water, pat dry, and set aside. In a medium saucepan, combine the sachet, bay leaf, thyme, chicken stock, and lemon juice. To clean each artichoke, peel away the outer leaves and trim the stem to about 1½ inches in length. Using a sharp paring knife, remove the skin from the stem and any tough leaf remnants from the base. Immediately submerge in the liquid to keep from oxidizing. If needed, add water to keep artichokes submerged. With a mandoline, thinly slice half of 1 of the artichokes length-wise into a small container, submerge with some of the liquid from the saucepan, and reserve for the garnish, chilled. Once all the artichokes are cleaned, bring to a simmer and cook for 20 minutes, or until tender. Remove from the heat and cool in the liquid. Use a spoon to scoop and discard the chokes from the artichokes and cut the flesh into ¼-inch dice. Transfer to a container and stir in enough cooking liquid to coat. Reduce the remaining liquid to 1 cup; adjust the season-ing with salt and pepper if needed, and reserve, chilled.

For the Lemon Croquettes

Grease an 8½ x 4½-inch loaf pan and line it with parchment paper. In a large saucepan over medium-high heat, bring the stock to a light simmer. In a medium saucepan, melt the butter over medium heat and add the onion. Cook, stirring, until translucent, about 2 minutes. Add the rice and stir with a wooden spoon for 2 minutes, or until well coated. Ladle 1 cup of the stock into the pan and simmer. Stir often and add more stock, ½ cup at a time, as it is absorbed by the rice while it cooks. The rice should cook in 16 to 18 minutes and be moist but not runny. When the rice is cooked, stir in the Parmesan, mascarpone, lemon zest, and lemon juice. Season with salt and pepper.

Evenly spread the mixture into the prepared pan and chill until firm. Invert the rice onto a cutting board and cut into at least twelve 1-inch cubes.

For the Dijon Tapioca Sauce

In a small saucepan, bring 2 cups water to a simmer and stir in the tapioca pearls. Cook for 20 minutes, or until the pearls are cooked and translucent. Strain and reserve the pearls. In a blender, puree the reserved artichoke cooking liquid and the mustard, then slowly stream in the olive oil to emulsify. The mixture should be thick enough to coat the back of a spoon. Transfer to a saucepan over medium heat and stir in the tapioca until heated through. Reserve, kept warm. Just before serving, stir in the cilantro pistou and sliced cilantro.

To Finish

Preheat the oven to 300°F. Fill one-third of a medium saucepan with canola oil and heat to 350°F. Allow the fish to rest at room tem-perature for 15 minutes, season on all sides with the olive oil and salt and pepper, and wrap individually with sheets of parchment paper. Transfer to a baking sheet and bake the fish for 6 to 7 minutes, until cooked through. Remove the parchment paper, sprinkle with lemon juice, and brush the tops of the fish with cilantro pistou.

Toss the lemon croquette squares in cornstarch until evenly coated and fry until golden brown. Transfer to a paper towel–lined tray and sprinkle with salt.

In a medium sauté pan, heat the diced artichokes and fava beans in 3 tablespoons of the sauce; season with salt and pepper.

Strain the reserved artichoke slices.

For each serving, spoon 2 tablespoons of the artichoke–fava bean mixture onto the bottom of each plate. Top with a bass fillet and arrange 3 croquettes on top. Spoon a pool of sauce around the fish and arrange a few artichoke slices and leaves of micro cilantro on top.

CEDAR-WRAPPED KAMPACHI
ROMANO BEANS, SAUCE DIABLE

SERVES 4

FOR THIS DISH, I imagined good old Kentucky bourbon aging in cedar barrels, taking their flavor from the old wood. Now, we take a flavorful sheet of that cedarwood wrapped around a log of kampachi, the firm, white fish from the yellowtail family. In fact, the thin cedar "paper" is soaked for 12 hours in the liquor and then another 12 hours in olive oil. When it touches the fish, it is already rich with spirit. Simply grilled, it will yield a light smoky flavor that intensifies as it's presented to the table on top of smoldering coals before its final undressing. The sauce diable, a classic in the French repertoire, is the spiciest of all sauces, but to tame it and just enhance the fish, we pair it with a touch of sesame tahini.

CEDAR-WRAPPED KAMPACHI
ROMANO BEANS, SAUCE DIABLE

Cedar-Wrapped Kampachi

¼ cup bourbon

4 sheets Japanese cedar paper, soaked in water overnight

½ cup olive oil

4 (5-ounce) portions kampachi fillet

1 pinch of piment d'Espelette

1 pinch of smoked paprika

Salt and freshly ground white pepper

Eggplant Chips

Canola oil for frying

1 (10-inch-long) Japanese eggplant

Salt

Pickled Red Onion

1 small red onion

1 cup Pickling Liquid (page 377)

½ teaspoon black peppercorns

½ teaspoon chili flakes

½ teaspoon coriander seeds

Paprika Oil

1 tablespoon smoked paprika

3 tablespoons olive oil

Romano Beans

Salt

3 (7-inch-long) Romano beans

Creamy Tahini Sauce

¼ cup tahini

3 tablespoons heavy cream

1 teaspoon salt

2 tablespoons lemon juice

Tabasco sauce

Sauce Diable

1 cup dry white wine

3 tablespoons brunoised shallot

½ teaspoon piment d'Espelette

½ teaspoon cayenne pepper

1 teaspoon coarsely ground black pepper

1 tablespoon sherry vinegar

1 cup Chicken Jus (page 369)

1 teaspoon finely chopped parsley

Honey-Glazed Eggplant

1 (10-inch-long) Japanese eggplant, skin on

3 tablespoons olive oil

2 tablespoons honey

3 tablespoons sherry vinegar

Salt and freshly ground white pepper

To Finish

Grilled Eggplant Puree (page 371)

2 tablespoons chopped parsley

1 tablespoon olive oil

4 petals Tomato Confit (page 376), cut into thirds lengthwise

Salt and freshly ground white pepper

Charcoal (we recommend Japanese Sumi Charcoal), optional

2 cups wood chips, optional

12 small nasturtium leaves

For the Cedar-Wrapped Kampachi

Pour the bourbon into a shallow dish and submerge the cedar paper for 12 hours. Strain, then submerge in the olive oil for another 12 hours.

At least 4 hours before cooking the kampachi, season it on all sides with the piment d'Espelette, paprika, and salt and pepper. Wrap the fish in the cedar paper and secure with butcher's twine; reserve, chilled.

For the Eggplant Chips

Fill one-third of a large saucepan with canola oil and heat to 300°F. Preheat the oven to 190°F. Using a mandoline, slice the eggplant lengthwise into thin strips. Fry the slices one at a time, keeping them submerged in the oil just until limp. With tongs or a heatproof strainer, transfer the slices to a Silpat-lined baking sheet in a single layer. Pat dry and sprinkle with salt. Bake for 4 hours, or until the eggplant slices are crisp but not colored. Store in an airtight container (you can add rice or stale bread to the container to keep the chips crisp).

For the Pickled Red Onion

Cut the onion in half and separate it into layers. Cut the layers into ¼-inch triangles and transfer them to a heatproof container. Combine the pickling liquid and spices in a small saucepan and bring to a simmer. Pour over the onion and store, chilled.

For the Paprika Oil

In a small saucepan, combine the paprika and olive oil over low heat. Bring to a simmer, while whisking, for 1 minute, being sure not to let it burn. Remove from the heat. Line a sieve with a coffee filter and set over a dry container. Strain the oil through the filter and set aside.

For the Romano Beans

Bring a large pot of salted water to a boil and set a bowl of ice water on the side. Cut the beans on a bias into ¼-inch-thick pieces. Boil for 3 to 4 minutes, until tender, and then chill in the ice water. Reserve, chilled.

For the Creamy Tahini Sauce

In a small bowl, whisk to combine the tahini, cream, salt, and lemon juice. Adjust the seasoning with Tabasco sauce. Transfer to a squeeze bottle or pastry bag with a small tip.

For the Sauce Diable

In a medium saucepan, combine the white wine, shallot, piment d'Espelette, cayenne, and black pepper and bring to a simmer. Reduce until almost dry, and add the vinegar and jus. Bring to a simmer and reserve, kept warm. Just before serving, stir in the chopped parsley.

For the Honey-Glazed Eggplant

Quarter the eggplant lengthwise and slice away the seeds. Cut the remaining strips into at least twelve ½-inch triangles. Heat the olive oil in a sauté pan over medium-high heat. Add the eggplant skin side up and sear until golden, about 1 minute. Strain any excess oil from the pan and add the honey and vinegar. Simmer, while stirring, until the eggplant is tender, about 2 minutes. Season with salt and pepper. Keep warm.

To Finish

Allow the fish to rest at room temperature for 15 minutes and preheat a grill or cast-iron grill pan to high heat. Transfer the grilled eggplant puree to a small saucepan over medium heat and stir to heat through; add the parsley. Warm the olive oil in a small sauté pan over medium-low heat and add the Romano beans and tomato confit; toss to heat through and season with salt and pepper. Grill the fish in the wood for 1 minute on each of the 4 sides. Rest in a warm place for 3 minutes before serving.

If desired, line a serving dish or dinner plate with charcoal and wood chips and ignite them until they smoke. Place the fish on top as a presentation.

For each serving, paint a long straight streak of paprika oil on one side of a large dinner plate and pipe around its perimeter with creamy tahini sauce. Unwrap a portion of fish and set in the center of the plate. On the opposite side of the plate from the paprika, arrange 4 eggplant triangles, 3 spoonfuls of grilled eggplant puree, 3 pieces of tomato confit, and 4 pieces of Romano beans in a rectangle set parallel to the oil. Stand 2 eggplant chips against the long sides of the vegetables. Garnish the vegetables with 3 nasturtium leaves and spoon the sauce on top of the kampachi.

DANIEL ON STOCKS AND SAUCES

BEFORE THE SAUCE, THERE WAS STOCK! THE STOCK IS THE flavor foundation of French cuisine. As a young apprentice, that was one of the first things I had to learn: prepping, simmering, filtering, chilling, and storing stock—all important, daily duties. The recipe is straightforward and the process is simple, but the whole composition of a plate often rests on those basic, ancestral references. In the kitchens of France, it is often declared that great chefs make great stock.

There are many schools of thought for making the perfect one. Some chefs roast the bones, others don't; roast the vegetables, or not; blacken the onions, or not. At Daniel, we make veal stock with backbones, roasted vegetables, and bouquet garni and employ it as a base for many of our braised items. It also serves as the main support element in many sauces. Chicken stock with fresh chicken bones is often the base of many of our soups.

Thinking back to my years as a young apprentice at Nandron in Lyon, I remember a fabulous old-fashioned sauce Nantua with crayfish stock served with pike dumplings, the famous Lyon specialty. It was so good that some customers (and a few cooks) drank it as if it were soup. The large dumplings wallowed in two pints of sauce and as we heated the timbale on the stove, you could see the dumplings breathing it in, drinking it and puffing up like a soufflé. We served this in a bowl with as much sauce as possible.

Yes, I will drink a sauce Nantua by the spoonful, but guess what? A sauce both French and American cultures love is mayo. Dip your finger into this French mayonnaise (page 370) I just whipped up. Do you taste the Dijon mustard? That's la grande différence; the strength of our mayonnaise is in the mustard. The perfect mayo is fluffy, light, bright, and delicious by itself but also can be a base for black olive paste, sweet garlic, herbs, and even truffles. One of my favorite sauces for cold shellfish plateau is based on ketchup and it's called French cocktail sauce: a mayo base, ketchup, Worcestershire sauce, Tabasco, a drop of lemon juice, and crème fraîche, but finished with a splash of Cognac. Coat a piece of shrimp with it and tell me what you think!

Before we go further, I need to dispel a myth: Today's sauce, an essential part of French cuisine, is not gravy! It's not thickened with roux anymore and it's not heavy. Most often it results from a reduction of wine and concentration of flavors, meaning that some of our best ingredients cook together very slowly for a very long time. In Chinese cuisine, the sauce is mixed into the dish. In Italian cuisine, it's often hidden in the braise. But in French cuisine, every ingredient, from mussels to veal, has one sauce as a partner. There are dozens of entries in the *Larousse Gastronomique* under "sauce." No other cuisine is richer and more complex in sauce repertoire. I feel the sophistication of French cuisine often originates in the sauce.

"It is the sauce that distinguishes a good chef. The saucier is a soloist in the orchestra of a great kitchen." —Fernand Point

*"Burgundy makes you think of silly things, Bordeaux makes
you talk about them and Champagne makes you do them."*
—*Jean Anthelme Brillat-Savarin*

DANIEL ON WINE

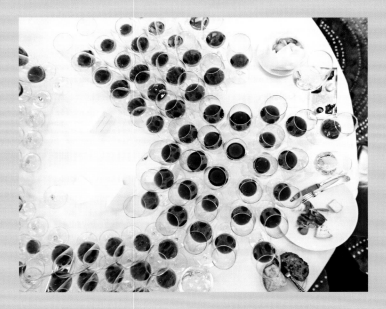

AT HOME ON THE FARM, I WAS IN CHARGE OF THE WINE. I DON'T mean choosing from a wood-paneled showroom cellar. No, what that meant was that each September, I would help my father make the two barrels of the deep, black baco we produced annually, and then every day I went to the cellar and poured enough for our daily consumption out of the barrel. I've been drinking wine since the age of seven, cut with water, of course—and believe me, it's better than soda!

To me, a visit to a winemaker's home is the first step to understanding and appreciating a wine. Sharing a meal, discussing the soil, tasting different crus are all critical ways to forge bonds that can last a lifetime.

There was a memorable rabbit stew cooked by Gérard Chave at the Hermitage vineyard, and the warm and fluffy gougères (warm Comté cheese puffs) served by Madame D'Angerville during my jaunt at the Marquis d'Angerville Estate in Volnay. And to this day, we cook this specialty as a welcoming treat for diners at Bar Boulud—a taste of Burgundy even before the wine is poured.

The bond between the cook and the vintner is unique and strong. We share the same work ethic and the same palate sensibility. That is the reason why I encourage my sommeliers to travel and meet the men and women who stand behind the wine we share with you.

The first word that comes to mind when I think of how we built the wine cellar at Restaurant Daniel is *passion*. First and foremost, passion for the vintners who nurture the vineyards in all weather, all year long; and at harvesttime, touch, feel, and know to wait just long enough before launching the vendanges. Passion for the French grands crus, of course, but also for international wines fitting all kinds of budgets. Passion for the best possible combination between a dish and its wine partner, so that the wine can enhance it, frame it, and, I hope, make for an indelible culinary memory.

At Daniel, the wine program offers selections covering a wide spectrum: Old and New Worlds, classic and modern, rare vintages and great value. We never stop seeking what is unique. We offer serious depth when it comes to the classic wine regions of Burgundy and the Rhône, my native terroir, and, of course, choice vintages from Bordeaux's leading estates.

Our wine cellar includes more than 25,000 bottles and more than 2,500 individual selections. We are delighted to offer the largest selection of Château d'Yquems in New York City, with more than 50 individual bottlings. In addition, 24 wines from around the world are available to our guests by the glass every day and for a wine pairing tasting menu.

Our sommeliers regularly meet with our waitstaff for training and tasting sessions as well as seminars with winemakers. We have four sommeliers at our guests' disposal, led by our head sommelier, Raj Vaidya, whose enthusiasm and great knowledge of fine wine is a perfect match for our cuisine. He works under the tutelage of wine director Daniel Johnnes, aka DJ, a friend and colleague since 1985 whose fame in the wine world is legendary and who represents the quintessential Burgundian born in America.

When guests send a glass of their selections for us to taste in the kitchen, I know that we've understood each other. We speak the same language.

Parker and Boulud

HOW WOULD YOU LIKE TO HAVE LUNCH WITH BOB PARKER? THE preeminent American wine critic whose palate and rating system revolutionized the international wine industry? At Daniel, we have been hosting such lunches for the last twenty years!

Picture this: Several times a year (after auctioning our collaboration for charity purposes) my friend Bob would arrive carrying loads of wine, sometimes as many as sixty bottles. Whether for a benefit for Citymeals-on-Wheels or the Navy Seals, Bob and I would concoct the perfect menu to match the phenomenal wines, often Rhônes, dug out of his legendary cellar for the occasion.

With the list of wines I had gotten in advance, and based on the season and the market, I would let my imagination run wild and plunge into recipes of the past, from tête de veau en tortue, to whole stuffed turbot or canard à la presse, and roasted venison saddle, each course on a parade of silver platters—the kind of feast reminiscent of the table of Louis the XIV!

These memorable meals would turn into full-fledged events, starting at noon and lasting until nearly dinnertime. Twelve to sixteen passionate gourmands would savor classic, often iconic preparations steeped in the French tradition, as the "Million-Dollar-Nose," as Bob is often called, would introduce each wine:

a unique, live Parker masterclass. We also cooked the more rustic dishes that pair best with complex and nuanced wines, such as a smoked suckling pig's head braised with cabbage and root vegetables or Alain Chapel's gâteau de foies blonds with crayfish, cockscombs, and morels.

Our skilled maître d', Bernard Vrod, officiated as the master of carving; portioning, filleting, and even scooping out the steamy broth of a poulet en vessie.

We would often start with chilled shellfish to underscore the best white Burgundy—a 1995 Coche Dury Meursault Les Rougeot, perhaps—then evolve toward hot appetizers such as mussels and bay scallops vol-au-vent for Hermitage blanc from Jean-Louis Chave, or lobster civet paired with a 1990 Châteauneuf-du-Pape cuvée spéciale from Henri Bonneau. I remember a menu based entirely around black truffles with a lot of red wine—French, American pinots, and syrah, finished with the greatest cabernets of Bordeaux and California. What a wine education for me and my sommeliers!

Throughout the years, each of these special events took on a unique dimension. At a recent horizontal tasting of twenty-six of the best Bordeaux château wines from the 1982 vintage, fifty people drank 125 bottles, and five hours later no one was drunk on wine. But we got drunk on life, on the incredibly unique atmosphere, on the feeling that this was a historic moment we would all remember for the rest of our lives. Bob Parker: great lover of wine, food, and terroir—a true wine advocate!

MEAT

CAILLE AUX RAISINS
CHANTERELLES, SAUTERNES JUS

SERVES 4

CAILLE AUX RAISINS, a classic French combination, has been served for centuries, maybe because during the grape harvest, plump quails often gorge on the sweet globes. There are many ways to present this dish, originally from Gascony, from simply roasting the birds on the bone, to stuffing them, to flambéeing them in Cognac. For special occasions in the late summer, I have often stuffed quail with figs and spices. Here, we mold a succulent mixture of mushrooms, quail, liver, heart, leg meat, bacon, and chicken livers into a farce under the breasts and then serve the birds with confit grapes.

CAILLE AUX RAISINS
CHANTERELLES, SAUTERNES JUS

Grape Confit

½ pound green seedless
grapes, peeled

1 cup sugar

Pearl Onion Confit

1 cup duck fat

1 bay leaf

5 juniper berries

1 clove garlic, peeled and crushed

8 white pearl onions

Salt and freshly ground white pepper

Roasted Chanterelles

¾ pound chanterelle mushrooms

2 tablespoons duck fat

1 tablespoon butter

1 tablespoon brunoised shallot

1 clove garlic, peeled and smashed

Salt and freshly ground white pepper

Stuffed Quail Breast

1 tablespoon olive oil

2 ounces onion, cut into ⅛-inch dice

4 bone-in whole quail

2 ounces bacon, cut into ⅛-inch dice

2 ounces chicken liver, cut into ⅛-inch dice

2 ounces chanterelles, chopped,
reserved from above

1 tablespoon Cognac

1 tablespoon Sauternes wine

*Seasoning mix per pound of quail
and stuffing:*

1¼ teaspoons (6 grams) salt, plus
more for the breasts

¼ teaspoon (1 gram) freshly ground white
pepper, plus more for the breasts

Sauternes Quail Jus

Bones from 4 quail, reserved from above

2 tablespoons duck fat

3 shallots, sliced

2 sprigs thyme

½ cup Sauternes wine

2 cups Chicken Stock (page 368)

Duxelle-Filled Potatoes

2 large Yukon gold potatoes, peeled

Salt

1 tablespoon butter

2 tablespoons milk

2 tablespoons heavy cream

1 ounce chanterelle duxelle,
reserved from above

Freshly ground white pepper

3 tablespoons duck fat

1 clove garlic, peeled

2 sprigs thyme

To Finish

2 tablespoons duck fat

2 tablespoons butter

1 clove garlic, peeled and smashed

2 sprigs thyme

½ tablespoon chopped parsley

½ cup purslane sprigs

Crispy Shallot Rings (page 372)

For the Grape Confit

Preheat the oven to 190°F. Thinly slice 10 of the grapes and reserve, chilled, for garnish. In a small saucepan, combine the sugar and 3 cups water and bring to a simmer. Place the grapes in a small baking dish, pour in the syrup, and bake uncovered for 3 hours, stirring every 30 minutes; the liquid will reduce slightly. Reserve at room temperature.

For the Pearl Onion Confit

In a small saucepan, heat the duck fat to 185°F. Add the bay leaf, juniper berries, and garlic. Season the onions with salt and pepper, submerge in the fat, and cook for 1 hour, or until tender. Strain and store, chilled.

For the Roasted Chanterelles

Scrape away any tough or woody parts of the mushroom stems. Wash the chanterelles several times in tepid water and pat dry.

Heat the duck fat and butter in a large sauté pan over medium heat. Add the shallot and garlic and cook, stirring, until translucent, about 2 minutes. Add the mushrooms, season with salt and pepper, and sauté for 10 minutes, or until any liquid has evaporated. Weigh 3 ounces of the mushrooms, transfer to a cutting board, and finely chop; set aside for the stuffing. Reserve the remaining mushrooms, chilled.

For the Stuffed Quail Breast

Fold 8 squares of aluminum foil into 7-inch-long x ¾-inch-wide strips.

Heat the olive oil in a small sauté pan over low heat and add the onion. Cook, stirring, until translucent. Extract the quail hearts and livers if they still remain in the cavities; chop them into ⅛-inch dice and transfer to a medium bowl with the onion. Cut off the wing tips and reserve for the jus. Carve off the breasts, leaving the wings attached, and set aside. Carve the legs from the quails and debone them; reserve the bones for the jus. Remove the skin from the legs, cut the meat into ⅛-inch dice, and add to the bowl with the heart and liver along with the bacon, chicken liver, two-thirds of the reserved chopped chanterelles, the Cognac, and the wine. Weigh the stuffing and scale the seasoning needed according to the ratio

listed in the ingredients. Sprinkle the quail breasts on both sides with salt and pepper.

Lay the breasts skin side down on a cutting board, evenly divide the farce onto the breasts, and pack it down firmly. Wrap aluminum foil strips around their edges, folding the ends tightly to form the breasts into taut eye-shaped portions. Reserve, chilled.

For the Sauternes Quail Jus

Chop the quail bones into 1-inch pieces, rinse, and pat dry. Heat the duck fat in a large saucepan over high heat. Add the bones in a single layer and sear on all sides until browned, about 10 minutes total. Reduce the heat to medium and add the shallots and thyme. Cook, stirring, until the shallots are caramelized, about 3 minutes. Add the Sauternes and simmer, stirring, until almost dry. Add the chicken stock and reduce by half. Strain through a fine-meshed sieve into a small saucepan and simmer until the sauce coats the back of a spoon; keep warm.

For the Duxelle-Filled Potatoes

Cut the potatoes into ¾-inch slices and punch out at least 8 discs with a ¾-inch ring cutter. With a Parisienne scoop, carve out cavities to form cups. Transfer the potato trim to a small

saucepan and cover with salted water. Simmer until tender, strain, and return to medium heat, stirring until dry. Add the butter, milk, cream, and the remaining chopped chanterelles and mash with a fork. Season with salt and pepper.

In a medium sauté pan over medium heat, melt the duck fat and add the garlic and thyme. Season the potato cups with salt and pepper and add them to the pan. Brown on all sides, about 8 minutes total, until cooked through. Strain onto a paper towel–lined tray and season again with salt and pepper.

Stuff each potato cup with a mound of the mushroom-potato mixture. Transfer to a baking sheet and set aside.

To Finish

Preheat the oven to 325°F.

Heat the duck fat in a large sauté pan over medium-high heat. Add the aluminum foil–wrapped quail breasts skin side down (you may need to do this in batches) and sear undisturbed for 2 minutes.

Add 1 tablespoon of the butter, the garlic, and thyme; once the butter foams, reduce the heat to medium and baste the butter over the stuffing for 3 minutes. Remove the pan from the heat and carefully flip the quail breasts.

Allow them to rest for 3 minutes in the warm pan, then transfer to a paper towel–lined plate. Strain the fat from the pan. Remove the foil from the breasts, return them to the pan, and spoon jus over the breasts to glaze; keep warm.

Spoon jus on top of the stuffed potatoes and bake for 5 minutes, or until heated through.

Melt the remaining 1 tablespoon butter in a medium sauté pan over medium heat. Add the reserved roasted chanterelles and pearl onion confit and toss to heat through. Adjust the seasoning with salt and pepper and add the parsley.

Strain the confit grapes and stir them into the remaining jus to heat through. For each serving, arrange 2 onions and 2 stuffed potatoes in the center of a warm dinner plate. Top the onions with purslane leaves and crispy shallots. Arrange 2 quail breasts on opposite sides of the plate. Spoon the mushrooms next to the breasts and garnish with some sliced grapes and purslane leaves.

SQUAB VADOUVAN PASTILLA
YOUNG RADISHES, AVOCADO CHUTNEY

SERVES 4

DANIEL IS a French restaurant, but our flavor palette knows no geographic boundaries. This started as a summer dish, a roasted bird infused with vadouvan, set on a warm and cold salad. Vadouvan is a fragrant, mild, sweet, and smoky curry blend with fenugreek, fried onions, shallots, garlic, and cardamom.

I love the peppery and crunchy qualities of the French breakfast and red radishes—some left raw, some cooked— and the cooling taste of the avocado next to the warm squab. To increase its tenderness, the breast is marinated overnight in yogurt, crème fraîche, and vadouvan, then broiled. The leg is stuffed with ground breast meat, liver, heart, and a bit of foie gras, then wrapped with brik dough to create our version of a crispy pastilla.

SQUAB VADOUVAN PASTILLA
YOUNG RADISHES, AVOCADO CHUTNEY

Vadouvan-Marinated Squab Breasts

2 squabs (about 7 ounces each),
with heart and livers

¼ cup thick lamb's or goat's milk yogurt

2 tablespoons heavy cream

1½ teaspoons vadouvan spice (we
recommend La Boîte à Epice)

2 tablespoons crème fraîche

Salt and freshly ground white pepper

Squab Leg Pastilla

2 ounces fresh grade A foie gras,
cut into small dice

1 teaspoon vadouvan spice

½ teaspoon salt

⅛ teaspoon freshly ground white pepper

4 sheets brik dough (feuille de brique)

1 egg, beaten

Vadouvan Jus

1 tablespoon olive oil

Bones from 2 squabs, reserved
from above

1 tablespoon vadouvan spice

1 cup Chicken Stock (page 368)

Avocado Chutney

1 ripe avocado, pitted and peeled

1 tablespoon lemon juice

1 tablespoon seeded and diced jalapeño
pepper

½ teaspoon vadouvan spice

1 splash of Tabasco sauce

1 pinch of piment d'Espelette

½ teaspoon salt

Freshly ground white pepper to taste

Glazed Radishes

14 large red radishes

4 small breakfast radishes with stems

¼ cup Chicken Stock (page 368)

1 tablespoon butter

Salt and freshly ground white pepper

To Finish

3 tablespoons olive oil

Vadouvan spice

8 small nasturtium leaves

For the Vadouvan-Marinated Squab Breasts

Extract the hearts and livers from the squab cavities. Carve the breasts and legs from the squabs. Pull the tenderloins from the breasts and reserve, chilled, with the hearts, livers, and legs for the pastilla. Chop the wings and bones into 1-inch pieces, rinse with cold water, pat dry, and reserve, chilled, for the jus.

In a small saucepan, combine the yogurt, cream, and vadouvan spice and bring to a simmer. Remove from the heat, cover, and infuse for 5 minutes. Pour through a fine-meshed sieve and chill. Stir in the crème fraîche and season with salt and pepper. Transfer half of the sauce to a resealable bag and add the squab breasts, turning them to coat. Marinate, refrigerated, overnight. Reserve the remaining sauce for finishing, chilled.

For the Squab Leg Pastilla

Carve the thigh bones from the legs, being sure not to puncture the skin; reserve the bones for the jus. Leave the remaining bones and feet attached.

Finely chop the tenderloins, hearts, and livers and transfer them to a medium bowl. Add the foie gras, vadouvan, salt, and pepper and mix well.

Cut the brik dough into 4 isosceles triangles with a 4-inch-wide base and a 3-inch height. Keep the sheets covered with plastic wrap while working.

Assemble the pastillas one at a time by laying a dough triangle on a flat surface with the middle point facing down, then lightly brush it with the egg. Place a leg skin side down in the middle of the triangle with the foot pointed up so that the top edge of the dough is aligned where the joint would be. With your fingertips, press approximately 2 tablespoons of stuffing onto the thigh. Wrap one top corner of dough down over the thigh. Fold the opposite top corner down over the top and press to adhere. Fold the bottom tip of dough up and press to seal into a packet. Repeat the process to make 4 pastillas.

For the Vadouvan Jus

Heat the olive oil in a medium saucepan over high heat. Add the squab bones and sear on all sides, about 5 minutes total. Add the vadouvan spice and cook, stirring, for 1 minute, or until very fragrant. Add the chicken stock and simmer until reduced; the thickness should be enough to coat the back of a spoon. Strain through a fine-meshed sieve and keep warm.

For the Avocado Chutney

Place all the ingredients in a small bowl. Mash with a fork until well combined but small chunks of avocado still remain. Season with salt and pepper. Place a sheet of plastic wrap on the surface of the avocado chutney and store, chilled.

For the Glazed Radishes

Trim the radishes, leaving a bit of the stem, and rinse. With a mandoline, shave 2 of the red radishes from stem to tip into a small bowl of ice water. Trim the breakfast radishes, leaving a small leaf sprig attached, then quarter them lengthwise halfway up from the tips; submerge them in the ice water and reserve for the garnish.

Cut the remaining red radishes in half. Use a ¾-inch ring cutter to cut 4 cylinders from 8 of the halves. Transfer the halves and cylinders to a medium sauté pan with the chicken stock and butter and bring to a simmer. Season with salt and pepper and cook over medium heat until the chicken stock and butter have reduced to a glaze and the radishes are tender, about 10 minutes. Keep warm.

To Finish

Preheat the broiler.

Heat the olive oil in a large sauté pan over medium heat and sear the pastilla legs for 4 minutes on each side, until crispy and golden brown.

Remove the squab breasts from the marinade and place on a baking sheet lined with aluminum foil. Broil the breasts for 6 to 8 minutes, flipping halfway through, until medium rare (internal temperature of 135°F). Spoon the reserved yogurt sauce onto the breasts in the last 2 minutes of cooking.

For each portion, set a breast on the bottom of a warm plate and set a large spoonful of avocado chutney alongside it. Set 1 leg pastilla against the breast, with the foot sticking up. Arrange 2 glazed radish halves, 2 radish cylinders, and 1 breakfast radish around the squab. Spoon a few dots of jus around the squab and sprinkle a pinch of vadouvan spice onto the plate. Garnish with 2 nasturtium leaves and a few radish shavings.

PEPPERED MAGRET OF DUCK
RHUBARB VARIATIONS

SERVES 4

WE MAKE THIS dish with Liberty Duck, hailing from the exceptional Sonoma County Poultry in California, which was founded by Jim Reichardt, a fourth-generation duck farmer. Seared on the skin and finished in the broiler, the meat is the perfect foil for a medley of rhubarb—confit, pureed, and pickled. Szechuan pepper brings a sophisticated, aromatic heat rather than straight fire. Around the plate, candied pistachios, pistachio oil, and pistachio powder add crunch and nuttiness.

"In French cuisine, marriage of duck and fruit is our own sweet and sour affair."

PEPPERED MAGRET OF DUCK
RHUBARB VARIATIONS

Rhubarb: Poached, Confit, and Coulis

6 large stalks (about 1½ pounds) red rhubarb, about 16 inches long, halved crosswise

2 cups port wine

¾ cup grenadine syrup

1 cup sugar

Daikon Radish and Baby Turnips

Salt

One 2-inch-thick slice of daikon radish

4 baby turnips, peeled and with their stems, halved

Pickled Rhubarb and Daikon Radish (makes extra)

1 small stalk rhubarb

1 cup Pickling Liquid (page 377)

1 star anise

½ teaspoon coriander seeds

Rhubarb Glaze

3 teaspoons rhubarb syrup, reserved from above

1½ teaspoons sugar

1 teaspoon sherry vinegar

¼ teaspoon Szechuan peppercorns

Pinch of salt

6 tablespoons Chicken Jus (page 369)

To Finish

Candied Sicilian Pistachios (see Caramelized Nuts, page 379)

4 (8-ounce) duck breasts

1 teaspoon duck fat

Salt and freshly ground white pepper

1 tablespoon ground Szechuan peppercorn

2 tablespoons butter

Fleur de sel

¼ cup micro shiso

3 tablespoons pistachio oil

For the Rhubarb: Poached, Confit, and Coulis

Poached: Preheat the oven to 200°F. Peel the rhubarb and place the peels in a saucepan with the port. Simmer to reduce by half and add the grenadine, sugar, and 3 cups of water. Return to a simmer. Arrange the rhubarb in a single layer in a shallow baking pan. Strain the liquid over the top. Bake uncovered for 2 hours, basting the rhubarb with the liquid every 15 minutes, until the rhubarb is tender. Scoop half of the rhubarb from the liquid onto a cutting board and trim into at least eight 1-inch squares; reserve the trim. Transfer the squares in a single layer into half of a shallow baking pan; reserve, chilled.

Confit: Return the baking pan with the remaining rhubarb stalks and liquid to the oven and bake, turning the rhubarb every 15 minutes, for 2 hours, or until the liquid is syrupy and the rhubarb is dark red and very tender. Remove from the oven and cool at room temperature. Scoop the confit rhubarb onto a cutting board and use a 2-inch ring cutter to cut and shape 4 discs; reserve the trim. Transfer the discs in a single layer to the other half of the baking dish with the poached rhubarb squares, cover, and reserve, chilled. Strain the liquid and reserve, chilled.

Coulis: Transfer all of the rhubarb trim to a blender and puree, adding just enough of the cooking liquid to make a thick, smooth puree; reserve the remaining cooking liquid. Pass the puree through a fine-meshed sieve and transfer to a squeeze bottle with a small tip; set aside.

For the Daikon Radish and Baby Turnips

Bring a small pot of salted water to a boil and place a bowl of ice water on the side. Cut the daikon radish into desired shapes (the daikon in the photo was cut into tubes with ¾-inch- and ½-inch-diameter cannoli forms; the insides were kept for pickling). Boil half of the daikon radish (or the tubes) and turnips in separate batches until tender. Chill in the ice water. Pat dry and set aside.

For the Pickled Rhubarb and Daikon Radish

Use a mandoline to cut the rhubarb into thin ribbons and place in a heatproof container with the remaining half of the daikon radish (the pickled daikon in the photo is the center of the tubes). In a small saucepan, bring the pickling liquid to a simmer with the star anise and coriander seeds. Pour over the rhubarb and reserve, chilled.

For the Rhubarb Glaze

In a small saucepan, combine the rhubarb syrup, sugar, vinegar, peppercorns, and salt. Bring to a simmer and add the chicken jus. Reduce to a thick glaze and remove from the heat.

To Finish

Preheat the broiler. Use a blender or spice grinder to pulse half the candied pistachios to a fine powder. Score the duck breast skin into a crosshatch pattern. Allow the duck breast to rest at room temperature for 15 minutes.

In a medium sauté pan, heat the duck fat over medium heat. Season the breasts with salt, white pepper, and Szechuan pepper, and add skin side down to the pan. Slowly sear the skin while basting the breasts with the fat from the pan, about 10 minutes. Drain all but 1 tablespoon of the fat and continue cooking until the skin crisps, about 2 minutes. Flip the breasts and sear for 1 more minute, or until the internal temperature reaches 127°F. Transfer the breasts to a foil-lined baking sheet, brush with an even coating of the rhubarb glaze, and broil skin side up for 1 minute, or until the glaze is caramelized and shiny. If desired, trim the edges of the breasts into straight lines.

Melt the butter in a small sauté pan and add the boiled daikon radish and turnips. Toss to heat through and season with salt and pepper. Cover the baking dish of poached and confit rhubarb with aluminum foil and transfer to the lower rack of the oven for 5 minutes, or until heated through.

For each serving, set a disc of confit rhubarb in the center of a warm dinner plate and top with a duck breast, a few candied pistachios, and a sprinkling of fleur de sel. Wrap the ribbons of pickled rhubarb around a piece of pickled daikon and place in one corner of the plate. Pipe a dot of rhubarb coulis in an opposite corner, top with a piece of glazed daikon (if you made tubes, fill the center with rhubarb coulis), and sprinkle with some of the ground pistachios. Place 2 pieces of poached rhubarb on the other 2 opposite corners of the plate and top each with 1 or 2 pieces of glazed turnip; garnish each with a leaf of micro shiso. Drizzle a couple of dots of pistachio oil on the plate.

TRUFFLED POULARDE
CHESTNUT-STUFFED CABBAGE, SALSIFY

SERVES 4

THROUGHOUT THE YEAR, our menu offers chicken, guinea hen, squab, pheasant, or other fowl recipes, ranging from a simply roasted bird stuffed with loads of garlic to spicy and refreshing summer preparations. During black truffle season, celebratory winter dishes like this roasted poularde really stand out. A poularde is a fat, meaty young hen with very tender meat. Since they aren't widely available in the United States, a large chicken is a perfect substitution.

Truffle is the highlight of the dish, and to give it even more strength, we have paired chestnut and cabbage, earthy elements that bring sweetness, rusticity, and refinement at the same time. The nutty flavor of the crispy skin mixes with the breast coated with truffle, elevating the simple roast to an haute dish.

Truffled Poularde Breasts and Thighs

1 (5-pound) poularde or chicken

2 medium black winter truffles

Olive oil as needed

Salt and freshly ground white pepper

Liver and heart from the poularde (or chicken), finely chopped

1 splash of Cognac

Chestnut-Stuffed Cabbage and Stuffed Garganelli Pasta

4 baby carrots with stems, peeled

1 stalk celery with leaves

Salt

1 small (1-pound) savoy cabbage

6 ounces garganelli pasta

Truffle Coulis (page 371)

2 tablespoons butter

1 medium onion, finely chopped

4 fresh or vacuum-sealed peeled chestnuts, finely chopped

Glazed Salsify

4 stalks salsify

¾ cup Chicken Stock (page 368)

2 tablespoons butter

Salt and freshly ground white pepper

To Finish

Salt and freshly ground white pepper

¼ cup Chicken Stock (page 368)

5 tablespoons butter

Sauce Périgueux (page 369)

2 tablespoons olive oil

4 Salsify Spirals (page 373)

For the Truffled Poularde Breasts and Thighs

Remove and reserve the liver and heart from the cavity of the poularde. Carve the breasts and legs from the poularde. Separate the thighs and drumsticks and debone without cutting through the meat and skin. If desired, chop the leg bones and remaining carcass and wings into 1-inch pieces, rinse with cold water, and pat dry; reserve, chilled, for chicken stock (see page 368).

Cut the truffles with a ring cutter slightly smaller than their circumference to make cylinders. Using a truffle slicer or mandoline, cut 24 very thin discs from the cylinders, transfer 8 to a plate, and wrap very tightly with plastic wrap; reserve, chilled. Lightly season the remaining 16 slices with olive oil, salt, and pepper and divide them under the skin of the breasts, arranging them in a single layer. Finely chop all the remaining truffle and trim, transfer to a covered container, and reserve, chilled (for chestnut-stuffed cabbage, stuffed thigh, truffle coulis [page 371], glazed salsify, sauce périgueux [page 369], and finishing the poularde).

With an immersion circulator, preheat a water bath to 144°F. Season the breasts on all sides with salt and pepper. Wrap the breasts in plastic wrap to tighten their form, place in a sous-vide bag, and vacuum-seal. Submerge the breasts in the water and cook until the internal temperature reaches 140°F, about 65 minutes. Remove from the water bath and chill in ice water.

Increase the water temperature to 150°F. Remove the skin from the drumsticks and finely dice the meat; transfer to a bowl and combine with 1 tablespoon of the chopped black truffle, the liver, heart, Cognac, and salt and pepper. Lay the thighs skin side down on a square of plastic wrap, season with salt and pepper, and divide the meat mixture on top of them. Use plastic wrap to roll them into cylinders and tie off the ends. Place in a sous-vide bag and vacuum-seal. Submerge in the prepared water bath and cook for 3 hours. Remove from the water bath and chill in ice water.

Reserve the breasts and thighs overnight in the refrigerator.

For the Chestnut-Stuffed Cabbage and Stuffed Garganelli Pasta

Using a mandoline, cut 1 baby carrot lengthwise into thin slices. Pick the celery leaves and cut eight ¼-inch cubes from the stalk. Reserve the shaved carrot, celery leaves, and cubed celery, wrapped and chilled. Finely chop the remaining carrots and celery.

Bring a large pot of salted water to a boil and place a bowl of ice water on the side. Peel the 4 largest leaves from the exterior of the cabbage. Boil them for 2 minutes, or until tender, and chill in the ice water. Boil the pasta until tender and chill in the ice water. Drain and pat dry the cabbage leaves and pasta. Transfer the truffle coulis to a squeeze bottle or piping bag and fill the garganelli; reserve, covered and chilled.

Thinly slice the remaining cabbage. In a large sauté pan over medium-low heat, melt the butter and add the onion and carrot. Cook, stirring, until the onion is translucent. Add the sliced cabbage, chestnuts, and 1 tablespoon chopped black truffle. Cook, stirring, until the cabbage is tender, about 15 minutes. Season with salt and pepper.

Lay the boiled cabbage leaves on a flat surface and divide the mixture onto them. Roll the cabbage up, tucking in the sides to form long packets. Reserve, chilled.

For the Glazed Salsify

Peel the salsify, rinse with cold water, and cut on a bias into 2-inch lengths. In a small sauté pan over medium heat, bring the chicken stock and butter to a simmer. Add the salsify and season with salt and pepper. Cook, stirring occasionally, until the salsify is tender and the liquid reduces to a glaze, about 20 minutes. Add spoonfuls of water as necessary if the liquid reduces before the salsify is cooked. Stir in 1 teaspoon chopped truffle, check the seasoning, and keep warm.

To Finish

Season the cabbage roulades on all sides with salt and pepper and transfer to a medium sauté pan in a single layer. Add the chicken stock and 2½ tablespoons of the butter and bring to a simmer. Reduce the heat to low and cover. Simmer, basting occasionally, until warm, about 10 minutes. Add 1 tablespoon of the reserved chopped truffle and swirl to coat.

Place the sauce périgueux in a small saucepan over medium heat and bring to a simmer.

Unwrap the poularde breasts and thighs and pat dry. Heat the olive oil in a large sauté pan over high heat. Add the breasts and thighs and sear until golden brown on all sides, about 3 minutes total. Reduce the heat to medium, add 1½ tablespoons of the butter, and continue cooking, turning the chicken and basting with the butter on all sides, about another 4 minutes. Slice each breast and thigh in half crosswise and return to the pan. Toss in 1 tablespoon reserved chopped black truffle trim to coat. Adjust the seasoning with salt and pepper if needed.

In a separate sauté pan, melt the remaining tablespoon butter over medium heat and add the reserved celery cubes. Cook, stirring, until tender and add the pasta; toss to heat through. Season with salt and pepper and stir in 1 tablespoon reserved chopped truffle. If you have any remaining chopped truffle, use it to coat the sliced ends of the thighs.

For each serving, trim the ends from a cabbage roulade and set 2 truffle slices against them. Set on one side of a warm dinner plate and place a thigh half in the center and a breast half on the other side. Set 2 celery cubes on top of similar-size cubes of truffle in between the cabbage and the meat; top them with a celery leaf. Place a garganelli noodle and a glazed salsify baton on the plate and drizzle a few spoonfuls of sauce around. Top the thigh with a salsify spiral and place a carrot shaving on the cabbage.

ROASTED GUINEA HEN
MOREL AND GIBLET–CRUSTED WHITE ASPARAGUS, VIN JAUNE JUS

SERVES 4

AT THE FARM in Saint-Pierre de Chandieu, near Lyon, I literally grew up on guinea hen, and I remember that if we didn't clip their wings, at sunset they would climb into the trees for the night! It was a real frustration to keep them domesticated and away from the foxes! This wild bird's size is a cross between a pheasant and a chicken; it doesn't taste gamy but has a nuttier flavor than chicken. Cooked on the rotisserie, the skin crisps up, the perfect mirror for the tender leg meat wrapped in fried kataifi.

ROASTED GUINEA HEN
MOREL AND GIBLET–CRUSTED WHITE
ASPARAGUS, VIN JAUNE JUS

Sautéed Morels and Vin Jaune Jus

20 medium fresh morel mushrooms
(about 8 ounces)

2 tablespoons butter

1 medium shallot, minced

¾ teaspoon salt

1 cup vin jaune wine

¼ cup Chicken Stock (page 368)

1 cup Chicken Jus (page 369)

Freshly ground white pepper

**Morel and Giblet–Crusted
White Asparagus**

1 tablespoon butter

1 small shallot, minced

1 liver, gizzard, and heart from
the guinea hen, finely chopped

1 splash of vin jaune wine

Chopped morels, reserved from above

½ tablespoon Fine White Breadcrumbs
(page 373)

Salt and freshly ground white pepper

1½ teaspoons finely chopped parsley

1 tablespoon sugar

8 jumbo white asparagus (about 1 pound)

Guinea Hen

Canola oil for frying

2 guinea hens (about 2½ pounds
each), refrigerated uncovered for
1 day to dry their skin

Salt and freshly ground white pepper

2 bay leaves

4 sprigs thyme

2 heads garlic, halved

4 tablespoons butter, softened

1 herb bouquet (4 large sprigs each
rosemary, parsley, and thyme tied with
butcher's twine to make a brush)

4 ounces kataifi (shredded phyllo) dough

Fleur de sel

Sauce Vin Jaune

See Chicken Jus (page 369), and
substitute 2 cups vin jaune wine for
the white wine.

To Finish

1 tablespoon butter

Salt and freshly ground white pepper

12 Parsley Chips
(see Herb Chips, page 373)

For the Sautéed Morels and Vin Jaune Jus

To clean the morels, submerge them in a bowl
of cold water, leave for 2 minutes, strain from
the top, and repeat until the water that settles
at the bottom is clear. Strain and pat dry with
a towel. Melt the butter in a medium sauté pan
over medium heat and add the shallot. Cook,
stirring, until translucent, about 2 minutes.
Add the morels, sprinkle with the salt, and
cook, stirring occasionally, for 5 minutes. Add
the vin jaune and simmer with the morels for
10 minutes. Scoop out the morels and set
aside. Continue simmering until reduced to
about 2 tablespoons. Add the chicken stock
and simmer until the liquid has reduced by
half. Add the chicken jus and simmer until the
sauce coats the back of a spoon. Check the
seasoning and add salt and pepper if
necessary. Strain the sauce into a bowl set
over ice; stir until chilled and reserve. Set aside
12 morels for garnish and finely chop the rest
for the asparagus crust. Reserve, chilled.

*For the Morel and Giblet–Crusted
White Asparagus*

In a small sauté pan, lightly brown the butter
over medium-high heat. Add the shallot and
cook, stirring, for 1 minute. Add the liver,
gizzard, and heart and sauté for 1 minute.
Add the vin jaune and simmer until almost
dry. Reduce the heat to low and stir in the
chopped morels and breadcrumbs. Season
with salt and pepper and fold in the parsley.
Remove from the heat and scrape the mixture
onto a sheet of parchment paper. Top with
another sheet of parchment and spread into
a sheet about 8 inches long and a width that
is two-thirds the length of an asparagus stalk.
Refrigerate, keeping flat, until hardened.

Pour 1 gallon of water into a large pot,
season with salt, and add the sugar; bring
to a boil. Set a bowl of ice water on the side.
Prepare each asparagus by laying it flat on
a cutting board and lightly peeling from just
below the tips to the end, rolling it clockwise
as you work. Trim and discard the bottom
fibrous 1 inch. Use butcher's twine to secure
the stalks into a bunch. Boil for 9 minutes, or
until easily pierced with a cake tester. Chill in
the ice water, strain onto paper towels, and cut

away the twine. Cut three ½-inch-thick discs from the end of each asparagus and set aside for finishing. Transfer the asparagus stalks to a foil-lined baking dish and season them with salt and pepper. Cut the chilled sheet of crust widthwise into 8 rectangles, peel off the paper, and press each one onto the bottom two-thirds of each stalk. Reserve, chilled.

For the Guinea Hen

Preheat a rotisserie to high and preheat the oven to 200°F. (*Alternately, preheat the oven to 400°F.*) Fill one-third of a medium saucepan with canola oil and heat to 350°F.

Use a paring knife to remove the wishbones from the guinea hens. Season the inside and outside of the hens with salt and pepper and stuff them with the bay leaves, thyme, and garlic. If desired, truss the hens. Rub the butter on their skin to coat.

Mount the hens to the rotisserie spit according to the manufacturer's directions. (*If cooking in the oven, transfer to a roasting pan with a rack.*) Start by roasting on high until the skin is browned. Baste the skin often with the melted butter using the herb bouquet. Once browned, reduce the rotisserie heat to medium (or reduce the oven temperature to 300°F). Remove from the rotisserie or oven when the temperature of the center of the breasts reaches 125°F. Heat the oven to 200°F, whether using the rotisserie or the oven.

Transfer the birds to a cutting board and carve off the legs. While preparing the legs, transfer the breast cages to a roasting pan with a rack, cover with foil, and transfer to the oven until cooked through. Debone the legs and cut each into 2 equal-size squares, leaving the skin attached. Wrap each square in a layer of kataifi dough. Fry the squares until golden brown, about 1½ minutes. Strain onto a paper towel–lined tray and sprinkle with salt; keep warm.

Carve the breasts from the breast cage and, if desired, trim the sides into straight lines. Sprinkle with fleur de sel.

To Finish

Preheat the broiler. In a small saucepan over medium heat, bring the vin jaune jus to a simmer.

Broil the morel and giblet–crusted white asparagus until the crust is crispy and the asparagus is heated through.

Melt the butter in a medium sauté pan over medium heat. Transfer the reserved sautéed morels and sliced asparagus discs to the pan and toss to heat through. Adjust the seasoning with salt and pepper.

For each serving, set a hen breast on one side of a warm plate and a crusted white asparagus on the other side. Arrange 2 crispy leg pieces, alternating with roasted morels standing on top of white asparagus discs in the center. Spoon jus onto the plate and top the morels with parsley chips.

SCOTTISH GROUSE FARCIE
POACHED QUINCE, HUCKLEBERRY

SERVES 4

DO YOU KNOW that August 12 marks the start of grouse hunting season in Scotland? I grew up in the Lyon country-side and treasure vivid memories of going hunting with my father. But now, as an occasional hunter living in New York, I look forward to the arrival of the fragrant game bird, redolent of heather and wild plains. It's a date our team still gets excited about, a happy feast signaling the start of the rich game season.

Grouse has a rare taste, and purists often would accent its flavor by letting the birds hang for a week in their cold rooms. We favor a more subtle approach achieved by bathing the bird in a milk marinade infused with juniper, orange peel, and herbs. Foie gras, truffles, and a drop of Scotch whisky later mingle with the meat, resulting in a delicate but pungent tasting experience.

SCOTTISH GROUSE FARCIE
POACHED QUINCE, HUCKLEBERRY

Butchering the Grouse

2 cups milk

1 teaspoon juniper berries

1 teaspoon black peppercorns

1 bay leaf

2 thyme sprigs

Peel from 1 orange

3 grouse

Parsnip Chips

Canola oil for frying

1 large parsnip, peeled

Salt

Breast Stuffing and Assembly

1 tablespoon olive oil

1½ tablespoons minced shallot

1½ ounces pork fatback

¾ ounce pancetta

6 ounces grouse meat (breasts from the smallest bird and thigh meat from all 3)

¾ ounce fresh grade A foie gras

¾ ounce chicken liver

1 tablespoon chopped black truffle

1 tablespoon crème fraîche

1 tablespoon Scotch whisky

Salt

½ teaspoon coarsely ground juniper berries

Freshly ground white pepper

1 pinch of freshly grated nutmeg

1 cup flour

2 eggs, beaten with 1 tablespoon water

1 cup Fine White Breadcrumbs (page 373)

Grouse Jus

1 cup dry red wine

2 tablespoons duck fat

Reserved bones from the grouse

¼ cup small-diced button mushrooms

¼ cup small-diced onion

¼ cup small-diced shallot

2 tablespoons small-diced carrot

2 tablespoons small-diced celery

2 tablespoons Scotch whisky

2 quarts Chicken Stock (page 368)

2 teaspoons cracked peppercorns

1 tablespoon red wine vinegar

Salt and freshly ground white pepper

Huckleberry Coulis

1 cup fresh or frozen huckleberries

½ cup dry red wine

½ cup port

2 tablespoons butter

Poached Quince (makes extra)

2 quinces, peeled and halved

3 cups sugar

½ cup grenadine syrup

2 star anise

2 small cinnamon sticks

½ teaspoon Szechuan peppercorns

Foie Gras Béchamel

2 sheets gelatin

2 tablespoons butter

2 tablespoons flour

1 cup milk

3½ ounces Foie Gras Terrine (page 375)

1½ teaspoons sherry vinegar

Cayenne pepper

½ teaspoon salt

Freshly ground white pepper

Glazed Root Vegetables

12 (½-inch) cubes rutabaga

1 cup Chicken Stock (page 368)

3 tablespoons butter

8 (¼-inch-thick) ¾-inch discs celery root

8 (¼-inch-thick) ¾-inch squares parsnip

Salt and freshly ground white pepper

To Finish

3 tablespoons duck fat

2 tablespoons butter

2 sprigs thyme

2 cloves garlic, peeled and smashed

Fleur de sel

Cracked black peppercorns

8 Breadcrumb Cups (page 373)

8 curly mustard leaves

For Butchering the Grouse

Pour the milk into a small saucepan and add the juniper berries, black peppercorns, bay leaf, thyme, and orange peel. Bring to a simmer, cover, and remove from the heat. Rest for 30 minutes, then strain into a heat-proof container and chill.

Set the grouse breast side up on a cutting board. If still attached, remove the innards from the cavities and discard. Carve off the legs and debone the thighs, reserving the meat for the stuffing and the bones for the sauce, and discard the skin. Carve the breasts from the rib cages and discard their skin. Submerge the thigh meat and breasts in the milk, cover, and refrigerate overnight or up to 24 hours.

Chop all the bones into 1-inch pieces, rinse with cold water, dry, and reserve for the jus.

Remove the meat from the marinade, pat dry, and reserve, chilled.

For the Parsnip Chips

Preheat the oven to 190°F. Fill one-third of a medium saucepan with canola oil and heat to 300°F. With a mandoline, slice the parsnip lengthwise into at least four ½-inch-wide very thin ribbons. Fry until the ribbons are tender and the edges turn a light golden color but do not crisp. Strain onto a paper towel–lined tray and pat off excess oil. Transfer the parsnip ribbons in a single layer to a parchment paper–lined baking sheet and bake for 8 hours, or until crispy but not colored. Sprinkle with salt, cool, and reserve in an airtight container.

For the Breast Stuffing and Assembly
Heat the olive oil in a small sauté pan and add the shallot. Cook, stirring, until translucent, about 2 minutes, then transfer to a large mixing bowl. Trim the sides of 4 of the largest breasts to form straight-edged rectangles; reserve, chilled. Use the trim for stuffing.

Roughly chop the fatback and pancetta; combine, cover, and chill well. Dice the thigh meat, the remaining 2 breasts, the breast trim, foie gras, and chicken liver into ¼-inch pieces and transfer to the bowl with the shallot. Pass the chilled fatback and pancetta through a meat grinder fit with the coarse plate into the bowl of diced meats. With your hands, mix the meats and shallots with the truffle, crème fraîche, whisky, 1 teaspoon salt, ground juniper berries, ¼ teaspoon pepper, and nutmeg until well combined. Divide the mixture into 4 approximately 3-ounce portions.

Season the undersides of the trimmed breasts with salt and pepper and pack 1 portion of meat mixture onto each, using your hands to mold into a rectangular shape. Chill for at least 1 hour, then freeze for 30 minutes, just to firm before breading. Place the flour, eggs, and breadcrumbs into separate shallow bowls. Dredge the grouse on the farce and sides only (leaving the breast uncovered) in the flour, then the egg, and then coat them in the breadcrumbs. Reserve, chilled.

For the Grouse Jus
Pour the red wine into a small saucepan and simmer until reduced by two-thirds; set aside. Heat the duck fat in a large Dutch oven over high heat. Add the bones in a single layer and roast on all sides until browned, 6 to 8 minutes. Add the mushrooms, onion, shallot, carrot, and celery. Reduce the heat to medium-high and cook, stirring, until the vegetables are golden brown. Add the whisky and, with a wooden spoon, scrape the pan to loosen any browned bits from the bottom; reduce by half. Add the reduced wine, the chicken stock, and the peppercorns and simmer lightly for 1 hour, skimming as

needed. Strain the liquid through a fine-meshed sieve into a large saucepan. Continue simmering the sauce to reduce by three-quarters, about 30 minutes, until it coats the back of a spoon. Add the vinegar and season with salt and pepper. Reserve, chilled.

For the Huckleberry Coulis
In a small saucepan, combine all the ingredients and bring to a simmer over medium heat. Cook for 1 hour, or until the berries have broken down and the liquid reduces by one-third. Transfer the mixture to a blender and puree until smooth. Pass through a fine-meshed sieve and set aside, covered.

For the Poached Quince
In a large saucepan, combine all the ingredients with 4 cups of water, making sure the quince is submerged. Bring to a simmer. Cut a round of parchment paper the same diameter as the saucepan and rest on top of the liquid. Lightly simmer the quince for about 1 hour, stirring occasionally, until easily pierced with a cake tester. Remove from the heat and cool the quince in the liquid. Cut the quince into ¼-inch-thick slices and, with a 1½-inch-diameter ring cutter, cut at least 8 discs. Transfer to a shallow container, with enough poaching liquid to cover, and reserve, chilled.

For the Foie Gras Béchamel
Soak the gelatin sheets in ice water for 10 minutes; squeeze dry. In a small saucepan over medium-low heat, melt the butter. Add the flour and cook, whisking, for 5 minutes without browning. Gradually add the milk to make a smooth sauce and simmer, whisking, for 4 minutes. Cool the sauce to lukewarm, then transfer to a blender with the gelatin, foie gras terrine, and vinegar. Puree until smooth and season with the cayenne, salt, and pepper. Pass through a fine-meshed sieve and transfer to a piping bag. Keep warm.

For the Glazed Root Vegetables
In a large sauté pan, combine the rutabaga cubes with the stock and butter and simmer for 5 minutes. Add the celery root and parsnip

and continue simmering until the vegetables are tender and the liquid has reduced to a glaze (if the liquid reduces before the vegetables are tender, add spoonfuls of water). Season with salt and pepper and keep warm.

To Finish
Preheat the oven to 350°F. Allow the grouse to rest at room temperature for 15 minutes.

Transfer the grouse jus into a small saucepan and stir over medium heat until heated through. Transfer the quince discs to a small sauté pan over medium heat with a few spoonfuls of their poaching liquid; toss until heated through.

In a large nonstick sauté pan, heat the duck fat over medium-high heat. Add the grouse stuffing side down and cook until the breadcrumbs turn golden brown, about 3 minutes, while basting the breasts with the fat in the pan. Gently turn the grouse so they brown on each of the 4 remaining breaded sides, about 2 minutes each. Turn the grouse stuffing side down, add the butter, and once it begins to foam, reduce the heat to medium-low, add the thyme and garlic, and continue basting the fat over the breasts, cooking for 2 minutes. Transfer to the oven for 2 to 3 minutes, until the internal temperature reaches 125°F. Remove from the oven and rest for 3 minutes in a warm place before slicing in half lengthwise.

For each serving, set 2 grouse slices cut side up on opposite sides of a warm dinner plate, top each with a quince disc, and sprinkle with fleur de sel and cracked black pepper. Line 3 glazed rutabaga, 2 celery root, and 2 parsnip pieces in the center of the plate. Pipe 1 dot of foie gras béchamel next to each grouse slice and place a breadcrumb cup on top, with the opening facing up. Pipe béchamel into the cups to fill. Spoon 2 dots of huckleberry coulis onto the plate, drizzle a couple of spoonfuls of sauce around the grouse, and garnish with 2 curly mustard leaves and a parsnip chip.

SPRING RABBIT RISSOLÉ
MOUSSERONS, FAVA BEANS

SERVES 4

OFTEN PREPARED in civet with a mustard sauce, rabbit has been savored in Europe for centuries. As described by nineteenth-century gastronome and poet Fulbert-Dumonteil, "Rabbit is the delight of the farmer and the workman . . . it finds its place at all the feasts." Today rabbit may be the most sustainable, leanest meat on the butchers' counters. In this ode to spring, the saddle is stuffed with mint, minced rabbit leg meat, and pork; the rack is simply roasted and surrounded by mousseron mushrooms, fava beans, and asparagus.

SPRING RABBIT RISSOLÉ
MOUSSERONS, FAVA BEANS

Butchering the Rabbit

1 (about 2½-pound) rabbit,
with liver and kidneys

Mint-Stuffed Loins

2 teaspoons olive oil

3 tablespoons small-diced onion

1 teaspoon minced garlic

5½ ounces diced rabbit leg meat,
reserved from above

1 rabbit liver, diced, reserved
from above

2 rabbit kidneys, diced, reserved
from above

1 ounce pancetta, diced

2½ teaspoons riesling wine

1 splash of Cognac

½ ounce chopped Tomato Confit
(page 376)

½ teaspoon Mint Oil
(see Green Herb Oil, page 376)

Seasoning ratio per pound of meat:

1 teaspoon (6 grams) salt

½ teaspoon (2 grams) freshly ground white
pepper

8 large mint leaves

Fava Beans and Asparagus

Salt

½ bunch jumbo asparagus

½ bunch pencil asparagus

2 cups peeled fava beans

Mousseron Tempura

Canola oil for frying

½ cup mousseron mushrooms,
trimmed and washed

Tempura Batter (page 374)

Salt

Mint-Roasted Mousseron Mushrooms

1 tablespoon olive oil

1 cup mousseron mushrooms, trimmed and
washed

Salt and freshly ground white pepper

1 clove garlic, peeled and smashed

1 sprig thyme

1 tablespoon butter

2 mint leaves, chiffonade

To Finish

Rabbit Jus (page 370)

2 teaspoons wild mustard seeds,
soaked in water overnight

Salt and freshly ground white pepper

1 splash of sherry vinegar

2 tablespoons olive oil

3 tablespoons butter

1 sprig thyme

1 clove garlic, peeled

Fleur de sel

Mint Oil (see Green Herb Oil, page 376)

8 micro Greek mint leaves

For Butchering the Rabbit

On a large cutting board, lay the rabbit on its back, remove the kidneys and liver from the body cavity, and pull away and discard the fat surrounding them; dice and reserve for the stuffing. Trim and reserve the tenderloins from under the rack.

With a butcher's knife, trim away the shoulders (forelegs) by cutting flush up against the neck bone, then bend each foreleg forward to pop the bone from the joint. Carve through the joint toward the ribs to completely remove.

Remove the legs by carving inward to separate the thigh from the tailbone, pop the bone from the joint, and then carve through the joint toward the tailbone to completely remove. Debone the legs, reserve the bones, and dice the meat for the stuffing.

Separate the saddle from the ribs by chopping crosswise through the backbone halfway up the carcass where the ribs begin to protrude.

Carve the 2 loins (leaving the belly flaps intact) from the saddle's backbone.

With a large knife, split the racks by laying them belly side up and chopping down both sides of the backbone. Shorten the tips of the rib bones to the desired length. French the racks by cutting a line across the top of the rib bones ½ inch from where the loin is attached. Score along the back of each rib bone and use your fingers to push the meat down, then trim it away. If desired, wrap the rack bones in aluminum foil to prevent browning. Reserve the racks, chilled. Chop all the bones, forelegs, and rack trim into rough 1-inch pieces, rinse with cold water, pat dry, and reserve for the rabbit jus.

For the Mint-Stuffed Loins

Be sure that all the meat parts are well chilled. Heat the olive oil in a small sauté pan over medium-low heat and add the onion and garlic. Cook, stirring, until translucent, about 2 minutes, then transfer to a large bowl; chill. Add the diced meats, the wine, Cognac, tomato confit, and mint oil. Weigh the mixture and measure the seasoning according to the ratio listed in the ingredients. Pass the mixture through a meat grinder fit with the coarse plate. Mix until slightly pasty, cover with plastic, and keep chilled.

Lay the loins on a cutting board so that the belly flaps are spread out, facing inside up. Lightly pound the belly flaps with a flat meat tenderizer and lightly score them in a crosshatch pattern. Lightly sprinkle the loins, the belly flaps, and the tenderloins with salt and pepper.

Make a ¼-inch-deep cut down the center length of each loin. Stuff each cut with a single layer of 4 mint leaves and top with a tenderloin. Divide the ground meat onto the belly flaps and spread into flat layers. Roll the loins over the belly flaps, forming a log. Secure by tying with butcher's twine at ½-inch intervals; reserve, chilled.

For the Fava Beans and Asparagus

Bring a large pot of salted water to a boil and place a bowl of ice water on the side. Trim and discard about ½ inch of the fibrous stems from the jumbo and pencil asparagus. Using a mandoline, thinly shave 2 stalks of jumbo asparagus lengthwise to make at least 8 ribbons. Cut 2-inch tips on a bias from the remaining asparagus. Cut the stalks into small dice and set aside.

Boil the jumbo asparagus tips for 1 minute, or until tender; transfer to the ice water. Boil the fava beans and pencil asparagus for 30 seconds, or until tender, then transfer to the ice water. Strain and pat dry the vegetables; reserve, chilled.

For the Mousseron Tempura

Fill one-third of a medium saucepan with canola oil and heat to 350°F. Using a toothpick as an aid, dip the mushrooms into the tempura batter to coat. Slide into the oil and fry until golden brown (you will need to do this in several batches). Transfer to a paper towel–lined tray and sprinkle with salt. Keep warm.

For the Mint-Roasted Mousseron Mushrooms

Warm the olive oil over medium-high heat in a large sauté pan. Add the mushrooms and sauté for 1 minute. Lower the heat, season with salt and pepper, and add the garlic, thyme,

and butter. Continue to cook, stirring occasionally, for 4 more minutes. Discard the garlic and thyme and toss in the mint just before serving.

To Finish

Transfer the rabbit jus to a small saucepan and bring to a simmer. Stir in the mustard seeds and adjust the seasoning with salt, pepper, and the vinegar.

Season the racks on all sides with salt and pepper. Heat the olive oil over medium-high heat in a large sauté pan. Add the racks and sear on all sides until browned, about 6 minutes. Remove the racks and add the loins to the pan. Sear the loins over medium-high heat on all sides until browned, about 5 minutes total. Reduce the heat to medium, return the racks to the pan, and add 2 tablespoons of the butter, the thyme, and the garlic. Cook the meats while turning every minute and constantly spooning the butter from the pan to baste them. Remove the racks after 4 minutes and transfer to a platter; rest in a warm place. Continue cooking the loins for another 2 to 4 minutes, until their internal temperature reaches 140°F. Transfer the loins to the platter with the racks, cover loosely with foil, and rest for 10 minutes. Remove butcher's twine and cut each loin into 8 slices and each rack into 6 chops.

Heat the remaining 1 tablespoon butter in a medium sauté pan over medium heat. Add the diced asparagus stalks and sauté for 1 minute. Add the fava beans and asparagus tips and toss to heat through. Season with salt and pepper.

For each serving, place a spoonful of diced asparagus and fava beans on one side of a warm dinner plate. Fan 4 loin slices on top and garnish them with 2 asparagus ribbons and 2 mousseron tempura pieces. Fan 3 chops of rack on the other side of the plate and sprinkle with fleur de sel. Arrange a few asparagus tips and a spoonful of roasted mousseron around the meats, drizzle jus in the center, and pipe a line of mint oil on the plate. Garnish the meat with 2 micro mint leaves.

ESCALOPE VIENNOISE
VEAL QUENELLES, GREEN ASPARAGUS

SERVES 4

WHAT IS CALLED escalope viennoise in France is every French child's favorite. Breaded veal slices originated in Austria as Wiener schnitzel but made it into the French repertoire more than a century ago. We offer this dish in honor of both Marcus Draxler, our legendary past maître d', and our marvelous photographer Thomas Schauer, who grew up together in the small village of Wilden in Austria.

To lighten things up, I prefer to bread just one side of the meat, and with the veal left from cutting a perfect disc, we make light mousse dumplings, called quenelles. Crispy seared sweetbreads and a sprinkling of hard-boiled eggs complete this classic dish.

ESCALOPE VIENNOISE
VEAL QUENELLES, GREEN ASPARAGUS

Sweetbreads

10 ounces veal sweetbreads, submerged in ice water for 24 hours

Crispy Sage

Canola oil for frying

12 fresh sage leaves

Veal Escalopes

4 (6-ounce) veal loin slices, trimmed of sinew and fat

Salt and freshly ground white pepper

1 cup flour

1 egg, beaten with 1 tablespoon water

1 cup Fine White Breadcrumbs (page 373)

2 tablespoons sage chiffonade

Veal Mousse Quenelles

5 ounces veal trim, reserved from above

½ teaspoon salt

Freshly ground white pepper

1 pinch of grated nutmeg

1 egg white

5 tablespoons heavy cream

Asparagus

Salt

12 jumbo green asparagus

Brown Butter Jus

2 tablespoons butter

1 teaspoon lilliput capers

1 splash of sherry vinegar

1 cup Veal Jus
(see Basic Meat Jus, page 370)

Salt and freshly ground white pepper

Glazed Morels

12 large morel mushrooms, trimmed

2 tablespoons butter

1 medium shallot, minced

Salt

3 tablespoons vermouth

¼ cup Chicken Stock (page 368)

2 tablespoons Veal Jus
(see Basic Meat Jus, page 370)

Freshly ground white pepper

To Finish

1 quart Chicken Stock (page 368)

Salt and freshly ground white pepper

6 tablespoons olive oil

6 tablespoons butter

2 sprigs thyme

1 clove garlic, peeled and smashed

½ bunch parsley, leaves picked

2 hard-boiled eggs, peeled and passed through a drum sieve

2 tablespoons lilliput capers

1 lemon, cut into supremes and diced

For the Sweetbreads

Strain the sweetbreads, transfer to a large saucepan, and cover with cold water. Simmer for 5 minutes, skimming any foam that rises to the surface. Remove from the heat and rest in the hot water for 5 minutes. Remove the sweetbreads from the water, pat dry, and transfer to a cutting board. Use a paring knife to trim away the fat and outer membranes. Place the sweetbreads in a shallow baking dish lined with paper towels, top with more paper towels, and place another baking dish on top. Fill the second baking dish with heavy objects (such as canned goods) to gently press on the sweetbreads. Refrigerate overnight. Cut the sweetbreads into 12 similarly sized morsels and reserve, chilled.

For the Crispy Sage

Fill one-third of a medium saucepan with canola oil and heat to 300°F. Fry the sage leaves, keeping them submerged for 1 minute, or until the bubbles subside. Strain onto a paper towel–lined plate and cool at room temperature. Store in an airtight container.

For the Veal Escalopes

Lay the veal slices on a cutting board in a single layer and cover with plastic wrap. With a flat meat mallet, pound the veal to reach ⅛-inch thickness and trim into a circle with a paring knife by tracing a 6-inch-diameter template. Reserve the trim for the mousse. Reserve the meat, chilled.

Up to 1 hour before serving, season the escalopes on both sides with salt and pepper. Place the flour, egg, and breadcrumbs mixed with the sage on separate shallow plates. Dredge one side of the veal escalope with the flour, pat off excess, dip into the egg, then coat with breadcrumbs. Reserve, chilled.

For the Veal Mousse Quenelles

Chill the bowl and blade of a food processor and make sure the meat trimmings, cream, and egg white are cold. Pulse the meat in the food processor with the salt, pepper, and nutmeg until finely chopped. Add the egg white and continue pulsing until pasty. Scrape the sides of the bowl with a rubber spatula. With the machine running, stream in the

cream to form a smooth mousse. Pass the mousse through a fine-meshed drum sieve and store, chilled.

For the Asparagus

Bring a large pot of salted water to a boil and set a bowl of ice water on the side. Cut the tips of the asparagus on a diagonal into 1½-inch lengths. With a mandoline, thinly slice 2 of the tips lengthwise into a small container of ice water and reserve for the garnish. Trim and discard the fibrous ½ inch from the base and slice the rest into ⅛-inch-thick discs. Boil the discs for 30 seconds, or until tender, and chill in the ice water. Boil the tips for 1 minute, or until tender, and chill in the ice water. Strain and pat dry the asparagus and reserve, chilled.

For the Brown Butter Jus

In a small saucepan over medium heat, brown the butter with the capers. Add the vinegar and veal jus and bring to a simmer. Adjust the seasoning with salt and pepper and keep warm.

For the Glazed Morels

To clean the morels, submerge them in a bowl of cold water, leave for 2 minutes, strain from the top, and repeat until the water that settles at the bottom is clear. Strain and pat dry with a towel. Melt the butter in a medium sauté pan over medium heat and add the shallot. Cook, stirring, until translucent, about 2 minutes. Add the morels, sprinkle with salt, and cook, stirring occasionally, for 5 minutes. Add the vermouth and reduce until almost dry. Add the chicken stock and simmer until the morels are cooked and the liquid has reduced to a glaze, about 12 minutes. Add the veal jus and toss. Check the seasoning for salt and pepper and keep warm.

To Finish

Bring the chicken stock to a simmer, season with salt and pepper, and remove from the heat. Using a pair of matching spoons, scoop a spoonful of veal mousse and scrape the insides of the spoons together in a rolling motion to compact the mousse into a football-shaped quenelle. Gently drop the quenelle into the stock and repeat to make at least 8 quenelles. Adjust the stock to just below a simmer and poach the quenelles for 3 to 4 minutes, gently stirring and basting them with the stock, until they are firm and cooked through. Turn off the heat and cover; keep warm.

Season the sweetbreads with salt and pepper. Heat 2 tablespoons of the olive oil in a sauté pan over medium-high heat. Sear the sweetbreads on all sides until light golden brown, then add 2 tablespoons of the butter, the thyme, and the garlic and baste, turning occasionally, for 4 minutes, or until the sweetbreads are firm to the touch.

Heat the remaining 4 tablespoons olive oil in a large sauté pan over medium heat. Add the escalopes, breaded side down (you will need to do this in batches), and sear until the crust is browned. Flip over, add 1 tablespoon of the butter, and continue cooking for 1 minute, while basting the butter over the meat.

In a medium sauté pan over medium heat, melt the remaining 1 tablespoon butter and add the asparagus tips and slices. Stir until heated through and adjust the seasoning with salt and pepper.

For each serving, place a veal escalope in the center of a warm dinner plate. Arrange on top 3 sweetbreads, 3 morels, 2 mousse quenelles, 3 asparagus tips, a spoonful of asparagus discs, 2 shaved asparagus tips, and a few leaves of parsley and fried sage. Sprinkle with the egg, capers, and lemon.

WHITE TRUFFLE VEAL BLANQUETTE
POLENTA TARAGNA, CROSNES

SERVES 6

I AM ALWAYS EAGER to dip into our French culinary legacy, to revisit the dishes of my childhood and use them as the foundation of a new dish. Here I was inspired by veal blanquette, a bourgeois, creamy stew named in reference to the prized "blanc" (white) of the meat and the sauce, often made with veal shoulder, and first described in 1735 by Vincent la Chapelle in *Le Cuisinier Moderne*.

For extraordinary tenderness, we choose veal cheek and poach it until the natural marbled gelatin dissipates, creating a lush melt-in-your-mouth kind of pleasure. In the sauce, we add a splash of vin jaune du Jura for a slight oaky taste with hints of hazelnut and hay.

We give our diners the opportunity to taste three different cuts and preparations to contrast the texture of the braised cheek, the crisp sweetbread, and a roasted, thyme-infused veal fillet. And at the table, as part of a truffle menu, we shave a white truffle from Alba on top of the blanquette for a touch of magic.

WHITE TRUFFLE VEAL BLANQUETTE
POLENTA TARAGNA, CROSNES

Sweetbreads

1 pound veal sweetbreads, submerged
in ice water for 24 hours

Veal Cheek Blanquette

2 quarts Veal Stock (page 368)

4 boneless veal cheeks, trimmed

1 small white onion, chopped

1 small leek, white and light green
part only, chopped and rinsed

1 small carrot, peeled and chopped

1 stalk celery, chopped

1 sachet (½ teaspoon white peppercorns,
2 sprigs thyme, 3 cloves garlic, peeled,
6 parsley stems, and 1 bay leaf tied in
cheesecloth and secured with butcher's
twine)

Salt

2½ tablespoons butter

¼ cup flour

1 cup heavy cream

½ cup vin jaune du Jura

Freshly ground white pepper

Comté Croutons

3 thin slices Comté cheese

6 (1-inch) round Melba Croutons (page 372)

White Truffle Polenta Taragna

2 cups veal cheek poaching liquid,
reserved from above, or Veal Stock
(page 368)

2 cups milk

1 cup polenta taragna (we recommend
Molino Riva)

½ cup mascarpone cheese

¼ cup freshly grated Parmesan cheese

2 tablespoons finely chopped white truffle

Salt and freshly ground white pepper

Glazed Pearl Onions and Crosnes

9 white pearl onions

1½ cups Chicken Stock (page 368)

3 tablespoons butter

4 ounces crosnes, washed and trimmed

Salt and freshly ground white pepper

White Truffle–Infused Veal Jus

2 teaspoons butter

1 tablespoon finely chopped white truffle

1 cup Veal Jus
(see Basic Meat Jus, page 370)

To Finish

½ pound veal tenderloin, trimmed and tied
with butcher's twine at ½-inch intervals

Salt and freshly ground white pepper

4 tablespoons olive oil

7 tablespoons butter

4 sprigs thyme

2 cloves garlic, peeled and smashed

1½ cups Spinach Puree (page 371)

1 shallot, finely minced

½ pound chanterelle mushrooms,
trimmed and washed

2 tablespoons thinly sliced parsley

Shaved white truffle, as desired

Fleur de sel

Cracked black pepper

1 ounce micro parsley leaves

For the Sweetbreads

Strain the sweetbreads, transfer to a large
saucepan, and cover with cold water. Simmer
for 5 minutes, skimming any foam that rises
to the surface. Remove from the heat and rest
in the hot water for 5 minutes. Remove the
sweetbreads from the water, pat dry, and
transfer to a cutting board. Use a paring knife
to trim away the fat and outer membranes.
Place the sweetbreads in a shallow baking
dish lined with paper towels, top with more
paper towels, and place another baking dish
on top. Fill the second baking dish with heavy
objects (such as canned goods) to gently
press the sweetbreads. Refrigerate overnight.
Cut the sweetbreads into 6 approximately
1½-inch cubes and reserve, chilled.

For the Veal Cheek Blanquette

In a large saucepan, combine the veal stock
with the veal cheeks. Simmer for 2 minutes,
skimming any foam that rises to the surface.
Add the onion, leek, carrot, celery, sachet, and
a sprinkle of salt. Poach the cheeks at a light
simmer for 1½ hours, or until fork-tender,
skimming as needed. With a slotted spoon,
transfer the cheeks to a shallow baking dish,
wrap in plastic, and keep warm while making
the sauce. Strain the poaching liquid through
a fine-meshed sieve; measure 2 cups for
cooking the polenta and reserve, chilled. Pour
the remaining liquid into a large saucepan
and reduce to 2 cups; set aside to cool.

In the saucepan that you cooked the
cheeks in, melt the butter over low heat. Add
the flour and cook, while whisking, for 3 to 4
minutes, without coloring. In 3 or 4 additions,
slowly whisk in the reduced poaching liquid to
make a smooth sauce. Simmer for 5 minutes,
stir in the heavy cream, and return to a
simmer. Add the vin jaune and season with
salt and pepper. Pour the sauce over the
cheeks and reserve, chilled.

For the Comté Croutons

With a ¾-inch-diameter ring cutter, cut at least 6 discs from the cheese and place on top of the croutons. Arrange on a baking sheet and, just before serving, transfer to a hot oven for about 1 minute to lightly melt the cheese.

For the White Truffle Polenta Taragna

In a large saucepan, bring the 2 cups reserved poaching liquid or veal stock and the milk to a simmer. Gradually whisk in the polenta. Reduce the heat to low and cook until the mixture thickens and the polenta is tender, stirring often, about 20 minutes. Just before serving, stir in the mascarpone, Parmesan cheese, and white truffle. Adjust the seasoning with salt and pepper and reserve, kept warm.

For the Glazed Pearl Onions and Crosnes

In a medium saucepan, combine the onions with the stock and butter. Simmer for 5 minutes, then add the crosnes. Continue cooking at a low simmer until the vegetables are tender and the liquid has reduced to a glaze (if the liquid reduces before the vegetables are tender, add spoonfuls of water). Season with salt and pepper. Remove 3 pearl onions from the pan and cut into quarters. Return to the pan and reserve, kept warm.

For the White Truffle–Infused Veal Jus

In a small saucepan over medium heat, brown the butter. Add the truffle and sauté for 20 seconds. Add the veal jus, bring to a simmer, and keep warm.

To Finish

Preheat the oven to 300°F. Transfer the veal cheeks to the oven and heat, stirring every 5 minutes, for 30 minutes, or until heated through.

Rest the veal tenderloin and sweetbreads at room temperature for 15 minutes, then season them on all sides with salt and pepper.

Heat 2 tablespoons of the olive oil in a large sauté pan over medium-high heat and add the tenderloin. Sear on all sides until browned, then add 2 tablespoons of the butter, 2 sprigs of the thyme, and 1 clove garlic. Cook, basting and turning, until the tenderloin

reaches an internal temperature of 125°F. Transfer to a platter, cover with foil, and rest in a warm place for 10 minutes.

Meanwhile, heat the remaining 2 tablespoons olive oil in the sauté pan over medium-high heat. Add the sweetbreads to the pan and sear on all sides to a light golden brown. Add 3 tablespoons of the remaining butter and the remaining thyme and garlic and baste until the sweetbreads are firm to the touch.

Remove the butcher's twine from the loin and slice into 6 portions.

Transfer the spinach puree to a small saucepan over medium heat and stir until heated through.

Melt the remaining 2 tablespoons butter in a medium sauté pan over medium-low heat and add the shallot. Sauté until translucent, about 2 minutes; increase the heat to medium-high, add the mushrooms in a single layer, and sprinkle with salt and pepper. Sauté until the mushrooms are cooked and any moisture they may have released is evaporated. Add the glazed pearl onions and crosnes to the pan

and toss to heat through. Adjust the seasoning if needed and stir in the sliced parsley.

For each serving, place 2 spoonfuls of polenta on opposite sides of a warm dinner plate. Place a braised veal cheek on one spoonful of polenta and a roasted sweetbread on the other. Cover the cheek with shavings of fresh white truffle. Place a spoonful of spinach puree and 1 slice of veal tenderloin in between the cheek and the sweetbread. Top the spinach puree with a whole pearl onion and a Comté crouton, and the veal with a sprinkle of fleur de sel and cracked black pepper. Arrange 2 spoonfuls of chanterelles and crosnes on opposite sides of the plate and garnish with 2 pearl onion quarters and a few leaves of micro parsley. Drizzle veal jus around the tenderloin.

VERMONT SPRING LAMB
PEAS À LA FRANÇAISE

SERVES 8

AFTER WE BUTCHER half of a twenty-pound lamb, every piece finds its place with this classic spring combination of peas, lettuce, carrot, and oregano. The glazed confit shoulder supports a perfect disc made with the saddle wrapped around oregano and slices of lamb kidney. On either side, a lamb chop bookends a perfect gigot. The front of the plate holds a barbajuan, a sort of crispy dumpling, filled with braised lamb to add richness and crunch to this tender spring specialty, delivered to us from Lydia Ratcliff, a member of the Fancy Meats from Vermont co-op.

VERMONT SPRING LAMB
PEAS À LA FRANÇAISE

Sous-Vide Braised Shoulder

1 (2-pound) lamb shoulder, deboned

Salt and freshly ground white pepper

Piment d'Espelette

2 tablespoons olive oil

3½ ounces button mushrooms, trimmed, rinsed, patted dry, and quartered

1 small onion, small-diced

1 clove garlic, peeled and chopped

1 lamb heart, diced

1½ ounces lamb liver, diced

½ ounce chopped Tomato Confit (page 376)

1 tablespoon white wine

Lamb Jus and Braised Shank

3 tablespoons olive oil

Lamb bones (about 6 pounds) from ½ lamb, chopped into 1-inch pieces, rinsed and patted dry

2 (5-inch-long) lamb shanks (from the front and back legs)

1 small onion, sliced

2 shallots, sliced

1 small carrot, peeled and sliced

4 cloves garlic, peeled and halved

2 Roma tomatoes, quartered and seeded

2 cups dry white wine

1 bay leaf

2 sprigs thyme

1 sachet (½ teaspoon each coriander seeds, black peppercorns, and crushed red pepper wrapped in cheesecloth and secured with butcher's twine)

4 quarts Chicken Stock (page 368)

Salt and freshly ground white pepper

Piment d'Espelette

Stuffed Lamb Loin

1 boneless lamb loin with belly flap attached (about 1 pound)

1 lamb tenderloin

1 lamb kidney

Seasoning ratio per pound of meat:

1 teaspoon (6 grams) salt

¼ teaspoon (1 gram) freshly ground white pepper

¼ teaspoon (1 gram) piment d'Espelette

10 oregano leaves

Lamb Shank Barbajuan (makes extra)

1½ cups 00 pasta flour, plus extra for dusting

2½ tablespoons olive oil

½ teaspoon salt

Braised lamb shank cubes, reserved from above

Artichoke Barigoule

Juice of 2 lemons

11 baby artichokes

1 tablespoon olive oil

1 small onion, thinly sliced

½ small carrot, peeled and thinly sliced

1 clove garlic, peeled and halved

½ cup white wine

1 cup Chicken Stock (page 368)

1 sprig parsley

1 bay leaf

1 sprig thyme

½ teaspoon salt

Ragout of Peas and Romaine Lettuce

Salt

4 cups fresh shelled English peas

½ cup heavy cream

1 tablespoon olive oil

2 cippolini onions, thinly sliced

¼ cup thinly sliced romaine lettuce

2 teaspoons chopped oregano

Freshly ground white pepper

Roasted Lamb Leg (makes extra)

1 (5-pound) lamb leg

Salt and freshly ground white pepper

Piment d'Espelette

2 tablespoons olive oil

2 cloves garlic, peeled and smashed

2 sprigs thyme

1 (2-inch) sprig rosemary

1 (2-inch) sprig oregano

2 tablespoons butter

Cippolini Onions and Baby Carrots

7 medium cippolini onions

7 small baby carrots, peeled and trimmed

1 cup Chicken Stock (page 368)

2 tablespoons olive oil

Salt and freshly ground white pepper

To Finish

Canola oil for frying

5 tablespoons olive oil

1 lamb rack (with 8 bones, ½ pound), Frenched and tied

Salt and freshly ground white pepper

2 sprigs thyme

2 sprigs oregano

2 sprigs rosemary

4 cloves garlic, peeled and smashed

4 tablespoons butter

Artichoke Chips (page 372)

¼ cup yellow pea shoots

¼ cup green pea shoots

1 baby carrot, peeled and shaved through a fine-toothed comb on a mandoline

For the Sous-Vide Braised Shoulder

Lay the shoulder on a cutting board. Lay a sheet of plastic wrap on top of the shoulder and use a flat meat mallet to pound it to a ½-inch thickness. Cut the shoulder into a 7 x 7-inch square; weigh and reserve 12 ounces of the trim for the stuffing, chilled. Sprinkle the pounded shoulder on both sides with salt, pepper, and piment d'Espelette; reserve, chilled.

Heat 1 tablespoon of the olive oil in a medium sauté pan over high heat. Add the mushrooms and sauté for 3 minutes, or until browned. Transfer the mushrooms to a paper towel–lined plate and chill. Return the pan to medium-low heat and add the remaining 1 tablespoon olive oil. Add the onion and garlic. Cook, stirring occasionally, until tender but not colored, about 4 minutes. Transfer to a large bowl with the mushrooms, the 12 ounces reserved shoulder trim, the lamb heart and liver, the tomato confit, and the white wine. Sprinkle with ½ teaspoon salt, 1 pinch of pepper, and 1 pinch of piment d'Espelette. Mix well, cover, and refrigerate until well chilled.

Using an immersion circulator, preheat a water bath to 144°F. Pass the meat mixture through a chilled meat grinder fit with the coarse plate. Spread the ground meat in an even layer onto the shoulder and roll into a log. Line a flat surface with a 1-foot double layer of plastic wrap and set the rolled shoulder in the center. Tightly wrap the shoulder in the plastic and tie off the ends to secure. Place in a sous-vide bag and vacuum-seal. Submerge the bag in the prepared water bath and cook for 3 hours. Remove from the water, chill in a bowl of ice water, and reserve, chilled.

For the Lamb Jus and Braised Shank

In a large Dutch oven, heat the olive oil over medium-high heat. Add the bones and shanks in a single layer (you may need to do this in batches) and sear on all sides until well browned, about 15 minutes total. Reduce the heat to medium and add the onion, shallots, carrot, and garlic to the pan. Cook, stirring, for 6 minutes. Add the tomatoes and white wine and simmer until almost dry. Add the bay leaf, thyme, sachet, and chicken stock. Bring to a boil and skim any foam that rises to the surface. Reduce the heat to a simmer and cook for 3 hours, skimming as necessary. Strain the liquid through a colander set over a bowl, reserve the shanks, and discard the bones and vegetables. Pass the liquid through a fine-meshed sieve into a medium saucepan and reduce for 45 minutes, or until it coats the back of a spoon.

Meanwhile, pick and shred the meat from the shanks into a medium bowl and mix in a few spoonfuls of the cooking liquid to moisten. Season with salt, pepper, and piment d'Espelette. While still warm, pack the mixture into an 8½ x 4½-inch loaf pan. Press the surface into an even layer, cover, and reserve, chilled. Once reduced, chill and reserve the sauce.

For the Stuffed Lamb Loin

Weigh the loin, tenderloin, and kidney and scale the needed amount of seasoning according to the ratio listed in the ingredients. Lay the loin on a cutting board so that the belly flap is spread out, facing inside up. Lightly pound the flap with a flat meat tenderizer and, with a paring knife, score it with a crosshatch pattern. Slice the kidney lengthwise into 3 pieces. Sprinkle the seasoning evenly over the loins, flaps, and kidney. Line the tenderloin and kidney against the loin on top of the belly flap and top with a line of oregano leaves. Tightly roll the flap up and around the meats to form a log. Tie the log at 1-inch intervals with butcher's twine. Reserve, chilled.

VERMONT SPRING LAMB
PEAS À LA FRANÇAISE

For the Lamb Shank Barbajuan

In the bowl of an electric mixer fitted with a dough hook, combine the flour, olive oil, and salt with 5 tablespoons water and mix on low speed until a dough comes together. Increase the speed to medium and knead for 5 minutes. Remove the dough, divide it in half, cover, and chill for at least 30 minutes.

Cut the reserved braised shank mixture into ½-inch cubes.

Pass one-half of the dough through a pasta machine, gradually reducing the thickness until it is ⅟₁₆ inch thick and approximately 16 inches long and 7½ inches wide. Repeat with the second half of the dough. Sprinkle the counter with flour, lay 1 sheet of dough horizontally on top, and line the cubes of braised lamb onto the dough, leaving 1 inch of space between them. Lightly brush in between the cubes with water and set the second sheet of dough on top; press lightly to seal. Cut between the mounds to separate them. Use a small offset spatula or the back of a paring knife to press the dough flat around each mound of filling to make tight, square pockets. Cut the edges of the dough around the filling to ⅛-inch borders. Store, frozen.

For the Artichoke Barigoule

In a large bowl, combine the lemon juice and 1 gallon of ice water. To clean each artichoke, trim the end of the stem and ½ inch from the tip. Peel away the rough outer leaves, leaving the pale yellow tender leaves intact. Using a vegetable peeler, remove the skin from the stem and any tough leaf remnants from the base. Submerge the artichokes in the lemon water immediately after cleaning.

Heat the olive oil in a large saucepan over medium heat, and add the onion, carrot, and garlic, and cook, stirring, for 2 minutes. Add the white wine and simmer for 1 minute. Strain 8 of the artichokes, reserving 3 for artichoke chips, and add to the pan along with the chicken stock, parsley, bay leaf, thyme, and salt. Simmer for 15 minutes, or until the artichokes are tender. Cool at room temperature, halve the artichokes, and store submerged in the cooking liquid, chilled.

For the Ragout of Peas and Romaine Lettuce

Bring a large pot of salted water to a boil and set a bowl of ice water on the side.

Boil the peas for about 20 seconds, until tender, and chill in the ice water. Peel the skins from 3 cups of the peas and set aside. Pour the cream into a medium saucepan and bring to a simmer. Transfer to a blender with the remaining peas and puree until smooth; pass through a fine-meshed sieve into a bowl set over ice. Stir until chilled.

When ready to serve, heat the olive oil in a medium sauté pan over medium heat and add the onions. Cook, stirring, until soft but not colored, about 2 minutes. Add the reserved peeled peas and romaine lettuce and stir until heated through. Stir in half of the pea puree and the oregano; season with salt and pepper and keep warm.

For the Roasted Lamb Leg

Preheat the oven to 300°F. Rest the leg at room temperature for 15 minutes, then season on all sides with salt, pepper, and piment d'Espelette. In a large roasting pan, heat the olive oil over medium-high heat. Add the lamb and sear on all sides until golden brown. Reduce the heat to medium and add the garlic, thyme, rosemary, oregano, and butter. Continue to cook, basting with the butter and turning occasionally, for 5 minutes. Transfer to the oven and continue to roast, basting every 10 minutes for 1 hour, or until the internal temperature reaches 122°F. Cover with aluminum foil and rest in a warm place for 20 minutes. Keep the oven on for finishing.

For the Cippolini Onions and Baby Carrots

In a small sauté pan, combine the onions, carrots, chicken stock, and olive oil. Sprinkle with salt and pepper and cook at just below a simmer for 45 minutes, or until tender. Strain, then cut a ⅛-inch cap from the tops of the onions. Scoop a small cavity from the middle of the onions and fill with reserved pea puree, return to the pan with the carrots; cover and keep warm.

To Finish

Fill one-third of a medium saucepan with canola oil and preheat to 350°F. Rest the stuffed lamb loins and racks at room temperature for 10 minutes.

Slice the shoulder roulade into 8 pieces, place in a shallow dish, top with the reserved sauce, and cover. Transfer to the oven to heat through, about 20 minutes.

Heat 2 tablespoons of the olive oil in a large sauté pan over medium-high heat. Season the reserved stuffed loin and the rack with salt and pepper and sear on all sides, about 6 minutes total. Reduce the heat to medium and add the thyme, oregano, rosemary, garlic, and butter. Continue cooking, basting with the butter, for 2 minutes. Transfer to the oven and roast for about 10 minutes, flipping and basting every 2 minutes, until the internal temperatures of the loin and rack reach 116°F.

Cover the rack and loin and rest in a warm place for at least 10 minutes.

Meanwhile, strain the artichoke barigoule and pat dry. Heat the remaining 3 tablespoons olive oil in a large sauté pan over medium-high heat and sear the artichokes cut side down until browned. Flip and continue cooking until heated through, about 2 minutes. Season with salt and pepper.

Deep-fry the barbajuans until golden brown, transfer to a paper towel–lined plate, and sprinkle with salt. Slice the leg into bite-size portions and slice the rack and stuffed loin into 8 portions each.

For each serving, place a large spoonful of pea and romaine lettuce ragout on one side of a warm dinner plate. Arrange 1 slice each of rack, loin, shoulder, and leg on top of the ragout. Arrange 2 halved carrots and an artichoke half around the meat. Set 1 barbajuan, 1 pea puree–stuffed onion, and a piece of artichoke barigoule in a line on the other side of the plate. Place an artichoke chip on the artichoke, a few yellow and green pea shoots on the lamb, and some shaved carrot on the onion. Spoon sauce from the pan with the shoulder onto the plate.

"In this spring lamb tasting, a variety of preparations, textures, and flavors come forth."

ELYSIAN FIELDS FARM LAMB RACK
SPICED TOMATO CHUTNEY, SUMMER SQUASH, BLACK OLIVES

SERVES 4

I CANNOT EAT LAMB without thinking back to Roger Vergé, who, at his Moulin de Mougins on the French Riviera, cooked some of the best lamb chops I've encountered: seasoned with herbes de Provence and grilled over petrified grapevines. Today we are honored to work with one of the best lamb purveyors in the United States, Elysian Fields Farm in Pennsylvania, where Chef Thomas Keller is a partner. The lamb, raised humanely and fed a perfectly balanced diet, yields delicate meat with just the right amount of gaminess. Today's trend is to cook it sous-vide, but I like to roast the meat to a perfect medium-rare, well seared on the outside and juicy on the inside. Zucchini, yellow squash, tomato chutney, and chickpea panisses complete this Provençale combination.

ELYSIAN FIELDS FARM LAMB RACK
SPICED TOMATO CHUTNEY,
SUMMER SQUASH, BLACK OLIVES

Crispy Squash Blossoms

3 tablespoons olive oil

4 squash blossoms

Salt and freshly ground white pepper

Chickpea Panisses (makes extra)

2 cups chickpea flour

2 teaspoons salt, plus
extra for seasoning

½ cup olive oil

Canola oil for frying

1 cup rice flour

Spiced Tomato Chutney

2½ pounds plum tomatoes
(about 8)

1 tablespoon honey

1 small onion, minced

2 cloves garlic, peeled and smashed

1 (¼-inch) slice peeled ginger

¼ teaspoon ground cumin

¼ teaspoon ground coriander

Salt

½ teaspoon piment d'Espelette

2½ tablespoons balsamic vinegar

Finely ground white pepper

Summer Vegetables

8 small pattypan squash
(8 ounces)

2 green zucchinis (1 pound)

2 yellow gold bar squash (1 pound)

½ pound haricots verts

Salt

Grilled Baby Zucchini

8 baby zucchini

1 tablespoon olive oil

Salt

Lamb Rack

3 tablespoons olive oil

1 lamb rack (about 5 pounds),
Frenched and tied with butcher's twine

Salt and freshly ground white pepper

3 tablespoons butter

2 cloves garlic, peeled

3 sprigs thyme

To Finish

Lamb Jus (see Basic Meat Jus,
page 370)

1 sprig rosemary

Piment d'Espelette

2 tablespoons olive oil

Salt and freshly ground pepper

Fleur de sel

Black Olive Mosto Oil (page 377)

¼ cup micro basil leaves

½ cup finely chopped
Taggiasca olives

For the Crispy Squash Blossoms

Preheat the oven to 190°F. Brush the olive oil onto 2 Silpat sheets and place 1 on a baking sheet, oiled side up. Gently open the squash blossoms (you will need to make a small tear down the side) and remove the pistil, stem, and stem leaves. Trim each blossom into 3 petals and lay in a single layer on top of the prepared baking sheet. Sprinkle with salt and pepper. Top with the second Silpat, oiled side down. Bake for 1 hour and remove the top Silpat. Bake for 1 more hour, then gently flip the petals. If they are still a little floppy, return to the oven for another hour, or until crispy. Transfer to a paper towel–lined plate, cool, and store in an airtight container at room temperature.

For the Chickpea Panisses

Lightly grease an 8½ x 4½-inch loaf pan. In a blender, combine the chickpea flour with 2 teaspoons salt and 2½ cups water and puree until smooth. In a medium saucepan, bring 2½ cups water to a simmer. Whisk the puree into the simmering water and reduce the heat to low. Cook, whisking occasionally, for 15 minutes, to a polenta-like texture and until the mixture no longer tastes starchy. Transfer to a food processor and blend in the oil. While still hot, transfer to the prepared loaf pan, flatten the surface with an offset spatula, and chill for 4 hours, or until set. Turn the panisse onto a cutting board and cut into ¼-inch-wide x 3-inch-long batons.

When ready to serve, fill one-third of a large saucepan with canola oil and heat to 375°F. Gently coat the panisse batons in rice flour and fry them until golden brown. Strain onto a paper towel–lined plate and sprinkle with salt. Keep warm.

For the Spiced Tomato Chutney

Bring a large pot of water to a boil and place a bowl of ice water on the side. Core the tomatoes and mark their bases with an X. Boil the tomatoes for 5 seconds, or until the skins loosen. Submerge them in ice water and peel the skins. Quarter and seed the tomatoes and then cut the flesh into ¼-inch dice.

Heat the honey in a medium saucepan until it bubbles. Add the onion and cook, stirring, for 2 minutes. Add the tomatoes, garlic, ginger, cumin, coriander, 1 teaspoon salt, piment d'Espelette, and vinegar and simmer for 30 minutes, or until the juice has cooked down to a syrup and the tomatoes are the texture of a chutney. Remove the garlic cloves and ginger. Season with salt and pepper and set aside.

For the Summer Vegetables

Trim the pattypan squash and halve crosswise. Quarter the zucchinis and squash lengthwise, trim and discard the seeds, and cut the strips into small triangles. Trim the ends of the haricots verts.

Bring a large pot of salted water to a boil and set a bowl of ice water on the side. Boil the vegetables in separate batches until tender; chill them in the ice water. Allow the water to return to a rolling boil in between batches. Strain, pat dry, and reserve the vegetables, chilled.

For the Grilled Baby Zucchini

Heat a grill or cast-iron grill pan over high heat. Using a mandoline, cut the zucchini lengthwise into thin slices into a bowl. Toss with the olive oil and season with salt; marinate for 5 minutes. Grill the slices to mark well on both sides; set aside and keep warm.

For the Lamb Rack

Preheat the oven to 325°F. If desired, wrap the rack bones in aluminum foil to prevent browning.

Heat the olive oil in a large ovenproof sauté pan over high heat. Season the lamb on all sides with salt and pepper. Sear all sides of the lamb rack until browned, about 5 minutes total. While searing, baste often with the oil from the pan, especially in the areas around the bones. Once seared, reduce the heat to medium and add the butter, garlic, and thyme. Allow the butter to foam, and continue basting for 2 minutes. Transfer to the oven for 5 minutes, flip, and return to the oven for 3 more minutes, or until the internal temperature reaches 125°F. Rest the lamb in a warm area, covered with foil, for 10 minutes, or until the internal temperature reaches 138°F. Remove the twine and keep warm.

To Finish

Transfer the lamb jus to a small saucepan with the rosemary and bring to a simmer. Season with piment d'Espelette and keep warm. Heat the olive oil in a large sauté pan over medium heat. Add the summer vegetables and toss to heat through. Season with salt and pepper. Slice the lamb rack into 8 chops.

For each serving, place 2 spoonfuls of tomato chutney on a warm dinner plate, set 2 lamb chops on top, and sprinkle the meat with fleur de sel. Scatter the sautéed summer vegetables and a few grilled baby zucchini slices around the lamb. Spoon several dots of mosto oil onto the plate and lean 2 crispy panisses against the lamb. Garnish with 3 crispy squash blossoms, a few micro basil leaves, and a sprinkling of black olive. Spoon the jus around the lamb.

WILD HARE À LA ROYALE

SERVES 8

LEGEND HAS IT that lièvre à la royale, a gut-warmer fall dish, was first invented for Louis XIV, who loved the gamy beast but had no teeth left, thus requiring that the meat be cooked long and slow until it became so tender that he could savor it with a spoon.

Culinary luminaries tell us that there are two different lineages for this icon of French gastronomy: Senator Couteaux's recipe—a slow-braised whole animal huddled in a dark, heady sauce; and Marie-Antoine Carême's, which favors, as I do, a completely deboned version. Like many great classic recipes, this preparation requires three days to complete. Today at Daniel, we harness the power of the hare with silky foie gras, specks of truffle, and a drop of deep Cognac for a noble stuffing.

WILD HARE À LA ROYALE

Butchering the Hare

2 (2½-pound) wild Scottish hare

Braised Hare Leg Roulade and Hare Sauce

4 hare legs, bone-in, reserved from above

4 ounces bacon, cut into large dice

2 cups full-bodied red wine

¼ cup Cognac

1 medium carrot, peeled and diced

1 large onion, diced

1 stalk celery, diced

4 cloves garlic, peeled

1 sachet (1 tablespoon juniper berries, 1 tablespoon black peppercorns, and 2 sprigs thyme wrapped in cheesecloth and secured with butcher's twine)

Salt and freshly ground white pepper

2 tablespoons duck fat

Hare bones, reserved from above

3 quarts Veal Stock (page 368)

Hare Sauce Liaison

9 tablespoons butter

2½ ounces Foie Gras Terrine (page 375)

4½ ounces fresh pork blood

1 teaspoon Cognac

Hare Royale Farce

2 tablespoons olive oil

6 ounces fresh black trumpet mushrooms, trimmed, rinsed, and patted dry

Salt and freshly ground white pepper

2 cloves garlic, peeled and thinly sliced

3 ounces diced crustless white bread

¼ cup hot milk

1 pound fresh deveined grade A foie gras lobe, cut lengthwise into four 4-ounce slices

20 ounces hare meat, reserved from above (14 ounces roughly chopped and 6 ounces cut into small dice)

12½ ounces fatback (3½ ounces roughly chopped and 9 ounces cut into small dice)

4 hare kidneys, small-diced

2 hare livers, small-diced

2 hare hearts, small-diced

7 ounces chopped fresh black truffle

1½ ounces truffle juice

2½ ounces hare sauce, reserved from above

Seasoning ratio for each pound of hare farce:

1 teaspoon (6 grams) salt

½ teaspoon (1.5 grams) freshly ground white pepper

½ teaspoon (2.5ml) Cognac

Foie Gras Melba

8 very thin slices brioche

2 tablespoons foie gras fat, reserved from above

Salt and freshly ground white pepper

Hare Royale Ballotine

2 hare loins, reserved from above

Salt and freshly ground white pepper

3 ounces fresh black truffle, chopped

1 egg white, beaten

Chestnut-Parsley Pasta

1 cup plus 3 tablespoons chestnut flour

1 cup plus 3 tablespoons type 00 soft wheat flour

7 ounces egg yolks

½ cup parsley leaves

Salt

1 tablespoon olive oil

Porcini Marmalade

1 pound large porcini mushrooms (about 6), caps separated and wiped clean, stems peeled

2 cups dry white wine

Salt

2 sprigs thyme

3 cloves garlic, peeled and smashed

Freshly ground white pepper

3 cups olive oil, or as needed

¼ cup heavy cream

White balsamic vinegar

Roasted Chestnuts

2 tablespoons butter

12 fresh or vacuum-sealed peeled chestnuts

Salt and finely ground white pepper

2 tablespoons Cognac

3 tablespoons hare sauce, from above

To Finish

½ ounce unsweetened baker's chocolate

Salt and freshly ground white pepper

8 small porcini mushrooms, cleaned and halved

4 tablespoons olive oil

2 cloves garlic, peeled and smashed

2 sprigs thyme

2 tablespoons butter

2 hare loins, trimmed

24 small celery leaves

½ cup lightly whipped heavy cream

For Butchering the Hare

On a large cutting board, lay the hare on their backs. Pull the kidneys, livers, and hearts from the belly cavities and peel off and discard the fat surrounding the kidneys; reserve for stuffing.

With a butcher's knife, trim away the shoulders (forelegs) by cutting flush up against the neck bone, and then bend the shoulder forward to pop the bone from the joint. Carve through the joint toward the ribs to completely remove. Debone the forelegs, reserving the meat for the farce and bones for the sauce.

Remove the legs by carving inward to separate the thigh from the tailbone, pop the bone from the joint, and carve through the joint toward the tailbone to completely remove; reserve for braising.

Carve the tenderloins from underneath the saddle; reserve for the farce. Turn the saddles over and carve the loins from the backbone. Cut away the silver skin from the loins in strips and discard. Trim the loins to 5-inch lengths and reserve for roasting; reserve the trim for the stuffing.

Chop all the bones into rough 1-inch pieces, rinse with cold water, dry, and reserve for the farce.

For the Braised Hare Leg Roulade and Hare Sauce

In a shallow container, combine the hare legs, bacon, red wine, Cognac, carrot, onion, celery, garlic, and sachet. Cover and marinate, refrigerated, overnight or up to 24 hours.

Preheat the oven to 300°F. Strain and reserve the liquid from the marinated ingredients and pat them dry. Separate the bacon and legs from the vegetables and sachet. Season the legs with salt and pepper on all sides. Place a large heavy-bottomed Dutch oven over medium heat and add the duck fat and bacon. Cook, stirring, until the bacon is browned, 4 to 5 minutes, then remove with a slotted spoon and set aside. Add the hare legs and sear on all sides until golden brown,

8 to 10 minutes; remove and set aside. Add the bones in a single layer (you may need to do this in batches). Roast on all sides until browned, 10 to 12 minutes. Remove the bones, set aside, and reduce the heat to medium. Add the marinated vegetables and sachet to the pot. Cook, stirring, for 5 minutes. Add the reserved marinating liquid to the pot, bring to a simmer, and reduce by half, about 20 minutes. Return the bacon, hare legs, and bones to the pot and stir in the veal stock. Bring to a simmer, cover, and transfer to the oven. Braise for 2 to 2½ hours, until the leg meat easily separates from the bones. Remove the legs from the liquid, transfer to a baking dish, cover with plastic wrap, and reserve in a warm spot. Strain the braising liquid through a fine-meshed sieve into a large saucepan and discard the solids. Bring to a simmer and reduce, occasionally skimming away any foam that rises to the surface, for 2 hours, or until it is thick enough to coat the back of a spoon. Reserve the sauce, chilled.

Meanwhile, pick the hare meat from the legs into a medium bowl and add a few spoonfuls of cooking liquid to keep it moist. If needed, adjust the seasoning with salt and pepper. Line a flat surface with a horizontal 2-foot-long double layer of plastic wrap. Spoon the braised hare meat into the center of the plastic in a 1-foot-long horizontal mound. Lift the bottom edges of the plastic wrap and fold over the meat to meet the top edges. Using your fingers, form the meat through the plastic into a 1¼-inch-diameter log, then roll the log forward to enclose in the plastic. Tie off the ends of the plastic to secure and refrigerate until fully chilled.

For the Hare Sauce Liaison

In the bowl of a food processor, pulse the butter with the foie gras terrine until well combined. With the machine running, slowly stream in the blood and Cognac until homogeneous. Transfer to a small container, cover, and reserve, chilled.

For the Hare Royale Farce

Be sure that all meats are well chilled. Heat the olive oil in a large sauté pan over medium-high heat. Add the mushrooms and sprinkle with salt and pepper. Sauté until tender, about 4 minutes, adding the garlic halfway through, and transfer to a cutting board. Finely chop and reserve, chilled. In a small bowl, soak the bread in the milk for 5 minutes. Squeeze out excess milk, weigh out 4 ounces of bread, and set aside.

Heat a large dry sauté pan over high heat until very hot. Add the foie gras and sear for 10 to 20 seconds on each side, until lightly colored (it should not cook through). Transfer to a plate and refrigerate, reserving the fat in the pan for the foie gras melba. Once chilled, cut the foie gras into small dice.

Pass the 14 ounces of roughly chopped hare meat and 3½ ounces of roughly chopped fatback through a meat grinder fit with the coarse plate. Transfer to a large bowl and add the chopped mushrooms, soaked bread, 6 ounces diced hare meat, 9 ounces diced fatback, the kidneys, livers, hearts, diced foie gras, black truffle, truffle juice, and hare sauce. Weigh the mixture and measure the needed amount of seasoning according to the ratio listed in the ingredients; sprinkle it over the top. Mix well, cover with plastic wrap, and refrigerate overnight.

For the Foie Gras Melba

Preheat the oven to 225°F. Using a 2½-inch ring cutter, cut the brioche slices into discs. Brush 2 sheets of parchment paper with foie gras fat on one side. Place 1 on a baking sheet, fat side up, and line the brioche on top in a single layer; sprinkle with salt and pepper. Top with the second sheet of parchment fat side down. Top with another baking sheet and bake for 18 to 20 minutes, until they are crisp but not colored. Cool, then store in an airtight container.

For the Hare Royale Ballotine

Using an immersion circulator, preheat a water bath to 144°F. Season the 2 hare loins with salt and pepper. Line a flat surface with a 2-foot-square double layer of plastic wrap. Spread the hare royale farce in the center of the plastic into a flat, approximately 1-foot-long and 10-inch-wide rectangle. Sprinkle the truffle evenly over the top. Brush the hare loins with the egg white and lay on the stuffing in a horizontal line approximately 3 inches from the bottom edge. Lay the braised hare log on top of the loins. Using the plastic wrap as an aid, begin rolling the farce away from you, up and around the top of the braised hare loins and roulade, and then roll forward to completely enrobe. Roll the ballotine in the plastic a few times to tighten and then tie off the ends. Transfer to a sous-vide bag and vacuum-seal. Submerge in the prepared water bath and cook for 24 hours. Transfer the bag to an ice bath until fully chilled through the center and remove from the bag. Unwrap the plastic and slice the roulade into 8 equal portions; reserve, chilled.

For the Chestnut-Parsley Pasta

Sift the chestnut and 00 flour into the bowl of a stand mixer fitted with a hook. Begin mixing on low speed; gradually add the yolks until just combined. Increase the speed to medium and mix until the dough comes together and begins to pull from the sides of the bowl. Remove the dough and continue to knead by hand for 3 minutes. Flatten the dough into a 3 x 4-inch rectangle, wrap in plastic, and rest in the refrigerator for at least 2 hours or overnight.

Pass the dough through a pasta machine, gradually reducing the thickness until it is thin enough to see your hand through. Lay the sheet of dough horizontally on a flat surface and line the parsley leaves on top of half of the length, facing outward, touching but not overlapping. Lightly brush the other half of the pasta with water and carefully fold on top, pressing lightly to stick together. Increase the thickness on the pasta machine three notches and run the pasta through

twice, then decrease the thickness one notch and run through again, being careful not to tear; you should be able to see the parsley through the sheet. On a lightly floured cutting board, using a 5-inch ring cutter, cut out at least 8 discs of pasta.

Bring a large pot of salted water to a boil and place a bowl of ice water on the side. Boil the pasta for 2 to 3 minutes, until al dente; immediately chill in the ice water. Strain and lay the pasta on a lightly oiled baking sheet; wrap in plastic and reserve, chilled.

For the Porcini Marmalade

Cut ½ cup of batons from the porcini stems and reserve, chilled, for garnish. In a large saucepan, combine 2 quarts water with the white wine and a pinch of salt; bring to a boil. Boil the porcini caps and stems for 30 seconds (you may need to do this in batches). Remove with a slotted spoon and drain on paper towels. Transfer the porcinis to a large saucepan with the thyme, garlic, and a pinch of salt and pepper. Add enough olive oil to cover the mushrooms, cover, and place over low heat. Cook at just below a simmer until the mushrooms are fork-tender, about 1 hour. Remove from the heat and, with a slotted spoon, transfer the stems to a blender. Puree with the cream until smooth and transfer to a medium bowl. Scoop the caps from the oil and place on a cutting board; reserve the oil for other uses. Cut the caps into small dice and toss with the puree. Adjust the seasoning with the vinegar, salt, and pepper, and reserve, chilled.

For the Roasted Chestnuts

In a medium sauté pan over medium heat, brown the butter. Add the chestnuts and sauté until lightly browned, about 4 minutes. Sprinkle with salt and pepper, carefully add the Cognac, and simmer until almost dry. Add the hare sauce and reduce the heat to medium-low; cook, stirring occasionally, for 8 minutes, or until the chestnuts are tender and glazed. Cut the chestnuts in half and reserve, chilled.

To Finish

Preheat the oven to 250°F. Place the reserved hare sauce in a large saucepan and bring to a simmer. Place the sliced ballotine in a baking or casserole dish and pour in one-third of the hare sauce. Cover and transfer to the oven. Bake for 45 minutes, or until the ballotine is heated through, basting with the sauce every 15 minutes.

Meanwhile, remove the remaining sauce from the heat and gradually whisk in the liaison, a spoonful at a time, and then the chocolate until it melts. Season with salt and pepper and keep warm (be careful not to boil, as the sauce may break; if it does, whisk in a spoonful of hot water).

Using a small knife, lightly score a cross-hatch pattern on the cut sides of the small porcini mushrooms. In a medium sauté pan, heat 2 tablespoons of the olive oil over medium-high heat. Add the mushrooms cut side down and sear until golden brown. Flip the mushrooms and sprinkle with salt and pepper. Add 1 clove garlic and 1 sprig thyme and continue to cook, basting the mushrooms and turning occasionally, until the mushrooms are tender, about 4 minutes. Reserve, kept warm.

Transfer the porcini marmalade to a medium saucepan over medium heat and stir until heated through. Transfer the roasted chestnuts to a small sauté pan, add a few spoonfuls of hare sauce, and place over low heat, stirring to heat through. Combine 1 tablespoon butter with ⅓ cup water in a medium sauté pan and place over medium-low heat. Add the chestnut-parsley pasta and toss just to heat though.

In a medium sauté pan, heat the remaining 2 tablespoons olive oil over high heat. Season the hare loins on all sides with salt and pepper. Sear on all sides until browned, reduce the heat to low, and add the remaining 1 tablespoon butter, garlic, and thyme. Cook, turning and basting with the butter, for 3 to 4 minutes, until the hare loin is medium-rare (130°F). Rest in a warm place for 3 to 4 minutes before slicing each one into 12 medallions.

For each serving, place a pasta round in the center of a warm dinner plate and top with a portion of ballotine. Place a spoonful of porcini marmalade and a few of the reserved porcini batons on top of the ballotine. Arrange 3 hare loin medallions, 2 pieces of roasted porcini, and 3 halves of braised chestnut on the pasta next to the ballotine. Garnish with 3 celery leaves. Swirl the whipped cream into the sauce and spoon onto the ballotine; top with a foie gras melba.

GRAIN-CRUSTED VENISON
LAMBIC-BRAISED RED CABBAGE, HONEYCRISP APPLES

SERVES 4

INSPIRED BY ONE of his mother's specialties, marinated red cabbage, Chef de Cuisine Eddy Leroux, who hails from northern France near the Belgian border, bathes a julienne of red cabbage in raspberry lambic beer before braising it with apples and onions, a nod to traditional sweet but sharp Belgian fare. In contrast, the thick loin of ruby-rare venison is crusted with nutty oat flakes, pumpkin seeds, flaxseeds, and cocoa nibs, and supports three cubes of silky seared foie gras.

GRAIN-CRUSTED VENISON
LAMBIC-BRAISED RED CABBAGE, HONEYCRISP APPLES

Foie Gras

Half of a fresh grade A foie gras lobe
(the smaller section, about 10 ounces)

Honeycrisp Apple Cubes

2 Honeycrisp apples

1 teaspoon lemon juice

Salt and freshly ground white pepper

Lambic-Braised Red Cabbage

1 head red cabbage

1 (750-ml) bottle framboise
lambic beer

1 orange, 3 (1-inch) peels and juice

½ cup small-diced Honeycrisp apple,
reserved from above

3 tablespoons foie gras fat,
reserved from above

1 Vidalia onion, finely diced

1 pinch of chili flakes

1 cinnamon stick

3 tablespoons butter

Salt and freshly ground white pepper

Grain-Crusted Venison

3 tablespoons oat flakes

2 tablespoons pumpkin seeds

2 tablespoons cocoa nibs

2 tablespoons flaxseeds

2 tablespoons sunflower seeds

1½ pounds venison loin, trimmed
and cut into 4 portions

2 tablespoons flour

1 egg, beaten

To Finish

2 Lady apples

2 tablespoons apple mustard
(we recommend Thiercelin Green
Apple Mustard)

½ cup Venison Jus
(see Basic Meat Jus, page 370)

Raspberry vinegar
(we recommend Huilerie Beaujolaise)

1 tablespoon butter

2 tablespoons Clarified Butter
(page 377)

1 clove garlic, peeled

1 sprig thyme

Salt and freshly ground white pepper

12 Apple Skin Chips (page 372)

12 yellow celery leaves

2 tablespoons melted foie gras fat,
reserved from above

4 large sprigs chervil

For the Foie Gras

Cut the foie gras into twelve ¾-inch cubes; wrap tightly and reserve, chilled. Roughly chop the remaining trim, place in a small saucepan, and place over low heat. Cook, without coloring, until the fat has rendered, about 30 minutes. Strain through a fine-meshed sieve and reserve the fat, chilled.

For the Honeycrisp Apple Cubes

Preheat a steam oven or stovetop steamer. Peel at least twelve 3-inch strips from the apples and square off the edges; reserve for apple skin chips. Cut the apples into at least twelve ¾-inch cubes; cut ½ cup of the trim into small dice and reserve for the cabbage. Toss the apple cubes with the lemon juice and a pinch of salt and pepper and steam for 10 minutes, or until tender. Reserve, chilled.

For the Lambic-Braised Red Cabbage

Quarter the cabbage, remove the core, and slice the leaves into a thin julienne. Transfer to a large bowl and mix with the beer, orange peel, orange juice, and apple trim. Cover and marinate refrigerated overnight, or up to 24 hours.

Strain the cabbage, reserving the liquid. Heat the foie gras fat in a large heavy-bottomed saucepan or Dutch oven over medium-low heat and add the onion, chili flakes, and cinnamon stick. Cook, stirring, without coloring, for 10 minutes. Add the cabbage and cook, stirring occasionally, for another 10 minutes. Add the marinating liquid, bring to a boil, and cook at a light simmer, stirring occasionally, until the cabbage is tender and the liquid is reduced to a syrupy consistency, about 45 minutes. If needed, add spoonfuls of water if the liquid glazes before the cabbage is tender. Stir in the butter and adjust the seasoning with salt and pepper; reserve, warm.

For the Grain-Crusted Venison

In a shallow bowl, combine the oat flakes, pumpkin seeds, cocoa nibs, flaxseeds, and sunflower seeds. Lightly dust the top side of each venison portion with the flour, brush with the beaten egg, then dip into the grain crust mixture, pressing to adhere.

To Finish

Preheat the oven to 325°F. Rest the venison at room temperature for 15 minutes.

Slice the Lady apples into very thin half-moons into a small bowl and toss with the apple mustard.

Transfer the venison jus to a small saucepan over medium-low heat and bring to a simmer. Season to taste with raspberry vinegar.

In a large sauté pan over medium heat, melt the butter with the clarified butter until it foams. Place the venison portions crust side down in the pan and sear for 3 minutes, to brown the crust, while basting with the butter. Turn the venison over, add the garlic and thyme, and continue to sear over medium heat while basting the top, about 3 more minutes or until the venison is medium-rare, 130°F. If needed, transfer the pan to the oven to finish cooking.

Transfer the apple cubes to a small sauté pan with the reserved foie gras fat over medium heat and toss to heat through; adjust the seasoning.

Heat a medium sauté pan over high heat. Season the reserved foie gras cubes on all sides with salt and pepper and brown on all sides, about 10 seconds each.

For each serving, place a large spoonful of cabbage in the center of a warm deep dinner plate. Place a portion of venison on top and spoon venison jus around. Line the side of the dish with 3 apple cubes, 3 slices of mustard-coated Lady apple, 3 apple skin chips, and 3 yellow celery leaves. Drizzle a few drops of foie gras fat on the jus and top the venison with a sprig of chervil.

FIVE-SPICED PORCELET
BLACK TRUMPET MUSHROOMS, CRISPY CHICHARRONES

SERVES 8

ONCE AGAIN our trusted purveyors and their pristine products inspire our dishes. Nourished for four weeks with warm milk only and fortified porridge for the next four, the piglets of St-Canut Farm in Quebec offer an incomparable flavor and tenderness not only in the meat (we use loin, belly, and the chop here), but also in the skin. As a wink to South America, we fry the skin and make chicharrones, a wonderful, crisp contrast to the soft, velvety consistency of the meat.

FIVE-SPICED PORCELET
BLACK TRUMPET MUSHROOMS,
CRISPY CHICHARRONES

Suckling Pig Rack, Sirloin, and Belly

1 (11-bone) Frenched rib rack, 1 sirloin, and skin-on belly from a 45-pound suckling pig

Seasoning ratio per pound of sirloin and belly:

1¼ teaspoons (7 grams) salt

¼ teaspoon (1 gram) five-spice powder

¼ teaspoon (1 gram) white pepper

⅛ teaspoon (0.5 gram) piment d'Espelette

Chicharrones (makes extra)

Skin from the pork rack and sirloin, reserved from above

1 quart Chicken Stock (page 368), or water

2 sprigs thyme

2 cloves garlic, peeled and smashed

Salt and freshly ground white pepper

Canola oil for frying

Roasted and Powdered Black Trumpet Mushrooms

1 pound black trumpet mushrooms

2 tablespoons butter

1 sprig thyme

1 clove garlic, peeled

Salt and freshly ground white pepper

Crispy Potato Cylinders

Canola oil for frying

1 large russet potato, peeled

Salt

Fingerling and Purple Potatoes

8 fingerling potatoes

4 sprigs thyme

4 cloves garlic, peeled and smashed

Salt

8 golf ball–size Peruvian purple potatoes

1 cup (2 sticks) butter

Baby Leeks

Salt

8 baby leeks, rinsed well, cut into 4-inch batons from the stem end

Shallot Confit

½ cup minced shallot

3 tablespoons butter

1 tablespoon white balsamic vinegar

½ teaspoon salt

Gingered Five-Spice Pork Jus

1 teaspoon butter

1 tablespoon minced ginger

2 teaspoons five-spice powder

2 cups Pork Jus
(See Basic Meat Jus, page 370)

Chicken Stock (page 368), if needed

Salt and freshly ground white pepper

To Finish

Five-spice powder

Salt and freshly ground white pepper

Cracked black pepper

2 tablespoons olive oil

4 tablespoons butter

3 sprigs thyme

3 cloves garlic, peeled and smashed

4 small leeks, white and light green parts only, cut into small dice and rinsed

2 tablespoons Chicken Stock (page 368)

1 head frisée lettuce, trimmed, rinsed, and cut into bite-size pieces

Mustard Vinaigrette (page 376)

Fleur de sel

For the Suckling Pig Rack, Sirloin, and Belly

With an immersion circulator, preheat a water bath to 144°F.

Remove and reserve the skin from the rack and sirloin for chicharrones. Shave the fat from the top of the rib rack down to ¼-inch thickness and score it in a crosshatch pattern. Reserve the rack, chilled.

Weigh the sirloin meat and measure the needed amount of seasoning according to the ratio listed in the ingredients. Sprinkle the seasoning over all sides of the meat, transfer to a sous-vide bag, and vacuum-seal.

Weigh the belly and measure the needed amount of seasoning according to the ratio listed in the ingredients. Sprinkle the seasoning over all sides of the meat, transfer to a sous-vide bag, and vacuum-seal.

Submerge the bags of sirloin and belly in the prepared water bath and cook for 12 hours. Transfer the bags to a bowl of ice water until fully chilled through the center, then remove the contents from the bags. Cut the belly into at least 8 cubes. Reserve the belly and sirloin, chilled.

For the Chicharrones

Preheat the oven to 190°F. Trim the skin of any excess fat, cut it into large (about 5-inch) pieces, and transfer to a large saucepan with the stock (or water), thyme, garlic, and a sprinkle of salt and pepper. Simmer covered for 2 hours, or until the skin is very tender.

Strain the skin, pat dry with paper towels, and lay in a single layer on a parchment paper–lined tray. Bake in the oven for 8 hours, or until dry and crispy but not colored (you can dry the chicharrones at the same time as the black trumpet mushrooms; see below).

Fill one-third of a medium saucepan with canola oil and heat to 400°F. Fry the chicharrones (you will need to do this in batches) until puffed and crispy but not browned. Drain them onto a paper towel–lined tray, sprinkle with salt, break into bite-size pieces, and cool. Store in an airtight container.

For the Roasted and Powdered Black Trumpet Mushrooms

Preheat the oven to 190°F. To clean the mushrooms, submerge them in a bowl of cold water, leave for 2 minutes, strain from the top, and repeat until the water that settles at the bottom is clear. Strain and pat dry with a towel. Transfer half of the mushrooms to a parchment paper–lined baking sheet and bake in the oven for 8 hours, or until dry. Using a blender or spice grinder, grind the dried mushrooms to a fine powder, pass through a fine-meshed sieve, and reserve.

Brown the butter in a large sauté pan over medium-high heat. Add the thyme and garlic and heat until aromatic. Add the remaining mushrooms with a sprinkle of salt and pepper and sauté until they become tender, 3 to 4 minutes. Drain the fat from the mushrooms, discard the garlic and thyme, transfer the mushrooms to a cutting board, and finely chop. Reserve, chilled.

For the Crispy Potato Cylinders

Fill one-third of a medium saucepan with canola oil and heat to 275°F. Use a mandoline to cut a ⅛-inch-thick slice from the long side of the potato. Trim the slice into a 4 x 2½-inch rectangle. Sprinkle the slice lightly with salt to soften it. Lightly oil the exterior of a ¾-inch-diameter stainless steel tube (or cannoli form) and wrap the potato around it. Place this tube in the center of another, slightly larger stainless steel tube about 1 inch in diameter. Lower into the oil and fry for 4 to 5 minutes, until the potato is golden and crispy. Slide the potato onto a paper towel–lined tray and sprinkle with salt. Repeat to make at least 8 cylinders. Cool and store in an airtight container.

For the Fingerling and Purple Potatoes

Place the fingerling potatoes in a saucepan with 2 sprigs thyme, 2 cloves garlic, and a pinch of salt; cover with water. Simmer 15 minutes, or until tender. Strain, and while still warm, peel and discard the skins.

Cut the ends of the purple potatoes so they stand at a flat 1-inch height and use a 1½-inch-diameter ring cutter to punch a disc

out of each one. In a medium saucepan over medium-low heat, melt the butter with the remaining thyme, garlic, and ½ teaspoon salt. Submerge the potato discs in the butter and cook over medium heat (the butter should be 190°F) for 15 minutes, or until easily pierced with a cake tester. Add the fingerling potatoes to the saucepan and keep warm.

For the Baby Leeks

Bring a large saucepan of salted water to a boil and place a bowl of ice water on the side. Boil the leeks for 2 to 3 minutes, until tender. Chill in the ice water, drain, and reserve.

For the Shallot Confit

In a medium saucepan over low heat, combine all ingredients. Cook, stirring occasionally, for 20 minutes, or until the shallot is tender but not colored. Reserve, chilled.

For the Gingered Five-Spice Pork Jus

Melt the butter in a small saucepan over medium heat. Add the ginger and five-spice and cook, stirring, for 1 minute. Add the pork jus and simmer lightly for 20 minutes. Strain through a fine-meshed sieve and, if needed, thin the consistency with chicken stock. Season with salt and pepper and keep warm.

To Finish

Preheat the oven to 325°F. Remove the fingerling potatoes from the pan with the butter, lightly crush each with a fork, and season with five-spice, salt, and white pepper; keep warm.

Rest the pork rack at room temperature for 15 minutes. Season on all sides with salt and cracked black pepper. If desired, wrap the rack bones in aluminum foil to prevent browning. Heat the olive oil in a large heatproof sauté pan over medium heat. Sear the rack on all sides, using a spoon to continually baste the meat with the rendering fat. Once the rack begins to turn golden brown, turn, fat side down, and add 2 tablespoons of the butter, the thyme, and the garlic. Continue to baste for another 2 minutes, then transfer the pan to the oven. Roast until the fat is browned and crispy, basting every 2 minutes. Flip the rack and return to the oven for 3 more min-

utes, or until the meat reaches an internal temperature of 130°F. Remove from the pan and allow it to rest in a warm area for 10 minutes.

Meanwhile, warm a heatproof medium nonstick sauté pan over medium-high heat. Add the pork belly cubes in a single layer and sear on all sides until golden brown, about 4 minutes. Arrange the belly cubes skin side down and transfer to the oven for 4 minutes. Transfer the belly to a baking sheet, strain excess fat from the pan, glaze the belly with a couple of spoonfuls of the jus, and keep warm. Return the sauté pan to high heat, add the pork sirloin, and sear on both sides until golden brown, about 6 minutes total. Slice the sirloin into 8 square portions and keep warm.

Melt the remaining 2 tablespoons butter in a medium saucepan over medium heat and add the diced leeks. Cook for 1 minute, stirring, then add the stock. Simmer until the leeks are tender and the butter and stock have reduced to a glaze. Add the reserved shallot confit, baby leek batons, and chopped mushrooms, toss to heat through, and season with salt and white pepper.

Slice the rack into 8 equal-size portions, with 1 bone each (trim off extra bones as needed). In a small bowl, toss the frisée lettuce with the mustard vinaigrette and season with salt and pepper.

For each serving, place a crushed fingerling potato topped with a spoonful of diced leek on one side of a warm dinner plate. Place a piece of pork belly next to the potato and top the potato with a portion of rack; sprinkle the rack with fleur de sel. Slide a baby leek baton inside a crispy potato cylinder and place in the center of the plate. Place a piece of seared sirloin and a purple potato on the other side of the plate. Arrange some frisée and a few pieces of chicharrones on top of the sirloin and purple potato. Sprinkle a straight line of black trumpet powder between the rack and the rim of the plate and spoon a line of sauce onto the plate at a 90-degree angle to the powder.

DUO DE BOEUF
BONE MARROW–CRUSTED TARDIVO, SWEET POTATO DAUPHINE

SERVES 4

OF COURSE I WAS familiar with the short ribs of France, boiled in the iconic pot-au-feu and served with mustard for a typical Sunday lunch, but braised in sauce? Never. At Le Cirque, I started braising them in red wine and created a signature entrée in the form of a luscious melt-in-your-mouth texture, earthy and robust at the same time. This dish exemplifies the duality of my background: the countryside of my childhood contrasted with the refined, seasoned tenderloin of my now urban life.

At Daniel, this duo of beef, which changes slightly each season, became an instant classic, a reference for other chefs, and our preferred beef preparation.

DUO DE BOEUF
BONE MARROW–CRUSTED TARDIVO,
SWEET POTATO DAUPHINE

Seasoning Oil

1 teaspoon cracked black pepper
(we recommend Pierre Poivre)

1 teaspooon fleur de sel

1 tablespoon olive oil

**Shallot and Bone Marrow Crust
(makes extra)**

3 (2-inch-long) beef marrow bones,
soaked in ice water for at least 12 hours

½ cup (1 stick) butter

1 cup minced shallot

3 ounces Fine White Breadcrumbs
(page 373)

¼ teaspooon salt

⅛ teaspoon piment d'Espelette

⅛ teaspoon white pepper

Balsamic Braised Tardivo

2 heads radicchio di Treviso

2 tablespoons olive oil

Salt and freshly ground white pepper

¼ cup balsamic vinegar

¼ cup Chicken Stock (page 368)

Sweet Potato Puree

2 sweet potatoes
(about 1 pound peeled)

4 tablespoons butter

2 cups milk

Salt and freshly ground white pepper

Sweet Potato and Black Garlic Dauphine

1 large (about 12 ounces) russet potato

½ cup kosher salt

3 tablespoons butter

1¾ ounces sweet potato, cut into
small dice, reserved from above

¾ teaspoon salt

5 tablespoons flour

1 egg

Freshly ground white pepper

2 cloves black garlic, peeled
and halved lengthwise

To Finish

Canola oil for frying

4 servings Braised Short Ribs
(page 374)

1 pound whole filet mignon,
trimmed and tied with butcher's
twine at ½-inch intervals

Salt and cracked black pepper
(we recommend Pierre Poivre)

2 tablespoons olive oil

1 tablespoon butter

1 sprig thyme

1 clove garlic, peeled

1 ounce bresaola, cut into matchsticks

4 Crispy Shallot Rings (page 372)

4 parsley leaves

For the Seasoning Oil
Combine the ingredients in a small bowl
and set aside.

For the Shallot and Bone Marrow Crust
Using your thumbs or a small spoon, pop the
marrow out of the bones, pushing from the
narrow to the wider opening. Store the
marrow in ice water if not using immediately.

Melt 1 tablespoon of the butter in a small
sauté pan over low heat. Add the shallot and
cook, stirring occasionally, until soft but not
colored, about 10 minutes; add spoonfuls of
water as needed if the shallot sticks to the pan.

Pat dry and weigh 5 ounces of the marrow;
transfer to the bowl of a food processor fitted
with a blade with the remaining 7 tablespoons
butter and the shallot. Blend until smooth.
Stream in the breadcrumbs, salt, piment
d'Espelette, and pepper and pulse until well
combined. Remove the mixture and pack it
into a small container; cover and chill until
the butter is hard.

For the Balsamic Braised Tardivo
Heat a grill or cast-iron grill pan over high heat.
Trim four 1-inch tips from the radicchio and
reserve, chilled, for the garnish. Place the
remaining radicchio heads in a bowl and toss
with the olive oil; season with salt and pepper.
Grill until charred on all sides, about 4 minutes
total. Transfer to a small saucepan with the
vinegar and chicken stock. Bring to a simmer,
cover, and cook over low heat until the leaves
are tender, about 15 minutes. Transfer the
radicchio to a cutting board and simmer the
remaining liquid in a saucepan until reduced to
a glaze. Cut the radicchio into 4 approximately
1½-inch-wide x 1-inch-tall square portions.
Arrange the portions so that the longer leaves
are on top and tucked around the sides like a
packet. Transfer the packets to a baking sheet
lined with foil and coat with the reduced liquid.
Top each portion with a ⅛-inch-thick slice of
bone marrow crust. Cover and reserve, chilled.

For the Sweet Potato Puree
Cut 1¾ ounces of the sweet potato into a
small dice and reserve, submerged in water,
for the dauphine; cut the remaining into large
dice. In a large saucepan over medium heat,

brown the butter and add the large dice of sweet potatoes, the milk, and ½ teaspoon salt. Simmer for 30 to 35 minutes, until fork-tender. Using a slotted spoon, scoop the sweet potatoes into a blender, reserving the milk. Blend with enough of the milk to make a smooth, thick puree. Adjust the seasoning with salt and pepper; reserve, chilled.

For the Sweet Potato and Black Garlic Dauphine

Preheat the oven to 350°F. Wash the russet potato and pierce its skin several times with a fork. Make a bed of the kosher salt on an aluminum foil–lined baking sheet, place the potato on top, and transfer to the oven. In a small sauté pan, melt ½ tablespoon of the butter over low heat, add the reserved small-diced sweet potato, and cook, stirring, until tender, about 3 minutes; set aside.

After 45 minutes, begin making a pâte à choux: Combine the remaining 2½ tablespoons butter, ¼ cup water, and ¼ teaspoon of the salt in a small saucepan over high heat and bring to a simmer. Add the flour, reduce the heat to medium, and stir with a wooden spoon for 5 to 10 minutes, until the mixture begins to dry and form a film on the bottom of the pan. Remove from the heat and beat in the egg until well combined.

Cover and keep in a warm place until the potato is fork-tender, another 10 to 20 minutes. Cut the potato in half, scoop out the flesh, and pass through a food mill or ricer into a medium saucepan. Place over low heat and cook, stirring, for 2 minutes, to dry.

Set a medium bowl on a scale and combine 10½ ounces of the warm potato, 4 ounces of the warm pâte à choux, and the cooked small-diced sweet potato; season with the remaining ½ teaspoon salt and pepper to taste, and mix well. With the palms of your hands, form the dough into at least four 2-ounce, approximately 1¼-inch-wide x 1-inch-tall squares, and press a half of black garlic, cut side up, into the tops. Reserve, chilled.

To Finish

Preheat the oven to 325°F. Fill one-third of a medium saucepan with canola oil and heat to 350°F.

Place the short ribs in the oven and reheat gently, covered, occasionally basting the meat with the sauce until heated through, about 30 minutes.

Transfer the sweet potato puree to a medium saucepan over medium heat and stir until heated through.

Rest the filet mignon at room temperature for 15 minutes. Season on all sides with salt and cracked black pepper. Heat the olive oil in a large sauté pan over medium-high heat. Add the beef and sear on all sides until browned. Lower the heat to medium; add the butter, thyme, and garlic and continue to roast, while basting, until medium-rare (115°F). If needed, transfer to the oven to finish roasting for a few minutes. Allow it to rest for at least 5 minutes in a warm place before removing the string and slicing into 4 equal portions.

Remove the short ribs from the oven and reserve in a warm spot. Increase the oven temperature to broil. Broil the radicchio packets until the crust is crispy and golden brown.

Fry the pommes dauphine in the canola oil until golden brown, about 4 minutes. Drain onto a paper towel–lined tray and sprinkle with salt.

For each serving, place a spoonful of sweet potato puree on the bottom of a warm dinner plate and place a short rib on top. Top with a radicchio tip, 2 matchsticks of bresaola, a crispy shallot ring, and a leaf of parsley. Arrange 1 packet of crusted radicchio, 1 slice of filet mignon, and 1 sweet potato dauphine on the plate. Top the filet mignon with a streak of the seasoning oil. Spoon extra short rib sauce around.

VEAL KIDNEY À LA GRAISSE
MUSTARD SEEDS, BLACK RADISH, BUTTER LETTUCE

SERVES 6

I ENJOY TEASING our diners with dishes that they may not expect in a Michelin three-star restaurant, such as this kidney preparation. It is an homage to Alain Chapel, one of the pillars of starred nouvelle cuisine in the 1970s, who was known in culinary circles around the world for his simple but majestic dishes. Chapel was a champion of game and offal and was known for a fabulous rognon à la graisse. Roasted at high heat, the meat is protected by the fat, which doesn't melt but encases all the flavors. I feel that rognon or kidney calls for acidity and jazz, and I present it here with crushed pepper and mustard seeds. There's a real love affair between the French and their mustard!

"Veal kidneys (rognons) are an integral part of the cuisine lyonnaise. La Mère Brazier, the first woman to receive three Michelin stars, in 1933, and who once hired an apprentice named Paul Bocuse, was rumored to serve the best in the region."

VEAL KIDNEY À LA GRAISSE
MUSTARD SEEDS, BLACK RADISH,
BUTTER LETTUCE

Veal Kidneys

2 veal kidneys with fat attached
(approximately 3½ pounds each)

2 tablespoons crushed black pepper

2 tablespoons yellow mustard seeds,
soaked in water overnight

Salt and freshly ground white pepper

Black Radish

2 medium black radishes (about
2½ inches in diameter and
5 ounces each)

Lettuce Puree

Salt

2 heads Bibb lettuce

1 tablespoon grapeseed oil

2½ ounces finely diced onion

2 ounces peeled and diced
russet potato

Braised Lettuce Spheres

4 heads Bibb lettuce

1 tablespoon butter

2 tablespoons brunoised carrot

2 tablespoons brunoised celery

2 tablespoons brunoised onion

Salt and freshly ground white pepper

Peewee Potato Tempura

24 Peewee potatoes
(about 8 ounces total) or other
small variety, washed well

2 sprigs thyme

1 clove garlic, peeled

Salt and freshly ground white pepper

Canola oil for frying

Tempura Batter (page 374)

To Finish

1 cup Veal Jus
(see Basic Meat Jus, page 370)

1 tablespoon yellow mustard seeds,
soaked in water overnight

1 teaspoon Dijon mustard

Salt and freshly ground white pepper

3 tablespoons duck fat

2 tablespoons butter

3 tablespoons grainy mustard

For the Veal Kidneys

Pull off the layers of fat encasing each kidney.
Open both fat layers onto a flat surface lined
with parchment paper and cover with more
parchment paper. With a flat meat mallet,
pound the fat to make approximately ¼-inch-
thick sheets, being careful not to tear them.
Lift the parchment and sprinkle the fat on
both sides with the crushed black pepper and
mustard seeds. Gently press the seasoning
into the fat.

Peel any white membrane from the kidneys.
Use a paring knife to remove most of the large
veins and fat that extend through their seams,
being careful not to split them. Season the
kidneys on all sides with salt and white pepper
and wrap each in a sheet of fat, trimming away
excess with scissors. Secure the fat with
butcher's twine and reserve the kidneys,
chilled, for up to 1 day.

For the Black Radish

With a mandoline, slice at least 12 paper-
thin discs from the tops and bottoms of the
radishes, wrap in damp paper towels, and
reserve, chilled, for garnishing. Halve the
radishes and cut each half into 6 cubes;
reserve for roasting. Cut the remaining trim
into brunoise for the braised lettuce.

For the Lettuce Puree

Bring a large pot of salted water to a boil and
place a bowl of ice water on the side. Separate
the lettuce leaves and boil them for 20 seconds, or until tender. Strain and chill in the ice
water (reserve the boiling water and ice for
the braised lettuce). Heat the oil in a small
saucepan over medium-low heat and add the
onion and potato. Cook, stirring, without coloring, for 10 to 15 minutes, until very tender,
and set aside. Squeeze dry the lettuce and
transfer to a blender with the cooked potato
and onion. Puree, adding spoonfuls of water
if needed to make a smooth puree, then pass
through a fine-meshed sieve and chill over
ice. If needed, adjust the seasoning with salt;
reserve, chilled.

For the Braised Lettuce Spheres

Peel 3 of the largest leaves from each head of lettuce. Boil them for 10 seconds, then transfer to the ice water to chill, being careful not to tear. Pat dry and trim away the thick white stems.

Separate the remaining lettuce leaves and rinse them with cold running water. Dry in a salad spinner; pick 18 of the smallest yellow leaves and reserve them for garnish.

Melt the butter in a medium sauté pan over medium heat and add the carrot, celery, onion, and reserved brunoised black radish. Cook, stirring, until the onion is translucent. Add the remaining lettuce leaves and continue to cook, stirring, over medium heat until wilted and tender. Season with salt and pepper. Transfer everything to a cutting board and roughly chop. Divide into 12 equal mounds and chill.

Place a large square of plastic wrap on a flat surface and open a boiled lettuce leaf on top into a flat layer. Sprinkle it with salt and pepper and place a mound of braised lettuce in the center. Pull the edges of the plastic up to wrap the lettuce leaf around the filling and twist the plastic to form it into a tight sphere. Repeat to make 12 spheres. Reserve, chilled.

For the Peewee Potato Tempura

In a small saucepan, combine the potatoes, thyme, and garlic and cover with cold water. Season with salt and pepper and bring to a simmer. Cook for 15 minutes, or until the potatoes are easily pierced with a cake tester. Strain and, while still warm, peel the potatoes.

When ready to serve, fill one-third of a medium saucepan with canola oil and heat to 350°F. In small batches, coat the potatoes in tempura batter and fry until golden brown. Drain on paper towels and season with salt.

To Finish

Preheat the oven to 325°F. Rest the kidneys at room temperature for 15 minutes. Transfer the veal jus to a small saucepan and bring to a simmer. Add the mustard seeds and Dijon mustard. Reduce the heat to low, cover, and infuse for 15 minutes. If needed, adjust the seasoning with salt and pepper.

Transfer the lettuce puree to a small saucepan over medium heat and stir to heat through.

Heat the duck fat in a large, heavy-bottomed sauté pan over medium-high heat. Sear all sides of the kidneys until golden brown. Reduce the heat to medium and cook, while basting with the fat, 1 minute. Strain half of the fat and transfer the pan to the oven.

Roast the kidneys, turning and basting every 5 minutes, until they reach an internal temperature of 115°F, checking after 20 minutes. Remove the pan from the oven, cover with foil, and rest in a warm place until the internal temperature reaches 135°F.

Meanwhile, spoon approximately 2 tablespoons of the fat from the pan with the kidneys into a medium sauté pan and warm over high heat. Add the reserved radish cubes and sear on all sides until golden brown, about 3 minutes total. Reduce the heat to medium-low, add the butter, and season with salt and pepper. Continue to cook, stirring, until tender, about 8 more minutes.

Bring a medium saucepan of water to a simmer, remove from the heat, and immediately submerge the plastic-wrapped lettuce spheres for 3 minutes. Strain and carefully unwrap the spheres from the plastic.

Transfer the kidneys to a cutting board and trim and discard the strings and fat. Divide the kidneys into 6 portions by slicing along the natural seams, or slice them to desired thickness.

For each serving, place a portion of veal kidney in a large serving bowl, top with 2 lettuce spheres and 4 radish cubes, and cover with the jus. Arrange 4 pieces of potato tempura, 3 yellow lettuce leaves, 2 radish shavings, a few spoons of lettuce puree, and a few dots of grainy mustard on top.

DANIEL ON COOKING IT ALL

AS YOU BITE INTO A PUFFY LANGOUSTINE TAIL, A POINTY asparagus tip, or the perfect rectangle of sirloin, perhaps you wonder where the rest of the animal or vegetable went. At a restaurant like Daniel, we actually crave the rest of them, and we cook it all! The rest of the asparagus will nourish a light puree or perhaps a spring soup; and the heads of langoustines, together with their precious coral, will be cooked and squeezed into a creamy briny bisque.

Three lambs hang in the walk-in fridge today. Between the beautiful animals and the two stylish chops you will find on your plate, there are numerous steps, numerous uses, numerous dishes. Part of the lamb will be braised then shredded and perhaps stuffed into a barbajuan; another piece may become the basis of the fabulous meat stew we will serve at our family meal (130 staff members every day!); the bones and meaty trimmings will render a delicious jus, redolent of thyme, garlic, and rosemary. If you wonder what a young cook in whites is doing, running from Daniel to Café Boulud, our more casual restaurant a few streets away, he or she may be carrying some of our most tender lamb shank. While we keep the rack and loin at Daniel, the shoulder might go to Bar Boulud for its lamb tagine terrine. The leg can end up as gigot Provençal at DB Bistro Moderne, and some of the meat and fat could become the essential part of the fiery merguez at DBGB.

Each vegetable cutting, slicing, carving, dicing, and peeling creates more side dishes for our staff meals. And even the fish heads of our snappers, bass, or turbots are prized elements for the base of a delicious fish soup.

The most interesting scrap I ever tasted was in Collioure, the anchovy capital on the Mediterranean near Spain, where the prized fillets end up in olive oil jars, and I was served just the fried, crunchy bones sprinkled with salt, true head-to-tail delights!

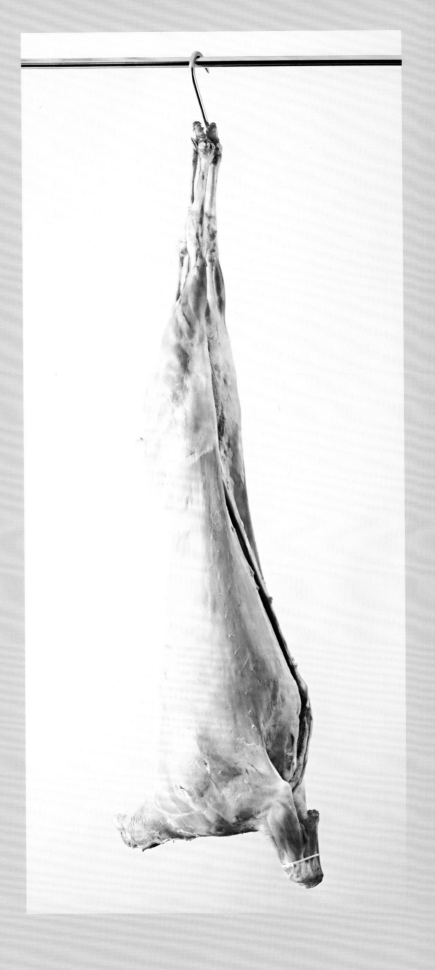

*"It would seem disingenuous to the animal not
to make the most of the whole beast: there
is a set of delights, textural and flavorsome,
which lie beyond the filet."*   —*Fergus Henderson*

"To me, life without veal stock, pork fat, sausage, organ meat, demi-glace, or even stinky cheese is a life not worth living."
—*Anthony Bourdain*

DANIEL ON CHEESE

THANKS TO OUR FABULOUS CHEESE STEWARD, PASCAL Vittu, the cheese cart at Daniel is a study in variety and excellence, but let's not detail what's on it quite yet. Before the cheese cart came the goats, forty maybe, and about twenty cows who frolicked in the barn at my parents' farm. In the summer, we enjoyed mostly goat cheese and sold the cow's milk, but in the winter, it was half goat's milk and half cow's milk cheeses.

Since each family member had different tastes, from the fromage frais our goats produced we made six to eight cheeses, from fresh to extra-dry. We counted the days, letting them age and, as we said, "flourish." My father liked it almost calcified; my sister would submerge the nuggets in olive oil and let them marinate with herbs. We ate cheese every day; it was an integral part of our seasonal way of life.

Perhaps you have heard about "la Mère Richard," the iconic Renée Richard and her daughter also named Renée, the unofficial exclusive cheese purveyor of the great chefs of Lyon. I still dream about her specialty, the soft and creamy St. Marcellin, and every time I am in Lyon, I make sure to visit her in Les Halles and buy a few dozen.

When I arrived in the United States, I found that few diners enjoyed a cheese course. The restaurateurs of the past generations believed, "Sommeliers are not necessary because wine sells itself. Oh, and cheese? Nobody is interested in eating cheese!" Boy, what an evolution! Over the course of the last twenty years, we have literally witnessed an explosion of passion for cheese, and hordes of world-class sommeliers.

At a Château-Latour event we held at the restaurant in 1998, Pascal Vittu, then one of our captains, met one of the best affineurs (the person who oversees the crucial aging and ripening process) in the world, Bernard Antony, who hails from Alsace, and still works exclusively with small farmers, monasteries, and artisanal cheesemakers. Vittu was inspired to help build the burgeoning cheese culture in New York, and from that moment on became our resident expert.

I may sound like a purist, but I like my cheese plain or with minimal garnish. The cheese course can be in harmony with a tasting menu, or for a splurge, why not sip a different wine with each cheese?

Here in New York, we take great care to source independent cheesemakers who have real talent and a solid philosophy about their craft, such as Mike and Carol Gingrich of Wisconsin's Uplands Cheese Company; and the mother-son team of Elizabeth MacAlister and Mark Gillman of Cato Corner Farm in Connecticut. These artisans help develop a true American cheese terroir. And now that I am also working in Canada, I am discovering a whole world of fabulous Canadian cheeses made in the old European style.

For a Frenchman, biting into a piece of cheese is a gustatory trip through the regions of France: Bleu d'Auvergne, Époisses from Bourgogne, Pont-l'Évêque from Normandy. My all-time favorites on the cart? A nutty, creamy Comté and a piece of bright, salty Mimolette.

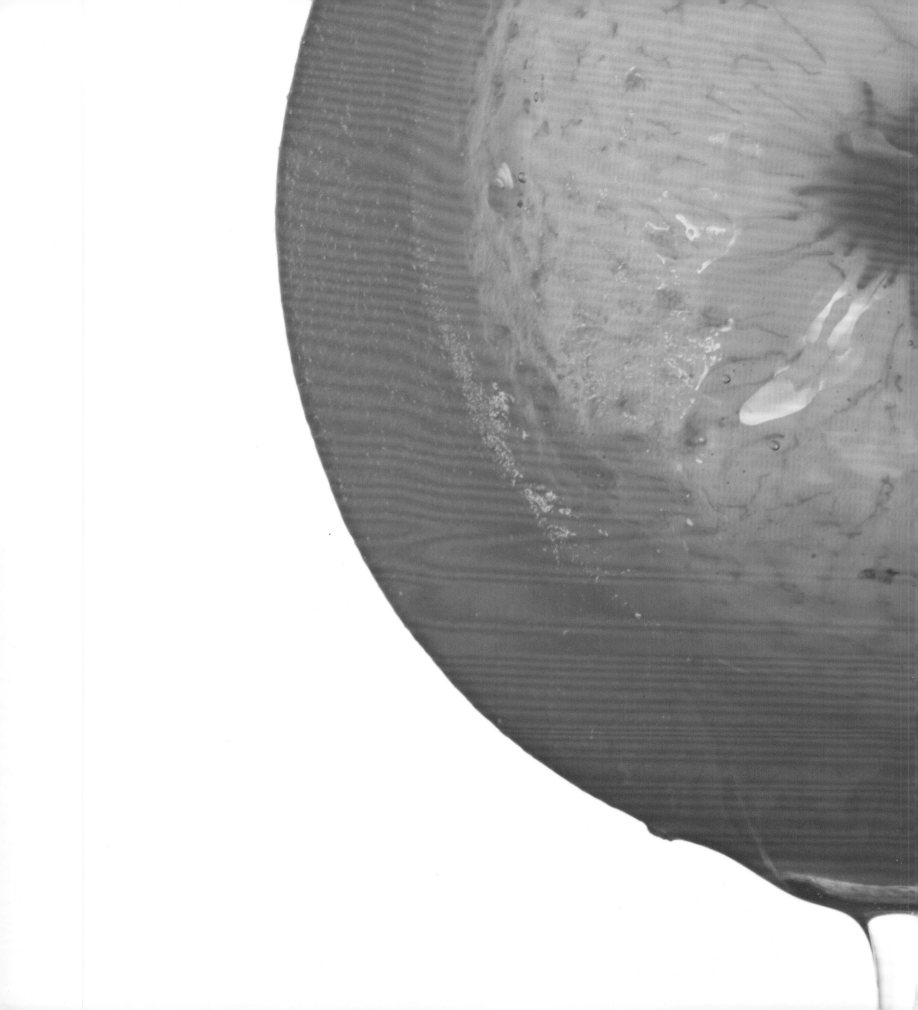

DESSERTS

POACHED RHUBARB
VANILLA PARFAIT, MICHEL GUÉRARD'S SAUTERNES-RHUBARB ICE CREAM

SERVES 6

IN EUROPE, rhubarb is often used in compotes and rustic tarts, but at Daniel it is found throughout both the sweet and the savory menus, as in our seared duck magret (page 159). Here the fibrous stems herald spring and bring a touch of acidity and tartness, but it's the sweetness of the Sauternes-rhubarb ice cream that rounds up the flavors. The Daniel gang who worked with Michel Guérard in Eugénie-les-Bains includes Sandro Micheli, Jean-François Bruel, and me. With this dessert we pay homage to Guérard, the master.

POACHED RHUBARB
VANILLA PARFAIT, MICHEL GUÉRARD'S SAUTERNES-RHUBARB ICE CREAM

Vanilla Sablé Breton
Vanilla Sablé Breton Dough
(page 378)

Vanilla Parfait
1 sheet gelatin
5 tablespoons sugar
4 egg yolks
⅔ cup heavy cream
1 Tahitian vanilla bean, split
and seeds scraped
1 cup mascarpone cheese

**Poached Rhubarb, Sauce, Foam,
and Gelée**
16 (15-inch-long x 1-inch-wide)
rhubarb stalks (about 2 pounds)
1 cup plus 7 tablespoons sugar
5 tablespoons butter
2 sheets gelatin
3 tablespoons Sauternes wine
1 scant teaspoon soy lecithin powder

**Michel Guérard's Sauternes-Rhubarb
Ice Cream**
14 (15-inch-long x 1-inch-wide)
rhubarb stalks (about 21 ounces)
1 Tahitian vanilla bean, split,
seeds scraped
½ cup plus 1½ tablespoons sugar
3½ tablespoons Sauternes wine
5 egg yolks
5 tablespoons butter

For the Vanilla Sablé Breton

Preheat the oven to 350°F. Unwrap the dough and place it on a sheet of parchment paper on a flat surface. Top with another sheet of parchment and roll into a ⅛-inch-thick sheet. Slide the dough with the paper onto a baking sheet and remove the top layer of paper. Bake for 8 minutes, or until the edges begin to color. Using a ruler, cut the hot dough into 1¼-inch squares. Return to the oven for 5 more minutes, or until the whole surface of the sablé is golden brown. Transfer the squares to a tray to cool and store, covered.

For the Vanilla Parfait

Soak the gelatin sheet in ice water for 10 minutes and squeeze dry. Line an 8½ x 4½-inch loaf pan with nonstick cooking spray and acetate paper.

In a medium heatproof bowl, whisk the sugar and egg yolks until smooth. In a medium saucepan, combine the cream and vanilla seeds and bring to a simmer. While whisking, gradually pour half of the hot cream into the egg yolk mixture. Gradually whisk the mixture back into the saucepan. Return the saucepan to the heat and cook, while whisking, until it reaches 185°F. Remove from the heat and stir in the gelatin until dissolved. Let the mixture cool to 104°F and whisk in the mascarpone. Pour the mixture through a fine-meshed sieve into the prepared loaf pan. Transfer to the freezer and chill until solid. Turn the parfait onto a cutting board, peel off the acetate paper, and cut into at least eighteen 1¼-inch squares. Reserve, frozen.

For the Poached Rhubarb, Sauce, Foam, and Gelée

Trim the tips and base of the rhubarb, peel, and reserve the skin and trim. Cut the stalks into thirds crosswise.

To make the poached rhubarb, combine the rhubarb trim and peels in a medium saucepan with 3¼ cups water. Simmer for 5 minutes, then remove from the heat, cover, and infuse for 30 minutes. Strain and discard the peels and trim from the liquid, add 1 cup plus 2 tablespoons of the sugar, and return to a simmer. Remove from the heat and chill the syrup.

Arrange the rhubarb sections in a single layer in a large sauté pan, pour in enough syrup to cover, and bring to a simmer. Cover and cook over low heat until tender, about 20 minutes. Cool in the cooking liquid.

Once cooled, strain the rhubarb, reserving the liquid for the gelée and foam. Place 2 lengths of rhubarb side by side on a cutting board and cut widthwise to form 1¼-inch squares; reserve the trim. Repeat to make 24 squares. Transfer the squares to a tray, wrap, and reserve, chilled.

For the sauce, weigh 5 ounces of the reserved cooked rhubarb trim and transfer to a small saucepan. Place over low heat and stir until heated through. Add the butter, stir until melted, and mix with a hand blender until smooth; pass through a fine-meshed sieve and reserve, chilled.

For the gelée, line an 8½ x 4½-inch loaf pan with nonstick cooking spray and acetate paper. Soak the gelatin sheets in ice water for 10 minutes and squeeze dry. Measure ⅓ cup of the reserved rhubarb syrup into a small saucepan with the Sauternes and the remaining 5 tablespoons of sugar and simmer until dissolved. Remove from the heat, stir in the gelatin until dissolved, and pour through a fine-meshed sieve into the prepared loaf pan. Refrigerate until set and cut into at least sixteen 1¼-inch squares.

For the foam, pour ½ cup of the remaining rhubarb syrup into a small saucepan. With a hand blender, puree in the soy lecithin; reserve at room temperature.

Michel Guérard's Sauternes-Rhubarb Ice Cream

With a vegetable juicer, juice the rhubarb and pass through a fine-meshed sieve. Measure 1 cup plus 1 tablespoon juice into a small saucepan with the vanilla seeds, sugar, and Sauternes. Simmer until the sugar is dissolved, remove from the heat, and cool to 158°F. In a medium heatproof bowl, whip the egg yolks until smooth. While whisking, gradually pour half of the hot rhubarb syrup into the egg yolks. Gradually whisk the mixture back into the saucepan. With a hand blender, puree in the butter. Return the pan to medium

heat and whisk until it reaches 185°F. Pass through a fine-meshed sieve into a bowl set over ice and stir until well chilled. Spin in an ice cream machine according to the manufacturer's instructions.

To Finish

Stack the vanilla parfait on top of the sablé breton squares and place a square of poached rhubarb on the parfait. Position the head of a hand blender just below the surface of the rhubarb foam liquid and blend to produce a light foam.

For each serving, set 3 rhubarb stacks on a chilled dessert plate and top each with a spoonful of foam. Alternate 2 pieces of rhubarb gelée in between the stacks. Set a square of poached rhubarb in the center of the plate. Trace a line of rhubarb sauce on the other side of the plate. Top the rhubarb square with a scoop of ice cream.

WARM RUBY RED GRAPEFRUIT
CANDIED POMELO, BERGAMOT HONEY

SERVES 4

DURING THE WINTER, we are blessed with the most fragrant citrus. By baking the ruby red grapefruit, we bring a sweeter underlying tone to its natural bitterness, while bergamot honey adds a floral note. The segments are set on a smooth crème fraîche parfait and a moist and fruity mirliton biscuit. Pomelo rinds are candied slowly in the traditional method and bring a variation of tanginess. Use extra candied rinds to make other treats, such as dipped in chocolate, rolled in sugar, or mixed into cakes.

Slow-Candied Pomelo Rind (makes extra/4-day process)

2 pomelos

12 cups sugar

3 tablespoons corn syrup

Earl Grey Ice Cream

2½ cups milk

1 cup heavy cream

6 tablespoons loose-leaf Earl Grey tea

½ cup plus 3 tablespoons sugar

8 egg yolks

Biscuit Mirliton

1 tablespoon bergamot honey (we recommend Solmielato), warmed

4 eggs

5 egg yolks

Zest from ½ grapefruit

1 Tahitian vanilla bean, split and seeds scraped

1 cup plus 2 tablespoons almond flour

¾ cup sugar

2 tablespoons flan powder (or substitute 1 tablespoon flour and 1 tablespoon cornstarch)

Croustillant Tuile (makes extra)

Croustillant Tuile Powder (page 379)

Bergamot Crème Fraîche Parfait

1 sheet gelatin

¾ cup heavy cream

5 tablespoons sugar

3 egg yolks

1 cup crème fraîche

⅓ teaspoon bergamot extract

Baked Grapefruit

3 ruby red grapefruits, peeled and cut into supremes

6 tablespoons bergamot honey, warmed

Crunchy Grapefruit Supremes

2 cups isomalt

1 ruby red grapefruit, peeled, cut into supremes, and patted with a paper towel

For the Slow-Candied Pomelo Rind

Cut the pomelos in half, squeeze and reserve the juice, and carve out the flesh from the interior with a spoon, taking care to not puncture the rind.

Place the rind in a medium saucepan, cover with cold water, and simmer for 5 minutes. Strain and repeat 4 more times. Strain the water from the pan; pour in the reserved juice, 1½ quarts of water, and 7½ cups of the sugar; simmer until the sugar is dissolved.

Remove from the heat, cover, and rest at room temperature overnight, making sure the rinds are submerged. For each of the next 2 days, add another 1½ cups sugar, simmer until dissolved, and cover again. On the third day, add the corn syrup with the 1½ cups remaining sugar and simmer until dissolved. Reserve the rinds in the liquid, refrigerated, for up to 1 month. Strain one-half of a rind and cut into bite-size slices before serving.

For the Earl Grey Ice Cream

In a medium saucepan, bring the milk and heavy cream to a simmer; remove from the heat, add the tea, cover, and infuse for 3 minutes. Strain and discard the tea. Return the liquid to medium heat. In a medium heatproof bowl, whip the sugar and yolks until smooth. While whisking, gradually pour half of the hot cream into the egg yolk mixture. Gradually whisk the mixture back into the saucepan. Return the pan to medium heat and cook, while whisking, until the mixture reaches 185°F. Remove from the heat and pass through a fine-meshed sieve into a bowl set over ice. Stir until well chilled and spin in an ice cream machine according to the manufacturer's instructions.

For the Biscuit Mirliton

Preheat the oven to 350°F. Line a rimmed 9½ x 13-inch baking sheet with a Silpat or parchment paper and coat with nonstick cooking spray. In a mixing bowl, whisk together the honey, eggs and yolks, zest, and vanilla seeds. In an electric mixer fitted with the paddle attachment, mix the almond flour, sugar, and flan powder on medium speed. Stream in the egg mixture and continue to mix for 2 minutes, stopping to scrape the

through a fine-meshed sieve and let cool to 104°F. Whisk in the crème fraîche and bergamot extract. Pour the mixture into the prepared loaf pan and freeze until solid, about 2 hours. With a 2¼-inch ring cutter, cut out at least 4 circles from the parfait. Transfer the circles to a plate and refrigerate to thaw, about 30 minutes.

For the Baked Grapefruit

Preheat the oven to 350°F. Arrange the grapefruit supremes in a single layer in a nonreactive baking pan. Drizzle the honey over the top and bake for 10 minutes. Remove the pan from the oven, drain the juice into a small saucepan; cover the grapefruit and keep warm. Bring the juice to a simmer and reduce to a syrupy texture; reserve, kept warm, for sauce.

For the Crunchy Grapefruit Supremes

In a small saucepan, heat the isomalt to 340°F, remove from the heat, and cool to 285°F. With a chocolate fork (or regular fork), pierce a grapefruit supreme and dip it into the sugar. Transfer to a tray lined with a Silpat. Repeat with the remaining segments. Rest the segments at room temperature for 5 minutes but no longer than 30 minutes before serving.

To Finish

For each serving, top a piece of mirliton biscuit with a tuile, a portion of parfait, another tuile, and 5 to 6 segments of baked grapefruit. Top with a few slices of candied pomelo rind. Alongside the biscuit, scoop a spoonful of ice cream onto another piece of pomelo rind. Arrange 2 crunchy grapefruit supremes and 2 slices of pomelo rind, and dot the sauce on the plate.

bowl with a rubber spatula halfway through.

Pour the batter into the prepared baking sheet, spread into a flat layer with an offset spatula, and bake for 14 minutes, or until golden brown. Remove from the oven, turn the cake out onto a cooling rack, and turn off the oven. Once cooled, cut 4 circles from the biscuit with a 2¼-inch ring cutter. Store in an airtight container until ready to use. Return the biscuit trim to the warm oven until dried, about 30 minutes. Cool, and transfer the trim to a food processor. Pulse into fine crumbs and reserve for the croustillant tuile powder.

For the Croustillant Tuile

Preheat the oven to 350°F. Line a baking sheet with a Silpat. Sift half of the powder over the prepared baking sheet in an even layer. Bake for 3 minutes, or until the sugar is melted. Remove from the oven, cover with a sheet of parchment paper, and carefully flip the Silpat onto a flat surface. Peel off the Silpat and, with a 2¼-inch ring cutter, cut at

least 8 discs from the sugar. While still warm, lift the discs off the parchment with an offset spatula and transfer to a flat tray. If the sugar becomes too brittle when cut or lifted, slide the parchment back onto the baking sheet and place in the oven for 30 seconds to soften. Cool the tuiles at room temperature and store in an airtight container.

For the Bergamot Crème Fraîche Parfait

Line an 8½ x 4½-inch loaf pan with nonstick cooking spray and acetate paper. Soak the gelatin sheet in ice water for 10 minutes; squeeze dry. In a medium saucepan, bring the cream to a simmer. Meanwhile, in a medium heatproof bowl, whip the sugar and yolks until smooth. While whisking, gradually pour half of the hot cream into the egg yolk mixture. Gradually whisk the mixture back into the saucepan. Return the saucepan to the heat and cook, while whisking, until it reaches 185°F. Remove from the heat and stir in the gelatin until dissolved. Pass the mixture

SLOW-BAKED APPLE MILLE-FEUILLE
CONFIT HONEYCRISP ICE CREAM

SERVES 4

THE UPSIDE-DOWN tarte tatin is as emblematic to the French as apple pie is to Americans. Many variations have evolved from this classic, but what remains as the most important factors are the choice of apple and the degree of darkness of the caramel. For this rendition, we cook New York's Hudson Valley Honeycrisp and serve alongside the tart raw Granny Smith. A crunchy Breton shortbread supports the apple mille-feuille, with paper-thin layers of apple confit topped with beads of Calvados cream.

Vanilla Sablé Breton

Vanilla Sablé Breton Dough (page 378)

Croustillant Tuile (makes extra)

Croustillant Tuile Powder (page 379)

Baked Apple Confit

1½ cups sugar

8 Honeycrisp apples

Confit Honeycrisp Ice Cream

3 egg yolks

3 tablespoons sugar

⅔ cup milk

¼ cup plus 1 teaspoon heavy cream

8 ounces baked apple confit trim, reserved from above

Calvados Cream

2 tablespoons mascarpone cheese

3 tablespoons powdered sugar

¾ cup heavy cream

2 tablespoons calvados

Green Apple Sauce

2 Granny Smith apples

1 teaspoon lemon juice

½ teaspoon xanthan gum

To Finish

1 Granny Smith apple

4 rings Pulled Sugar (page 379), optional

For the Vanilla Sablé Breton

Preheat the oven to 350°F. Unwrap the dough and place it on a sheet of parchment paper on a flat surface. Top with another sheet of parchment and roll into a ¼-inch-thick rectangular sheet. Slide the dough with the paper onto a baking sheet and remove the top layer of paper. Bake for 8 minutes, or until the edges begin to color. Using the aid of a ruler, cut the hot dough into at least four 3½ x ¾-inch rectangles. Return to the oven for 5 more minutes, or until the whole surface

of the sablé is golden brown; turn off the oven. Remove the sablé and transfer the rectangles to a rack to cool to room temperature; store them in an airtight container. Return the sablé breton trim to the warm oven until dried, about 30 minutes. Cool, and transfer the trim to a food processor. Pulse into fine crumbs; reserve for the croustillant tuile.

For the Croustillant Tuile

Preheat the oven to 350°F. Line a rimmed 18 x 13-inch baking sheet with a Silpat. Sift half of the powder over the baking sheet in an even layer. Bake for 3 minutes, or until the sugar is melted. Remove from the oven, cover with a sheet of parchment paper, and carefully flip the Silpat onto a flat surface. Peel off the Silpat, and with the aid of a ruler, cut the sugar into 4 triangles that are 3½ inches long and have a base of ¾ inch. Lift the triangles with an offset spatula and transfer to a flat tray. If the sugar becomes too brittle when cut or lifted, slide the parchment back onto the baking sheet and place in the oven for 30 seconds to soften. Cool the tuiles at room temperature and store in an airtight container.

For the Baked Apple Confit

Preheat the oven to 350°F. Line a baking sheet with parchment paper or a Silpat. Line an 8½ x 4½-inch loaf pan with nonstick cooking spray.

Put half the sugar in a large, heavy-bottomed saucepan over medium heat. Melt until golden brown, stirring occasionally. Add the remaining sugar and continue to heat to a dark caramel, 340°F. Pour onto the prepared baking sheet and cool at room temperature until hardened, about 3 hours. With a blunt object, crack the hardened sugar into small pieces and transfer to a food processor. Pulse into a fine powder and shake through a fine-meshed sieve. Store in an airtight container; use as soon as possible to prevent clumping.

Peel the apples and, using a Japanese Ciba Peel S turning slicer or a mandoline, cut into thin slices one at a time. Line the bottom of the prepared loaf pan with a single layer of apple slices, trimming the edges as needed, and use a fine-meshed sieve to dust the top with an even layer of caramel powder. Repeat the

process until all of the apples have been layered.

Cover the loaf pan with aluminum foil and bake for 1½ hours, or until the apples are dark caramel in color and tender when pierced with a cake tester. Remove from the oven and cool at room temperature. Freeze in the mold overnight and cut into four 3½ x ¾-inch rectangles; reserve the trim for the ice cream.

For the Confit Honeycrisp Ice Cream

In a heatproof bowl, whisk the yolks and sugar until smooth. In a medium saucepan, bring the milk and cream to a simmer. While whisking, gradually pour half of the hot cream into the egg yolk mixture. Gradually whisk the mixture back into the saucepan. Return the pan to medium heat and cook, while whisking, until it reaches 185°F. Remove from the heat and transfer the mixture to a blender with the reserved apple trim. Puree until smooth and strain through a fine-meshed sieve into a bowl set over ice; stir until well chilled. Spin in an ice cream machine according to the manufacturer's instructions.

For the Calvados Cream

Up to 30 minutes before serving, in the bowl of an electric mixer fitted with a whisk, whip the mascarpone and powdered sugar until smooth. Stream in the cream while whisking on high speed to medium peaks. Add the calvados and transfer the cream to a piping bag fitted with a small tip; keep chilled.

For the Green Apple Sauce

Core and quarter the apples and juice them with a vegetable juicer. Combine the juice with the lemon juice and xanthan gum and blend with a hand blender. Chill until ready to serve.

To Finish

Slice the apple into very thin half-moons.

For each serving, set a rectangle of apple confit on a sablé breton. Pipe the calvados cream on top in a zigzag pattern. Top with a croustillant tuile and transfer to a dessert plate, inside of a sugar ring set upright (if using). Garnish the plate with dots of green apple sauce topped with fresh sliced apple and a scoop of ice cream set on top of an apple slice to the side.

SWEET BING CHERRIES
KIRSCH CHANTILLY, SICILIAN PISTACHIO ICE CREAM

SERVES 8

IN MY MIND, it is impossible to imagine a real cherry dessert without drops of Kirsch. Whether from the Black Forest of Germany, the valleys of Switzerland, or the orchards of Alsace, the clear liquor always creates a sweet whiff. A pistachio dacquoise biscuit supports a crown of poached bing cherries under a spiraling disc made of Kirsch chantilly and mascarpone. And on top? A cherry, of course!

SWEET BING CHERRIES
KIRSCH CHANTILLY, SICILIAN PISTACHIO ICE CREAM

Vanilla Poached Cherries

1 pound fresh Bing cherries

1¼ cups sugar

1 Tahitian vanilla bean, split and seeds scraped

Sicilian Pistachio Ice Cream (makes about 1 quart)

2 cups Sicilian pistachios

2 cups milk

½ cup plus 2 tablespoons heavy cream

2 tablespoons trimoline

½ teaspoon ice cream stabilizer, optional

4½ tablespoons milk powder

¼ cup sugar

4 egg yolks

Pistachio Dacquoise

5 egg whites

¾ cup powdered sugar

1½ tablespoons pistachio paste (we recommend Trablit), or pistachio butter, at room temperature

1 cup pistachio flour

¼ cup sugar

Croustillant Tuile (makes extra)

Croustillant Tuile Powder (page 379)

Sour Cherry Sauce

1 pint (4 ounces) halved, pitted sour morello cherries

3 tablespoons sugar

⅓ teaspoon apple pectin

Kirsch Cream

¼ cup powdered sugar

½ cup mascarpone cheese

1⅓ cups heavy cream

2 tablespoons Kirschwasser

To Finish

Caramelized Pistachios (see Caramelized Nuts, page 379)

For the Vanilla Poached Cherries

Pick 8 cherries for garnish, leave the stems attached, and scoop the pits from their bottoms; set aside. Stem, halve, and pit the remaining cherries and place in a heatproof container. In a medium saucepan, combine 2 cups of water, the sugar, and the vanilla seeds and pod and bring to a simmer. Pour over the top of the cherries, cool to room temperature, cover, and refrigerate for 2 days.

For the Sicilian Pistachio Ice Cream

Place the pistachios in a dry medium saucepan and set over medium heat. Cook, stirring, to toast, for 5 minutes, being careful not to burn. Remove the pan from the heat to cool slightly, then add the milk and heavy cream; bring to a simmer. Transfer the mixture to a blender with the trimoline and stabilizer. Puree until smooth and return to the saucepan. In a heatproof bowl, whisk the milk powder, sugar, and egg yolks until smooth.

While whisking, gradually pour half of the hot cream mixture into the egg yolk mixture. Gradually whisk the mixture back into the saucepan. Return the pan to medium heat and cook, while whisking, until it reaches 185°F. Remove from the heat and pass through a fine-meshed sieve into a bowl set over ice. Stir until well chilled and spin in an ice cream machine according to the manufacturer's instructions.

For the Pistachio Dacquoise

Preheat the oven to 350°F. Line a rimmed 9½ x 13-inch baking sheet with a Silpat or parchment paper and nonstick cooking spray.

In an electric stand mixer fitted with a whisk, whip the egg whites with one-third of the powdered sugar until frothy. Continue whipping at medium speed while gradually streaming in the remaining powdered sugar until the whites reach soft peaks.

With a rubber spatula, fold the pistachio paste (or butter) into the whites until no streaks remain. Sift the pistachio flour and sugar into the mixture in 3 additions, folding with a spatula each time until well combined but still fluffy. Spread the batter onto the prepared baking sheet in an even layer and bake for 14 minutes, or until the edges turn dark brown and the center is springy. Turn off the oven, cool at room temperature, and flip onto a cutting board. Remove the parchment or Silpat, and use a 2½-inch ring cutter to cut out 8 discs and eight 1-inch ovals from the dacquoise. Return the dacquoise trim to the warm oven until dried, about 30 minutes. Cool, then transfer the trim to a food processor. Pulse into fine crumbs; reserve for croustillant tuile powder.

Croustillant Tuile
Preheat the oven to 350°F. Line a baking sheet with a Silpat. Sift half of the powder over the prepared baking sheet in an even layer. Bake for 3 minutes, or until the sugar is melted. Remove from the oven, cover with a sheet of parchment paper, and carefully flip the Silpat onto a flat surface. Peel off the Silpat, and with a 2½-inch ring cutter, cut at least 8 circles from the sugar. Lift the circles with an offset spatula and transfer to a flat tray. If the sugar becomes too brittle when cut or lifted, slide the parchment back onto the baking sheet and place in the oven for 30 seconds to soften. Cool the tuiles at room temperature and store in an airtight container.

For the Sour Cherry Sauce
Fill one-third of a large saucepan with water and bring to a simmer. In a large heatproof bowl, toss the cherries with half of the sugar, cover with plastic wrap, and set over the pan of simmering water. Heat the cherries until they release their juices, about 1 hour. In a small bowl, combine the remaining sugar and the pectin and stir into the juicy cherries. Heat for 5 minutes, transfer the mixture to a blender, and puree until smooth. Pass through a fine-meshed sieve, chill, and transfer to a piping bag or squeeze bottle.

For the Kirsch Cream
Up to 30 minutes before serving, in the bowl of an electric mixer fitted with a whisk, whip the powdered sugar and mascarpone until smooth. Stream in the heavy cream, continuing to whip on high to reach stiff peaks. Whisk in the Kirschwasser and transfer to a piping bag fitted with a St. Honoré tip (Ateco #880 tip). Store chilled.

To Finish
For each serving, set a croustillant tuile on top of a dacquoise round. Pipe about 2 tablespoons of cream onto the tuile and stick about 16 cherry halves in a tightly coiled spiral on top. Pipe more cream onto the cherries in a circular pattern and top with a cherry with a stem and a few caramelized pistachios. Transfer to a chilled dessert plate and pipe the sour cherry sauce onto the plate in a decorative fashion. Set a small piece of pistachio dacquoise on the side and top with a scoop of ice cream.

RASPBERRY AND YUZU VERRINE
SWIRLED SORBET

SERVES 8

OUR OWN glorified sundae at Restaurant Daniel is a dessert in a "verrine," a thin glass jar or cup, where transparency has become part of the design. The vanilla panna cotta supports almond crumble and a swirl of yuzu and raspberry sorbet: a harmony of textures and colors. At DBGB Kitchen and Bar, we offer a more classic sundae, but no matter where we feature the dish, the combination of crispy, creamy, fluffy, and fruity elements always brings a smile to my face.

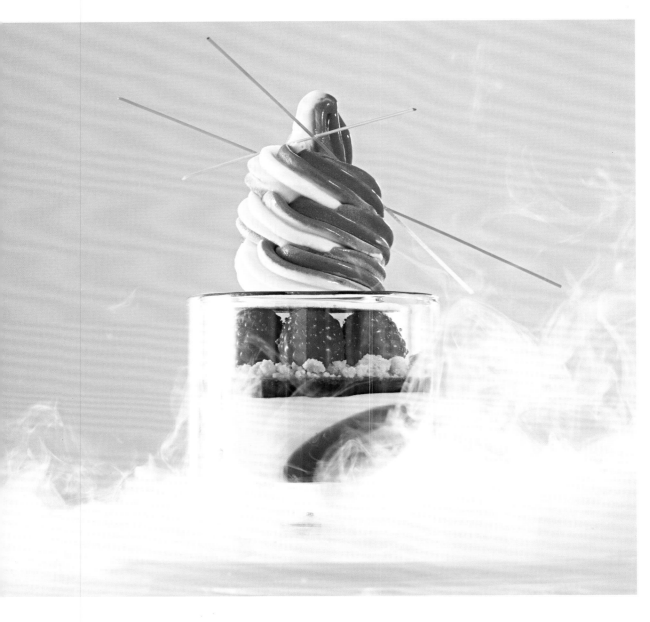

Raspberry Puree

5 pints fresh raspberries

¾ cup sugar

Crunchy Raspberry Meringue

5 egg whites

¾ cup sugar

¾ cup powdered sugar

3 tablespoons raspberry puree, reserved from above

Yuzu Sorbet

1 cup sugar

6 tablespoons glucose powder

2 cups yuzu juice (fresh, or we recommend bottled yuzu juice by Yakami Orchard)

Raspberry Sorbet

1 cup sugar

6 tablespoons glucose powder

2 cups raspberry puree, reserved from above

Raspberry Gelée

3 gelatin sheets

1½ cups raspberry juice, reserved from above

6 tablespoons sugar

Vanilla Panna Cotta

4 gelatin sheets

2 cups milk

1 Tahitian vanilla bean, split and seeds scraped

½ cup sugar

To Finish

Almond Crumble (page 378)

2 pints fresh raspberries, rinsed

24 (3½-inch) Sugar Sticks (see Pulled Sugar, page 379), optional

For the Raspberry Puree

Fill one-third of a medium saucepan with water and bring to a simmer. In a heatproof bowl, toss the raspberries with the sugar, cover with plastic wrap, and place over the simmering water. Heat the raspberries until they release their juices, about 1 hour. Line a fine-meshed sieve with cheesecloth, place over a bowl, and pour in the raspberry mixture. Strain well (do not press the berries or the juice will turn cloudy). Measure 1½ cups juice, chill, and reserve for the gelée.

Pour the strained berries with any remaining juice into a bowl and puree with a hand blender on its lowest setting to avoid chopping the bitter seeds. Pass the puree through a fine-meshed sieve and reserve for the sorbet and meringue.

For the Crunchy Raspberry Meringue

Preheat the oven to 200°F. Line 2 large 13 x 18-inch baking sheets with Silpats.

In the bowl of an electric mixer fitted with a whisk, whip the egg whites on medium speed until frothy, about 30 seconds. While continuing to whip, add one-third of the granulated sugar. Whip for 30 more seconds, add the remaining granulated sugar, and continue whipping until they reach soft peaks. With a rubber spatula, fold in the powdered sugar in 3 additions until well combined. Fold in the raspberry puree until no streaks remain. With a circular flat plastic stencil slightly smaller than the diameter of the sundae or verrine glasses you will use and a small offset spatula, spread the mixture evenly onto the Silpat. Repeat to make 10 circles per tray. Bake for 3 hours, or until the meringues are crisp. While still warm, loosen the meringues from the Silpat with an offset spatula (this makes extra since they are fragile). Finish cooling, and store in an airtight container for up to 3 days.

For the Yuzu Sorbet

In a medium saucepan, combine 1 cup water, the sugar, and the glucose powder and bring to a simmer. Pour into a bowl set over ice and stir until well chilled. Add the yuzu juice and pass through a fine-meshed sieve. Spin in an ice cream machine according to the manufacturer's instructions. Transfer to 2 disposable pastry bags and freeze.

For the Raspberry Sorbet

In a medium saucepan, combine 1 cup water, the sugar, and the glucose powder and bring to a simmer. Pour into a bowl set over ice and stir until well chilled. Add the raspberry puree and pass through a fine-meshed sieve. Spin in an ice cream machine according to the manufacturer's instructions. Transfer to 2 disposable pastry bags and freeze.

For the Raspberry Gelée

Soak the gelatin sheets in ice water for 10 minutes; squeeze dry. In a small saucepan, combine the raspberry juice and sugar, and simmer until the sugar is dissolved. Remove from the heat and stir in the gelatin. Pass through a fine-meshed sieve. Divide half of the gelée into the bottom of 8 sundae glasses or verrines and refrigerate until set, about 2 hours. Reserve the remaining gelée for topping the panna cotta.

Vanilla Panna Cotta

Soak the gelatin sheets in ice water for 10 minutes; squeeze dry. In a small saucepan, combine the milk, vanilla seeds, and sugar. Simmer until the sugar is dissolved, remove from the heat, and stir in the gelatin. Strain through a fine-meshed sieve and allow to cool to about 86°F. Pour approximately ¼ cup into each glass with the gelée. Refrigerate until set, about 2 hours.

To Finish

In a small saucepan, warm the remaining raspberry gelée, then cool at room temperature to about 86°F. Divide the mixture into the glasses with the panna cotta and refrigerate until set, about 1 hour.

Place a large star tip into a pastry bag. Cut a large tip from one each of the yuzu and the raspberry sorbet pastry bags and slide them side by side into the bag with the star tip so that both flavors come out of the tip when piped.

For each serving, sprinkle a layer of almond crumble onto the gelée and stand about 6 raspberries on top. Set a meringue disc on top of the raspberries and, if needed, press to make it level. Pipe a swirl of sorbets on the meringue and, if using, garnish with 3 sugar sticks.

BLACKBERRY AND CRÈME FRAÎCHE VACHERIN

SERVES 6

EVERY SEASON we feature a different kind of vacherin, one of my childhood favorite desserts. I see it as almost a cross between a pavlova and an ice cream sandwich, with less whipped cream and more sorbet, but always with meringue for the crunch. This particular one, with blackberry-infused meringue and crème fraîche–blackberry swirled sorbet, may be my all-time favorite. Clouds of crème fraîche coiffe a thin disc made of meringue, while blackberry pearls float on a bed of panna cotta.

Blackberry Puree (makes 2 cups)

3½ pounds (about 5 pints) fresh blackberries

¾ cup sugar

Crunchy Blackberry Meringue

5 egg whites

¾ cup sugar

¾ cup powdered sugar

3 tablespoons blackberry puree, reserved from above

Blackberry Sorbet

5½ tablespoons sugar

1 tablespoon glucose powder

2 cups blackberry puree, reserved from above

Crème Fraîche Sorbet

½ cup sugar

3 tablespoons glucose powder

7 tablespoons crème fraîche

3 tablespoons plain yogurt

1 tablespoon plus 1 teaspoon lemon juice

Blackberry Pearls and Gelée

1½ sheets gelatin

5 tablespoons sugar

2 grams agar-agar powder

1½ cups blackberry juice, reserved from above

1 quart grapeseed oil, poured into a deep container and frozen overnight

Vanilla Panna Cotta

1 sheet gelatin

½ cup crème fraîche

1 Tahitian vanilla bean, split and seeds scraped

2 tablespoons sugar

Whipped Crème Fraîche

1½ cups crème fraîche

6 tablespoons powdered sugar

To Finish

18 blackberries

For the Blackberry Puree

Fill one-third of a medium saucepan with water and bring to a simmer. In a heatproof bowl, toss the berries with the sugar, cover with plastic wrap, and place over the simmering water. Heat the berries until they release their juices, about 1 hour. Line a fine-meshed sieve with cheesecloth, place over a bowl, and pour in the berry mixture. Strain well (do not press the berries or the juice will turn cloudy). Measure 1½ cups juice, chill, and reserve for the pearls and gelée.

Pour the strained berries with any remaining juice into a bowl and puree with a hand blender on its lowest setting; avoid chopping up the bitter seeds. Pass the puree through a fine-meshed sieve and reserve for the sorbet and meringue.

For the Crunchy Blackberry Meringue

Preheat the oven to 200°F. Line two 13 x 18-inch baking sheets with Silpats.

In the bowl of an electric mixer fitted with a whisk, whip the egg whites on medium speed until frothy, about 30 seconds. While continuing to whip, add one-third of the granulated sugar. Whip 30 more seconds, add the remaining granulated sugar, and continue whipping until soft peaks form. With a rubber spatula, fold in the powdered sugar in 3 additions until well combined. Fold in the blackberry puree until no streaks remain. Using a 2½-inch-diameter round plastic stencil and a small offset spatula, spread the mixture evenly onto the Silpat. Repeat to make 10 circles per tray.

Transfer the remaining meringue to a piping bag and cut a small hole at the tip. Pipe small dots of the meringue around the circles on the Silpats.

Bake for 3 hours, or until the meringues are crisp. While still warm, loosen the meringues from the Silpat with an offset spatula (this makes extra since they are fragile). Finish cooling, and store in an airtight container for up to 3 days.

For the Blackberry Sorbet

In a medium saucepan, combine 5 tablespoons water, the sugar, and the glucose powder. Bring to a simmer, then transfer to a bowl set over ice and stir until well chilled. Whisk in the blackberry puree. Pass through a fine-meshed sieve and spin in an ice cream machine according to the manufacturer's instructions.

For the Crème Fraîche Sorbet

In a medium saucepan, whisk to combine ¾ cup plus 1 tablespoon water, the sugar, and the glucose powder and bring to a simmer. Set aside to cool and whisk in the crème fraîche, yogurt, and lemon juice. Pass through a fine-meshed sieve into a bowl set over ice. Stir until well chilled and spin in an ice cream machine according to the manufacturer's instructions.

Assembling the Sorbets

For a swirling effect, stir each sorbet to reach soft-serve consistency. Fill a piping bag with alternating spoonfuls of each flavor. Pipe the sorbets into at least six 2½-inch-diameter and ¾-inch-tall metal ring molds, or muffin tins lined with plastic wrap. Flatten the surfaces with a small offset spatula. Freeze until solid.

For the Blackberry Pearls and Gelée

Soak the gelatin sheets in ice water for 10 minutes, then squeeze dry.

In a small bowl, mix the sugar with the agar-agar powder. In a small saucepan, bring the blackberry juice to a simmer, add the sugar mixture, and cook, while whisking, for 1 minute. Remove from the heat and stir in the gelatin. Pour enough of the mixture onto a flat, rimmed plate to reach about ⅛-inch thickness, and transfer to the refrigerator to set.

Transfer the remaining mixture to a squeeze bottle with a fine tip. Cool to room temperature. If the frozen grapeseed oil has coagulated, let it sit at room temperature just until it becomes liquid again, about 5 minutes. Squeeze the blackberry mixture from the bottle in droplets into the cold oil; they will form firm pearls as they sink into the oil. Work quickly so the oil doesn't get too warm (or the droplets won't set). Refrigerate for 20 minutes, then pour the oil through a fine-meshed sieve into a clean, dry container (the oil can be reused). Rinse the pearls in the sieve with cold running water. Store, chilled.

Cut the blackberry gelée into desired shapes; store, chilled.

For the Vanilla Panna Cotta

Soak the gelatin sheet in ice water for 10 minutes, then squeeze dry.

In a small saucepan, combine the crème fraîche, vanilla seeds, and sugar; bring to a simmer. Remove from the heat and stir in the gelatin until dissolved. Pass through a fine-meshed sieve and pour onto a flat, rimmed tray or baking dish to reach a thickness of approximately ¼ inch. Refrigerate until set, and cut into desired shapes. Store, chilled.

For the Whipped Crème Fraîche

Up to 1 hour before serving, whip the crème fraîche and sugar to stiff peaks. Transfer to a piping bag fitted with a large tip (Ateco #807 tip).

To Finish

For each serving, set a disc of meringue on a chilled dessert plate and top with a portion of sorbet. Top with another meringue disc and pipe dollops of crème fraîche cream on top. Sprinkle the top with meringue dots. Garnish around the vacherin with blackberry pearls, blackberry gelée, vanilla panna cotta, and 3 fresh blackberries.

APRICOT AND LAVENDER CLAFOUTIS
FRESH GREEN ALMONDS

SERVES 4

AS THE APRICOTS BAKE within this custardy tart, they release their luscious juices into the batter. In this preparation, we chose to make small individual clafoutis rather than the traditional family-sized treat to enjoy more of the buttery crust, the best part! Sweet almond milk ice cream finishes this delicate dessert, and edible lavender flowers dot the plate.

Almond Milk Ice Cream

8 egg yolks

½ cup plus 2 tablespoons sugar

2 cups unsweetened almond milk
(we recommend Pacific Brand Organic)

1 cup heavy cream

Clafoutis

6 tablespoons butter,
at room temperature

6¾ tablespoons powdered sugar

½ cup plus 2 tablespoons
almond flour

1 egg

4 egg yolks

7 tablespoons sugar

2 tablespoons flan powder
(or substitute 1 tablespoon flour
and 1 tablespoon cornstarch)

¾ cup milk

1 Tahitian vanilla bean,
split and seeds scraped

1 tablespoon dried lavender,
wrapped in cheesecloth and
secured with butcher's twine

1 apricot, skin on, pitted
and cut into 8 wedges

To Finish

20 fresh green almonds, halved
lengthwise

1 ounce fresh lavender

1 apricot, halved, pitted, and
cut into 12 thin slices

For the Almond Milk Ice Cream

In a medium heatproof bowl, whip the yolks and sugar until smooth. In a medium saucepan, bring the almond milk and heavy cream to a simmer. While whisking, gradually pour half of the hot milk into the egg yolk mixture. Gradually whisk the mixture back into the saucepan. Return the saucepan to the heat and cook slowly, while whisking, until it reaches 185°F. Strain into a bowl set over ice and stir until well chilled. Spin in an ice cream machine according to the manufacturer's instructions.

For the Clafoutis

In an electric stand mixer fitted with a whisk, whip the butter until creamy. Sift the powdered sugar and almond flour into the bowl and whip until well combined. Add the egg and whip until homogeneous. Transfer the batter to the refrigerator and chill overnight.

In a heatproof bowl, whip the yolks, granulated sugar, and flan powder until smooth. In a small saucepan, combine the milk and vanilla seeds and bring to a simmer; remove from the heat, add the lavender sachet, cover, and rest for 3 minutes. Remove the sachet, return to a simmer, and while whisking, gradually pour half of the hot milk into the egg yolk mixture. Gradually whisk the mixture back into the saucepan. Return the saucepan to medium heat while whisking. Bring to a simmer for about 1 minute, until thickened, to make a pastry cream. Transfer the mixture to a bowl, cover the surface with plastic wrap, and refrigerate until chilled.

Preheat the oven to 350°F. Spray the inside of eight 3-inch oval cake rings or other medium-size ring molds with nonstick cooking spray and line with a strip of parchment paper; arrange on top of a Silpat-lined baking sheet.

Alternately, butter 8 cupcake or muffin tins. In a large bowl using a rubber spatula, fold the almond batter and pastry cream together until no streaks remain. Spoon into the prepared molds until two-thirds full and nestle 1 wedge of apricot into each of their centers.

Bake for 15 minutes, or until the tops are golden brown.

To Finish

For each serving, arrange 2 clafoutis on a dessert plate and top each with an almond half and a lavender flower. Arrange 3 slices of apricot through the center of the plate and garnish them with 3 more almond halves and lavender flowers. Serve with the almond milk ice cream.

STRAWBERRY GRANITÉ ROSACE
SZECHUAN PEPPERCORN SORBET

SERVES 6

A CYLINDRICAL FAN made of thin slices of strawberries hides a crunchy almond crumble under a frozen strawberry granité. On the buttery sablé breton, strawberries find their place in an array of textures. A citrusy Szechuan pepper sorbet brings a lingering pleasant spice that balances the naturally sweet strawberries.

Vanilla Sablé Breton

Vanilla Sablé Breton Dough (page 378)

Strawberry Juice (makes 4 cups)

2½ pounds strawberries, cleaned, trimmed, and cut into thin slices

9½ tablespoons sugar

Strawberry Gelée

2½ sheets gelatin

¾ cup strawberry juice, reserved from above

6 tablespoons sugar

Strawberry Sauce

6 tablespoons plus 2 teaspoons sugar

⅓ teaspoon apple pectin

½ cup strawberry juice, reserved from above

Strawberry Granité

2 cups strawberry juice, reserved from above

6¼ tablespoons sugar

3 tablespoons lemon juice

Szechuan Pepper Sorbet (makes 1 quart)

¾ cup plus 2 tablespoons sugar

5½ tablespoons glucose powder

1 tablespoon Szechuan peppercorns

1¼ cups sour cream

3 tablespoons lemon juice

To Finish

6 (4-inch-long x 1-inch-wide) clear acetate strips, rolled and taped to form 2½-inch-diameter rings

24 large strawberries

Powdered sugar

Almond Crumble (page 378)

For the Vanilla Sablé Breton

Preheat the oven to 350°F. Unwrap the dough and place on a sheet of parchment paper. Top with another sheet of parchment and roll the dough into a ¼-inch-thick sheet. Transfer the dough to a baking sheet, remove the top sheet of parchment paper and, bake for 8 minutes. Remove from the oven and, using a ruler as an aid, cut the sablé while still hot into 3 x 1-inch rectangles. If desired, use a ¼-inch-diameter ring cutter to remove about 8 holes from the sablé rectangles in a free-form pattern.

Return to the oven for 8 minutes, or until the entire surface is golden brown. Cool at room temperature, then transfer the rectangles to an airtight container.

For the Strawberry Juice

Fill one-third of a large saucepan with water and bring to a simmer. In a large heatproof bowl, toss the strawberry slices with the sugar, cover with plastic wrap, and set over the simmering water. Heat until the strawberries release their juices, about 1 hour. Line a fine-meshed sieve with cheesecloth, place over a bowl, and pour in the strawberry mixture. Strain well (but do not press the berries or the juice will turn cloudy) at room temperature for 2 hours. Reserve the juice, chilled.

For the Strawberry Gelée

Soak the gelatin sheets in ice water for 10 minutes; squeeze dry. In a medium saucepan, whisk together the strawberry juice and sugar and simmer until dissolved. Remove from the heat and stir in the gelatin until dissolved. Pour onto a rimmed plate to reach ⅛-inch thickness. Refrigerate until the gelée is set, about 1 hour. Use a ¼-inch ring cutter to cut discs from the gelatin, lift them with an offset spatula, transfer to a plate, and keep chilled.

For the Strawberry Sauce

In a small bowl, mix the sugar and pectin. In a small saucepan, bring the strawberry juice to a simmer. Whisk in the sugar mixture and simmer, continuing to whisk for 2 minutes. Transfer to a bowl set over ice and stir to chill.

For the Strawberry Granité

In a small saucepan, simmer the strawberry juice with the sugar until dissolved. Cool, stir in the lemon juice, and pour into a bowl or container to form an approximately ¼-inch-thick layer. Freeze for 3 to 4 hours, stirring with a fork every 30 minutes, to form ice crystals. When finished, the granité should have a fine, crumbly texture.

For the Szechuan Pepper Sorbet

In a medium saucepan, bring 1¾ cups water, the sugar, and the glucose powder to a simmer. Remove from the heat, add the Szechuan peppercorns, cover, and infuse for 4 minutes. Strain through a fine-meshed sieve into a bowl set over ice. Stir to chill, then whisk in the sour cream and lemon juice. Continue stirring until well chilled. Spin in an ice cream machine according to the manufacturer's instructions.

To Finish

Set acetate rings on a flat tray. Cut each strawberry lengthwise into about 8 slices and fan them into the interior of the plastic rings, overlapping them with the tips facing upward; save 6 slices for setting a scoop of ice cream on top. Sift powdered sugar onto the vanilla sablé cookies in a decorative pattern.

For each serving, place a vanilla sablé breton rectangle in the center of a chilled dessert plate and decorate it with discs of strawberry gelée and dots of strawberry sauce. Place a strawberry ring on one side of the plate and place a spoonful of crumble inside. Scoop a spoonful of strawberry granité onto the crumble, forming a mound at the top; lift away the acetate ring. Scoop a spoonful of Szechuan pepper sorbet onto a strawberry slice on the other side of the plate.

ICE WINE SABAYON
POACHED YELLOW PEACH, RED CURRANT

SERVES 6

IN THE EARLY SUMMER, peaches, nectarines, and red currants ripen at the same time. So we thought to marry them again and turn them into jewels dotting an ice wine sabayon crown. Its Italian cousin, the zabaglione, is typically made with Marsala wine, but our version incorporates an ice wine, a very sweet wine made from grapes left to freeze on the vine.

Poached Peaches

6 yellow peaches

1 cup ice wine

3 cups dry white wine
(we recommend a dry riesling)

2½ cups sugar

Ice Wine Sabayon

3 sheets gelatin

¾ cup plus 2 tablespoons heavy cream

12 egg yolks

¾ cup sugar

½ cup ice wine

Ice Wine Syrup

6 tablespoons sugar

⅓ teaspoon apple pectin

½ cup ice wine

Currant Gelée

2 sheets gelatin

½ cup currant juice (fresh,
or we recommend R.W. Knudsen)

6 tablespoons sugar

To Finish

2 yellow peaches

2 white peaches

2 nectarines

2 yellow nectarines

1 cup red currants

1 cup gooseberries, peeled

¼ cup bush basil leaves

For the Poached Peaches

Bring a large pot of water to a simmer and place a bowl of ice water on the side. Score an X on the bottoms of the peaches with a sharp paring knife. Boil the peaches for 1 minute, or until the skins start to loosen around the scored bottoms. Scoop the peaches from the water, chill in the ice water, and peel the skins. Combine 1 quart water, the wines, and the sugar in a saucepan, bring to a boil, and boil until the sugar dissolves. Cool the syrup, submerge the peeled peaches, and marinate, chilled, for 3 days.

For the Ice Wine Sabayon

Soak the gelatin sheets in ice water for 10 minutes; squeeze dry. In a medium bowl, whip the cream to soft peaks, cover, and keep chilled. In the bowl of an electric mixer fitted with a whisk, whip the yolks with ¼ cup of the sugar on medium speed until pale and fluffy. Meanwhile, in a medium saucepan, heat two-thirds of the ice wine with the remaining ½ cup sugar to 250°F. While whipping, pour the hot ice wine mixture into the yolks in a slow stream until well combined. Add the gelatin and whip until dissolved. Add the remaining ice wine and continue to whip on medium speed until the mixture cools to room temperature.

With a rubber spatula, fold the whipped cream into the sabayon until no streaks remain, being careful not to overmix. Divide the sabayon into six 6- to 8-ounce molds of your choice: We recommend Flexipan silicone molds (in the photo we used Demarle Flexipan mold Ref 402); or use ramekins or parfait glasses. If using Flexipan molds, freeze for 1 hour, or until set, unmold, and transfer to the refrigerator for 1 hour. If using ramekins or glasses, chill in the refrigerator until set, about 2 hours.

For the Ice Wine Syrup

In a small bowl, mix 1½ tablespoons of the sugar with the pectin. In a medium saucepan, combine the ice wine with the remaining 4½ tablespoons sugar, and simmer until dissolved. Whisk in the pectin mixture and simmer for another 2 minutes. Reserve, chilled.

For the Currant Gelée

Spray an 8½ x 4½-inch loaf pan with nonstick cooking spray and line with acetate paper. Soak the gelatin sheets in ice water for 10 minutes; squeeze dry. In a small saucepan, combine the currant juice and sugar, and simmer until dissolved. Remove from the heat, stir in the gelatin, and pour into the prepared baking pan. Refrigerate for 2 hours, or until set. Use a ¼-inch ring cutter to punch out at least 18 circles from the gelée. Keep chilled.

To Finish

Pit the stone fruits and cut into wedges.

For each serving, place a serving of ice wine sabayon on a plate and set a poached peach on the side. Scatter the fruit wedges, currants, and gooseberries around the sabayon and peach in a decorative fashion. Add a few dots of ice wine syrup and 3 discs of currant gelée. Garnish the poached peach with a sprig of bush basil.

CHOCOLATE PRALINÉ PALET D'OR

SERVES 8

INSPIRED BY the chocolate palet d'or, a bonbon created by French chocolatiers at the turn of the century, we have reinvented this delicacy as a dessert hidden inside a gold-dusted, chocolate-glazed orb. Our own palet d'or reveals a classic gianduja filling, the historical hazelnut paste mixed with chocolate. A hazelnut-coated hazelnut ice cream extends the theme even further.

CHOCOLATE PRALINÉ
PALET D'OR

**Dark Chocolate Rings
(optional; makes extra)**

1 (15 x 12-inch) sheet of clear acetate

Tempered Chocolate (page 378)

1-foot-long section of 4¾-inch-diameter PVC piping (or similar-size cylindrical object such as a full paper towel roll)

Praliné Ice Cream (makes 1 quart)

2 tablespoons sugar

½ teaspoon ice cream stabilizer, optional

2 cups milk

½ cup plus 1 tablespoon heavy cream

1¼ tablespoons trimoline

3 tablespoons milk powder

5 egg yolks

¾ cup plus 2 teaspoons Valrhona 50% Praline Paste

Hazelnut Coating

⅔ cup sugar

2 cups skin-on hazelnuts, toasted

Praline Sauce

½ sheet gelatin

3 tablespoons plus 1 teaspoon milk

5 tablespoons Valrhona 50% Praline Paste

Chocolate Sablé

¼ cup powdered sugar

1 Tahitian vanilla bean, split and seeds scraped

2 tablespoons almond flour

3½ tablespoons cornstarch

¾ cup flour

1 pinch of salt

5½ tablespoons butter

1 egg

3½ ounces Valrhona 33% Hazelnut Gianduja Chocolate

2 large sheets of clear acetate

Dark Chocolate Crémeux

6 egg yolks

2 tablespoons sugar

½ cup milk

½ cup plus 2 teaspoons heavy cream

5¼ ounces Valrhona Guanaja 70% Chocolate

Dark Gianduja Pâte à Bombe

1½ gelatin sheets

1 cup plus 3 tablespoons heavy cream

4 egg yolks

1 egg

4¾ tablespoons sugar

6½ ounces Valrhona Dark Gianduja Chocolate

To Finish

Dark Chocolate Glaze (page 378)

1 pinch of gold luster dust

For the Dark Chocolate Rings

Set the sheet of acetate on a smooth, flat surface. With an offset spatula, evenly spread tempered chocolate across the sheet to approximately 1 millimeter thickness. Run a ¹⁄₁₆-inch-gauged chocolate comb crosswise across the acetate to form 12-inch-long strips. Allow the chocolate to cool slightly, about 4 minutes, then wrap the sheet of acetate, chocolate side out, around the tube; secure with tape. Allow to set for 24 hours before removing.

For the Praliné Ice Cream

In a small bowl, mix 1 tablespoon of the sugar with the ice cream stabilizer. In a medium saucepan, combine the milk, cream, trimoline, and milk powder and place over medium heat. Once the milk mixture reaches 122°F, whisk in the sugar-stabilizer mixture. Continue to heat until the milk mixture begins to simmer; remove from the heat. In a medium heatproof bowl, whip the egg yolks with the remaining 1 tablespoon sugar. While whisking, gradually pour half of the hot cream into the egg yolk mixture. Gradually whisk the mixture back into the saucepan. Return the saucepan to medium heat and cook slowly, while whisking, to 185°F. Remove from the heat and whisk in the praline paste until well combined. Pass the mixture through a fine-meshed sieve into a bowl set over ice. Stir until well chilled and spin in an ice cream machine according to the manufacturer's instructions.

For the Hazelnut Coating

Line a baking sheet with a Silpat. In a medium saucepan, melt the sugar with 1 tablespoon water and heat, until lightly caramelized, to 250°F. Stir in the hazelnuts with a wooden spoon. Continue cooking the hazelnuts over medium heat, stirring until the sugar turns from a frosted white color to a glossy caramel. Transfer the nuts to the prepared baking sheet and spread into an even layer. Cool at room temperature for about 30 minutes, until hardened.

Transfer the nuts to a food processor fitted with a blade and pulse into crumbs. Transfer the nuts to a shallow baking dish.

Scoop a ball of ice cream into the nuts and roll until evenly coated; transfer to a plate and return to the freezer. Repeat the process to make 8 scoops.

For the Praline Sauce
Soak the gelatin in ice water for 10 minutes; squeeze dry. In a small saucepan, bring the milk to a simmer. Stir in the gelatin to dissolve, then mix in the praline paste. Cool, and transfer to a piping bag. Reserve, chilled.

For the Chocolate Sablé
In a large bowl, whisk the powdered sugar and vanilla seeds until well incorporated and no lumps remain. Add the almond flour, cornstarch, flour, and salt and whisk to combine. In the bowl of an electric mixer fitted with a paddle, mix the butter until creamy. On low speed, gradually add the dry ingredients to the butter and mix until combined. Scrape the bowl with a rubber spatula, then add the egg and mix on medium speed until combined. Scrape the dough from the bowl, pat into a rectangular shape, wrap in plastic wrap, and refrigerate for at least 1 hour or up to 3 days.

Preheat the oven to 350°F. Set the dough on a sheet of parchment paper, top with another paper, and roll into a ¹⁄₁₆-inch-thick rectangular sheet. Slide the bottom sheet of parchment along with the dough onto a baking sheet and remove the top layer of paper. Bake for 4 minutes, or until a light golden brown. Remove from the oven and cool at room temperature. When the sablé has cooled, break it into small chunks.

Fill one-third of a small saucepan with water and bring to a simmer. Place the chocolate in a heatproof bowl and set it over the water. Heat the chocolate, stirring, until melted and it reaches 104°F.

Transfer the chocolate and sablé chunks to a standing electric mixer fitted with a paddle attachment and mix on medium speed until the sablé is broken down into crumbs. When the chocolate and crumbs have come together, scoop onto a sheet of acetate, top with another sheet, and roll to a thickness of 2 millimeters. Transfer to a flat tray and refrigerate until the chocolate is set. With

eight 3-inch-wide ring cutters, cut discs from the gianduja crust. Keep the crust in the bottoms of the rings, chilled.

For the Dark Chocolate Crémeux
In a heatproof bowl, whisk the egg yolks with the sugar until smooth. In a medium saucepan, bring the milk and cream to a simmer. While whisking, gradually pour half of the hot milk into the egg yolk mixture. Gradually whisk the mixture back into the saucepan. Return the saucepan to the heat and cook slowly while whisking until it reaches 185°F. Put the chocolate in a high-sided container such as a pitcher. Pour the hot cream mixture through a fine-meshed sieve over the chocolate and rest for 1 minute. Use a hand blender to mix until smooth, keeping the mixer head submerged to avoid air bubbles. Cover and refrigerate for at least 3 hours or overnight, until set. Transfer the crémeux to a piping bag and pipe ¼-inch-high discs onto the tops of the sablé discs inside of the metal rings, leaving a ¼-inch gap between the crémeux and the rings. Refrigerate the rings.

For the Dark Gianduja Pâte à Bombe
Soak the gelatin sheets in ice water for 10 minutes; squeeze dry. In a medium bowl with a whisk, whip ¾ cup plus 2 tablespoons of the heavy cream to soft peaks. Cover and keep chilled.

In the bowl of an electric standing mixer, whisk to combine the yolks, egg, and sugar with 2 tablespoons water. Place the chocolate in a separate heatproof bowl and set aside.

Fill half of a medium saucepan with water and bring to a simmer. Set the mixer bowl with the egg mixture over the simmering water and heat, while whisking, until it reaches 185°F. Transfer the bowl to the electric mixer fitted with a whisk and continue whipping on high speed until the eggs cool to 104°F.

While the egg mixture is whipping, place the bowl of chocolate over the pot of simmering water and heat, stirring, until it is melted and reaches 113°F; remove from the heat. Transfer the remaining heavy cream to a small saucepan, bring to a simmer, remove

from the heat, and stir in the gelatin until dissolved. Stir into the melted chocolate until combined.

Whisk one-third of the egg mixture into the chocolate. Fold in the remaining egg mixture in 2 batches with a rubber spatula until just combined. Fold in the reserved whipped cream until no streaks remain.

Remove the rings from the refrigerator and divide the mousse inside them to reach the rims. Use an offset spatula to spread the mousse so it is flush against the top of the molds. Freeze until the mousse is solid, about 4 hours.

To Finish
Remove the mousse rings from the freezer. Warm the sides of the rings with your hands and pop out the palets. Set the frozen palets on a baking rack set over a baking sheet 1 inch apart; return to the freezer. Transfer the glaze to a heatproof bowl and warm in a microwave or over a saucepan of simmering water until it reaches 95°F. Ladle the chocolate glaze over the palets to coat. Refrigerate the palets for 2 hours so the glaze sets and the interior thaws. Dust the palets with powdered gold.

For each serving, stand 2 dark chocolate rings on a plate in a crisscross pattern and, with an offset spatula, slide a palet into the center. Dot the plate with praline sauce and set a scoop of hazelnut-coated ice cream on the side.

CHOCOLATE-COFFEE BAR
MASCARPONE WHIPPED CREAM

SERVES 6

IN MY MIND there is no real celebration unless it is capped with the sinful combination of chocolate and whipped cream. Here we expand the flavor profile, adding to the plate mascarpone and coffee elements, similar to a tiramisu. The mascarpone cream holds itself better than a simple whipped cream and brings some structure to this luscious modern dessert.

Tempered Dark Chocolate Rectangles

Tempered Chocolate (page 378)

2 (19 x 5-inch) rectangles of clear acetate

Coffee-Chocolate Krispies

3½ ounces Valrhona Guanaja 70% chocolate, chopped

1 teaspoon Nescafé instant coffee

2 cups Rice Krispies

Coffee Crémeux

4 egg yolks

1 tablespoon sugar

3½ tablespoons milk

3½ tablespoons heavy cream

1 tablespoon coffee extract (we recommend Trablit)

3 ounces Valrhona Guanaja 70% Dark Chocolate

Chocolate Pâte Sablée

4½ tablespoons powdered sugar

⅓ teaspoon salt

1 cup plus 2 tablespoons flour

3½ tablespoons cornstarch

¼ cup Valrhona cocoa powder

1½ sticks (¾ cup) butter

3 egg yolks

Espresso Ganache

Clear acetate

5¼ ounces Valrhona Guanaja 70% Chocolate, chopped

5½ tablespoons milk

1½ tablespoons heavy cream

1 tablespoon freshly brewed espresso

3 tablespoons butter, softened

Whipped Mascarpone Cream

3 tablespoons mascarpone cheese

¼ cup powdered sugar

½ cup heavy cream

To Finish

1 tablespoon Nescafé instant coffee

Dark Chocolate Glaze (page 378)

For the Tempered Dark Chocolate Rectangles

Use a large offset spatula to spread a 1-millimeter layer of tempered chocolate across each acetate sheet. Run a ¹⁄₁₆-inch chocolate comb widthwise through the first sheet of acetate to make 5-inch-long x ¹⁄₁₆-inch-wide strips. Allow the second sheet to cool for 3 minutes so that it is set but still pliable. With a chef's knife, score the second sheet of chocolate at ¾-inch intervals widthwise to create at least twenty-four 5 x ¾-inch rectangles. For best results, allow the chocolate to rest at room temperature for 24 hours before removing from the acetate with an offset spatula.

For the Coffee-Chocolate Krispies

Place the chocolate in a heatproof bowl and microwave on high, checking every 10 seconds, until melted. Stir in the instant coffee until well incorporated. Fold in the Rice Krispies with a rubber spatula until well coated. Pour onto a parchment paper–lined tray, arranging in clumps. Cool at room temperature until hard. Store in an airtight container.

For the Coffee Crémeux

In a heatproof bowl, whisk the egg yolks with the sugar until smooth. In a medium saucepan, combine the milk, cream, and coffee extract and bring to a simmer. While whisking, gradually pour half of the hot milk into the egg yolk mixture.

Gradually whisk the mixture back into the saucepan. Return the saucepan to the heat and cook slowly, while whisking, until it reaches 185°F.

Remove from the heat and, using a hand blender, puree the chocolate in until smoooth. Strain through a fine-meshed sieve into a heatproof container. Cover with a sheet of plastic wrap and transfer to the refrigerator. Chill overnight, then transfer to a piping bag fitted with a large tip (Ateco #801 tip).

For the Chocolate Pâte Sablée

In a medium bowl, whisk the powdered sugar, salt, flour, cornstarch, and cocoa powder to combine. In the bowl of an electric mixer fitted with a paddle, mix the butter on medium speed until creamy. Gradually add the dry ingredients, mixing until well combined, stopping to scrape the sides of the bowl with a rubber spatula at least once. Mix in the egg yolks one at a time until well combined. Scrape the dough from the bowl, pat it into a square, and wrap in plastic wrap. Refrigerate until firm, at least 1 hour.

Preheat the oven to 350°F. Unwrap the dough and place it on a sheet of parchment paper and top with another sheet of parchment. Roll the dough through the paper to a ¼-inch-thick sheet. Transfer the dough to a baking sheet, remove the top layer of paper, and bake for 6 minutes. Remove from the oven and, with a large knife, cut the hot dough into at least six 5 x ¾-inch rectangles. Return to the oven to bake for 5 minutes, or until the rectangles start to look dry around the edges. Remove from the oven and cool at room temperature.

For the Espresso Ganache

Line an 8½ x 4½-inch loaf pan with cooking spray and acetate. Place the chocolate in a heatproof mixing bowl. In a small saucepan, combine the milk, heavy cream, and espresso, bring to a simmer, and pour over the chocolate. Rest for 30 seconds, then whisk until it is smooth and shiny. Whisk in the butter in 3 additions, until well combined. Pour into the prepared loaf pan, wrap with plastic, and transfer to the freezer until solid, about 3 hours. Loosen the sides of the frozen ganache with an offset spatula and flip it onto a cutting board. Peel away the

acetate and cut into at least eight 4 x ½-inch rectangles, transfer to a tray, wrap in plastic, and refrigerate until ready to use.

For the Whipped Mascarpone Cream

Up to 1 hour before serving, transfer the mascarpone and powdered sugar to an electric stand mixer fitted with a whisk. Whip on medium speed until combined and stream in the heavy cream. Continue whipping until medium peaks form. Transfer to a piping bag fitted with a medium star tip (Ateco #823 tip).

To Finish

For each serving, set the chocolate pâte sablée on a chilled dessert plate and set 1 tempered chocolate rectangle on top. Stack a rectangle of espresso ganache followed by another tempered chocolate rectangle on top. Pipe the coffee cream on top in a zigzag pattern to cover the rectangle and top with another tempered chocolate rectangle. Pipe mascarpone cream on top in a swirly line. Sift instant coffee on top. Pipe 2 lines of chocolate glaze on the plate, lean a few tempered chocolate strips against the bar, and set a piece of coffee-chocolate Krispies on the side.

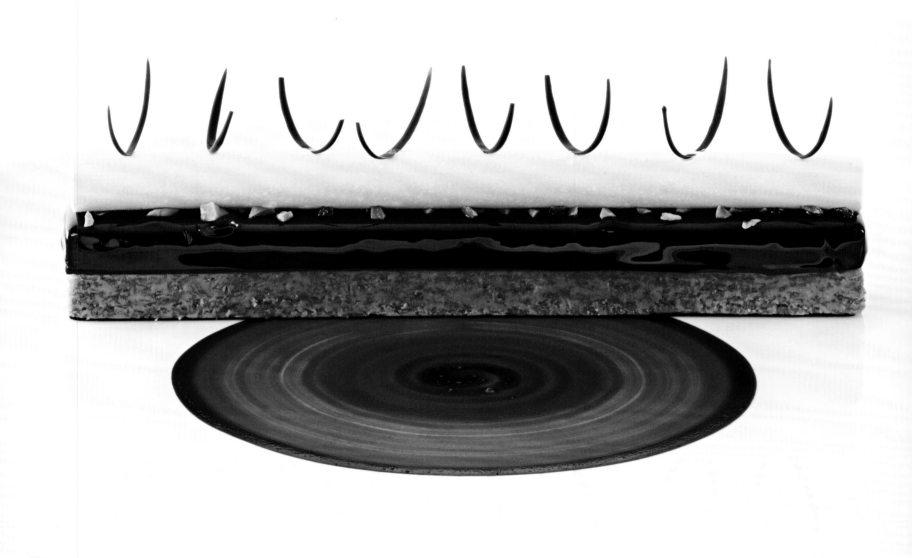

PEANUT CROUSTILLANT
TURRÓN CANDY ICE CREAM

SERVES 8

EVERY CHRISTMAS, my nephew, who lives in Valencia, Spain, sends me a 15-pound box of Turrón, the delicious Spanish Marcona almond and honey candy, similar to nougat. I share it with the chefs and staff, and one year, our wonderful pastry chef Sandro Micheli was inspired to create this dessert around it. A declination of taste: peanuts, chocolate, and Turrón, unusual and delicious.

Chocolate Décor

2-foot piece of clear acetate

8 ounces Tempered Chocolate (page 378)

Peanut Butter Feuilletine

1 cup creamy peanut butter

3½ ounces milk chocolate (we recommend Valrhona Jivara 40%)

1½ cups feuilletine (we recommend Cacao Barry Pailletté Feuilletine)

Turrón Ice Cream (makes 1 quart)

8 (5-inch) squares of clear acetate sheets

2 cups milk

½ cup plus 2 tablespoons heavy cream

7 ounces Turrón candy, chopped

3 tablespoons milk powder

¼ cup sugar

4 egg yolks

Glazed Chocolate Ganache

Clear acetate

9 ounces Valrhona Caraïbe 66% Chocolate

½ cup milk

2 tablespoons heavy cream

4½ tablespoons butter, cubed

Dark Chocolate Glaze (page 378)

To Finish

Dark Chocolate Glaze (page 378)

Caramelized Peanuts (see Caramelized Nuts, page 379), chopped

For the Chocolate Décor

Roll the piece of acetate into a 2-inch-diameter roll and tape to secure on the sides. Fill a piping bag cut with a very small tip or cornet with chocolate and drizzle thin lines widthwise across the acetate tube. Allow the chocolate to set overnight and carefully remove the décor.

For the Peanut Butter Feuilletine

Fill one-third of a medium saucepan with water and bring to a simmer. Combine the peanut butter and chocolate in a medium heatproof bowl and set on top of the saucepan. Heat, stirring occasionally, until melted. Remove from the heat and fold in the feuilletine; cool for a few minutes. Scoop the mixture onto a sheet of parchment paper and set another sheet of parchment on top. Roll the mixture to an approximately ¼-inch-thick sheet. Transfer to a baking sheet. Refrigerate until hardened, then remove the top layer of parchment. Using the aid of a ruler, cut the sheet into at least eight 3¾ x ½-inch bars. Reserve, chilled.

For the Turrón Ice Cream

Roll the acetate sheets into eight ½-inch-diameter tubes, secure the sides with tape, and then tape off one of the open ends to seal. Stand the tubes in a container that will keep them upright with the open end facing up. In a small saucepan, bring the milk, heavy cream, and Turrón to a simmer, cover, and remove from the heat to rest for 5 minutes. Transfer the mixture to a blender and puree until very smooth; return to the saucepan over medium heat. In a heatproof bowl, whisk the milk powder, sugar, and egg yolks until smooth. While whisking, gradually pour half of the hot cream mixture into the egg yolk mixture. Gradually whisk the contents back into the saucepan. Return the pan to medium heat and cook, while whisking, until it reaches 185°F. Remove from the heat and pass through a fine-meshed sieve into a bowl set over ice. Stir until well chilled, then spin in an ice cream machine according to the manufacturer's instructions.

Transfer the ice cream to pastry bags immediately after spinning. Cut small tips from the bags and fill the acetate tubes. Freeze, making sure they stay upright, until solid, at least 2 hours.

For the Glazed Chocolate Ganache

Grease an 8½ x 4½-inch loaf pan with nonstick cooking spray and line with acetate paper. Fill one-third of a medium saucepan with water and bring to a simmer. Place the chocolate in a heatproof bowl and set on top of the saucepan. Stir until melted, then remove from the heat. In a small saucepan, combine the milk and heavy cream and bring to a simmer. Whisk into the melted chocolate. Cool the mixture to 115°F and, with a hand blender, puree in the butter until smooth. Pour into the prepared loaf pan and transfer to the freezer until solid, about 4 hours. Invert onto a cutting board, peel off the acetate, and with the aid of a ruler, cut into at least eight 3¾ x ½-inch bars. Set the bars on a rack set over a baking sheet. Ladle the chocolate glaze over the frozen bars to coat. Refrigerate the bars for 2 hours so the glaze sets and the interior thaws.

To Finish

For each serving, spread a circle of chocolate glaze in the center of a chilled dessert plate. Stack a rectangle of glazed chocolate ganache, sprinkled with chopped caramelized peanuts, on a rectangle of feuilletine and set on the plate. Unwrap a tube of Turrón ice cream and set on top of the ganache. Garnish the top with several pieces of chocolate décor.

CHOCOLATE, BANANA, AND HAZELNUT GÂTEAU
LIME CONFIT, VANILLA-LIME SORBET

SERVES 8

SO MANY PEOPLE love bananas, and combined with chocolate it's a match made in heaven for children and adults alike. But sadly, as all of my chefs have learned, I haven't yet trained my palate to enjoy the soft, rich fruit. That, however, doesn't mean I will deny my guests the opportunity to enjoy it! Here we ponder, will a chocolate cake cut into thirds weigh less than the sum of its parts? For the look, certainly. This destructured chocolate ganache cake mingles with fresh bananas, a vanilla-lime sorbet, and lime zest confit. Smooth and vibrant, intense and creamy—a flourless sweet and sour composition that is so popular, I might change my mind!

Lime Zest Confit
(makes extra/4-day process)

6 limes

7 cups sugar

1½ tablespoons corn syrup

Dark Chocolate Décor

Tempered Chocolate (page 378)

One 24 x 3-inch sheet of acetate

One 24-inch-long x 2-inch-diameter section of tubing, or similar-size cylindrical object

Flourless Cocoa Biscuit

11 egg yolks

1 cup plus 3 tablespoons sugar

¾ cup unsweetened cocoa powder (we recommend Valrhona 100% Pure Cacao Powder)

11 egg whites

Chocolate-Banana Ganache

3 sheets gelatin

5½ ounces milk chocolate (we recommend Valrhona Jivara 40%)

2¾ ounces dark chocolate (we recommend Valrhona Manjari 64%)

1 large ripe banana, peeled and diced (about 6 ounces)

6 tablespoons heavy cream

3 tablespoons sugar

Caramel Chocolate Crémeux

4 ounces bitter chocolate (we recommend Valrhona Manjari 64%)

½ cup plus 1 tablespoon sugar

2 teaspoons corn syrup

1 cup heavy cream

3 tablespoons butter, melted

Lime Sauce

6 tablespoons sugar

⅓ teaspoon apple pectin

½ cup lime juice

Vanilla-Lime Sorbet
(makes about 1 quart)

3 Tahitian vanilla beans, split and seeds scraped

¾ cup sugar

1 tablespoon trimoline

5½ tablespoons glucose powder

¾ cup lime juice

To Finish

2 ripe bananas

Finely grated zest and juice of 1 lime

For the Lime Zest Confit

Cut the limes in half, extract and reserve the juice, and carve out the flesh from the interior, taking care to not puncture the rind.

Place the rind in a medium saucepan, cover with cold water, and bring to a simmer. Simmer for 5 minutes. Strain and repeat 4 more times. Strain the water from the pan and pour in the reserved juice, 1 quart of water, and 4 cups of the sugar; simmer until the sugar is dissolved.

Remove from the heat, cover, and rest at room temperature overnight. For each of the next 2 days, add another 1 cup of sugar, simmer until dissolved, and cover again. On the third day, add the remaining sugar with the corn syrup and simmer until dissolved. Reserve the rinds in the liquid, refrigerated, for up to 1 month. Strain the rind and cut into triangles before serving.

For the Dark Chocolate Décor

Spread a 1-millimeter layer of chocolate to cover the acetate. Rest for 5 minutes, or until the chocolate has begun to set but still remains flexible. With a paring knife, quickly form triangles from the chocolate by scoring on a diagonal at 2-inch widthwise intervals, then drape the acetate, chocolate side out, over the tube. Let the chocolate harden overnight for best results.

For the Flourless Cocoa Biscuit

Preheat the oven to 390°F. Line the bottom of a 9½ x 13-inch rimmed baking sheet with a Silpat and coat with a thin layer of nonstick cooking spray.

In the bowl of an electric mixer fitted with a whisk, whip the egg yolks with 7 tablespoons of the sugar until it forms ribbons, sift in the cocoa powder, and whip on low speed until no streaks remain. Transfer the mixture to a large bowl and set aside. Clean the bowl of the electric mixer and add the egg whites with one-third of the remaining sugar. Whip on medium speed until foamy. Gradually stream in the remaining sugar, while continuing to whip to reach soft peaks.

Gently fold the egg whites into the yolk mixture in 3 additions, until no streaks remain but it is still light and fluffy. Pour the batter onto the prepared baking sheet and spread into a flat layer with a spatula. Bake for 8 to 10 minutes, until a cake tester inserted into the center is clean when removed. Run a knife along the edges of the biscuit to loosen and flip it out onto a rack to cool.

Return the biscuit to a parchment paper–lined 9½ x 13-inch rimmed baking sheet and freeze.

For the Chocolate-Banana Ganache

Soak the gelatin sheets in ice water for 10 minutes; squeeze dry.

Fill one-third of a medium saucepan with water and bring to a simmer. Place the chocolate in a heatproof bowl and set on top of the saucepan. Warm until melted, stirring occasionally, then remove from the heat. With a spatula, pass the banana through a drum sieve into the chocolate. In a small saucepan, bring the heavy cream and sugar to a simmer. Add to the melted chocolate and puree with a hand blender until smooth to make a ganache. Pour the ganache over the chocolate biscuit, spread to an even layer, and return to the freezer until solid, then cover.

For the Caramel Chocolate Crémeux

Fill one-third of a medium saucepan with water and bring to a simmer. Place the chocolate in a heatproof bowl and set on top of the saucepan. Stir until melted; keep warm. In a medium heavy-bottomed saucepan, combine the sugar and corn syrup and heat, stirring occasionally, to a dark caramel color, 355°F. Remove from the heat and carefully (it will spatter) add the heavy cream and butter. Return to low heat and stir until smooth. Pour the caramel mixture into the chocolate and puree with a hand blender until smooth. Pour onto the tray of frozen biscuit and ganache and spread into an even layer to finish layering the gâteau. Return to the freezer until solid, about 4 hours.

To Portion the Gâteau

Run a knife around the edges of the layered gâteau and lift onto a cutting board. Cut lengthwise into two 3-inch strips and trim the edges. Cut each strip into 8 triangles with 2-inch bases, making 24 total. Transfer to the refrigerator to thaw, about 3 hours.

For the Lime Sauce

In a small bowl, combine the sugar and pectin. In a small saucepan, bring the lime juice to a simmer and whisk in the sugar mixture. Simmer for 1 minute, strain through a fine-meshed sieve, and reserve, chilled.

For the Vanilla-Lime Sorbet

In a medium saucepan, combine 1½ cups water with the vanilla seeds, sugar, trimoline, and glucose powder. Stir until the sugar is dissolved. Pour into a bowl set over ice and stir until well chilled. Stir in the lime juice. Spin in an ice cream machine according to the manufacturer's instructions.

To Finish

Just before serving, cut the bananas into 1-inch batons and toss with the lime zest and juice.

For each serving, arrange 3 slices of gâteau, several dots of lime sauce, and a few lime confit triangles on a chilled dessert plate. Top each slice of gâteau with a piece of banana and a chocolate décor triangle. Scoop a spoonful of ice cream on top of a piece of lime zest confit.

CONTEMPORARY CHESTNUT MONT-BLANC

SERVES 6

UNDER THIS SHINY glazed dome hides our interpretation of the Mont-Blanc, the typical French early winter dessert that celebrates sweet chestnuts. Here, layers of chestnut cream, mandarin marmalade, and vanilla bavarois sit on top of a chestnut biscuit. Candied chestnuts anchor the plate.

Chestnut Biscuit

¾ cup plus 2½ tablespoons sugar

½ cup flour

½ cup chestnut flour

¾ tablespoon baking soda

⅓ teaspoon salt

1 egg

5½ tablespoons Clarified Butter
(page 377), melted

½ cup chestnut puree
(we recommend Clément Faugier)

10 candied chestnuts
(we recommend Clément Faugier),
drained well and finely chopped

Mandarin Jam

3 tablespoons plus 1 teaspoon sugar

1 teaspoon apple pectin

1 cup fresh mandarin orange juice

1 tablespoon glucose syrup

Vanilla Bavarois

4 sheets gelatin

3 tablespoons plus 1 teaspoon sugar

4 egg yolks

¾ cup heavy cream

¾ cup milk

1 Tahitian vanilla bean, halved
and seeds scraped

Chestnut Mousse

2 sheets gelatin

1⅓ cups heavy cream

1 cup chestnut puree

2 tablespoons bourbon

2½ tablespoons butter, at
room temperature

White Chocolate Glaze

5½ sheets gelatin

6 ounces chopped white chocolate
(we recommend Valrhona Ivoire 35%)

1¼ cups sugar

7 tablespoons glucose syrup

⅓ cup condensed milk

1 drop white food coloring, optional

To Finish

Dark Chocolate Glaze
(page 378), optional

6 candied chestnuts, strained

12 sticks Pulled Sugar
(page 379), optional

For the Chestnut Biscuit

Preheat the oven to 350°F. Line a 9 x 13-inch rimmed baking sheet with a Silpat or parchment paper and spray with nonstick cooking spray. Sift the sugar, flour, chestnut flour, baking soda, and salt into the bowl of an electric mixer fitted with a paddle attachment. On medium speed, add the egg and stream in the melted butter until well combined. Add the chestnut puree, and then the candied chestnuts, and mix to incorporate well. Spread the batter in an even layer on the prepared baking sheet. Bake for 10 minutes, or until golden brown. Cool at room temperature, then chill in the refrigerator and, with a ring cutter, cut at least 6 circles slightly smaller than the circumference of 6 individual dome molds (a 2.6-inch Flexipan half sphere form and a ring cutter were used for the photograph).

For the Mandarin Jam

In a small bowl, mix the sugar with the pectin. In a small saucepan, bring the mandarin juice and glucose to a simmer. Add the sugar mixture, and simmer for 2 minutes, while whisking. Pour into at least 6 small Flexipan dome molds (a 1¾-inch-diameter Flexipan mold was used for the photograph) and freeze.

For the Vanilla Bavarois

Be sure the mandarin jam domes are frozen solid before preparing the bavarois. Soak the gelatin sheets in ice water for 10 minutes; squeeze dry. In a medium heatproof bowl, whip the sugar and yolks to combine. In a small bowl, whip the cream to medium peaks. In a small saucepan, combine the milk, vanilla seeds, and vanilla pod and bring to a simmer. While whisking, gradually pour half of the hot milk into the egg yolk mixture. Gradually whisk the mixture back into the saucepan. Return the saucepan to medium heat and cook, while whisking, until it reaches 185°F. Remove from the heat, mix in the gelatin to dissolve, and strain through a fine-meshed sieve into a medium bowl. Cool to room temperature and fold in the whipped cream until no streaks remain. Scoop the bavarois into a piping bag with a large tip and fill one-third of at least 6 medium Flexipan dome molds (a 2.6-inch Flexipan half sphere form was used for the photograph). Press a frozen mandarin dome onto the surface of the bavaroise and pipe the remaining bavaroise on top to coat. Lightly press a piece of biscuit onto the mousse until flush with the rim of the mold. Smooth the tops with an offset spatula. Freeze until set, about 1 hour.

For the Chestnut Mousse

Be sure the bavarois domes are frozen solid before preparing the mousse. Soak the gelatin sheets in ice water for 10 minutes; squeeze dry. In a medium bowl, whip 1 cup of the heavy cream to soft peaks; cover and keep chilled.

In a medium saucepan over medium heat, combine the chestnut puree with the remaining ⅓ cup of heavy cream. Stir until combined and the paste reaches a simmer. Remove from the heat and mix in the gelatin, bourbon, and butter; cool to room temperature. Transfer the mixture to a large bowl and fold in the whipped cream until no streaks remain.

Transfer to a piping bag and fill one-third of at least 6 large dome molds (a 3-inch Flexipan half sphere form was used for the photograph). Press a frozen bavaroise dome into the center of each until the biscuit is level with the top of the mold, and pipe more mousse around the edges if needed to fill. Spread the mousse with an offset spatula until flush with the rim to form the bombes. Freeze until solid.

For the White Chocolate Glaze

Soak the gelatin sheets in ice water for 10 minutes; squeeze dry. Fill one-third of a medium saucepan with water and bring to a simmer. Place the chocolate in a heatproof bowl, cover with plastic wrap, and set over the water. In a small saucepan, combine the sugar, glucose, and ½ cup plus 2 tablespoons of water and set over medium heat. Heat, stirring, until it reaches 221°F. Remove from the heat and stir in the condensed milk and gelatin. Remove the chocolate from the heat and stir in the liquid until well combined to make a glaze.

Stir in the white food coloring, if using.

Unmold the frozen bombes and set them on a rack set over a baking sheet. Cool the glaze to 95°F. Using a large ladle, pour the glaze onto the bombes, allowing it to coat all the way down the sides. Refrigerate the bombes for 4 hours to thaw before serving.

To Finish

If using the chocolate glaze, transfer it to a heatproof bowl and warm in a microwave or over a saucepan of simmering water until it reaches 95°F. Transfer to a piping bag fitted with a small tip and drizzle over the bombes in a decorative fashion.

For each serving, slice a bombe in half and set on a chilled dessert plate; slice a chestnut in half and use to garnish the plate. If using the sugar sticks, rest them against the dome.

"It takes more than three months to candy the chestnuts that hide inside the classic Mont-Blanc, named for the pride of the Alps."

DANIEL ON DESSERTS

AT THE END OF A MEAL, DESSERT SHOULD BE ART, HARMONY, and sweet substance in one bite!

This might surprise you: I adore sweets, but I hate too much sugar! I've always loved desserts, but I prefer ones that are not cloying. During my apprenticeship at Nandron, I received a solid training in pastry but quickly felt I belonged closer to the salt box. I admired the precision and joy that come with the creation of desserts and pastries, but I craved the creative freedom I discovered on the savory side.

Then I went to work for Michel Guérard in Eugénie-les-Bains. Guérard had been the pastry chef at the starred Crillon Hotel on Place de la Concorde and then at the Lido in Paris before he opened Le Pot-au-Feu, the simple restaurant in the suburbs of Paris that would ignite his fame at the forefront of nouvelle cuisine, in 1970. He worked with the precision and technique of a pastry chef, but when he worked with savory foods, it resulted in a unique creativity and sensitivity. He would make the most beautiful and delicious puff pastry or create the lightest possible soufflés. He used vegetables as if they were music notes and always considered himself to be a true artist in the kitchen.

When I arrived in Eugénie-les-Bains, there was no pastry chef. Under Guérard's mindful guidance, each chef rotated, three months in pastry and three in savory.

My own "saga des chefs pâtissiers" started in New York City at the Plaza Athénée, where my pastry chef was Joël Boulay, who now owns a pastry shop in St. Nazaire. It was the mid-1980s and we were rolling the entire pastry menu to the table on a cart. Can you imagine? Fifteen or twenty choices on the "chariot de desserts."

My dessert sensibilities kept evolving: My uneasiness with too much sweetness evolved into a search for the ideal way to cap off a meal and not overwhelm it, to seek a feeling of balance and elegance. Dessert is addictive, and if you're going to be sinful at the table, dessert is the time to let go!

Accompanied by a smooth dessert wine or port, I learned that dessert should be light, but its taste should linger. It should contrast with the meal and, instead of a loud bang, leave a refined note in the mind.

When I became executive chef at Le Cirque, the revered "temple" where Dieter Schorner refined the crème brûlée, owner Sirio Maccioni introduced me to Markus Farbinger, a twenty-two-year-old wunderkind who turned out to be one of the most talented pastry chefs I ever met, and who now owns Isle de Pain, a pastry shop near Cape Town. But Farbinger wanted to be a teacher at the CIA, and soon I found myself asking Alain Ducasse for a recommendation.

"You know," he answered, "Jacques Torres is at the Ritz-Carlton in Atlanta." He picked up the phone and five minutes later, the deal was made. Jacques was playful and soulful; he had been one of the youngest Meilleur Ouvrier de France, winners of the best French Craftsman competition, and already his mastery of chocolate was unparalleled. In celebration of Pierre Franey's sixtieth birthday, we created a miniature chocolate stove that revealed an opera cake underneath, a huge hit with our customers.

When Jacques needed a sous chef, we hired François Payard, a third-generation pastry chef from Nice whose imagination and creativity knew no boundaries. Later, I lured François Payard again, having missed his opinionated temper and his boundless energy. He became my pastry chef at Daniel on 76th Street, and together we opened the Payard Pâtisserie and Bistro on Lexington Avenue.

Over the years, I have worked with many talented pastry

chefs: Rémy Fünfrock; Thomas Haas, another young prodigy who now works in Vancouver; Johnny Iuzzini, who rose from apprentice to chef in his decade with us; and Dominique Ansel, a thoughtful and refined colleague who now runs his own bakery in SoHo.

Today, thanks to Eric Bertoïa, our fabulous corporate pastry chef, and Sandro Micheli, whom I consider to be a true artisan, our desserts are often inspired by classic pastry, but have become complex multisensorial experiences. Keep in mind, though, that with all the technical innovations, we still rely on the basics: eggs, flour, and sugar. It's all about the balance between sweet and sour; crunchy and creamy; smooth and flaky. Pastry is a science similar to chemistry, where components are carefully measured for size and volume, and the scale is an integral part of this delicious architectural equation.

At service time, the chefs assemble what was painstakingly prepared earlier that day; they play with contrasting temperature, textures, and tastes, as in the slow-baked apple mille-feuille. The sablé breton is crunchy, the apple is syrupy, and the sweet ice cream is a welcome contrast to the tart, crisp Granny Smith apple slices.

At Daniel, half of our dessert offerings follow a chocolate theme, the other half a seasonal fruit focus. Desserts allow me to take my guests to exotic locales around the world: South American treasures within a chocolate ganache, Provence in a lavender-spiked clafoutis, and Spain with a Turrón candy ice cream. And then there are what we call "the fruits of the moment": How many ways can we tempt you with a stone fruit or a berry? We may also explore the full range of chocolate paired with spices, coffee, hazelnuts, or even candied fruits.

Still, most simple—and maybe most memorable—at Daniel, for the last two decades, your meal ends with lemon-infused madeleines dusted with a snow of powdered sugar and nestled into a beautiful folded linen napkin.

"There are only four great arts: music, painting, sculpture, and ornamental pastry-architecture being perhaps the least banal derivative of the latter."
—Julia Child

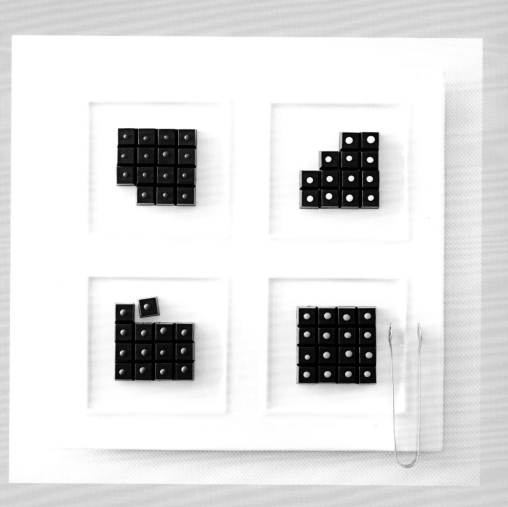

PART II
ICONIC SESSIONS

BILL BUFORD

ICONIC SESSIONS

icon. noun. [ORIGIN: Latin from Greek *eikōn* likeness, image, similitude.] A person or a thing regarded as a representative symbol of something. *Oxford English Dictionary*.

On a Saturday in February, I arrived in New York City, dropped off my bags, got a ride to the Upper East Side, knocked on a heavy unmarked door that was a service entrance to the kitchens of Restaurant Daniel, presented myself, put on a chef's jacket, apron, and clogs, and became the last and least qualified member of a team of cooks who, in the next eighteen days, would produce over a dozen elaborate, technically flamboyant, and historically evocative French dishes. I was the amateur, and I was in trouble. I knew that. The others involved in what I was already thinking of as "Project Iconic" must have known that as well, and in the self-conscious, formal moments that followed—my being introduced to project managers AJ and Chad (who had researched the dishes and had been making and remaking them for weeks), shaking their hands, chit-chatting, smiling; and then to photographers Thomas and Sahinaz, not shaking their hands but bowing, since they were Austrian, and I had become convinced that in Austria this is what people do when they meet, they bow; and then to project "coaches" Jean-François, Fabrizio, Eddy, Olivier, Sebastien (all of them chefs, all at the top of their game, all loyally employed by their boss for around a decade, except Jean-François, who had been employed for nearly two decades), my trying to be witty, and failing, and then laughing heartily at everyone else's being witty—I had a nervous feeling that, as awkward as this ritual might be, my meeting these strangers, knowing that we were about to spend many hours in each other's company, I was in a familiar behavioral box. I knew what to do. I could acquit myself with an illusion of competence and dignity. After today, it would be ugly. Of the two dozen dishes, I had made one, once. I knew some by name. Many I'd never heard of. Chartreuse? Coulibiac? My ignorance wasn't surprising. It was the ignorance of the others. This was surprising. I wasn't the one in trouble. We all were.

It is accepted that French food is normally challenging to prepare, that it can be inflexible in its orthodoxies, obsessive in its attention to detail. But nothing about these dishes was normal. They were extreme. They were extreme versions of the extreme. They were wizardly, masterful, wacky, and often baffling. You knew this food, if you knew it, not by a recipe. You don't learn it from a book. The people who make this food are from a different era, anachronistic ghosts who grew up eating and cooking it, the summers of their childhoods spent in old empire French resorts, their fathers in a dinner jacket on Saturday nights, their mothers in an evening gown, the high-society soirées, or else because… Actually, who does know this food? As I mentally settled in, picturing the days ahead, I fell into wondering who, at this moment, might be making some, or one, or *any* of these dishes. A few people? Anyone? No one. Us.

Our itinerary was Daniel Boulud's doing. Daniel, who is on a first-name basis with the entire world, was also our Daniel, our boss, our patron, our team captain, our instructor, and the only person any of us knew who actually knew how to make everything.

For him, these dishes loomed gigantic. They were bigger than what they seemed to be, and what they seemed to be was already very big. They were food, and craft, and art, and metaphor. They were "iconic," he said.

"What does that mean?" I asked.

He shrugged.

I asked again.

He mumbled something that sounded French but may have been English and conveyed, more or less, that the dishes would do the talking. Watch, he seemed to be saying. Taste. Smell. Think. Find out what is being expressed in the food. A poet works with words, a painter with paint. These dishes are what he is.

We finished at eight o'clock that first evening. We were jazzed and jumpy and joyful. It felt historic, what we were about to do. I hesitate to describe our being on the eve of a journey, except that such a description captures what we felt. We were going to another country and time. Like all good journeys, it would change us. At the end we would know things that we didn't know now.

TURBOT SOUFFLÉ

WAS I NERVOUS? YES. DID I SLEEP? YES, BUT BADLY. I HAD
gone to bed knowing that in the morning I would be surrounded by
chefs, all of them staring at me, rubbing their chins, wondering if
I was up to the task, while I then mauled one of most expensive fish
in the world. A turbot soufflé? No, I had never made such a thing.
I had never eaten such a thing. I had never heard of such a thing.

And until last year, I hadn't eaten the fish. I had no idea that
it was prized. I was born in Louisiana. You don't see turbot in
Louisiana, mainly because there aren't any. What I knew was basic
in the extreme: a turbot was flat; it was big; it was ugly; it was a
bottom-feeder. Bottom-feeder? You don't hear "bottom-feeder"
and think *Yum! Yum!* What does a bottom-feeder eat? Anything.
Roadkill. Or whatever you call roadkill when it's under water.

It was only recently that I had become aware of the fish, and
that was because of a book and my children.

The book is *The Physiology of Taste*. It was written by Jean
Anthelme Brillat-Savarin and published in 1825, and is famous
because it is the first treatment of food that doesn't tell you how to
make it but how to think about it. Serious practioners of the
culinary arts inevitably acknowledge Brillat-Savarin at some
point, if only to establish their credentials, and so I feel compelled
to come clean: it took me fourteen years to read this book. I
finished it on September 17, 2008, and marked it in my calendar as
a hallelujah day. If you haven't read it (and take heart, you won't),
you may know its insufferably banal aphorisms ("You are what you
eat," etc.), which are bunched up at the beginning like a Hallmark
card. Then it is straight uphill. The book is long, very long, and is
pretty tough to read, although it gets better in the second half, and
by the end is not just good but probably very good, and full of food
stories. One involves a turbot and a dinner party.

The party is in the country, and the author arrives early to find
his hosts in a state of high distress. They have acquired a turbot of
gigantic dimensions. It is so large that it won't fit into a turbotière,
a weirdly shaped pot designed to accommodate a weirdly shaped
fish. What is to be done? The husband proposes cutting the fish
in half. The wife is adamant that a turbot must never be cut. The
Professor intervenes, raises his hand, and declares that a solution
will be found, and the implication is that a turbot cannot, will
not—Oh, no, no, no!—must never be severed. (Brillat-Savarin
refers to himself like this, as the Professor, a cute but revealing

piece of narcissism, since the author, whose other book was about
the art of dueling, wasn't in the least professorial.) The actual fix
involves a pot and a wood-burning washing machine, and is ably
described, but, for me, the powerful impression is in the author's
commitment to the uncut fish. It is absolute. And it got me
wondering: Why the fuss?

For instance, the Professor says nothing about the taste. Is
looking at the fish more rewarding than eating one? It *is* a peculiar
sight. A turbot is basically a lozenge. There are not many lozenges
alive in the world at large. Actually, apart from the turbot, there
don't seem to be any. One day, on a scholarly whim, I consulted the
first English-French dictionary, published in 1755, also the year of
Brillat-Savarin's birth. Here I learned that a "turbot" had two
senses: the fish *and* its shape. This was curious. More curious was
that the word's primary sense wasn't the fish. In 1775, when people
heard "turbot," their first thought may have been *trapezoid*. The
implications might be worth pondering. Is it possible that, in
matters turbotièrienne, the shape might matter more than we
appreciate—or at least that it did, once, at some point, in France,
between 1775 and 1825?

On October 1, 2008, my wife and I moved to Lyon, in France,
with our twin sons, George and Frederick, then three years old.
The following summer, my wife was away, the children were in

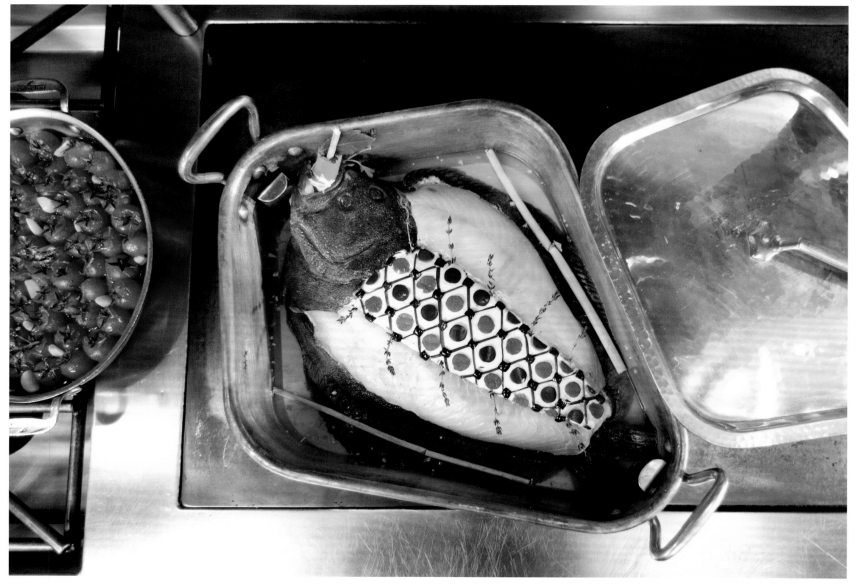

my care, and there was a heat wave. It was humid, 103 degrees, no AC because the Lyonnais regard it as an extravagance, and the boys and I found shelter at an aquarium. Every afternoon for a week, that is where we were. The aquarium included a simulated tide pool, with starfish, sea horses, and a school of turbot, close enough to touch, which my three-year-olds did daily. (Actually, they wanted to hug them, which proved impossible; they also wanted to bring one home as a pet.) Close up, the fish is blister-ingly ugly. The next time you are face-to-face with a turbot, check out the wonky eyes. Evidently, it has normal eyes when it is born, one on each side of the head, just like a normal fish. Then it grows up, and flattens out, and one eye (and the turbot never knows which one it will be) migrates to meet up with the other. That side, now furnished with a pair of eyes, becomes the top, the better to watch out for predators, while the ugly thing of a fish blindly pigs out on the bottom. But often the migrating eye gets lost. It ends up near the nose or just east of the gills, and gets stuck. A turbot is not like other fish. It is primordial and cartoonish and utterly compelling. Perhaps, in matters turbotièrienne, appearance, even a repugnant one, matters, too.

These lessons in what might be called "the aesthetics of the ugly" (or, maybe, "the beauty in the beast") took place without my tasting a single turbot morsel. It was a remarkably unlucky run. For instance, my fish class. I had moved to Lyon to become a French cook (the next eighteen days would be a measure, alas, of what I had learned) and had enrolled at l'Institut de Paul Bocuse, where one day, my seven fellow students and I cleaned and boned two hundred turbot for the canteen lunch. We were done by 9 a.m. The turbot were then whisked away. That was the protocol: a different class did the cooking. We never ate a single one.

Meanwhile, the anecdotes were accumulating: how a turbot is called "the most meatlike" of marine creatures, and is often eaten with a béarnaise, the sauce normally served atop a glistening piece of beef, and, unlike every other fish, can be accompanied by a bottle of a big hearty red.

This intrigued me: what properties make a fish so appealing to carnivores?

I found the answer in Harold McGee's *On Food and Cooking*: that just because all flat fish are flat doesn't mean that all flat fish are alike. Yes, most flat fish are lazy, scarcely moving, piggy

bottom eaters. The turbot, it turns out, is an exception. It eats athletically. It is aggressive and active, and pounces on its prey: that is, it is a hunter; it likes meat. We don't often eat the meat of meat-eaters. Grandma's roasted vulture? A center-cut of hyena? But we do eat a few crustacean-eating crustaceans and at least one crustacean-eating fish.

Before I accidentally convey the impression that I am more competent than incompetent, I should point out that a turbot is probably the easiest fish in the sea to dismantle, mainly because there is really only one bone to worry about, the spine, so big and obvious that it looks like the handle of a car door. There are irritating toothpick bones running around the "wings," which, in this preparation, are left intact, but if they're ever a problem you can have a go at them with a pair of heavy sewing shears, and they're history.

To begin, you flop the fish onto your cutting board, eyes up, mouth side down, except, in my case, there were two cutting boards because we had two fish. The other was for Jean-François, aka JFK, today's kitchen coach. He would be teaching me by example. What he taught me, mainly, was that I was slow, overcautious, and terrified of making a mistake on my first day, like accidently cut-ting my hand in half, or, worse, the fish, and then being haunted for the rest of my life by the ghost of Brillat-Savarin. I couldn't keep up. I fell behind. I panicked. I started sweating—I always sweat when I panic—and by "sweat" I mean full-on, wide-open, and dripping.

The fish is massive. Getting into it, and getting rid of that big bone, means first getting through the skin. In fact, it's not skin. You would never delicately peel it off with your fork at the table. It is more like a hide. You attack it dagger-style with a pointy knife—*Bam!*—then drag it round, pressing hard, tearing it up like an old leather coat (you can hear its ripping), making a rough oval inside the toothpick bones. When you are done, you take a breath (unless you are me, in which case you ask if you might take a shower), return to your handiwork, and discover that the oval skin can now be rolled back like a scroll of old parchment. Underneath are two puffy pouches: exquisite white pillows of deliciousness. These are the fillets, which you remove gently with a spoon. The giant bone that was in between them is the spine, and it comes away cleanly with a little wiggling. Everything else—head, belly,

belly skin, and that ring of toothpick bones—is left in place so that the fish can be, in effect, reconstructed. Lobster tails will go where the spine had once been (the perfect re-filler, a meat-eater inside of a meat-eater), the fillets are returned, and the rest of the space will be filled up with a light white mousse. (The mousse is made with sea bass and cream, and buzzed in a blender, or with turbot and cream, if you have an extra trapezoid lying around.) During the cooking, the whole thing puffs up gracefully. It is ridiculously pretty.

Daniel made a turbot soufflé at Le Moulin de Mougins, in the Côte d'Azur, working for Roger Vergé, the nouvelle cuisine chef of southern sunshine. This version, done in homage, was adorned with a Provençal checkerboard. The crisscrossing green lines? Chives, steamed and then iced. The green checker pieces? Zucchini. The red checker pieces? Oven-dried tomatoes. It was very fussy. Frankly, I had never fussed so much with a piece of food. I was surprised by how gratifying I found the experience.

Somehow, it seemed correct. It was what the fish deserved. (Did I really just say that?)

The "soufflé" is put into a turbotière and braised in its sauce, an homardine (made appositely with lobster shells), spooned over regularly, care taken not to splash the mousse and stain its puffy-white illusion. For Daniel, the turbotière is essential because an inset tray allows you to remove the fish without breaking it. A turbotière has another quality: its uniqueness. There is nothing else you can cook in it. In its effect, the turbotière is a stage prop in the historical spectacle of the fish, its brazen shape intact, utterly uncut.

For me, this dish completed a four-year education. I had moved to Lyon and learned about the turbot. I had returned to New York to learn how to cook one. This lesson alone justified the journey. I was spent. I was happy. I could return to France. But this was Day 1. (Oh, and the taste? Good. Like lobster but better.)

JAMBON AU FOIN

THE STORY SO FAR: FARM BOY, RESTLESS, BORED IN
school, a worry to the family, looking for meaning, wanting a mission, ready for his calling, finds higher purpose in a restaurant kitchen, displays culinary skills that most people need years to acquire, masters the basic five thousand recipes of French cuisine, excels beyond the excellent, seeks out and is trained by the undisputed champion chefs of the world, is driven (by who-can-possibly-know-what engine?) to learn and have at his intuitive command every variation of every dish ever, abandons Europe, arrives in the USA, seems unstoppable, will not be stopped, doesn't stop, succeeds and succeeds again, indefatigable, brilliant, possibly a genius, certainly a genius, and is admitted, in time, to culinary eternity. But was there a moment when he almost blew it?

In April 1997, for instance, when Daniel announced that, after the success of what was then called "Daniel," his first New York City restaurant, on East 76th Street, small, perfectly formed, and unanimously acclaimed (*New York Times* four stars, adoring critics, fame, fortune, groupies), he intended to open yet another, grander version, which, curiously, would also be called "Daniel," on Park Avenue, a massive establishment on a site once occupied

not only by Le Cirque but also by the old Mayfair hotel, plus two underground floors for yet-to-be-built prep and pastry kitchens, changing rooms, offices, a wine cellar, millions of dollars in renovations, a staff of hundreds? It seemed audacious and visionary, not really an announcement, but a manifesto ("History? Shall I save you the corner table?"). But, then, the moment when he had the attention of the world, surrounded by all things chic and long-legged and smelling of money, Daniel, lonely or nostalgic or confused, found that what he wanted to cook was farmhouse pig.

"The pig confuses people," Daniel concedes. "They read about the restaurant, its Michelin stars, and then they arrive . . ." Even now, preparing the most elaborately sophisticated dishes in the French repertoire, Daniel needed to call "time out" (it was Day 2) and make pig. "I can't help it."

Pig, of course! That was what I ate on my first visit to Daniel (le Grand!) when it opened finally, more than two years after it had been announced, and all the talk and the reviews were about "the room." You don't see it when you arrive. It is only after you have been greeted by someone on your left, then welcomed by someone on your right, then another person on your left, and don't notice, therefore, that two doors have been swung open and that you are now standing in a vast, flamboyant, brightly lit, drop-dead public dining space. The room is a proclamation: *What is our show tonight, ladies and gentlemen? You and your dinner!* And what did I order? Pork belly. It arrived, a fatty layered rectangle, beading juice and with an unctuous tendency to slide out from underneath my knife and fork. The brazen incongruity: here I was, me in this room of rooms, eating bacon.

"Breakfast," Daniel clarified. "It was what my grandmother put out on the table. We spread it on bread instead of butter. It is almost pure fat."

Daniel has pork issues. His restaurant is fancy. Pig is not fancy. Pig is not among the animal elite. But Daniel can't keep pig off his menus.

He was raised on a farm, a woody hilly plateau east of Lyon and near the airport and by the border of the historic region of the Dauphiné. He grew up with cows, horses, dogs, duck, quail, partridge, woodcock, rabbits, hare, guinea hens, chickens, and snails. And pigs. Pigs are farmhouse efficiency. A sow makes a dozen piglets; six months later, she makes a dozen more. You sell

some. You keep some. You pay nothing. You feed them leftovers, skins of carrots, onions, turnips, whatever is at the bottom of the soup pot. ("Oh, the pigs loved our soup.") You befriend them. You hang out with them on hot afternoons. You attend to their wounds and infections. You talk to them. You don't let them sleep in your bed, not normally, but you could, they're pets, and then you kill them and eat them, and your leftovers, vegetable skins, and bottom-of-the-pot soups are returned to you, in effect, in a new form, and feed you through the winter.

"Tomorrow, we will make something sophisticated," Daniel said, apologizing. He seemed to think that I would be disappointed—no mousse, no sauces, no truffle. The dish he proposed was "simple," he said, even though it was not simple and not one dish, but several: a butt, a shoulder, and a foot.

The foot was for the potatoes, a last-minute addition. Daniel pictured an occasion when he would cook a meal of this kind, a large table, family members crowded round, his father, Julien (eighty-five), mother, Marie (eighty-five), the five siblings, the nephews, the nieces, and saw that there would be potatoes done up as a local gratin. This is a rich food: the potatoes, peeled and sliced, are cooked in milk and cream, plus nutmeg and grated Gruyère. This, compared to what Daniel actually made (a "gratin dauphinois"), is a Weight Watchers special. Daniel starts with

that foot. It is boned, chopped, and sautéed until the bits of meat caramelize in the pan and the gelatin becomes sticky. Potatoes are arranged on the bacon-bumpy piggy bits, the milk poured over, the cream, the nutmeg, et cetera. *Then* a whole Reblochon is layered on top. What is a Reblochon? Imagine five gallons of the world's thickest milk—from an Alpine cow, eating high-altitude summer herbs—compressed and fermented and sunk into a wheel and so concentrated that it is a tenth of its original volume. Where can you buy it? In the United States, nowhere, because the milk is uncooked, and the Food and Drug Administration is convinced that the cheese is unsafe for American tummies. How can you get it? By e-mailing your friend in Lyon, the evening before he gets on a plane to New York, asking if he can slip a couple of wheels into his luggage.

"JAMBON AU FOIN" MEANS A "LEG IN HAY," BUT IT IS NOT really the leg, it is the butt, or what, in English, we politely prefer to call a "ham." Daniel first ate one at Paul Bocuse's eponymous three-star restaurant just outside of Lyon. Although Daniel had grown up on a farm, he had no idea that you could cook with hay. "It was what we fed the animals, not people," he told me, still conveying some of the shock he felt on finding some on his plate. Daniel was seventeen, and the experience was a culinary game-changer. "Paul showed me that you could actually use the rustic

in haute cuisine." In this, Daniel betrays his extraordinarily divided upbringing: his rustic had been really rustic; his haute-cuisine, really très haute. In Daniel's childhood, there had been no budget for food. Zero. Everything came from the farm. The exceptions were salt and olive oil, obtained by barter from relatives. Daniel's idea of travel was a county fair to sell garlic. Until he was fourteen, he had never seen the inside of a supermarket. Until he was fourteen, he had never seen the inside of a restaurant. He entered one for the first time in June 1969. It wasn't to eat but to work in the kitchen, where he was taught how to make dishes that could have come from Mars. Daniel's grandmother had never served Martian food at home.

According to Paul Bocuse, the hay in a hay ham shouldn't be anything special—nothing more exotic than what you will find in a pasture nearby—and an essential part of your kitchen prep is putting on your boots and filching some from a cow. On 65th and Park, there are no pastures. Chad asked a vegetable wholeseller for help but was disappointed with the samples. You just couldn't imagine that this was how happy cows started their day, eating this stuff, Chad told me. AJ approached the New York City Police Department, which keeps horses in a stable in Brooklyn and obviously has to feed them. The officer who took AJ's call was confused but ultimately saw no reason to keep their hay a secret. It was alfalfa, widely regarded as the best thing you can give a hay-eating animal. Chad arranged a tasting for me later, and there is no question that alfalfa has considerably more flavor and "green juice complexity" than any other grain on the livestock market. I cannot recommend it highly enough.

There are several ways to introduce that green juice complexity into the butt—or, more precisely, a butt en route to being made into a ham. One involves a "hay water" brine: a pot of alfalfa boiled with salt, pepper, and sugar, which is refrigerated overnight. The next morning you dip a rubber hose into the solution and connect it to a bicycle pump and an injection penetration-probe device: something like a livestock rectal thermometer with sprinkler holes. It is available from JB Prince, the kitchen specialist on East 31st Street, for $249.99. Thus enabled, you poke your way between the butt's tissues. It is a wet business. Afterward Daniel and I both smelled like a picnic caught in a thunderstorm.

The butt wants to be wet, wet, wet because it is always in danger of becoming dry, dry, dry. The butt is the animal's most worked muscles, and its leanest, and isn't happy in the unforgiving heat of an oven, which is why it is always first cooked in water, a long slow simmer. Chad undertook the task, arriving at 5 a.m. the next morning. He packed a pot with alfalfa and filled it up. Hay might be powerfully fragrant at first, but, once cooked, its dinner-plate aromatics are surprisingly fragile, and in every step of our preparations there was an implicit instruction: use as much

hay as possible, unless you're able to use more. Chad then brought his hay-water on a bed of hay to the quietest of quiet simmers (I thought of it as "hay squared") and watched it do nothing for the next three hours except steam languidly.

By the time the rest of us showed up with coffee, a little after eight, the butt was ready for its brief exposure to heat, or what in Louisiana we call the "baking." On this occasion, the butt really was baked. Before going into the oven, it was enveloped in a giant rustic dough sandwich: an oval on the bottom, an oval on top. There was more hay, invariably: some pressed into the dough, some twisted into a long hempy rope to seal the two ovals together at a seam. Once the dough had cooked through and become bread, the butt was no longer a butt. It was a ham. You can't look at this preparation, cracking open the crust, and being enveloped by smells of campfires and grassy late-summer meadows, without thinking, *Very clever, those country types.*

A SHOULDER, WITH ITS FAT AND ITS SMALLER MUSCLES, can stand up to a dry heat, and gets a different, drier treatment: hay smoke. To get the hay smoke into the meat, you need a handheld smoking gun ($79.90, at JB Prince). For the smoke itself,

you need a hash pipe. It would have been difficult not to observe that every member of the kitchen was at ease with the workings of paraphernalia: no high-grade Moroccan brick, of course, just plenty of the aforementioned NYPD alfalfa, packed solid. There was a lot of sucking and blowing and trying to get the damn thing to light. It was, for everyone, a highly nostalgic moment.

The shoulder was then roasted in a cast-iron pot atop root vegetables—an abundance of carrots and turnips, plus shallots, celery, and spring garlic—but *underneath* was more hay, of course, loads of it, braided tight to concentrate it. And even more hay, some braided, some by the handful, was rammed into every remaining gap in the pot.

It was an extraordinary feast. It evoked sweaty intimacies of a Sunday lunch on a humid day, and called out for blurry bottles of Beaujolais, and a salad made from the vivid vegetables in Julien's garden. Meanwhile, four of us gathered round Daniel in the kitchen, after all the plating and photos were done. This was for an impromptu lesson in root vegetables. Daniel removed a carrot from the cast-iron pot. Daniel doesn't skin his carrots. That's where you find the flavor, he said. The carrot was a brownish orange. It had been washed, I assume, but no amount of water

could hose off the compacted soil and who-knows-what that you find embedded in the lines of a carrot skin. It reminded me of an afternoon at the playground with my children, and the look of their hands afterward, the crevices blackly crusted up. Daniel sliced the carrot into precise one-inch pieces, on the diagonal, sprinkled some sea salt, and ladled porky hay fat from the roasting pan over them like a sauce. We tasted. The wet carrot collapsed between the middle of the tongue and the roof of the mouth, too flavor-soggy to chew. It squished orangeness and pig. Each one of us took another piece. Daniel prepared another carrot. It was a good moment.

TÊTE DE VEAU EN TORTUE

BY DAY 3, A ROUTINE WAS IN PLACE, OWING TO AJ'S DAILY worksheet. The worksheet was organized as a grid, which she filled in the night before and e-mailed out, often around midnight. It included a start time (8 a.m., for today's dish, being a veal's head), unusual ingredients (like two dozen live crayfish), serving props (the 1931 English silver platter that AJ had persuaded James Robinson Antiques to loan out on a promise, rashly made, that it wouldn't be scratched), and extra pieces of cooking kit (the Paul Bocuse pot, which was gigantic, more a "marmite" than a pot, in fact more bathtub than marmite, and big enough, in any case, to accommodate a cow's head, and several other members of the herd). The worksheet included photos of earlier efforts, because all dishes had been rehearsed; bibliographical references, because everything had a history, especially the tête de veau, which dates from the fourteenth century; and a "recipe," which was bracingly concise. I had already confessed to Daniel that I hadn't made a tête de veau in a long time. Actually, I'd added, I was struggling to remember what one looked like exactly, especially when done as a tortoise. "En tortue" means "like a tortoise." This was the "recipe":

1. Cook head.
2. Remove skin.
3. Remove tongue.
4. Remove cheeks, sweetbreads, head meat, and brain.
5. Combine cheeks, sweetbreads, head meat, and brain; cover with skin.

It was hard not to admire the understatement. Even so, I went to bed thinking: *Where is Julia Child when you need her?*

The bibliographical history intrigued me. This was on the subway, on my way in to the kitchen in the morning. The principal source was *Le Livre de Cuisine*, written in 1881 by Jules Gouffé, one of those end-of-the-Second-Empire, start-of-the-Belle-Époque kick-ass chefs. AJ's worksheet also included an illustration, an elaborate woodblock by a Mr. Etienne Antoine Eugene Ronjat (called "E" by friends, evidently).

The illustration was incomprehensible. No it wasn't. It looked like a hat. How did this help? We were not about to make a hat. It was also a wacky hat. You could imagine women of another era wearing one to a funeral. I put it away.

Then I thought: *It can't be a hat.*

I pulled it out.

It wasn't a hat. But what was it?

I had a sudden, uneasy suspicion that the picture was the instruction. How many words would you need to describe making a tortoise from a cow's head? And who could read it all? No. Our recipe was here. This was what we were meant to reproduce.

I studied it. There was a lot going on. The organizing principle was pile-it-on and pile-it-up. On the bottom was a flat pastry manipulated to look like a straw basket. In it was a giant gray slug. It was adorned with black rocks, yellow ovals, green marbles, and outsized red crustaceans. They looked inflamed. Were those the crayfish? They were the size of crows. The puzzle was the phrase "en tortue." That sluggy, lumpy oval, was that the tortoise? Wait a minute. Where was the head? I wasn't finding it. A headless tête?

In Daniel's version, there was a tête, and cooking it was the first order of business. "Veau," or "veal," is the food word for a "calf," and a calf is a calf until the age of three months—that is, a baby—and I was surprised by how unbaby-like a three-month-old head turns out to be. It was hefty. It was also unwieldy (when you move it, do you grab it by the ears?), and had an impossible-to-ignore visceral reality. I could pretend this was normal, to arrive and discover an

CALF'S HEAD "EN TORTUE"

animal head on my cutting board as I finished my coffee, but, no, it wasn't. Its features—eyelashes, lips, slightly sagging cheeks—were fresh and surprisingly pleasant-smelling, and evoked both its decapitation (a clean cut along the neck) and its recent milk-feeding life. Until Tuesday, or maybe the day before, this head had been attached to a cow. Until Tuesday, or the day before, this head had been a regular underbelly visitor of its big mama, drinking the very nutrient that I had added to my coffee. Modern cooks rarely come face-to-face with the animalness of the animals they cook. I liked that this morning we had an animal so animal-like in our kitchen. Then again, that was the dish, this head.

We wrapped it in cheesecloth, mummifying it, so that, after four hours at a low simmer, it would emerge from its Paul Bocuse pot as a head intact.

Meanwhile, we addressed the garnishes, the adorning "what-nots." AJ listed eleven on her midnight worksheet. There were more than eleven; even AJ couldn't keep track. They included buttered croutons, fried brains, cornichons, veal quenelles, an herbed Jell-O (bright green, an inch deep, in a tray), a poached tongue, olives, egg yolks (the soft kind, where the whites fall away, after eighteen minutes at 140°F), and a sauce tortue: "sort of a cross between a diable and an espagnole," in AJ's worksheet-speak. There were fluted mushrooms. They looked like so many miniature-ribbed umbrellas, easy enough to pull off if you have a light wrist and a light knife, not so easy if your wrist is made of clay. (My score: 27 assayed, 0 successful.) I was shown how to trim a tray of cockscombs (after first poaching them into chewability). I was instructed in crayfish. They arrived like bad weather, a locust-like invasion, running around in packs, zigzagging across cutting boards, until they fell off the edge, and we gave chase across the kitchen. Once rounded up, they underwent two minutes in a boiling broth, followed by two minutes in ice, and were then either mounted or moussed. How do you mount a crayfish? If you are Daniel, you bend one backward like an Olympic swimmer doing the butterfly, hook the small lower claw delicately into the body, and, "Voilà, you have done him proud." If you are me, you bend one backward like a fat man in his first Pilates lesson, and it breaks. Just like that ("Shit!"), right in half. You hope Daniel is not looking. You do it again. Snap. (Assayed: 12. Irreparably broken: 11.) The mousse was made from all the broken crayfish: that is, my

broken crayfish + cream + blender. It looks like a pink Cool Whip. It is then spooned into "timbales" (French fancy for "cupcake tins"), cooked in a pan of hot water, popped out, and eventually scattered artfully here and there on the tortoise head. Given the number of whatnots, there was a lot of artful scattering.

I consulted the picture again. Mr. E. Ronjat wasn't really the detail guy that you would have thought that the job description called for. He also had a very elastic sense of proportion. The yellow ovals: were those the egg yolks?

Our head was ready around midday ("It's when the nostril starts to pull away from the skull," Chad clarified). We put on three pairs of latex surgeon's gloves, because it would be hot, and began peeling the skin off slowly to ensure that it didn't tear. I didn't know why our not tearing the skin was important, probably because I didn't know what was going to happen next. Or maybe I did. I *was* asking questions, but everyone was suddenly very busy—"We have to move fast," Daniel kept repeating—and I was happy just to keep up and be allowed to do a task, a condition I think of as "participatory ignorance." At the risk of stating the obvious, I can confirm that the skin is kept intact because it goes back in place, re-enveloping the contents of the head—cheeks, tongue, lips, ear, gobs of gelatinous matter, plus a mousse whipped up from unaccounted-for bits of meat, milk-soaked bread, and cream—but without the skull.

"Eyeballs, Chef?" asked Chad, an American boy who understood the French concept that you should eat everything and like it.

"No, not the eyeballs," answered Daniel. "You don't eat the thing that was staring at you when you killed it." Daniel paused, reflecting on the transgression. "No. You would never eat an eyeball." He regarded Chad in a new way. "That's disgusting."

Meanwhile, I had become curious. The whole thing was so gummy to look at (brown-gray in "color," except for the spots, which were black-gray), and, frankly, so unappealing that I wanted to taste it out of a perverse curiosity. Was there a difference between what it was *there*, and what it would be in the mouth? But it wasn't ready.

"*Attends, attends.*" The veal pudding needs to set first, Daniel said. It won't be long.

Daniel lifted the skin—that is, the more-or-less miraculously still-intact skin—stretched it out with the extended fingers of both

his hands, and draped it over the slug, tucking it in on the ends, to get an oval. Then, in a delicately poised "flip," Daniel flopped the tray of green herby Jell-O on top, one of those do-it-right or do-it-again-all-night moments, since there was no backup. It was really a toupée. But why a green toupée? No one was explaining. I puzzled the question, staring at the dish, as Daniel completed the grooming. The flop, I began to suspect, was everything. The flop made the dish. Until the flop, the dish hadn't been so pretty to look at. It had been gray and jelly-wobbly and, frankly, just a bit too bald. Now, like a tortoise, it had a shell to hide inside of. Tortoise + green shell = oval-shaped lumpy thing in a green jelly toupée. Voilà! With the flop, a cow's brain became a turtle.

To slice, you use a broad flat knife, like a cake knife, to keep the wobble intact. To eat, you use a spoon. Or I did. And the taste: blurry. I had another bite: all middle. The texture: this was all middle as well, squishiness without variation. The dominant flavor was offal, but neutered. I spooned on some of the diable-espagnole confection. Wow! The sauce was a shocker. I looked around for Chad. Whose hand had been so heavy with the Tabasco? It burned up into the nose. This was not what I would have thought of as a French sauce, except that it obviously was, and the French do have sauces with heat, and they do love their mustards, but *this*: *this* was a lot of heat. It had everything that the tête didn't have: zip and red spice and peppery intensity. The sauce talked directly to the dish, its flavorful non-flavors, its mono texture. It now seemed risky.

Where would you find a food like this today? In a dining room by the sea, a grand hotel that no longer exists? There would be an acidic wine, an abundance, bottles and bottles, no label, a gamay or a pinot noir, then an eau-de-vie, maybe several, the essential digestif, a creeping crepuscular light, curtains about to be drawn, a place that is now no place, another era, not here.

People have described food as transporting. I hadn't. Now I could.

COULIBIAC

IT MAY HAVE BEEN CRAIG CLAIBORNE'S DOING. BECAUSE of Claiborne, New York had old-world French restaurants at a time when it wouldn't have been easy to find them in France. Because of Claiborne, these restaurants served the "classics," when in France, the word, like the food it described, was already out of favor. Claiborne, for nearly forty years the dining critic for the *New York Times*, and who died in 2000, never thought of himself as a guardian of the *old* French menu. He had no reason to believe that it needed protecting. He just regarded it as what French food should be, and was supported in this by a number of French-born, Manhattan-based, old-world chefs, the Claiborne "team."

Then, on October 12, 1982, Daniel arrived in Manhattan, by and large another old-world chef, but younger than his new New York colleagues and, maybe, more worldly. Unlike the colleagues, who had come decades ago by boat, Daniel came by airplane. Unlike the colleagues who stayed on in America, plying a craft that they had acquired long ago from some old-country grand chef now long gone, Daniel, who was twenty-seven, had already worked for a dozen cutting-edge masters in fifteen kitchens, each one radically different from the last, and most were *in* France. It had been a long time since a colleague had worked *in* France. But the colleagues had worked *in* New York, and prepared Daniel for a New York ritual, the "invitation," extended to every new French chef, to appear at Claiborne's home in East Hampton.

Daniel arrived on the Friday, bought his ingredients the next morning, and set up in Claiborne's kitchen. "Right away, Craig was putting questions to me, fast, one after another."

Claiborne wanted Daniel to explain every step. Claiborne wanted history, sources, background. Daniel, standing over a stove, pulling trays out of an oven, stacking dirties in the sink, replied as best as he could, while plating his food, as Claiborne, also standing (a manual typewriter on a high table, Hemingway-style, clack-clack-clacking), banged out the answers.

"A week after arriving, every French chef was summoned to East Hampton," Daniel told me after I'd asked if a Saturday morning demo was a test, like an entrance exam to the city. "Not at all," he said. "It was exhilarating."

It was also exhilarating in the surprising way that New York was now exhilarating, not necessarily for the familiar New York reasons, its edgy, never-sleeping modernity, but because, for a young chef

from France, it was *not* modern: its restaurants were backward. They had fallen off the calendar. They had time-warp menus that, having been created during the great restaurant flourishing before World War II (and "old-fashioned" then), had rarely been touched since. They were museums. In New York, Daniel made dishes that, until now, he had only heard of. Coulibiac would be one of them: popular in the 1870s, it disappeared in the 1970s, but remained, characteristically, a Claiborne favorite. And, in 1988, after announcing his retirement, and on then learning that the team was preparing a party at the Four Seasons to mark the occasion, he asked if someone might make the dish for him.

The names in the kitchen that night were a roll call of the Claiborne era: André Soltner, the patron-chef of Lutèce, the country's "best" restaurant (now closed); Roger Fessaguet, the patron-chef of La Caravelle (now closed); Alain Sailhac of Le Cirque, the 21 Club, and the Plaza (now retired); Georges Perrier of Le Bec-Fin in Philadelphia (now retired); and Gilbert Le Coze, a younger team member, who had just opened Le Bernardin on the ground floor of an insurance company. (Le Coze died five years later of a heart attack.) There were also New York's two honorary American Frenchmen, Jacques Pépin and Pierre Franey, and two honorary Francophiles, Paul Prudhomme from New Orleans and Patrick O'Connell from the Inn at Little Washington in Virginia. And the kid, Monsieur Smarty Pants, that Boulud boy. He had just turned thirty-three. "Tell him to make Craig's favorite. Tell him to do the coulibiac."

"It was an honor that the old guys trusted me," Daniel told me. The old guys may have found that their trust had been misplaced. Daniel had never made a coulibiac. He had never seen one.

He blames nouvelle cuisine. "The dish got lost in the aftermath." "Nouvelle cuisine"—the term was first used by the magazine *Gault & Millau*, in 1974—has come to mean many things, but its most general sense describes a kitchen revolution, when a generation of chefs rose up and challenged just about every aspect of their heritage. It has had many consequences, including a universal but unofficial code for what is no longer acceptable. Overcooked fish? Unacceptable. Salmon, cooked more than medium-rare? Unacceptable. Eggs boiled until they are cakey and hard and smell of a sulfurous hot springs? Unacceptable. At its most basic, a coulibiac is salmon and hard-boiled eggs in a pastry. The pastry prevents you from knowing what is going on underneath it during the cooking until (Hey! What happened?) it is too late.

DANIEL AND I WERE IN THE BASEMENT, ALONG WITH EDDY, the chef coach assigned to the dish, using the "Mercedes," the pastry kitchen's high-tech state-of-the-art steam convection oven with a hair-trigger thermostat. It was a fourth rehearsal. The hope was that a better cooking device would get a better result. The pastry was the head-banger: either it was cooked through and yummy but the insides were inedible, or it was undercooked and disgusting and the insides were yummy. Daniel, well into his third

decade with a coulibiac, was guided, and always had been guided, by *the* guide of guides, the 1903 *Guide Culinaire* by Auguste Escoffier. *Le Guide* is the equivalent of *Webster's* in Scrabble. Two cooks arguing about what goes with what? One opens *Le Guide*; end of argument. Escoffier makes his coulibiac with a puff pastry, a pâte feuilleté. As it happens, I had become a student of puff, making it on Saturday mornings for the last two years, and was convinced that everything (hot dogs for my sons? pizza?) is improved by a bit of it. But a puff needs a hot oven, takes as long as it takes, pools butter, and threatens cardiac arrest if it hasn't finished cooking. The fish and egg kept being ruined in the wait.

Daniel thought that there might be a fix in the dish's architecture, which was a variation on Russian dolls. An egg was wrapped by a salmon fillet. The salmon fillet was wrapped by sticky mushrooms. The sticky mushrooms were wrapped by rice, made especially sticky by a sturgeon glue called "vésiga" (the fish's spinal cord, boiled). And the whole sticky, fishy cylinder was wrapped in pastry. For the eggs, Daniel was trying quail—needing less time to cook than a chicken's—and burying them in between two salmon fillets to retard the heat penetration. But it wasn't working. He cut into the fourth effort—"*Merde!*"—and threw it away.

It is a peculiar dish, I said, trying to be upbeat.

It also had a peculiar name, obviously Russian. Maybe it just wasn't French. I asked Daniel: How did it even get here?

Oh, one of those nineteenth-century guys, he speculated. He didn't know who. "They were all in Russia then, hoping to get hired by a tsar."

"I'd heard it was Carême," I said. Marie-Antonin Carême was a great impresario of the French kitchen, probably the greatest, and author of the five-volume *L'Art de la cuisine française au XIXe siècle*, which began appearing a volume at a time, in 1833. (Actually, he was mainly the author. He subverted the project by dying midway through volume three.)

"Carême?" Daniel was surprised. "Carême discovered coulibiac?" This cheered him up. But he was also baffled. He hadn't known that Carême was the guy.

It was an awkward moment. "Actually I've got no idea."

Daniel looked at me, confused, clearly wondering: *why, then, did you say that?*

Why *did* I say that?

Carême is often credited with inventing every dish eaten in France, but it turns out that, no, he didn't invent every dish. But maybe I had read that somewhere, the coulibiac connection. Wasn't Carême the guy who replaced "service à la française" (banquet-style) with "service à la russe" (arriving in courses)? Wasn't he among those bombing off to Russia?

In fact, Carême did go to Russia once, and only because his mates were there, making bags of money. I discovered this later. Carême went in the way that a chef today says, "You're right, I deserve a private jet, let's open in Las Vegas." A Prince Orlov had said, Antonin, my dear friend, come to St. Petersburg. (Prince Orlov also said, I will give you a castle to live in, a fortune to squander, and treat you like a king.) But Carême was unhappy to be leaving Paris, very unhappy not to be writing his five-volume history, extremely unhappy en route, and utterly miserable on arrival, when he learned that Prince Orlov had buggered off, no details of a return date, suggesting only that the chef might want to hang out for a few months. He did, for a bit, mainly because there were so many French friends ("toute la fleur de la

cuisine française," according to one biographer). Then, just before Christmas, Carême couldn't take any more, and bolted. There were storms; he was convinced he would die at sea; he didn't; he arrived in Paris, finally, sometime in February 1832, where, eleven months later, he did die, aged forty-nine, the magnum opus incomplete.

DANIEL WAS HAVING SECOND THOUGHTS ABOUT ESCOFFIER.
This was three days later. Daniel is an Escoffier disciple. Disciples don't doubt. But Daniel couldn't stop thinking of that failed coulibiac, especially the pastry. It had been acting as though it were more important than the fish. This was wrong. So Daniel ditched it. Just like that. Bang! He abandoned Escoffier.

In the kitchen, no question, everyone was feeling a modest but undeniable buzz: Daniel ditched Escoffier? No way! DB, you go, dude. Whoa.

"Escoffier was never *not* in a suit and tie," Daniel observed, conceding that there was something suspicious about a chef who shows up for work dressed like a banker. Daniel was going with a brioche instead—easier to brown, quicker to cook, needing less heat, and made with less butter, although still plenty, especially in the preparation he settled on, Jean-Louis Palladin's. Palladin doubled the eggs, tripled the fat, and quadrupled the time to incorporate it all. Palladin had been a friend, the youngest member of the nouvelle-cuisine generation, and the first to open a restaurant in the United States: in Washington, DC, not New York, in 1978. Palladin died in 2002. By an uncanny coincidence, Eric Ripert, who had been Palladin's sous chef, was quoted in the *New York Times* on the day that we made our coulibiac. How do these things happen? The article lamented the disappearance of the French "classics." Like coulibiac, Ripert said. Why don't we see it anymore? (Ripert had become the chef at le Bernardin after Le Coze died.)

We were back in the basement, and a probe thermometer was inserted into our new coulibiac. The probe allows you to "see" the temperature inside a food—a wire runs out the side of an oven door to a digital device—including that of two salmon fillets wrapped around two half-cooked quail eggs inside a brioche. The whole thing then went back into the high-tech Mercedes. Then: we waited. We did nothing. The idea was, that with so much kit, no one needed to do a thing.

Then, I don't know, something happened, I'm not sure what, because after ten minutes Eddy seemed to be losing his nerve, and Daniel lost his, and everyone was in a state, and the coulibiac was touched, poked, turned this way, turned back, bumped, and, at every possible moment, fussed with.

The oven was too hot. It was turned down to 350.

The brioche has no color. The oven was turned up.

It's bubbling! I see a bubble! It was turned down.

Eddy opened the door and poked his head inside. Why? I don't know why. Did he know why? To see what it felt like? Because after that, the door was never left alone. The temperature rose, fell, and did everything except stand still.

The hope was to catch fish and pastry crossing a finish line, in different conditions of doneness, at the same time: the pastry, brown, crusty, crunchy, hot; the fish, rosy-red, warm, just. But after an hour the brioche wasn't cooked, and, according to the probe thermometer, the salmon was cold. It would take an hour and forty-five minutes. You don't cook salmon for an hour and forty-five minutes and get rare. It was ruined, obviously, when, at last, it emerged from the oven, a blast of buttery, yeasty seafood aromatics, and sat on a worktop untouched. What was the point? It was a long time before anyone cut into it and tasted it and acknowledged that this brioche coulibiac might be perfect.

I found, in all this, a resoundingly obvious lesson: that, if cooking knowledge is not carefully passed from one generation to the next, it doesn't last. If you look up "coulibiac" in the first, 1938 edition of *Larousse Gastronomique*, you will find plenty, including a simple account of the dish's origins, "a warm pastry (un pâté chaud) with fish inside," an acknowledgment that it is Russian, and a grainy photograph of a loaflike entity sitting bluntly on a platter, emanating rustic veracity. From the entry, you may not be able to replicate the dish, but you'll understand what it is. In the recent *Larousse Gastronomique*, published fifty-nine years later, and edited by Joël Robuchon, a high prince of nouvelle cuisine, the coulibiac passage has been rewritten. It has no picture, makes no mention of vésiga, or Russia, or salmon, doesn't specify the pastry, and describes the dish in terms that suggest a sack that can be filled with meat, vegetables, fish, whatever, yesterday's newspapers. I read the entry and thought: *no idea what is being described*. Even now, with all of human history compressed onto a hard drive, when a dish falls out of the repertoire, the know-how goes with it. In less than sixty years, it was gone: *pfiff*.

Chad prepared two plates. He sliced the coulibiac crosswise and then dressed the fish, which was between rare and medium-rare, with a butter sauce and caviar, an appositely Russian garnish, another food that Carême is said to have introduced to France.

I closed my eyes, I tasted, I thought: *home*.

In fact, it was nothing like what we eat at home, but had a quality that made me think: *home*. Was it because of the rice? Does rice say "home"? It was sticky and smelled lightly of the sea. This must have been the vésiga. I rolled a kernel in my mouth. It was swollen. Was this the best rice of my life? The salmon was flavoring everything as well. It was like a pink butter that had melted into the other ingredients. There were no pan juices. Maybe that is the pastry's purpose: to ensure that nothing escapes. It is like a mini-oven, locking in the gummy, buttery ocean flavors.

I GOT A SIMILAR "TAKEAWAY" IN A PASSAGE FROM *DEAD* *Souls* by the Russian novelist Gogol. It is quoted under "Coulibiac" in *The Oxford Companion to Food*, edited by the late Alan

Davidson. The entry was written by the editor's daughter, Pamela, whom I tracked down at the London School of Economics, where she is now professor of slavic studies. A French coulibiac is under no obligation to be faithful to the Russian original, of course, but since it obviously inspired the French version I found that I had loads of queries that I was keen to submit to an authoritative referee. The vésiga, for instance. Daniel got his from a fish supplier. The spine was long and white and a half-inch in diameter, and had a bungee-stretchiness, like an elastic lasso. The vésiga, I asked, basically, it's the dish, no?

Essential, Professor Davidson said. She repeated the word, silently correcting me: "*vyaziga*." She pronounced it like a sneeze. For many, she said, it is the taste of Russia. "It is like getting sturgeon without having to pay for it." No *vyaziga*, no coulibiac. Usually it was bought dried.

Dried sturgeon spine?

"All the shops had it." Davidson lived in Moscow in the eighties. It was a pantry item. "It came in a box."

In the passage from *Dead Souls*, which was published in 1843, the dish, a "four-cornered pie," is all about the sturgeon-ness. Pyotr Petrovich Petukh, who is short and fat, as round as a watermelon

(the stomach, in Gogol, is the body's noblest part), is telling a cook how to prepare a coulibiac for lunch. First of all, Petukh says, the fish should be sturgeon. (Both salmon and sturgeon are used, Davidson confirmed.) And the filling is almost like a savory pudding: yes, vésiga, but also brains and cheeks and the caviar, stirred together into something creamy and rich. And the pastry is important, too, because you want it to soak up all the rich sturgeon juices. "I mean, I don't want it to crumble," Petukh says. "I want it to melt in the mouth like snow, so that one shouldn't even feel it melting."

"It's not puff pastry, is it?" I asked Davidson.

"Puff pastry?" She was horrified. "No."

"Brioche?"

"Yes, brioche, but normally the dough is simpler." There was a coulibiac pastry. She would send me the recipe later—a yeast dough, with milk, a little butter, and extra eggs.

"And rice?" I confirmed.

"Yes, rice, but often kasha."

Kasha? Kasha is the hardy starch of a Slavic winter, buckwheat in fact, but when done properly it gets a nutty, deep-brown crust. (Like rice, you boil buckwheat; unlike rice, you then roast it first until it is crunchy.) A slice of coulibiac is already dressed in the

colors of the UPS man. These are the cozy chromatics of comfort. Kasha: the suggestion was thrilling and obvious. It was like adding a cello.

Restaurant food is not normally harmonic. It tends to be discordant (sweet and sour, soft and hard, fruit and savory) and intensified, more salt than you use at home, more pepper; it has texture, contrast, crackle; probably because, in a restaurant, food is a business transaction: it wants you to notice what you have paid for. A coulibiac, in contrast, is a food of no contrasts. It isn't a food of textures, because, in Petukh's description, all the textures dissolve. It is a winter food. It rewards you for getting home.

Daniel, meanwhile, was looking pleased. I had never seen him pleased before. Even when he is pleased, he would never say anything so bald as "I'm pleased." It would be more like: I'm not unpleased. ("*Ce n'est pas mal ça . . . peut-être.*") Craig Claiborne had not eaten this well.

It was later that I told Daniel my theory of how coulibiac reached France.

Once again, Carême is involved, at least indirectly, because the first French publication of a coulibiac recipe appears to have been

in volume five of Carême's very own *L'Art de la cuisine française au XIXe siècle*. This was in 1847. Alas, by 1847, Carême had been dead fourteen years. The recipe had been written by Armand Plumerey, a Carême acolyte. Not much is known about Plumerey, except that, with Carême's premature death, as volume three was being wrapped up, it fell to Plumerey to interpret Carême's intentions for posterity. It seems reasonable to wonder if that interpretation had been conducted via the occasional séance in a dark room, at least if Plumerey's coulibiac recipe is representative. It is not eccentric; it is outright bonkers. It is long, involves two fish, including a turbot, has a half-dozen eggs, an abundance of green herbs, a glass of Madeira, no vésiga, plus reductions, several sauces, and a beurre fondu popped under the pastry.

By an improbable-seeming coincidence, the genuine first French publication of a true coulibiac recipe *also* involves Carême, although, once again, only indirectly. The story originates with Prince Orlov. When he returned to St. Petersburg in December 1831, having been ditched by his trophy chef, he was in a tough spot. Who would prepare the New Year's Eve banquets? In a panic, he hired a twenty-nine-year-old Carême disciple named Urbain Dubois. You can imagine the logic: if you can't get the great man, you can at least get his recipes from the young guy who stole them. Dubois remained in Slavic employment for nearly two decades and became an advocate of all things Russian: caviar, the service à la russe, and coulibiac. It is recipe no. 1139 in Dubois's first book, *La cuisine classique*, published in 1856. It calls for vésiga, an egg, salmon or sturgeon, mushrooms, and a unique pastry, a "coulibiac pâte," basically a brioche with extra eggs. The dish is made with kasha, although rice is an acceptable substitute.

I finished my account.

Daniel looked unhappy: that is, not normally unhappy, but *really* unhappy. He was pacing.

It was the kasha that made Daniel unhappy. "You don't understand," he said. "I have been trying to make a coulibiac for thirty years. I have been haunted by this dish. Finally, I get it right. Or at least I believe that I have got it right. Now you tell me that, actually, what it needs is kasha?"

His distress was palpable. It was moving. I felt terrible. I apologized. I was so sorry. These old dishes, I said, really, they're good, they're very good—in fact, they are probably better—with rice.

CANARD À LA PRESSE

THIS IS NO ORDINARY DUCK. THIS IS A GRAND DUCK. THIS is a duck with a history, a highly ritualized service, *and* a flashy dining room toy.

The toy is a press. It is used to squeeze what people euphemistically refer to as the "juices" from a carcass of a scarcely roasted bird—that is, its blood. The blood is then added to a sauce. And that, in its fundamentals, is the dish: a duck and its bloody sauce.

The histories (and there are many, and all of them the same) begin in the middle to late nineteenth century, when the press was invented by Méchenet—a chef from Rouen, known for its big ducks. The actual date and Méchenet's first name haven't quite been nailed down. What Monsieur Méchenet invented is also unclear, if only because the invention had already been invented. In France, it is called a "presse-viande" (a meat press) or simply a "pressoir" (as in a "pressoir à fruit," or "à citron," or "à jus"): the principal is screw, squeeze down, filter out. Your great-grandfather may have used one to crush juice from orchard fruits. Your great-grandfather may also have used it for birds, especially pigeons, which used to be killed by smothering: a smothered bird is full of juice. In fact, before your great-grandfather's time, all birds were smothered. In the old days, bird dinners were very juicy.

What Monsieur Méchenet probably invented was a look. It wasn't a better duck dinner; it was a better duck show. We will never know for sure, because no historian has glimpsed the Méchenet machine. It was "appropriated" sometime before 1890 by Frédéric Delair, a restaurateur in Paris, who ran an establishment called la Tour d'Argent. Delair's version was gigantic, plated in white silver, and arrived tableside on a trolley draped in white linen. Unlike its farmhouse cousin, which often used a broomstick as an improvised handle to screw it down, Delair's version was a *machine*. It had a valve—one that required two hands to turn— and such an enduring sense of design that it would have been wholly apposite in an underwater vehicle devised by Jules Verne. It was a thing with bling.

Blood is an awkward ingredient in French dishes. Only one is prepared tableside: canard à la presse. In 1890, Delair enhanced the aura of the ducks by numbering them, as if each one was uniquely valuable. That year, for instance, Edward VII, then the Prince of Wales, ate number 328. Edward's niece, Princess Elizabeth, the future Queen of England, was number 185,387. Meanwhile, the rustic farmhouse tool is still available; you will find plenty on eBay.fr. Christofle offers the full-on silver-plated one: its price reduced, when I visited the website, to €69,460 (about $90,992).

Since 1890, the Tour d'Argent's basic "recipe" hasn't changed. If you find yourself at the Tour d'Argent tomorrow, you will eat duck in the confidence that it was what someone ate a hundred years ago. You will eat it in the expectation that someone else will serve it a hundred years from now. You will find the same preparation at Michel Rostang's. In fact, you will find it at any French restaurant still serving duck à la presse: that is, any establishment prepared to invest in the high theater of presentation confected by Frédéric Delair. You can even watch it demonstrated on one of the legendary shows of food television, a 1971 episode of *The French Chef,* featuring Julia Child's whacking away at a carcass at a long arm's length, her towering frame extended and tilting backward, maintaining an awkward distance, because she is wearing a dress and a uselessly petit apron, and bits of bone and lobs of fat are shooting off in unpredictable directions.

The duck made by Daniel, however, is different. Both the recipe and the press originate not in nineteenth-century France, but in 1930s New York, and arrived, circuitously, via a turn-of-the-century family from Ohio.

Charles Maxwell Robertson, born in 1902, was responsible for the press. He was the president of Ralph H. Jones Co., an advertising firm in Cincinnati. He liked to hunt and fish. With his wife, Ann, who was born in 1901, he traveled: transatlantic cruises, first class; New York, by train, weekly. They were Hemingway contemporaries and, like Hemingway, were at ease in the American Midwest of Sherwood Anderson and the Paris of Ford Madox Ford and the Prohibition New York of wise guys and journos. They were regulars at the 21 Club. It had a duck press, the silver-plated, wheel-it-out-on-a-trolley luxe apparatus. But after Prohibition was repealed on December 5, 1933, the 21 Club lost some of its edge and many of its big spenders, and the duck was no longer a menu item. Robertson had been eyeing the press. He offered $5 for it and took it back to Cincinnati on the train.

Alice Robertson was responsible for the recipe. In 2008, her daughter Ann, then seventy-three, found it in an attic, written out in her mother's fine, enfeebled hand. It was a ghostly discovery. It connected her instantly to her powerful parents, their glamour, their joy at the table, all now gone. Ann mailed the recipe to a friend, Joel Buchman. Buchman, a Daniel regular and friend of

the kitchen, brought it in and asked Eddy and Jean-François if they thought it might work.

Yes. But they needed a press. Ann volunteered the 21 Club contraption. Buchman delivered it.

Until now, the only "prep" in preparing a duck à la presse was acquiring the bird. Its juices were the sauce. Yes, there was veal stock, and a splash of Cognac and a knob of butter, but fundamentally the dish was the duck. The Robertson recipe includes a preliminary step so self-evident, it is baffling that it hasn't always been done. It is this: the duck is first marinated. The marinade is a bottle of port, a jar of red currant jelly, some orange and lemon zest, and a lot of pepper, which is boiled and then cooled, and into which the duck is then submerged and swells until saturated, its

own "juice" content now enriched. (Daniel intensifies the saturation by putting everything into a plastic bag and vacuuming out the air with a sous-vide machine; he also slits the skin with a razor blade to render the fat, another resoundingly obvious step not in the d'Argent textbook.) When the carcass is now pressed, the liquid is deep and dark. It produces a sauce so unusual that, on tasting it, I finally understood that the duck is almost immaterial. The dish is what you coat it with. What matters is the sauce.

In October 2008, a trial dinner was arranged, possibly the first of its kind in New York since 1933. Eddy and Jean-François prepared the duck; Daniel completed the sauce for a four top: Ann Robertson and her husband; Joel Buchman and his wife. Ann reminisced about her parents, and how they remained for her "so much larger than life," and how the annual duck dinners were the most extravagant social event at home. The birds were Canadian and wild, flying south. "Daddy shot them," she said, when, in a startling Banquo moment, the four top became six, and Ann was convinced that her parents had joined them "there, right there." Buchman recalls a spinal shudder. Daniel remembers the meal as the most complete he has made since arriving in the United States. Afterward, Ann Robertson gave the restaurant a gift: the duck press.

CHARTREUSE

la Chartreuse. noun, *feminine.* The mountains ninety minutes east of Lyon by car, between Chambéry and Grenoble.

l'Ordre des Chartreux. noun, *masculine.* A monastic "family" founded in 1084 by Saint Bruno and known for its lifelong vows of silence and solitude.

la Grande Chartreuse. noun, *feminine.* The "mother" abbey.

Chartreuse. noun, *feminine.* An herbal distillation originally made at the monastery from an anonymous *élixir de longue vie* recipe discovered in 1605, and now manufactured in Grenoble under the supervision of the Carthusian monks.

chartreuse. adjective. An unnaturally "natural" color inspired by the monastery distillation: a neon green.

la Chartreuse. noun, *feminine.* A dish cooked in a mold of vegetables and turned out on a plate, with a "surprise" inside. In an 1868 Urbain Dubois recipe, the surprise is bear.

DANIEL HAS A MODEST CONVERSATIONAL TIC, WHICH IS
that whenever he mentions "Nandron"—and it is always "Nandron," no first name, no "the Lyonnais chef," or "my former boss"—he assumes that you know whom he is talking about and is surprised when you don't. I witnessed this on the eve of my moving to Lyon, after I had dropped by the kitchen to get some last-minute tips, and Daniel, answering a question that I had put to him about the people he had worked for, ran through a list, then backed up, and added his first employer, not as an afterthought, but as a given. "And Nandron, of course."

Who?

"Nandron."

Who is that?

"You don't know Nandron? *C'est vrai?*" He stared at me to see if I was joking. "I don't believe you."

I looked the name up later, but didn't find much: a restaurant called "Nandron" and a man called "Nandron," who closed the restaurant in 1990 and died in 1999.

When I next saw Daniel, I was living in Lyon, and he was in town for the Bocuse d'Or, a biennial food competition. Nandron's name came up again, and I missed it again. "Who?" I asked, ever the dumbo. I resolved then and there to nail the story. It wasn't easy. When I asked Daniel what seemed like obvious questions, I got replies that were often vague, or anecdotal, or else stuck in the oddly myopic details of the restaurant itself: the precise location of the service entrance, or the slaughterhouse across the street ("Oh la la, the stink"), or the chefs' market so near that you ran the risk of being spotted by Paul Bocuse and getting boxed on the ear if you had stepped outside for a teenage smoke. What I was getting was incomplete. What I was getting was what a fourteen-year-old teenage apprentice saw. What I wasn't getting was the stuff a grown-up uses to complete a picture: that there had been *two* Nandrons, for instance, a father and a son, Joannès and Gérard; that they had been chef-proprietors of what was clearly a classy place on a quai by the Rhône; and that there had been two *female* Nandrons as well, the Madame, a widow when Daniel arrived in 1969, always parked in the dining room, handling cash and payroll ("A very large woman," in Daniel's description, "but, you know, elegantly large"); and Odette, Gérard's "slim,

cosmopolitan" wife, who organized the banquets. Meanwhile, the Nandron theme continued. Two years later I happened to witness *other* versions of the *c'est vrai* exchange ("Really, you don't know Nandron?"), involving Daniel's own kitchen staff. I had no reason to know about this cozy anachronistic family restaurant, because, with the exception of Daniel, no one else—outside of Lyon *and* under the age of, say, seventy—knew about it either.

No one will find out much more. There are no Nandron cookbooks. No bits of publicity, no newspaper stories, no interviews, scarcely a recipe: in effect, no paper trail. I found my first tidbit, on November 18, 2011, three years after that initial Daniel meeting. It was a photograph of Gérard, the son, in an exhibit on Lyonnais gastronomy at the musées Gadagne. It was also incorrectly labeled. (He was identified as the father, which seemed telling somehow.) Then, on March 10, 2012, *Le Progrès*, the local paper, announced a sale of plates and cutlery from the old Lyonnais restaurants. I went as Daniel's emissary, with instructions to buy only sets, not bits and pieces, but anything with Nandron's name on it. There was nothing, even though the paper had said there would be. It seemed like a mean trick.

Daniel remained at Nandron's until just before his eighteenth birthday. These were the last days of the old ways. Nouvelle cuisine was a rumor in Paris. Nandron Sr., a legendary Escoffier disciple, had died a few years before, but his son remained committed to making his father's old dishes, believing that they were essential to the restaurant's identity. It was, in any case, a great time to be a chef in Lyon. The younger Nandron was proudly, chauvinistically Lyonnais—the city was widely accepted as the "gastronomic capital of the world"—and in everything Gérard taught the new apprentice there was, therefore, a double lesson: old school and local. The lessons are evident in every one of the iconic bird dishes. (Lyon could also be called "the bird-eaters capital of the world.") They were especially evident in the weekly chartreuse.

It was made on Mondays. That was when the birds arrived. Gérard shot them over the weekend. He glided up to the service entrance, a ritual of autumn—a Citroën DS, de Gaulle's car, a proclamation of Frenchness and entitlement—and popped open the automated trunk, where Daniel, already waiting, gathered up the bounty, removed it to the basement, and began plucking. Daniel was the restaurant's first plucker.

For me, the challenge posed by a chartreuse was its name. I couldn't separate it from every other sense of the word: a mountain, a monastery, a religious order, a drink, a color. These words were related to each other in obvious ways. Chartreuse, the dish, didn't seem to be related to any of them. Daniel had none of these problems. For Daniel, a chartreuse was this, a game-bird confection that looks like a joke birthday cake.

It took three days.

On day one, we made the "farce"—the filling, which was chopped-up cabbage sautéed in pork belly, duck fat, and foie gras. Who could come up with a fattier cabbage? It was the meatiest vegetable I remember eating. It was insanely satisfying. It compounded my confusion.

Why chartreuse? I asked AJ.

"Because that's what it's called."

In the evening, I searched the digital holdings of the Bibliothèque Nationale de France for an edible chartreuse. I found several, all in the nineteenth century. Nothing explained how they came to be called what they are called. You don't name a dish after a bunch of monks for no reason, do you?

On day two, the birds were prepared. Most chartreuse recipes call for one bird, a fat one, like a pigeon or a partridge, secreted inside the casing, the vegetable mold that is then turned out onto a plate. Ours, being an extravagant tribute to Nandron's trunk, called not for one fat fowl but for a cacophonous flock—fat and skinny, big and small, quails, woodcocks, doves, pheasants, a guinea hen, and both a pigeon and a partridge. We used only the breasts, roasted pink. They would be stacked neatly inside the mold and then held in place by the farce, which would be shoveled in and pressed tight. Bernard Vrod, the restaurant's maître d', is a hunter.

Finally, we addressed the casing. This was day three. The casing was made from root vegetables—white turnips and yellow and orange carrots—which had been cut thin on a mandoline by Chad, steamed until pliable, and trimmed into shape with a knife. Chad had also determined the dimensions of each slice; in his spare time, Chad is a student of higher mathematics at Columbia University. He came up with a triangulation formula so precise that it eliminated overhangs and overlaps, each piece falling into place like a children's puzzle. In practice, the pieces shrank; the formula was useless; and there was much snipping to get the thing

to fit into its snug pastry cake illusion. At one point, five of us were bumping shoulders, squeezing our triangles into an increasingly small-seeming mold, lifting them out again to re-trim, our fingers becoming more balloon-like the closer we got to finishing. We then started in on a second mold, which was even smaller.

They went into the oven. We waited.

In Daniel's office, I came upon "Chartreuse" in a nineteenth-century food encyclopedia. This was *Le grand dictionnaire de cuisine* by Alexandre Dumas, the novelist (*The Count of Monte Cristo, The Three Musketeers*). Given his métier, Dumas is good at giving voice to strong feelings. He is less good at facts. He claims, for instance, that Antonin Carême created chartreuse. He didn't, although Dumas was probably just participating in the widespread practice of French wishful thinking that Carême is responsible for any dish that expresses the Gallic soul. (With the help of the food historian Jim Chevallier, I found accounts of chartreuse before Carême was born.) Dumas also speculates on the dish's origins, imagining that it would have been served to the Carthusian monks, the elaborate vegetarian casing hiding a piece of meaty contraband inside. (Among a monk's many lifetime vows was one never to eat meat.) This seemed not just unlikely but utterly ridiculous. In fact, Dumas was probably right.

Until the late nineteenth century, chartreuse was not a color because few people knew the drink. I learned this on discovering that, until 1838, the drink wasn't distributed any further than the donkey bearing it. It was the monks who were famous, owing to the notoriety of their extreme vows. Plenty of people didn't eat meat, of course, but not eating it was a ritualized sacrifice—the "lean" days, Lent—ordered by the church. Very few people ate meat *never*. (Jim Chevallier points out that the word "vegetarian" didn't exist yet.) That was what the word "chartreuse" evoked, these mountain freaks who would *never* know the fatty happiness of a steak frites and a glass of red. Was a chartreuse, with its secret meat tucked inside, actually served at a monk's table? No. It was a conceit, an eighteenth-century confection, a piece of wit invented by a clever chef somewhere, we'll never know who, this dish pretending to be made only of vegetables.

When the two molds had finished cooking, they were turned out. One was mounted atop the other. Daniel arranged roasted woodcock heads on top and stepped back. The effect was unlike anything I have witnessed in a kitchen. An instantaneous feeling of wonder. Wow! We were responsible for what we were staring at. The dish was almost incomprehensible in its unnatural natural beauty.

I wonder now if it is in this unnatural beauty that we find Carême: the lines and geometric shapes, as if confected by a machine, but smelling of the earth. He didn't invent the dish, but he made it his own. Carême is known for giant, preposterous foods that gobbled up space in three dimensions, having famously found inspiration in architectural plans that he copied out in the Bibliothèque Nationale. But the achievement that has endured is in two dimensions: how he made unnaturally straight lines out of natural ingredients. Carême's actual instructions for this dish are revealing. He recommends that it be made in late spring or summer ("*les mois de mai, juin, juillet et août*"), because the vegetables are then "tender" and "full of sunshine." This is a pastry chef's instruction, not a hunter's. You don't shoot birds in the spring; they are mating or about to give birth. But at the end of spring, a vegetable, even a lowly root, is at its most colorful. Color gives you the crisp line.

Daniel cut into the chartreuse. He was thrilled. He corrected himself. It was not that he was thrilled; he was not unthrilled. "*C'est pas mal,*" he said. He had a bite. The game birds, the fat, the forest scents, the autumnal flavors, late harvests and mushrooms and dirt. "*C'est du vrai medieval.*" He had another bite.

Despite an effort at restraint, Daniel was excited. Maybe he was hungry, because after a third bite he said, quietly, as though to himself, "This is actually country grand." He was jumping slightly. I had never seen this jumping thing before. Maybe he was merely shifting weight from one foot to the other, but it seemed that he was about to bounce through the kitchen, elflike, until finally and unequivocally, he declared, "Now *this* is the taste of the true France, *c'est le vrai goût de la France*."

I had a bite, trying to locate the flavors that Daniel was describing. I wanted to commit them to memory, this goût, this taste, this France.

VOLAILLE À NOELLE

IS A VOLAILLE À NOELLE THE MOST PLAYFUL OF THE playful foods? It *seems* to be a chicken ("volaille" often means chicken; "poultry" is probably the English equivalent). And it *is*, but it's a chicken with no bones. You can cut through it and serve it as a slice. The practice is sometimes referred to as trompe-l'oeil, but it's really just chefs' messing with our heads. Droll head-banging kitchen jokesters have been around since the 1400s, at least, but only during periods of culinary self-confidence. You tend not to play with your food during famine, war, cultural subjugation, financial collapse, enslavement, military siege, and epidemics of cholera, or bubonic plague. Lyon in the 1960s and 1970s must have been feeling pretty good about itself.

The dish rests on a cook's being able to bone a chicken entirely without breaking the skin. We had no recipe, only a video of Joannès Nandron. It was Nandron Sr.'s only television appearance, and was recorded in 1955, an extraordinary find in itself, and had been unearthed by the musées Gadagne for its gastronomic exhibit. Nandron Sr. is credited with being the dish's "inventor"—it was his party trick, evidently—and we all watched the demonstration. Afterward, no one said a word: for days, nothing. Finally, Daniel alluded to it, mumbling something about the production qualities: that, I don't know, maybe they weren't of the highest standards. As always, Daniel was being polite. But once the team captain had uttered a dissident sentiment, we all felt entitled to own up to what we really thought. There is no pretty way to say this. It looked like shit. *Merde.* Does it sound better in French? *C'était dégueulasse*, just plain disgusting.

The video features a rotund, impatient man of zero charisma, a round face, and a short-haired caterpillar moustache. He is both bored and imperious. He is possibly drunk. He slops together a dish that he has made a thousand times. He bones the chicken in three minutes—a sack of saggy skin, the meat still stuck to it, some hanging by a thread of stretched tendon—so that it's only a matter of dumping in the filling: a chickeny creamy mousse, one assumes (the old guy doesn't give a lot away), some carrots, some peas, gobs of butter (by the handful), followed by a slapdash surgery with a trussing needle. The bad lighting and black-and-white film are brutally unflattering. You can't look at this video and think: What a jolly treat, I can't wait to try it. You think: I'm glad I'm alive, and he's dead, and I don't have to eat *that*.

For me, the amateur, the boning of the chicken was the first challenge, and on Valentine's Day, our official Iconic Sessions having been suspended because the kitchen was so busy, I showed up early to practice, and set up in a corner. Me and a chicken: two hours. My chef's jacket was sodden. That was sweat, mainly. It had also been paintbrush flicked with yellow, red, and white. That was the splatter trail. I also kept having to swat my neck.

Otherwise it was straightforward enough. You need only a small sharp knife.

1. You flip the bird over, butt up, and look for the "pope's nose," just north of the anus, where the back narrows into an arrow. You poke it with your knife and separate the tissue from the bone, not much, then a little more, and carry on, scraping, scraping.
2. You move up the bird, scrapingly, until you reach a leg and work down it until you can turn it inside out. Inside out is easier.
3. You carry on until you reach the wings: inside out, same deal.
4. Then the neck: inside out, done.

For Chad, bird boning was Poultry 101. Filling the bird back up again wasn't so easy. The problem wasn't the bird; it was Chad's boss. The basic filling was a chicken mousse. There would be other stuff, but the mousse was the re-inflator: pump it in, and the chicken, no longer just a sack of skin, gets bigger and bigger until it looks chickeny again. But Daniel didn't like Chad's mousse. I don't know why. After six efforts, Chad didn't know why. ("Daniel can be a little particular about his mousse.") Suddenly, Chad remembered a classic flavoring: a heady quantity of vin jaune. Vin jaune, or "yellow wine," comes from a sheltered valley in the Jura Mountains where grapes should not be expected to grow. The wine is filthy-smelling, obviously oxidized, possibly hyperbacterial, and abrasively alcoholic until you get used to it, whereupon it becomes something that some of us are happy to drink with our morning coffee. Vin jaune is also an ingredient in a traditional dish, chicken with morel mushrooms and cream. Cooking is like a court of law: if there's a precedent, you have a case. Chad had found a wine with a chicken precedent to flavor his mousse, and was good to go.

A problem remained: what else to put inside? You can't fill up your chicken with only the mousse. That had been the Papa Nandron approach. In order to achieve a proper "ahaaaa" show-piece moment, you really want to follow up the surprise of slicing through a boneless chicken with the surprise of what you *then* find inside. But what? Chad and his boss settled on two pairs of arty radiating "teardrops." One pair was spinach-flavored and therefore green. The other pair was made from truffles and therefore black.

We got to work.

A flavored teardrop inside a boneless chicken might seem straightforward, Chad told me, as we set up our mise en place, but it had been pretty hard to figure out.

In an early rehearsal, Chad hadn't been thinking green and black teardrops. Instead, he had made perfect green and black circles. They weren't circles, really. They were tubes, achieved by rolling a green spinach or black truffle mousse until it stretched and grew snakelike. It was when you cut across one that it looked like a circle. But Chad's boss wasn't impressed. Anyone can make circles.

I drew an experimental teardrop in my notebook. It is like a water drop before it plops. There is a swelling round curve on the bottom, a stretched-out pointy stem on top. But how do you make it into a shape that, when sliced sideways, will deliver up a true lachrymose silhouette onto your plate?

Chad had devised a parametric equation, and was trying to execute it, when Aurelien Dufour, the in-house charcutier, happened to pass by.

What you need, Dufour told Chad, are aluminum bullnose stair edges. These are the metal guards that you find screwed down on a step to keep you from sliding off it on rainy days. Dufour keeps a set in his knife bag.

Here, he said, you can borrow mine.

Chad demonstrated. You take two bullnose stair edges and hold them against each other at a forty-five-degree angle. They make a wedge. Then you tape it.

I wrote in my notebook:

1. There is a charcuterie guy who goes everywhere with metal stair edges.
2. He uses blue duct tape to hold them together and then...
3. puts them in chicken. WTF?

Chad held up one of his taped-up stair-edge charcuterie devices and laid a sheet of plastic acetate inside. Plastic acetate is like plastic film, but heavy. It bends rather than folds, and once jammed into a forty-five-degree corner it curves rather than creases, and forms a swelling rounded crescent remarkably similar to the curve at the bottom of a teardrop. He squirted a quantity of mousse on top (the green spinachy kind, as it happens), and brought the two sides of the acetate together until they were touching, and then snapped them in place with an office binder clip. And *that* is the spot—the mousse squished up against the binder-clipped sheets of acetate—where you will find the pointy stem of a teardrop when it is sliced.

Remarkably, what followed was starting to seem normal. Two pairs of stair-edge charcuterie devices—now loaded, respectively, with a spinach and a truffle mousse—were frozen and then inserted into a chicken. The "normal" vin jaune–scented mousse was pumped inside, plumping up the bird, which could then be sewn up and roasted in the normal way. I say "in the normal way," but by now I sensed that I might be losing my sense of normal. Sometimes, when I am working alongside Chad, there is so little that is normal that the abnormal becomes a kind of visiting normal. Sometimes, when I am working alongside Chad, I find that it is a healthy practice to step back, hit a pause button, take a deep breath, and observe that, ladies and gentlemen, this was some very weird shit.

POULET EN VESSIE

VERY, VERY FEW PEOPLE OUTSIDE FRANCE HAVE EATEN
a poulet en vessie. Very, very few people will ever eat one. It is such
a peculiar concoction that it is worth recognizing what it isn't in
order to understand what it is. It is not art. There are no vegetables
turned into spheres. There are no straight lines. To make it, you
need to know only how to tie a string into a sturdy knot. It is dinner.
It is chicken.

It is a tasty chicken because it comes from Bourg-en-Bresse, the
poultry capital of France. In Lyon, the all-white Bresse chickens—
Bourg-en-Bresse is forty miles away, a straight Roman road, cutting through low-lying swamps and ponds—are so widely available
that they constitute the unofficial flavor of the region. A Bresse
chicken is the best of the best, and, in this preparation, it enjoys
a hard-to-miss affinity with the other ingredients: foie gras, black

truffles, truffle juice, Cognac, Madeira, port, even the white wine,
Condrieu, the region's most celebrated and its priciest. These are
totems of luxury eating. The list seems arbitrary, as if the criterion
is status, not taste, especially in the context of what it is all then
cooked in: a vessie; a pork bladder. You will look a long time before
finding ingredients so grand cooked in such a lowly vehicle. You
will look a long time before finding this dish in the United States.
The FDA already has hygiene concerns about poultry, but poultry
in a pig's pee-pee bag? Not a chance.

For Daniel's New York version, the chickens come not from
Bresse, but from Pennsylvania, said to have the most French of the
world's non-French chickens. An actual Bresse chicken wasn't going
to happen. Chickens are largish entities; Daniel needed several;
they would have to be fresh, with their innards intact. In France,

birds are cleaned at the last minute. All and all, it would be a formidable challenge, to convey such a parcel across the Atlantic, guts and whatnot bloating and starting, possibly, to ferment.

The bladders, however, you can't find anywhere in the United States, unless you own a pig and have the wherewithal to kill it, rescue the essential sack, and squeeze the liquid out. The bladders would have to come from France, and on a Thursday morning a clandestine package arrived in the kitchen. It was from a secret source in Paris, conveyed by DHL courier, and loosely described on the customs declaration as "documents." Another batch had already been supplied, "just in case." This was from a less secret source, yours truly, who had buried a half-dozen deep in his suitcase. Yours truly had been advised by his Lyonnais butcher to wrap them in newspaper. "Fools the dog." The dog in question is that mutt on a leash held by a U.S. Customs and Border Protection agent, sniffing in the baggage reclaim area, hoping to score.

You start by stuffing several of the luxury products into the chicken, the truffles first, which are cut thick, dipped into melted butter, and slipped underneath the skin at the front of the breast. I had worked in restaurants in Lyon, where the practice is to slice truffles as thin as possible and shove them in from the back. That's because the chefs are penny-pinching and ungenerous, Daniel explained and then, as if by illustration, he seized an additional truffle, quartered it and poached it briefly in a pot of already simmering port and inserted it into the bird's cavity. It was a flamboyant declaration of allegiance to the spirit of the dish.

He filled the rest with a duck liver, followed by generous splashes of Cognac and Madeira. The bird was sewn up, the legs and wings trussed up against the body, and inserted into the vessie.

It didn't fit. The task had fallen to Eddy. He just couldn't get the creature into the hole. He twisted the chicken, this way and that, until finally the vessie ripped, a long tear down the side. I tore one as well, but this was later, at Chez Billy, and from my own stash, after I had come to believe that trussing the bird, back to front to back again, was fussy, and that it would be sufficient to hold the wings and legs with my hands as I pushed it through: I was right, or appeared to be, until the bird's appurtenances opened out in the heat of cooking and the sharp tip of a wing punctured the vessie.

In general, a vessie is impressively commodious, there is no other word for it, and elastic up to a point. The hole, however, isn't. Eddy's solution was to cut small incisions around the perimeter of what he called the "orifice," just enough the pop the chicken through. This was probably "bird #3." We spun the orifice round, tied it up tight, and dropped the whole thing gently into a big pot of simmering chicken broth. The broth warmed the liquid in the sack, of course, which was mainly high-grade, high-percentage alcohols; and the sack, expanding to accommodate the mounting molecular hyperactivity, grew and grew until it was a round, fully inflated oven. This was miraculous to witness. I stood over it, this beach ball bobbing in a pot, and ladled broth over the top. A bladder, being what it is, should never be not wet. I continued

ladling. Then I became worried. I could see what was happening: the hot liquid, the alcohol inside, the taut thin muscle of the bladder expanding and expanding. It was going to burst.

It didn't. Instead, the highly pressured vapors inside pushed past the knot, and exited gently through the orifice, and the sack instantly deflated.

The first time this happened, our spirits deflated with it, while dark liquid poured out into the simmering broth, a brown tide of brandy and foie gras. Actually, our spirits deflated the second time as well.

A solution was proposed by a visiting chef, Dominique Gauthier, from the Beau-Rivage hotel in Geneva. He and his team had been using a corner of Daniel's kitchen to prepare large, raucous lunchtime banquets in a private dining room. Chef Gauthier knew all about poulet en vessie. Philosophically, Bourg-en-Bresse is halfway between Geneva and Lyon. The fix was simple: you need a knot that tightens under pressure. Ours had been done lasso-style, a string wrapped around the neck, over and over again, as tight as possible. But tight wasn't enough. He demonstrated. You take the vessie neck, as though it were a balloon, comme ça, but you don't knot it up as though it were a balloon. Instead, you flip it over, onto itself, making a lip, fold it over again, and *then* tie the string around, so that when the pressure increases the knot tightens.

Aaaaaaaaaaaaaaaaaaah.

Sometimes people ask me, What does the food of Lyon taste like? And I recall this dish, probably the most Lyonnais of all the distinctly Lyonnais preparations. Chicken, I say. It tastes like chicken, but different.

Left, volaille à Noelle. Right, poulet en vessie. Center, old rooster.

RILLETTE

I THOUGHT THAT I KNEW RILLETTE, BUT IMMEDIATELY
realized that my understanding was incomplete. It had been
fashioned in England, where I had moved as a university student,
when I was twenty-two years old, and where I remained until
I was forty. In England, they don't read Julia Child. They read
Elizabeth David. Elizabeth David did not go to cooking school.
Her recipes, inspired by farmhouses, or a small town's boulangerie
and its one rustic restaurant—the one that was always busy on
Sundays, at lunchtime—are written up as stories, and convey
the sense that they have been learned by long conversations at a
kitchen table with mothers about to make the family supper. One
such paragraph describes rillette, country-style, and how you
make it with your leftover goose, shredding the meat and mashing
it into the fat, heating it slightly, and fashioning it into a stick of
sorts. (What did I know? I was learning French cooking from a
book. Can you learn French cooking from a book?) One Christmas,
I cooked a goose, and afterward picked my way through the wings
and neck, and managed to make what I understood Elizabeth
David to be describing. Since then, I have yet to encounter anything even remotely resembling my fatty little dirty gray sticks.

In Daniel's kitchen, I learned that a rillette is not a repellent
gray stick, but one of the great dishes of the ancient kitchen, a
show-off piece, and that each region of France has its version.
The *Larousse Gastronomique* has a full-page table, describing

the variations. In Anjou, on the Loire, for instance, it is a beauti-
fully layered terrine, made from a pork belly and shoulder that have
been cooked slowly in pork fat; in Franche-Comté and around
Beaujolais, it is a leftover meat, lightly smoked.

Nothing, however, matches the audacious extravagance of
Daniel's preparation. It was created for the opening of his first
restaurant, more than two decades ago, and continues to be
served today. A rillette made by Daniel shares one feature with
my vaguely Elizabeth David version—the confiteness of it all (the
shredded meat, the salt, the fat)—but the detail ultimately has
nothing to do with Daniel's meticulous composition of slow-
cooked pork and rabbits, the shoulders, the duck and squab legs,
and the foie gras. The dish is extreme. The intention appears
to have been to take a luxurious dish and render it over-the-top
luxurious: a thing that you will never have eaten in your life, even
if it threatens to be the last thing you eat in your life, because, once
you see how the dish is made, you realize that you cannot eat it
often and contemplate a long future. You cannot eat it often and
contemplate any future. It should come with a health warning:
second helpings fatal. This is a food that you eat with a very small
spoon, every now and then, to give the palate some sense of what
the afterlife might taste like.

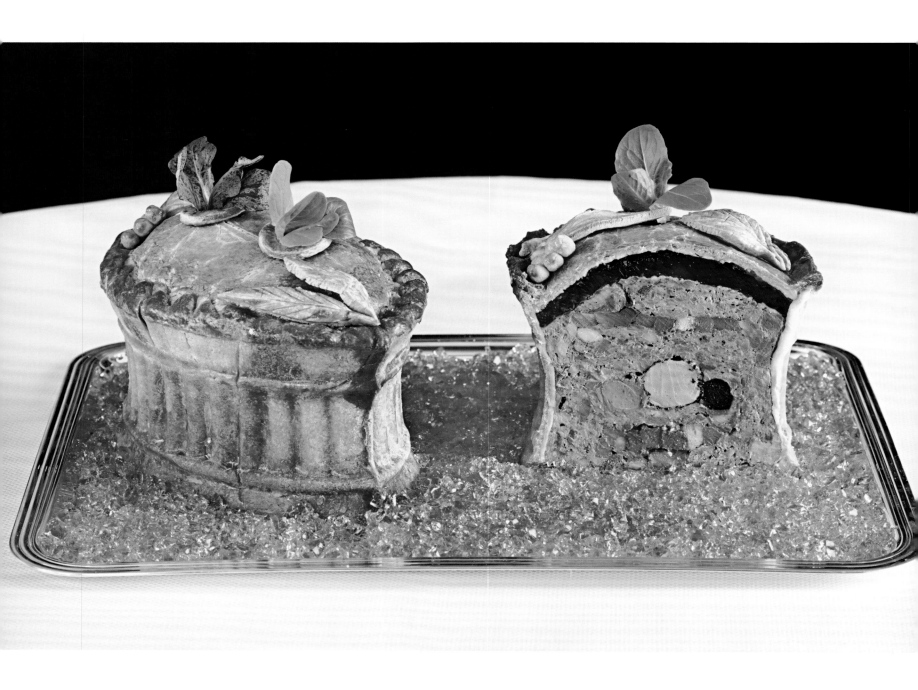

PÂTÉ EN CROÛTE

A PÂTÉ EN CROÛTE IS A DISH ITS NAME DESCRIBES. WHAT else in the French kitchen is so straightforward? The name is so plain it could be a cooking instruction: a pâté, which is basically morsels of meat, liver, and fat ground up and rendered smooth (or partly ground up and rendered both rough and smooth, or coarsely chopped and rendered chunky), is cooked in a crust, la croûte. *Voilà*. The dish is not merely a farmer's dish but a French farmer's dish. It combines an honest household husbandry—a bit of this and that, some leftover this and leftover that, plus a meat jelly for luxury—with Gallic kitchen flair, enveloping the whole thing in a pastry, the sum so much greater than its parts. It is ancient. It is rustic. It is grand.

It turns out that I am definitively and unequivocally wrong: Uh-uh, no way. In Daniel's kitchen, a pâté en croûte is art: end of discussion. Daniel and Jean-François were the masters—nobody else in the kitchen came close—*and* my instructors. Both, by coincidence, had grown up on a farm. Both, by coincidence, were the only ones in the kitchen who had grown up on a farm. Both, in fact, were the only people I knew living and working in New York City who had grown up on farms. And both assured me that they knew much more about farms than I had years in my life to learn, and that no farmer would ever make a dish this sophisticated.

I set up next to Jean-François, two cutting boards side by side, for his dish and my imitation.

I might as well confess that, for me, this tutorial (my limitations notwithstanding) was a privilege. Like Jean-François and Daniel, I've had a lifelong fascination with pâté en croûte. I can't entirely explain why. I did not grow up on a farm. I also never thought of it as art. But there is no other dish that I have longed more to master. I had made it at home and was shocked—*shocked!*—by how bad it had turned out *every* time.

At the very least, I knew what I should know in order to make the basic croûte. The recipe was ye ol' French tart pastry: namely, half butter. To be precise, it was a half-pound of butter for every pound of flour, plus two eggs yolks, salt, and a little water. But the recipe was irrelevant if you didn't know what to do with it, which was nothing. The best practitioners of French pastry, I now know, aspire to an intellectual ozone hovering between Zen master and mentalist, and hope never to touch a thing. (In effect, they put their ingredients in a pile and will them into being mixed.) For the rest of us, you just try to touch everything as little as possible. The issue is all that butter. Kneading might be good for good bread, but in a pastry it renders a brick: something, in any case, that your mouth will instruct you to spit out. Meanwhile, Daniel's basic pastry turned out not to be so basic at all—it was deep in color, and silky to touch—and was all about the recipe, after all. This is it (and until now an in-house secret): instead of a pound of flour, there is a mix of flour and cornstarch; and instead of two egg yolks, a staggering seven! (In its metric specifics: 384 grams of flour, 125 grams of cornstarch, 200 grams of butter, 9.5 grams of salt, 90 grams of cold water, and *seven egg yolks*.)

The pâté part of our pâté en croûte was supplied again by Bernard Vrod, the restaurant's forest forager. I was becoming so accustomed to finding his birds in the kitchen that it didn't seem remarkable that our worktop was again covered with woodcocks, quail, pheasant, partridges, grouse, doves, and pigeons. I will never be surrounded by so much again. In the United States, it is illegal to sell wild game, and if you have eaten some in a restaurant, it is because it wasn't wild but farm-raised, its health certified by the FDA. (Ours, which was wild, didn't count, because we weren't selling.) Jean-François marinated the birds in salt, boned them, put the breasts to one side, and filled up a bowl with the legs, hearts, lungs, and livers. These would constitute the "farce"— in effect, the tasty goop that the really good stuff floats in. The

really good stuff was those breasts, which were partially roasted and cut into beams with precise right angles: more LEGO than Lincoln Logs.

Jean-François then pulled out his "demo kit." I don't know how else to describe it. It included full-size diagrams, cutouts and flash cards illustrating where each item in the pâté en croûte was meant to go, propped up on our worktop so that they were always in view. He measured the LEGO pieces, checking their shape against one of the diagrams. He weighed his ingredients, not just carefully, but with a studious and solemn purposefulness. He could have been a chemist in a lab. The experience was humbling and intimidating. I had never seen someone so organized. He had an exacting picture in his head, not of the dish coming out of the oven, but of what it would look like when it was sliced. In my experiments, I hadn't paid much attention to what was underneath the croute; it was hidden, thankfully. For Jean-François, nothing mattered more.

The problem was the assembly. Actually, the problem was the mold. Frankly, when you think of a pâté en croûte, you imagine a terrine, no? Something long and rectangular. This is where a pâté en croûte obviously feels most at home. It is also easy. You roll out your pastry, flop it inside, trim out the corners so you're not doubling up, press and seal, done.

Jean-François put his pâté en croûte into a boat. Worse, it wasn't just a boat. It was a canoe. Actually, it was probably more Greek warship than canoe. The point is that a boat is pointy, and pointy means that there is only a tiny zone (the bow) where the two sides of your pastry meet and are then pressed together, flattened, and sealed. I have short fat planks for fingers. I couldn't get them into the bow of my Adriatic vessel. I couldn't flatten. I couldn't seal. I couldn't do anything except indiscriminate pressing, which wasn't working because it was making the pastry thicker. Thick is not

good. I began to panic, which I knew because I was sweating. I then used my pinky to *ram* the corner into thinness. This was a mistake. This seemed only to make the thickness thicker. I approached from the stern, and double-pinky punched it. Basically I was kneading the dough. This was the "big no-no," kneading a butter pastry, even if with the tips of my pinkies. I was treating it as though it were a loaf of bread.

This, alas, was the piece that Daniel first tasted, my corner, my rowboat all clogged up where the life jackets should have been stored, my distasteful wedge.

He called my name. He has a way of calling a name. It isn't a scream as such, but isn't conversational. It is an expression of pain. Daniel had just come across something that hurt, and rather than saying "ouch," he exclaimed my name, stretching out the sound slightly so that it was unclear if it was a question or a command.

I appeared. I felt sorry for him. Whatever he had eaten had my fingerprints all over it and was obviously indigestible. The Lyon question was next. Daniel has high expectations of the transformative powers of his city; I am living proof that they do not exist. When disappointed in me—the mushrooms I couldn't flute; the crayfish I had amputated; and now this lump (brownish on the outside, raw in the middle)—Daniel resorts to a hopeless interrogative formulation: "They didn't teach you this in Lyon, did they?"

WHAT HAPPENED NEXT MIGHT SOUND A LITTLE CORNY. I have gone back and forth about admitting it. Here goes: I was struck by a thunderbolt.

Yep, it's true. There was a white light, I was blinded, there was a resounding clatter, a tiny tintinnabulary deafness. I caught my breath, blinked, shook my head, et cetera. (What can I say? It's my story, and I'm sticking to it.) A thought then presented itself: it's the birds.

At the heart of everything: birds.

Of course. A pâté en croûte originates in a farmer's kitchen. Since when did these guys become so grand? What, having grown up on a farm, they now believe that their food is too refined to have come from one? This dish is old. It is older than history. It is a fundamental unit of the Mediterranean table.

But. It is usually made with pig. In Provence, pig. In Brittany, pig. In the Ardennes, pig. In the Alps, Italy, Spain: pig, pig, pig.

Although. Sometimes it is made with a goose (in the Dordogne), or a duck (in the southwest), or a lamb (in the Languedoc).

And. In the Rhône Valley, that endless-seeming basin of rivers and ponds, its hills and embankments covered with vines, one vineyard after another, like runners in a relay, bearing pinot in the north, and gamay, and then syrah and grenache and finally mourvèdre and the southern grapes: there it is a pâté en croûte with birds.

Why? I put the question to Daniel, realizing, even as I posed it, that never in my life would I find another person who thinks about birds more. You won't find him in among the reeds of Long Island's brackish backwaters, binoculars around his neck. He doesn't want to look at a bird; he wants to kill it, and eat it, and has been killing birds and eating them ever since he kept a slingshot in his back pocket to knock off crows on the way home from school.

"Why birds in Lyon?" Daniel repeated, the question so obvious that he needed to confirm that this was what I was asking. "Because of the vineyards. You didn't know that?"

No, I didn't know that. It was an invitation to think of the Rhône in a new way, and how the valley is a migratory corridor, and how the flocks start arriving in September, harvesttime, looking to rest, looking to drink, looking to land among ripened ready-to-eat grapes. Birds: the farmers hate them; the winemakers hate them. Wild birds are famously good with red wine, and I now understood why: because they are both dinner and pest control. What does the food of Lyon taste like? Bird pie.

POT-AU-FEU

I HAD BEEN LIVING IN LYON FOR THREE AND A HALF YEARS: not long enough for me to understand the French, not yet, not entirely, but long enough for me to observe that when you gather people round a French table (friends or strangers, it doesn't matter) and run these words together—*pot*, *au*, and *feu*—you will have some very animated company on your hands. Why? I didn't know why. I was sitting with Daniel, at a dining table adjoining his office, the "skybox," at the end of our marathon pot-au-feu session. Pot-au-feu is soup, isn't it? Soup with boiled meat. Wrong. It is a poem of the French soul, Daniel explained.

He was agitated and impatient. He was, after all, about to eat pot-au-feu. Even though he had made most of the pot-au-feu himself—tasting it the whole time, tweaking it, seasoning it, tasting it again—it was still, you know, *the* dish. He seemed afflicted and was showing symptoms of a modest motor mouth. I had spent three weeks in his company. I hadn't seen him so disturbed.

Okay. I was about to eat a poem. Actually, I was about to eat four poems, because this was not a normal pot-au-feu, but a pot-au-feu à la royal, a kingly spread, of four different pots-au-feu eaten in succession. Chad would be bringing the first one up the stairs shortly.

We waited.

I repeated the name. *Pot-au-feu*. Maybe it is a poem, a mini poem anyway, the way those three words—*pot*, *au*, and *feu*—rhyme and combine. (In French, you don't say POT-au-feu; the *t* is silent, but it elides with the next word and becomes its first sound: po-TAU-feu, almost a perfect internal assonance in triplet.) The dish is old—probably conceived not long after the discovery of fire and the invention of the pot. In any case, it is a hearth food—that much we know—that has outlasted the hearth, and has a legitimate claim to being France's primordial, first-out-of-the-box, there-before-anything-else national dish.

This, Daniel was saying, is what it is to be French, and then immediately punched the speakerphone. "Where is Chad?"

The dish earned its intellectual cred in the nineteenth century. Brillat-Savarin obsessed over it. So did Victor Hugo, Jules Verne, Alexandre Dumas, various mediocre poets, and several scientists. One chemistry lexicon, published in 1852, lists it in the "P" section, just before "potasse" and "potassium." In 1886, a Dr. J. Renegade argued for the dish's inherent morality.

I found an unexpected ally in Bayle St. John, an English author and social anthropologist of the French. His two-volume study, published in 1854, was called *The Purple Tints of Paris*. In fact, its principal but unofficial subject is French women, who had immediate access to Mr. St. John's unprotected heart and thoroughly trampled all over it. (His chapter on French married women's affairs—they have them with every man except Mr. St. John—reads like an Italian opera.) Since Mr. St. John spent his time principally in rooms frequented by the "fairer sex," including the kitchen, he was witness to the daily pot-au-feu schedule, which began around ten in the morning, when three or four pounds of beef were put in a marmite of cold water. This would be brought to a simmer and skimmed for seven hours. Around two, vegetables were added, "carrots, turnips, a bunch of leeks, and a small bit of garlic, with fragrant herbs, and a burnt onion," a trick still used today, to deepen the broth's caramel color. The result, poured into a tureen over crusty bits of bread, was "not at all disagreeable to eat with pickled gherkins." Mr. St. John's pot-au-feu is remarkably similar to the one made by Daniel's mother. The differences are in details that Mr. St. John probably missed: not three or four pounds of generalized beef, but three specific cuts: the shank, two sides of ribs, and the tenderloin. The shank, almost all bone, gives the

liquid its gelatin. The ribs are fatty and give it flavor. The tender-loin, held back until the end, so it comes out rare, adds an element of luxury.

Chad arrived, bearing a dish written in the flavors of duck. He set out the vegetables. These were not the broth's actual vegetables, which had long yielded up their bite and yumminess, but fresh imitations, cooked up at the last minute in a separate pot of the by-now thoroughly ducky broth, a French trick: the first batch of vegetables make the broth and are then tossed out; then the broth is used to cook a new batch of fresh vegetables. Chad added a morsel of duck breast and ladled on the consommé. I was struck by Chad's natural, down-home, lanky baseball-diamond chirpiness. He was relaxed and confident and reassuringly American. He was missing the tragic gene. He was also missing the fact that Daniel had been inserted into a faulty socket and was about to short-circuit.

"I used to get upset," Daniel said after Chad left. "I don't get upset anymore. Now, I . . ." But his voice trailed off. He was staring at the display of food. Items were missing.

He punched the speakerphone. "Maisie?" Maisie was Daniel's assistant. "There is no toast. Maisie, the toasts. Where are the toasts? Do you know? Maisie, we don't have the toasts."

The toasts were summoned.

Once again the speakerphone. "Where is the foie? You can't have a pot-au-feu à canard without foie. Maisie, tell Chad that we need the foie."

The foie, having been duly summoned, duly appeared.

"*La truffe, la truffe, la truffe.*" Daniel got up and shot off, muttering, "You need la truffe; you can't eat the dish without la truffe." I heard him in the kitchen below. "*La truffe, s'il vous plait!*" He was talking and moving fast, while trying to slow himself down because he seemed to know that he was on the verge of careening out of control. It was a peculiar condition, like a race driver who keeps hitting the brakes. Maisie leaned against a doorframe, an unflappable veteran, while we waited for Daniel's return. "I shouldn't say this, but don't you get tired of so many truffles?"

It is not known when pot-au-feu was first served in a royal court, and the anecdotes are difficult to substantiate. Henry IV, who ruled France from 1589 to 1610, is said to have been especially partial to the dish, and, for all we know, may well have been the

first king to insist on being served it. He liked it lean: vegetables okay; meat never. Meat was for flavoring. It was left in the pot for the kitchen staff. It was the consommé that mattered. I now understood this for the first time. The duck breast and liver: yes, tasty, obviously, but what made the dish was the liquid. It was so un-extreme. (Frankly, I would never have believed that this was something that I could have appreciated. My palate, dulled by years of hot chiles and frying fats, of nachos and Indian food, hadn't been trained for subtlety.)

I had another spoonful. What made it so good? The liquid had body and weight—this was probably the gelatin and the reduction from a long simmer. But what was the taste?

I closed my eyes. I was picking up multiple flavors rather than a single one; duck, yes, but not overwhelmingly so. There was some fat. The flavors were also long, in the way that a good wine is long. They lingered. They didn't go away.

"*Merde,*" Daniel said.

I opened my eyes. Daniel was eating frantically. He seemed to be chewing the liquid.

"I'm sorry," he said finally. "This pot-au-feu is not a tour de force." He looked at me to confirm that I agreed.

I didn't know what to say. Was it the dish that had been found wanting? Or me? Here I was, face-to-face with a great chef. He had prepared an exceptional plate of food. Clichés occur, one after the other—of my being blown away, my socks knocked off, et cetera, et cetera—and before I can utter a single banality he interrupts: "Sorry, it's shit, no?"

It wasn't shit.

What Daniel wanted to see was the basic etiquette for serving the dish. Nobody had this etiquette. Daniel had this etiquette. Nobody else knew it. Daniel knew that you made your veal broth with a shank from the foreleg and not the back leg. He knew that you don't serve the pork broth without a cabbage leaf. (There are fifteen ingredients in the pork broth. Who knew that the cabbage leaf was so important?) Yes, the herby green sauce is made with basil, parsley, tarragon, chives, and chervil, but not in equal quantities. It's the chervil that counts. "I can't really blame AJ and Chad," he sighed, while clearly thinking: *How could AJ and Chad not know this?* In moments like this, I looked at Daniel and thought: *You are a weirdo molecular-mutating time traveler. How did you squeak into our century?*

Pot-au-feu became interestingly royal in the kitchens of Louis XIV. This was the first great era of French cuisine, when many previously simple dishes were elaborated and complicated and rendered grand. Pot-au-feu can't be rendered grand. It can only

be varied. The pure flavor buzz that you get from beef is different from the one you get from veal or partridge or duck or pork or venison or wild boar or horse or goat or woodcock or squirrel or pheasant. In this simple discovery, the dish exploded. This is what intrigued so many nineteenth-century intellectuals, the varieties of the dish's purity. And this is what has been lost to everyone except time travelers. In the current *Larousse Gastronomique*, you will find basic instructions for a basic pot-au-feu, with two or three variations. In the first edition, there had been hundreds, each with its own condiment.

Pot-au-feu is not a date food, Daniel said. It is a table food. It is a food for twelve of your best friends, who have given over the day and the night to eating. The first multiple pot-au-feu he witnessed was in the kitchens of Roger Vergé. It wasn't served in the dining room; it wasn't on the menu, or available to diners. It was for friends. It was labor-intensive in the extreme—today, for Daniel's four dishes, thirty-seven pots were used—and was ultimately a gift that a cook, any cook, you, me, Daniel, fancy, not fancy, was able to prepare, in advance, and with much planning and many hours, for friends who understood the effort that goes into realizing a pure flavor. Over the course of the past eighteen days, we had made, counting sides and variations, twenty-one historically unique plates of food. Pot-au-feu was one of the last. It was the most iconic. It was cooking as gift giving.

THE DESSERTS

IT WOULD NOT BE ACCURATE TO SAY THAT, ONE MORNING,
I made a religieuse à l'ancienne, got started on a charlotte aux pommes, began assembling an omelette norvégienne, and then wrapped them all up by lunchtime. Such a statement wouldn't, in any technical sense, be true. Until now, just about everything else—a volaille à Noelle (savaged so badly that Daniel had to stitch it up); the turbot that took me an hour to bone—more or less, *c'était moi*. But the desserts: well, not exactly. On the other hand, it wouldn't be correct to say that I *didn't* make them.

The "prep" for the dishes that I didn't make but may have actually made began on a Saturday afternoon. At around 2 p.m., as I was explaining to Daniel how I had achieved my pâté en croûte, AJ appeared.

"Mymi and Eric are now ready for you."

Mymi is Mymi Eberhardt. She is the pastry chef at Daniel's DBGB, which is a French version of the hot dog palace of your dreams. (You go with your children; they are happy. You go without them; you are happy, and, maybe, a little guilty.) Eric is Eric Bertoïa. He is the pastry boss. Every week, he oversees the production of eight hundred croissants, one thousand mini hot-molten chocolate cakes, twenty-five thousand madeleines, plus another two hundred and thirty-one different desserts.

But I was confused. Isn't my day done?

"Daniel didn't tell you?"

I was led down two flights of stairs. There was a corridor, a ramp, and a white room. This was the prep kitchen. The prep kitchen is different from the service kitchen. The service kitchen is where your dinner comes together. It is noisy and dramatic. Sometimes, at a fancy place, after a fancy meal—a birthday, an anniversary—the maître d' drops by and invites you to take a tour of the kitchen. The kitchen you are shown is the service kitchen. The kitchen you are never shown is the prep kitchen. The prep kitchen is not in *Ratatouille*. A prep kitchen is not sexy. It is a factory.

As I was led through the factory, en route to an appointment that I hadn't known I had, I noticed several features about the environment. The first was a smell. It was a men's locker room *before* an athletic event. It wasn't the smell of a body well-exercised; it was a body in a nervous state. Next was a frenetic sense of purposeful activity. The activity: cube-making. At a

long steel table, laborers known as "*commis*" were slowly and systematically cutting carrots with big knives into identically shaped, one-millimeter-square tiny boxes. Further down the long steel table, another group was cutting parsnips. Then: carrots. (By word of explanation, a commis is the lowest of the low. A commis is a title verging on abuse, as in: "Oh, don't mind him, he's just a commis.")

I continued, past grills and ovens and rotisseries; a hot flattop and an empty salamander turned on to full burn; and arrived in a room that was cool and quiet, and where Eric and Mymi were waiting: the pastry kitchen.

In the next five hours, *I* made patisserie cream, crème anglaise, Italian meringue, French meringue, chocolate butter, and coffee butter. *I* made ice cream. *I* made cake. *I* made brioche. *I* made a pâte à choux. This was for the éclairs. *I* made the éclairs. A syrup? An applesauce? Was there nothing that *I* couldn't make, if *I* put my mind to it? In fact, *I* found myself in a position of unusual pampering. Two of the world's best pastry chefs had prepared everything ahead of time—separating eggs, measuring out flours, butters, creams, arranging sheet pans, a pot, a spatula, everything—so that *I*, over the course of a Saturday afternoon, could cook through a fat textbook of the French pastry kitchen.

My worst moment (when I had been so cosseted and provided for and overdeterminedly directed that a bad moment was a statistical improbability): the squiggly lines. The squiggly lines killed me.

This was on the Monday afternoon, when the desserts were finished and photographed and then devoured by my two sons, who had shown up with a babysitter. The squiggly lines run between the columns of the religieuse à l'ancienne. The columns themselves were made from éclairs. You can see the squiggly lines in the photograph, looking all symmetrical and silky-fabric-like. I did not do those. Those were done by Eric. Mine are on the other side. (If you think of a religieuse à l'ancienne like a moon, then mine, at least in this photographic history, will always be on the dark side.)

My greatest achievement? The *flop*. Every now and then, a dish has a do-or-die. The tête de veau had one. The green Jell-O toupée that Daniel *flipped* on top, everyone holding their breath, because you can't get it wrong? The omelette norvégienne (aka "Baked Alaska") also had a do-or-die: the roof. It is made of biscuit (or cake, as we refer to it in less refined circles). It is a perfect rectangle. You can't slide it on; you can't pick it up with your fingers. There is no choice. You line it up, and, in one motion . . . you *flip* and *flop* it. Have I had a more profound moment in a kitchen in my entire life?

As I was making these desserts, several thoughts occurred to me.

For instance, pastry chefs. Don't most of them have unresolved issues from their childhood? The good ones talk a lot about "art," of course. Carême spent his famous hours in the library stacks, searching for models to inspire his towering sugar temples. But, really, what was going on? He was making toys. Carême never knew his parents. What kind of childhood do you think he had?

Consider, for instance, the religieuse à l'ancienne. This is a solemn, earnest name for a hat. It is a bishop's headpiece. What culture makes a confection from children's food—an éclair, after all, is a schoolchild's snack food, a gouter—that invokes the highest authority in the national religion, and then eats it?

Those killer chops. To my right, I had the extreme South of France. To my left, the extreme North. (Eric Bertoïa? He's from Montauban, near the Pyrénées. Mymi Eberhardt? She is from Mulhouse, in Alsace.) I stood between them, pretending to be the Midi. Both were teaching me something at the same time, resuming the lesson during the other's pause. So, when the South was showing me how to make my pâte à choux, the North was waiting to start in on a crème anglaise. And when the South then moved on to a buttercream, and had to retrieve an ingredient from the back, the North pounced and told me the three essential points in making biscuit. If the pastry kitchen is about learning every possible preparation, and committing it to your deep never-need-to-look-it-up muscle memory, then I managed to do the opposite, and was taught everything so quickly that I have been able to commit nothing to any memory at all.

What gives with all the cookbooks?

You don't read a French pastry recipe in a cookbook and whip it up that night for dessert. You read it, study it, read it some more, and commit yourself to making it every day for a month. And then you start in on the next thing.

Tips. Oh, the tips. How to know when your brioche is ready, and how to keep your mango passion fruit soufflé from falling down. The tips, the tips, there were so many tips—the lemon that you add to your egg whites, the lard rather than butter for your puff pastry—and all of them conveyed by a hand-covered word of mouth and none of them published. I have pages of tips. Do you think I'm going to share them? (Na-na-na-naa-na.)

The wow factor. Imagine that you are at a table with friends. You are happy. You have eaten plenty, been surprised at every course, each one a giant platter of WOW. You are dizzy, the drink, the heat, the conviviality, when Daniel kicks open a door and brings out: the dessert! It is a showpiece, high in sugar, high in fat, and very high in wow. He returns to the kitchen, kicks open the door, and brings out: another dessert! He returns and brings out yet another one! And there would have to be three desserts, not

one, because, by generic necessity, there has to be more than you can imagine eating, because they have to have more WOW than anything that has come before. After all, they could not have less. In fact, they are not WOW. They are WOW-WOW.

A postscript. It is 2:30 p.m. We are running late. There are nutritional consequences. The photographer is still shooting, the religieuse à l'ancienne still intact, the omelette norvegienne alight, the charlotte aux pommes sliced but only for a beauty shot. My boys, aged six, are at a table. Frederick has risen from his seat and appears ready to be launched up to the ceiling on glucose fumes. It feels dangerous. I am uneasy. I haven't had lunch. Breakfast was a French carbohydrate affair. I find myself staring at the desserts, glistening and irresistible. Once I taste one, will I be able to stop? Daniel appears beside me and whispers: Do you have any sugar issues? (Yeah, maybe, I say, my mouth drying up. Who wouldn't?) Should we have a salad? he says. And I agree, yes, a good idea, but since this is Daniel, this is his restaurant, and he has only to say to no one, to the room, to the air, "Can I have a salad?" and instantly

one appears, a plate of lobster tails and grapefruit and avocados, with a handmade mayonnaise, and we sit down, a glass of white Burgundy materializing in my right hand, and the sugar urgencies fade, and the world becomes less wobbly, and even though I notice that one of my children has just roared past at great speed and is now ricocheting round the room, his little body in chemical overthrust, I am starting to relax and in my own time turn to the bishop's hat (by now demolished by my progenies' caretaker) and poke it with a fork and break up an éclair and pierce a morsel with the tine of my utensil and eat it. "Well," I say, turning to Daniel, who is equally restored, "it's not actually that good, is it? It's WOW-WOW, but not WOW-WOW-WOW. Do you know what I mean?"

PART III
DANIEL AT HOME

DANIEL AT HOME

Restaurant Daniel is the epicenter of my life. But on Sundays, when Daniel is closed, I often cook for friends and family. I have the incredible privilege to live above the "store" and, in an emergency, have access to the treasure chest of ingredients in the basement. I prepare spontaneous, intimate dinners but also more elaborate meals.

Here are four examples of soulful regional menus I enjoy preparing at home:

Alsace for its rustic, Franco-Germanic culinary tone—the crispy crust of tarte flambée, cabbage baeckeoffe covered with nutty bacon, and fluted kougelhopf redolent of candied fruits. **Normandy** for its briny mussels, salty coastal lamb, and apple orchards steered by the power of calvados. **Provence**'s delicate vegetables and seafood punched up by garlic aioli, my reinterpretation of the traditional loup de mer au fenouil, and honeyed fresh fig tart. Then on to **Lyon**, my hometown, where I imagined a real Bouchon Lyonnais: poireaux vinaigrette but dressed, garden-to-table-style, with a carrot emulsion, the emblematic recipe of poulet au vinaigre et à l'estragon, the first dish I made as an apprentice. And for dessert, a serious chocolate cake, the symbol of the gourmande city of Lyon.

ALSACE

MENU

Wild Mushroom Tarte Flambée

*Beer-Marinated Pork Rack
with a Barley-Mustard Crust*

Root Vegetable Baeckeoffe

Kougelhopf

ON A WINTRY SUNDAY NIGHT, I DECIDED TO COOK A RUSTIC MEAL, TAKING MY INSPIRA-tion from Alsace, where my brother Michel lives. Alsace is a mecca of hearty cuisine with great chefs. The *flammekueche*, otherwise known as tarte flambée, is as ubiquitous in Alsace as crêpes are in Brittany, and whether as a snack in a swinging Weinstube, or as an appetizer for a more familial dinner, there's always a good reason to devour it. If you're taking the pain to cook the dough and feed your friends, think of the big picture and make it for the whole village!

There are as many recipes for the tart as there are cooks, but I never featured it in one of my restaurants until the Alsatian chef Olivier Muller took the helm of DB Bistro's kitchen. Then every week, we celebrated "Sunday Night in Alsace," and the tarte flambée became the emblematic starter on the menu. This recipe is a vegetarian variation, using wild mushrooms rather than the usual bacon.

I love the rustic and delicate flavor of roast pork, a meat I find both lean and mean, and the rack is an easy cut to cook at home. Add a crust of barley, mustard seeds, bread-crumbs, and butter, and the meat takes on a toasted, spicy flavor. You will hear the fat and barley crackle and sizzle as it broils, always welcome music in the kitchen. But don't get me wrong, the most important part of the recipe is the forty-eight-hour brine in beer (amber ale, Alsatian if possible!), with salt, brown sugar, mustard, garlic, and herbs. To season and keep the meat moist while it cooks, nothing beats a good brine. One more tip: Before you serve the rack of pork, boil a few green outer cabbage leaves until tender, toss them with butter and horseradish, and fold them under the rack to present the feast to your guests before slicing it.

To accompany the rustic meat, I imagined a slow-cooked vegetable baeckeoffe—a casserole of layered onions, turnips, potatoes, and cabbage flavored with bacon and baked, but sadly, not in the baker's oven as in the past, the reason for its name. Start early, as it tastes better if assembled the night before and cooked rather slowly.

The most majestic baeckeoffe I tasted in my life was baked for one of my big birthdays when sixteen chefs, past alumni, and current colleagues each cooked a dish close to their heart. Olivier Muller, of course, was behind the fabulous veal baeckeoffe, full of vegetables, calves' feet, and tender veal shoulder marinated in Alsatian white wine.

For dessert: an Alsatian kougelhopf, a mix between a panettone and a brioche, often served as breakfast, but great as a light dessert after a hearty meal. Serve it with ice cream or cassis-poached pears. There will be leftover kougelhopf for the next day, so do as I do, and dunk it in your coffee!

WILD MUSHROOM TARTE FLAMBÉE

MAKES 6 TARTES (SERVES 6 TO 12)

Dough

1¾ cups 00 pasta flour

1 cup milk

¼ teaspoon salt

1 teaspoon colza oil

Topping

1 cup fromage blanc

½ cup crème fraîche

2 tablespoons flour

1 tablespoon colza oil

1 egg yolk

¼ teaspoon freshly ground nutmeg

Salt and freshly ground white pepper

3 tablespoons butter

1 pound hen of the woods or other wild mushrooms, cut into bite-size pieces, washed and patted dry

To Finish

1 large onion, finely chopped

½ bunch oregano leaves

½ bunch chives, thinly sliced

For the Dough

In an electric mixer fitted with a dough hook, combine the flour, milk, salt, and oil. Mix on medium speed for 3 minutes. If needed, add 1 tablespoon warm water to help the dough come together into a solid mass. Continue to knead the dough on medium speed until smooth, about 8 minutes. Wrap in plastic and refrigerate for at least 1 hour, or up to 3 days.

Divide the dough into 6 portions. Using a pasta machine, roll each portion, decreasing the thickness after each pass, into long, very thin 5-inch-wide sheets (setting #1 on most machines). You will need to do this in several batches. Trim the sheets into approximately 10- to 12-inch lengths. Transfer to a tray in between layers of parchment paper and refrigerate (or freeze until needed).

For the Topping

In a medium bowl, whisk to combine the fromage blanc, crème fraîche, flour, oil, egg yolk, and nutmeg until smooth. Season with salt and pepper and keep chilled.

Brown the butter in a large sauté pan over high heat. Add the mushrooms and season with salt and pepper. Sauté until tender, about 5 minutes. Drain onto a paper towel–lined plate.

To Finish

If you have a pizza stone, place it on the bottom of the oven; otherwise, an upside-down baking sheet can be substituted. Preheat the oven to 500°F.

Place a sheet of dough on a lightly floured pizza peel. Spread the cream topping in a thin layer over the dough, making sure it is evenly distributed. Leave a ¼-inch border around the edge of the dough. Sprinkle one-sixth of the onion, mushrooms, oregano, and chives evenly over the cream topping. Repeat to make all 6 tartes. Slide the flambées, one at a time, onto the pizza stone and bake until crispy on the bottom and lightly browned on top. Slice and serve immediately.

BEER-MARINATED PORK RACK
WITH A BARLEY-MUSTARD CRUST

SERVES 6

Barley-Mustard Crust (makes extra)

¼ cup pearl barley

1 cup Chicken Stock (page 368)

Salt

½ cup (1 stick) butter

1 cup Fine White Breadcrumbs (page 373)

2 tablespoons mustard seeds, soaked in water overnight

1 tablespoon mustard powder

2 tablespoons Dijon mustard

2 tablespoons grainy mustard

Freshly ground white pepper

Pork Rack

Salt

¾ tablespoon brown sugar

1½ tablespoons mustard seeds, soaked in water overnight

¾ tablespoon cracked black peppercorns

6 sprigs sage

8 sprigs thyme

4 bay leaves, torn

8 cloves garlic, peeled and smashed

1 (6-rib) pork rack (about 8 pounds), Frenched and tied

1 (12-ounce) bottle amber ale (such as Fischer's Bière D'Alsace)

Freshly ground white pepper

3 tablespoons canola oil

3 tablespoons butter

8 large green cabbage leaves, remaining head reserved for the baeckeoffe (page 340)

¼ cup grated fresh horseradish

For the Barley-Mustard Crust

Preheat the oven to 325°F. Rinse the barley with cold water until it runs clear. Place in a medium ovenproof saucepan with the stock and ½ teaspoon salt. Bring to a simmer, cover, and bake for 35 minutes. Remove, rest for 10 minutes, and fluff with a fork. Transfer the barley to a tray, spread into a thin layer, and chill uncovered in the refrigerator.

In an electric mixer fitted with a paddle, mix the butter until creamy. Add the cooled barley, the breadcrumbs, mustard seeds, mustard powder, Dijon mustard, and grainy mustard and season with salt and pepper; mix just until combined. Scrape the butter onto a sheet of parchment paper, set another paper on top, and roll into a ⅛-inch-thick sheet. Refrigerate until firm, or for up to 3 days.

For the Pork Rack

In a large saucepan, simmer 2¼ cups water with 2¼ tablespoons salt and the brown sugar until dissolved. Remove from the heat, add the mustard seeds, cracked peppercorns, and half of the sage, thyme, bay leaves, and garlic; allow to cool. Place the pork in a 2-gallon resealable bag and pour in the water–spice mixture and the beer. Seal and marinate refrigerated for 48 hours, turning the pork 4 times.

Preheat the oven to 300°F. Remove the pork from the marinade, scrape off any herbs or spices stuck to the meat, and pat dry. Season on all sides with white pepper. If desired, wrap the bones with aluminum foil to prevent browning.

Heat the oil in a roasting pan over medium-high heat. Add the pork and sear on all sides until golden brown, about 8 minutes total. While searing, baste often with the oil from the pan, especially in the areas around the bones. Reduce the heat to medium and add 2 tablespoons of the butter and the remaining sage, thyme, bay leaf, and garlic. Continue turning and basting for 3 minutes.

Transfer to the oven and roast until the internal temperature reaches 130°F, 45 minutes to 1 hour.

Meanwhile, bring a large pot of salted water to a boil and boil the cabbage leaves until tender, about 4 minutes. Strain off the water and add the remaining 1 tablespoon butter. Toss with the horseradish to heat through. Season with salt and pepper.

Remove the pork and increase the oven temperature to broil. Remove the barley crust from the refrigerator. Press the crust onto the meaty side of the pork and trim any overhanging edges if needed. Broil the pork for about 5 minutes, until the crust is golden brown.

Arrange the cabbage on a serving tray and set the roasted pork rack on top.

ROOT VEGETABLE BAECKEOFFE

SERVES 6 TO 8

3 tablespoons butter

1 head green cabbage, with 8 leaves peeled for the pork (page 338); and head cored, quartered, and sliced ¼ inch thick

Salt and freshly ground white pepper

2 large onions, sliced ¼ inch thick

4 Yukon gold potatoes (1¾ pounds), peeled and sliced ¼ inch thick

5 turnips (1¾ pounds), peeled and sliced ¼ inch thick

12 thick slices slab bacon

Half of a 12-ounce bottle amber ale

The night before serving, melt the butter in a large sauté pan over medium heat. Add the cabbage and stir until limp, about 10 minutes. Season with salt and pepper and remove from the heat.

Butter the interior of a 4½-quart baeckeoffe or casserole dish with a lid. Build 2 layers of the vegetables, starting with the onions, then potatoes, then turnips, and then cabbage. Layer the sliced bacon on top and pour in the beer. Refrigerate overnight.

Preheat the oven to 300°F. Transfer the baeckeoffe, covered, to the oven. Bake for 2½ hours, or until a knife inserted into the center yields no resistance. Remove from the oven and rest for 30 minutes before serving.

KOUGELHOPF

SERVES 6 TO 8

¼ cup dark rum

¼ cup small-diced dried apricots

3 cups flour

⅓ cup sugar

1¼ teaspoons salt

1½ tablespoons active dry yeast

¾ cup milk

2 eggs

18½ tablespoons (9¼ ounces) cold butter, cubed

¾ cup Sicilian pistachios

Powdered sugar

1 pint pistachio, apricot, or rum raisin ice cream, optional

In a small saucepan, bring the rum to a simmer, add the apricots, and stir. Remove from the heat, cover, and soak for 30 minutes. Transfer to the refrigerator to cool.

In the bowl of an electric mixer fitted with a dough hook, mix the flour, sugar, salt, and yeast on the lowest speed to combine. Add the milk, then the eggs, one at a time, allowing the dough to start gathering between additions.

Increase the speed one level to knead for about 5 minutes, until it resembles a sticky dough that pulls from the sides of the bowl and gathers around the hook. Continue kneading until the dough becomes slightly warm, another 5 minutes.

Add the butter a few cubes at a time, allowing it to be absorbed into the dough after each addition. Continue kneading the dough until homogeneous and it begins to pull from the sides of the bowl, about 8 minutes.

Strain the apricots and add them to the dough with ½ cup of the pistachios. Mix just to combine.

Grease a large bowl with nonstick cooking spray. Scrape the dough into the bowl, cover with plastic wrap, and refrigerate overnight. It should rise by about one-third.

Preheat the oven to 325°F. Grease a 9½-inch-diameter (3-quart) kougelhopf mold or Bundt cake pan with nonstick cooking spray. Line the grooves inside the bottom of the pan with the remaining pistachios. Turn the dough out onto a floured surface and shape into a smooth ball by rolling it between the palms of your hands. Poke a hole into the center of the dough and set inside the prepared mold. Set in a warm area (about 78°F), such as near the oven, and cover with a damp cloth. Allow the dough to rise to the rim of the mold, about 2 hours.

Bake for 10 minutes, turn the pan 180 degrees, and continue baking for 10 more minutes, or until a thin knife or cake tester inserted into the thickest part of the dough comes out clean. Remove from the oven and immediately invert the kougelhopf onto a cooling rack. Dust with powdered sugar and serve warm or at room temperature. Serve with ice cream, if desired.

NORMANDY

MENU

Mussel and Cauliflower Velouté

Garlic-Studded Gigot with Artichokes and Watercress

Tarte Normande

WHEN I THINK ABOUT NORMANDY, I SEE TOWERING CLIFFS, IMMENSE TIDES, AND THE history of our two countries intertwined since World War II in the ancient sand. On family trips, and when my daughter Alix visits her grandmother, who lives near Deauville, we never miss gulping down large pots of steaming mussels with their broth at Les Vapeurs in Trouville. And the ingredients of Normandy? Mussels, yes, but also the world's best crème fraîche, apples, butter, and of course the famous Camembert cheese.

Tonight at home, it's an intimate Normandy-inspired dinner. I think back to the first time I tasted Paul Bocuse's famous soupe de moules aux pistils de safran. I was amazed to see what I felt was a sophisticated version of a simple shellfish broth served in a three-star restaurant. It was simple, all right, but the briny mussels and the tender diced vegetables were elevated to the sublime with the powerful aroma of the saffron!

In my version, we use cauliflower to thicken a mussel and saffron soup. You can make it in advance, but cook the mussels first so they yield their delicious juice, which will become the basis for the soup. I pair it with a white Château-Grillet, a rare wine from the northern Rhône region and favorite of Fernand Point, Bocuse's mentor. Its mineral characteristics complement the salty mussels perfectly and the essence of the saffron underscores the fruitiness of the wine.

A leg of lamb studded with garlic, even if it's not a pré-salé from Mont-Saint-Michel, is the perfect main course. I love to butcher my own meat—it reminds me of my early days in the kitchen—but it's not everyone's cup of tea, so you can ask your butcher to remove the thigh bone and to tie it for you. Potatoes, artichoke hearts, and garlic, iconic ingredients from Normandy and Brittany, make for a luscious garnish for lamb. If you can find it, drink a Châteauneuf-du-Pape, Réserve des Céléstins 1989, from vintner Henri Bonneau, a good friend and a wonderful cook. Of course, you could also serve a fizzy apple cider.

Do you know why people grow apples in Normandy? It's not to make apple juice or cider only; it's to make calvados! As a dessert, I thought to make a simple tart celebrating apples and calvados. The fruits are sweetened with honey and butter, but I don't add sugar to the tart dough, a pâte brisée, to let the sweet calvados-spiked filling shine.

MUSSEL AND CAULIFLOWER VELOUTÉ

MAKES 3 QUARTS (SERVES 8 TO 10)

3 pounds fresh mussels

3 tablespoons butter

3 cups (about 2 small) sliced onions

2 sprigs thyme

3 cloves garlic, peeled and sliced

2 bay leaves

1½ quarts Chicken Stock (page 368)

2 cups dry white wine

1½ teaspoons saffron threads

2 heads (about 3 pounds) cauliflower,
woody stems removed, cut into
small florets

1 cup heavy cream

1 cup crème fraîche

Salt and freshly ground white pepper

2 cups ¼-inch cubed white bread, toasted

½ bunch chives, cut into batons

Discard any mussels that are cracked
or open and will not close with a tap on the
counter. Place the rest in a large container
and cover with cold water for 20 minutes to
filter out any sand. Lift the mussels from the
water, leaving all the sand behind. Remove the
beards by grasping them with a dry towel and
pulling toward the hinges of the shells. Scrub
the mussels under cold running water.

Heat 1 tablespoon of the butter in a large
saucepan over medium heat. Add half of the
onions, thyme, garlic, and bay leaves and
cook, stirring, for 3 minutes. Add 2 cups of
the stock and the wine and bring to a boil.
Toss in the mussels, cover, and simmer until
the mussels open. Drain the mussels through
a cheesecloth-lined colander set over a bowl
and reserve the liquid for the soup. Pick the
mussels from the shells, place in a shallow
container, and cover with enough cooking
liquid to keep them moist. *(At this point the
mussels and cooking liquid can be reserved,
chilled, overnight.)*

In a large Dutch oven or heavy-bottomed
pot, melt the remaining 2 tablespoons butter
over medium heat. Add the remaining onion,
thyme, garlic, and bay leaf and the saffron
threads and cook, stirring, until the onions
are translucent. Add the cauliflower and
cook, stirring, for another 5 minutes. Add the
reserved cooking liquid and the remaining
chicken stock. Simmer, stirring occasionally,
for 30 minutes, or until the cauliflower is very
tender. Add the heavy cream and crème
fraîche and bring to a simmer. Discard the bay
leaf and thyme and transfer the mixture to a
blender (you will need to do this in batches).
Puree until smooth and season with salt and
pepper. Return to the pan, bring to a simmer,
and stir in the mussels just before serving.

Serve, garnishing with the toasted bread
and chives.

GARLIC-STUDDED GIGOT WITH ARTICHOKES AND WATERCRESS

SERVES 8

1 (8-pound) lamb leg, thigh bone removed, tied with butcher's twine

2 heads garlic, 6 cloves peeled and quartered, remaining cloves with skin

1½ pounds fingerling potatoes (about 12)

Salt

2 lemons

6 large artichokes

Freshly ground white pepper

Piment d'Espelette

¼ cup olive oil

4 tablespoons butter

2 sprigs sage

1 bay leaf

18 cipollini onions, peeled

1 cup dry white wine

2 cups Chicken Stock (page 368)

1 bunch watercress, trimmed and washed

Mustard Vinaigrette (page 376)

Two hours before cooking the lamb, puncture the meat on all sides with a paring knife and stud with the quartered garlic cloves. Reserve, chilled.

Place the potatoes in a large saucepan, cover with cold salted water, and simmer until tender. Drain and, when cool enough to handle, peel the skins and set the potatoes aside.

Fill a large bowl with cold water and squeeze in the juice from the lemons. Clean the artichokes one at a time by peeling away the outer leaves and trimming the stems to about 1½ inches in length. Using a sharp paring knife, remove the skin from the stems and any tough leaf remnants from the base. With a spoon, scrape out and discard the chokes. Cut the artichokes in half. Immediately submerge in the lemon water after preparing each artichoke.

Preheat the oven to 300°F. Rest the lamb at room temperature for 30 minutes and pat dry. Season liberally on all sides with salt, white pepper, and piment d'Espelette. Heat the olive oil in a roasting pan over high heat.

Sear the leg on all sides until browned, about 12 minutes total. Reduce the heat to medium and add the butter, garlic cloves with skin, sage, and bay leaf. Roast, turning and basting the leg often with the butter, especially in areas that don't touch the pan directly, about 5 minutes total.

Transfer to the oven and roast for 35 minutes. Remove from the oven and transfer the lamb to a platter. Strain the artichokes, pat dry, and add to the roasting pan with the onions and set over medium heat. Cook, turning the vegetables on all sides to brown, about 5 minutes. Add the potatoes, toss, and season with salt and pepper. Continue cooking, stirring often, for 5 more minutes.

Nestle the lamb into the vegetables and return the roasting pan to the oven. Roast until the temperature at the meatiest part of the leg reaches 125°F, about 45 minutes. Transfer the leg to a platter, cover with aluminum foil, and rest in a warm place for at least 20 minutes before slicing. If the vegetables aren't tender, return them to the oven to finish cooking.

Scoop the vegetables into a serving dish; cover and keep warm. Set the roasting pan over medium heat. Add the wine and reduce until almost dry, using a wooden spoon to scrape the bottom of the pan. Add the chicken stock and reduce by half. Season with salt and pepper and pour into a serving bowl; use for saucing the meat.

Toss the watercress with the vinaigrette and serve alongside the lamb with the vegetables and pan sauce.

TARTE NORMANDE

SERVES 8

Dough

3 cups flour

1 teaspoon salt

¾ cup (1½ sticks) (6 ounces) chilled butter, cubed

2 egg yolks

Filling

6 Gala apples, each peeled, cored, and cut into 8 wedges

¾ cup powdered sugar

5 tablespoons (2½ ounces) butter

½ cup honey

¼ cup calvados

4 teaspoons cornstarch

⅓ cup sugar

3 eggs

1 egg yolk

⅓ cup crème fraîche

2 teaspoons vanilla paste

1 cup milk

For the Dough

In the bowl of a food processor, pulse the flour, salt, and butter until it resembles coarse meal. With the machine running, pour in the yolks and 3½ tablespoons cold water and mix just until the dough holds together. Turn the dough onto a flat surface and flatten into a disc. Wrap in plastic wrap and refrigerate for 1 hour, or until firm.

Preheat the oven to 350°F. Lightly flour a work surface and roll the dough into a round large enough to fit a 10- to 12-inch tart or quiche pan with 1½- to 2-inch-tall sides. Fit the dough in the bottom and up the sides of the pan. Trim excess dough even with the pan's rim. Line with parchment paper and fill with rice or beans to weigh down the dough. Bake for 15 minutes, remove the tart shell, and reduce the oven temperature to 325°F. Remove the weights and paper from the dough and return to the oven to bake for another 15 minutes, or until light golden brown.

For the Filling

In a large bowl, toss the apples with ¼ cup of the powdered sugar and set aside at room temperature for 30 minutes. In a large sauté pan over high heat, lightly brown the butter, add the apples, and toss to coat. Add the honey and cook, stirring, until the apples are golden brown and about halfway cooked. Remove the pan from the heat, pour in the calvados, and carefully flambé. Simmer, stirring, until glazed. Set aside.

In a medium bowl, whisk the cornstarch and sugar to combine. Add the eggs, yolk, crème fraîche, and vanilla paste and whisk until smooth. Stream in the milk, while whisking, to make a smooth batter.

Fan the apples into the tart shell in a single layer. Pour the batter over the top to the rim (reserve any extra). Bake for 30 to 35 minutes, until a cake tester inserted into the center comes out clean. If the filling sinks while baking, pour in the reserved batter about halfway through.

Remove from the oven and dust with the remaining ½ cup powdered sugar.

PROVENCE

MENU

Grand Aïoli

*Loup de Mer on Herbes
de Provence Citrus Salt*

*Fig, Pine Nut, and Mascarpone
Custard Tart*

THE ROSÉ IS CHILLED, THE LIGHT MUSIC IS ON, AND IT'S TIME TO RELAX. JUST A REGULAR Sunday afternoon, at home, still reeling from a busy night at the restaurant. I step into my urban kitchen above the "store" on 65th Street to prepare dinner for my friends.

Tonight I am taking them to Provence. We will start with a grand aïoli, the perfect Mediterranean appetizer to serve when you're not sure how many will show up.

I was reunited with aïoli the summer I spent a week at Michel and Betsy Bernardaud's home in St. Palais, on the Atlantic Coast. Betsy, a fabulous home cook, and I went shopping, and she made a huge aïoli bursting with steamed cauliflower, potatoes, and asparagus, as well as the traditional warm cod, poached mussels, and other shellfish. This meal of garlicky pleasure truly stayed with me, and when I opened Bar Boulud the following year, in honor of Betsy, I put aïoli on the menu. To this day, it's the first thing I taste when I go there.

As you know, the dish is named for the sauce, an addictive garlic and olive oil dip. In my recipe, I use a poached egg for added fluffiness and some water to emulsify this pseudo-mayonnaise. Also, I usually add a little more cooked garlic than raw for a delicate balance. The colorful, abundant display holds court at the center of the table, and the guests can linger over it, a perfectly convivial experience.

As a main course, I bake a classic loup de mer with fennel on a bed of citrusy herbes de Provence salt. An olive oil dressing full of raisins, grapes, lemon, lime, cherry tomatoes, and herbs adds freshness and a dash of tartness.

In the bread basket, fougasse, the Provençal olive oil bread. A close cousin of the focaccia, it shows how food seeps through the latitudes, skipping man-made boundaries.

Although fig trees are normally found in Provence, we had some at home in Lyon, and my grandmother Francine would often bake a tart with them on Sundays. In my mind, it still holds the taste of childhood. At home I would much rather bake a tart than a cake. A sweet dough, maybe a frangipane that can absorb the juices of the fruit, or as in this recipe, with pine nuts and a mascarpone custard.

What to drink in Provence? The Rolls-Royce of rosés: a young vintage from the intensely pink Château Simone in the countryside near Aix-en-Provence.

GRAND AÏOLI

SERVES 6 TO 8

Whelks

2 pounds whelks

1 cup white wine vinegar

1 tablespoon cracked black pepper

Salt

Olive oil

Freshly ground white pepper

Lobster and Shrimp

1 gallon Court Bouillon (page 369)

2 (1½- to 2-pound) live lobsters

1½ pounds large shrimp, in the shell

Vegetables

1 pound Peewee or fingerling potatoes

Salt

1 bunch jumbo green asparagus, stalks lightly peeled

2 bunches baby carrots, trimmed and peeled

1 head celery, stalks peeled and cut into 2-inch sticks

1 pound haricots verts, trimmed

1 pound broccoli rabe, trimmed into long florets

Aïoli Sauce

4 large cloves garlic, peeled

1 tablespoon white vinegar

Salt

1 egg

2 egg yolks

1 tablespoon Dijon mustard

½ cup olive oil

1½ cups canola oil

To Finish

2 heads romaine or baby lettuce leaves, washed

1 bunch breakfast radish, trimmed

1 pinch of piment d'Espelette

For the Whelks

Scrub the whelks under cold running water. Transfer to a large saucepan and cover with cold water, the vinegar, cracked black pepper, and 1 tablespoon salt. Bring to a boil, cover, reduce the heat and, simmer, skimming as needed, for 1½ hours. Strain and, when cool enough to handle, pick the meat from the shells. Separately rinse the meat and shells with cold water. Return the shells to the saucepan, cover with water, and boil for 10 minutes. Trim the guts from the meat, leaving just the muscle. Rinse the muscle, pat dry, and toss with olive oil, salt, and white pepper to taste. Strain the shells and chill under cold running water. Return the whelks to the shells for presentation.

For the Lobster and Shrimp

In a large stockpot, bring the court bouillon to a boil and place a large bowl of ice water on the side. Drop the lobsters into the pot, being sure they are submerged (add water if necessary), and cover with a lid. Simmer for 10 minutes. Transfer the lobsters to the ice water to chill. Return the court bouillon to a light simmer and add the shrimp. Poach at just below a simmer for 4 minutes. Chill in the ice water.

Strain and pat dry the lobsters and shrimp. Remove the meat from the claws and knuckles of the lobster. Cut off the tails, slice them in half lengthwise through the shell, and remove the veins. Cut the tail meat into pieces and return to the shells. Peel the shrimp. Reserve the seafood, covered and chilled.

For the Vegetables

Place the potatoes in a medium saucepan, cover with cold salted water, and bring to a simmer. Cook until the potatoes are tender. Strain, peel if desired, and chill in the refrigerator.

In a large stockpot, bring 2 gallons of salted water to a boil and set a bowl of ice water on the side. In separate batches, boil the asparagus, carrots, celery, haricots verts, and broccoli rabe until tender. Allow the water to return to a boil in between batches. Remove and chill the vegetables in ice water, strain, and pat dry.

For the Aïoli Sauce

Cut the cloves of garlic in half lengthwise and remove the germ. In a small saucepan, bring 6 halves of the garlic to a boil in cold water, then discard the water and repeat, cooking the garlic until tender the second time. Fill a small saucepan with a few inches of water and add the vinegar and a pinch of salt; crack the whole egg into a cup. Bring the water to a simmer and slide in the egg. Poach for 2 minutes (the white will solidify but the yolk will remain runny). Transfer the poached egg to a blender or food processor and add the cooked and raw garlic, the egg yolks, mustard, 3 tablespoons water, and ¾ teaspoon salt. Blend until well combined. While the machine is still running, add the olive oil and then the canola oil in slow, steady streams. The sauce should emulsify, with a thick, pale consistency similar to that of mayonnaise. Taste for seasoning, then transfer to a bowl.

To Finish

Assemble the lettuce, radishes, cooked whelks, lobster, shrimp, and boiled vegetables on a platter. Sprinkle aïoli sauce with piment d'Espelette and serve alongside for dipping.

LOUP DE MER ON HERBES DE PROVENCE CITRUS SALT
FENNEL AND GRAPE SAUCE VIERGE

SERVES 4

Loup de Mer

4 cups kosher salt, plus more for cooking the fennel

3 fennel bulbs, with their stalks

Olive oil

Salt and freshly ground white pepper

Piment d'Espelette

¼ cup plus 2 tablespoons dried herbes de Provence spice blend

2 (3- to 4-pound) loups de mer, scaled and gutted

4 lemons, sliced

4 limes, sliced

Grape Sauce Vierge

1 pint cherry tomatoes

⅓ cup minced shallot

3 cloves garlic, peeled and minced

½ cup yellow raisins

1 small bunch baby white grapes, or quartered large white grapes

Juice of 2 lemons

Juice of 2 limes

2 tablespoons chopped chervil

2 tablespoons thinly sliced chives

2 tablespoons chopped parsley

2 tablespoons piment d'Espelette

1 tablespoon cracked black pepper

1 cup olive oil

Salt to taste

For the Loup de Mer

Preheat the oven to 325°F. Bring a large pot of salted water to a boil. Trim the stalks from the fennel and set aside. Peel the bulbs and cut each one, root to tip, into 4 even slices. Boil the fennel slices for 4 minutes, or until just cooked; strain and pat dry (you can reserve the boiling water for the cherry tomatoes). In a bowl, toss the fennel with olive oil to coat and season with salt, pepper, piment d'Espelette, and 1 tablespoon of the herbes de Provence.

Score the skin of each fish fillet 3 to 4 times and season them on both sides and in the cavities with salt, pepper, piment d'Espelette, and 1 tablespoon herbes de Provence.

Stuff each fish with the reserved fennel stalks, half of the sliced lemon, and half of the sliced lime.

In the bottom of a baking or roasting dish large enough to hold the fish, combine the 4 cups kosher salt, the remaining ¼ cup herbes de Provence, the sliced lemons and limes, and ½ cup water. Top the salt mixture with a sheet of parchment paper and poke it several times with a knife. Line the fennel around the outer edges of the dish and nestle the fish into the middle with their bellies facing in. Cover with aluminum foil and bake for 20 to 30 minutes, until the thickest parts of the fish fillets reach 120°F. Remove from the oven and rest for 5 minutes before carving off the fillets.

For the Grape Sauce Vierge

Score the bottoms of the cherry tomatoes with an X and boil for 5 seconds. Rinse with cold water and peel the skins. Halve the tomatoes and put in a large bowl. Add the remaining ingredients.

To Finish

Serve the fish fillets with the fennel and drizzle grape sauce vierge on top.

FIG, PINE NUT, AND MASCARPONE CUSTARD TART

SERVES 6 TO 8

Dough

1¼ cups flour

1½ tablespoons sugar

½ cup (1 stick) cold butter, diced

1 egg yolk, whipped with
2 tablespoons water

Filling

⅓ cup sugar

4 tablespoons honey

1 teaspoon cornstarch

4 teaspoons flour

⅓ cup plus 2 tablespoons
mascarpone cheese

3 eggs

½ teaspoon orange blossom
water, optional

1 cup pine nuts

1 pound fresh figs, stemmed and halved

Honey Whipped Cream

1 cup heavy cream

⅓ cup mascarpone cheese

5 tablespoons honey

For the Dough

In the bowl of a food processor, pulse the flour, sugar, and butter together until it resembles coarse meal. With the machine running, pour in the yolk and pulse just until the dough holds together. Turn the dough onto a flat surface and flatten into a disc. Wrap in plastic wrap and refrigerate for 1 hour, or until firm.

Preheat the oven to 350°F. Lightly flour a work surface and roll the dough into a sheet large enough to fit a 9-inch-square tart pan with a removable bottom. Fit the dough in the bottom and up the sides of the pan. Trim excess dough even with the pan's rim. Line with parchment paper and fill with rice or beans to weigh down the dough. Place the tart pan on a baking sheet and bake for 20 minutes. Remove from the oven and reduce the oven temperature to 325°F. Remove the weights and paper from the dough and return to the oven to bake for another 10 minutes, or until golden brown.

For the Filling

With an electric mixer fitted with a paddle attachment, mix the sugar, 2 tablespoons of the honey, the cornstarch, and the flour until well combined. Add the mascarpone, eggs, and orange blossom water (if using) and continue mixing until smooth. In a small bowl, toss the pine nuts with the remaining 2 tablespoons honey.

Line the figs with their tips facing up in the tart shell. Evenly pour the batter in be-tween the figs. Sprinkle the honeyed pine nuts over the top. Return the tart to the oven for 20 minutes, or until the pine nuts are golden and the batter is cooked through; you can check with a cake tester.

For the Honey Whipped Cream

Up to 1 hour before serving, with an electric mixer, whip the heavy cream to soft peaks. Add the mascarpone and honey and continue whipping to reach stiff peaks. Keep, chilled, and serve alongside the tart.

LYON

MENU

Modern Salade Lyonnaise

Poulet à l'Estragon

*Cocoa-Dusted Dark
Chocolate Bombe*

TONIGHT I AM TAKING YOU HOME; I MEAN TO LYON AND ITS SOULFUL, UNIQUE CUISINE.
And I will confide in you that one of my dreams is to open a real bouchon there. An old-fashioned bistro where the Lyonnais can eat lunch every day, and where the menu gets written in the morning after the chef comes back from the market. One of my favorites is the Café des Fédérations, open for decades, where you start with a selection of charcuterie or a simple leek vinaigrette salad, and then choose between the meat or the fish of the day. Hungry for dessert? A big baking sheet holds the massive tarte du jour, just like the one we offer at Épicerie Boulud every day. There's one person in the kitchen, one in the front, and one bartender. Wine is Beaujolais, often bought by the barrel, or perhaps a Mâcon blanc, and served in the thick-bottomed bottles called "pot Lyonnais."

This menu's salad is my fantasy of a bouchon appetizer, a wink to the taste of the rich gateaux de foies blonds I had at Alain Chapel. Let the chicken livers marinate overnight in milk to mellow their bitterness, and do not cook them too long, so they stay pink and tender.

When the soft-boiled egg oozes onto the leeks, it will mix with the vinaigrette, which holds a good trick: carrots are cooked until tender with the leeks and then blended in the dressing to thicken it. Acidity is often an integral part of the Lyon repertoire, where the rich cuisine often needs to be cut with a zing of vinegar.

For this main course, instead of buying your chickens already cut up, get whole animals so you can make a flavorful stock with the carcass, feet, and trimmings. Imagine, for my apprentice exam, we needed to cut a whole chicken into eight perfect pieces. But this is really the meaning of a fricassée, where the meat itself, as it roasts, yields the sauce, browning and condensing all of its deep flavors into the dish. I learned this simple but classic recipe at my very first job, at Nandron, and it is still one of my favorite ways to braise a chicken.

Choose to roast your chicken in a wide, shallow casserole or a braiser so the pieces are not crowded. You'll see that the mix of vinegar, tarragon, and tomatoes will drown the meat in a delicious sauce.

In Lyon, the tradition of chocolate making dates back to the Middle Ages, and it's fair to say that Lyon makes some of the best chocolate in France. One of the most famous chocolatiers is Maurice Bernachon, who actually roasts his own raw cacao inside his shop. A few miles away down the Rhône in Tain-l'Hermitage lies the famous Valrhona chocolate factory that produces much of the chocolate we use in our desserts.

Tonight's intense chocolate bomb will endear you to your guests. Inspired by the Bernachon President's Cake presented to French president Valéry Giscard d'Estaing at the Légion d'Honneur lunch for Paul Bocuse in 1975, this simplified interpretation is lighter than you think with no butter and very little flour, but it still showcases the force of pure cocoa.

A noble Beaujolais Morgon Marcel Lapierre, with its wax-covered seal, will work magic to toast the flavors of my terroir.

MODERN SALADE LYONNAISE
LEEKS, LARDONS, AND OEUF MOLLET

SERVES 6

8 ounces chicken livers
(about 12), trimmed

2 cups milk

Salt

6 eggs

4 small carrots
(about 1 pound), peeled

6 small leeks

1 bay leaf

2 sprigs thyme

¼ cup Dijon mustard

2 tablespoons sherry vinegar

5 tablespoons olive oil

Freshly ground white pepper

6 (¼-inch-thick) slices of bacon

½ bunch chives, cut into 1-inch batons

Submerge the chicken livers in the milk and soak overnight in the refrigerator. Strain and pat dry with a paper towel.

Bring a large pot of salted water to a boil. Submerge the eggs and boil for 6 minutes. Strain and peel the eggs under cold running water.

Thinly slice 1 carrot and cut the slices into thin julienne.

Peel the tough outer leaves from the leeks and halve them lengthwise, starting ½ inch from their base to keep them intact. Rinse them with cold water to wash any sand from their layers. Bunch the leeks and tie together with butcher's twine. Place in a large pot with the remaining carrots, the bay leaf, and thyme and cover with cold salted water. Bring to a simmer and cook for 20 minutes, or until the carrots are tender. Strain, and discard the thyme and bay leaf.

Transfer the carrots to a blender with 5 tablespoons water, the mustard, and vinegar. Puree until smooth, then stream in the olive oil until emulsified. Season with salt and pepper.

Untie the leeks, pat dry with paper towels, and brush them with carrot dressing; sprinkle with salt and pepper.

In a large sauté pan over medium heat, sear the bacon on both sides until crispy, about 6 minutes total. Strain off all but 1 tablespoon fat, transfer the bacon to a cutting board, and cut the strips crosswise into ½-inch pieces. Season the chicken livers on all sides with salt and pepper. Return the sauté pan with the bacon fat to high heat and add the livers in a single layer. Sear the livers on both sides until cooked through but still light pink in the center, about 5 minutes total. Scoop onto a cutting board and slice the livers in half.

Spoon the carrot vinaigrette into the center of 6 salad plates and top each with a fanned-out seasoned leek and 1 egg. Divide the bacon, chicken livers, julienned carrot, and chives on top.

DANIEL AT HOME

POULET À L'ESTRAGON
RICE PILAF AND YELLOW WAX BEANS

SERVES 6 TO 8

Poulet à l'Estragon

Salt

15 golf ball–size tomatoes

1 tablespoon butter

2 tablespoons olive oil

2 (2- to 3-pound) farm-raised chickens, each cut into 8 pieces

Freshly ground white pepper

4 large shallots, sliced

10 ounces pearl onions

2 tablespoons tomato paste

3 tablespoons flour

½ cup tarragon vinegar

2 cups Chicken Stock (page 368)

½ bunch tarragon

Rice Pilaf

1½ cups basmati rice

2 tablespoons olive oil

1 shallot, minced

2 tablespoons butter

2½ cups Chicken Stock (page 368)

1 teaspoon salt

1 bay leaf

2 sprigs thyme

2 sprigs tarragon

Yellow Wax Bean Fricassée

Salt

1 pound yellow wax beans, trimmed

2 tablespoons butter

Freshly ground white pepper

½ bunch tarragon, leaves chopped

For the Poulet à l'Estragon

Bring a large pot of salted water to a boil and set a bowl of ice water on the side. Score an X on the bottoms of the tomatoes. Boil them for 5 seconds, or until the skins loosen on the bottoms. Strain and peel under cold running water; set aside.

In a 5-quart braising pan over medium-high heat, melt the butter with the oil. Season the chicken on all sides with salt and pepper.

Add the chicken to the pan skin side down and sear until golden brown on both sides, about 10 minutes total. Transfer the chicken to a platter, set aside, and strain all but 1 table-spoon fat from the pan.

Reduce the heat to medium and add the shallots and onions to the pan. Cook, stirring, until the shallots are soft. Add the tomato paste and flour and cook, stirring, for another minute. Add the vinegar, bring to a simmer, then stir in the chicken stock. Bring to a simmer, making sure to scrape the bottom of the pan. Return the chicken to the pan with half of the tomatoes and the tarragon. Cover and simmer for 10 minutes, stirring occasionally. Add the remaining tomatoes, cover, and simmer for another 20 minutes, or until the chicken is cooked through.

For the Rice Pilaf

Rinse the rice with cold water until it runs clear. Heat the olive oil in a medium saucepan over medium heat. Add the shallot and cook, stirring, until translucent. Add the rice and stir to coat. Add the butter, chicken stock, salt, bay leaf, thyme, and tarragon and bring to a simmer. Cover and cook undisturbed over low heat for 10 to 15 minutes. Turn off the heat and rest, covered, for 5 minutes. Remove the lid and fluff the rice with a fork.

For the Yellow Wax Bean Fricassée

Bring a large saucepan of salted water to a boil. Add the beans and boil for 4 minutes, or until tender. Strain, return the beans to the pan over medium-low heat, and toss with the butter. Season with salt and pepper and toss in the tarragon leaves just before serving.

COCOA-DUSTED DARK CHOCOLATE BOMBE

SERVES 8 TO 10

Chocolate Ganache Frosting

3¼ cups heavy cream

2¼ cups sugar

12 ounces unsweetened baker's chocolate (we recommend Valrhona cacao paste), chopped

Chocolate Syrup

¼ cup sugar

2 ounces dark chocolate (we recommend Valrhona Manjari 64%), chopped

Chocolate Genoise Cake

1½ cups flour, plus extra for coating the bowl

7 eggs

1 egg yolk

1¼ cups sugar

⅔ cup unsweetened cocoa powder (we recommend Valrhona 100% Pure Cacao Powder)

3¼ tablespoons milk

3½ tablespoons butter, melted

Chocolate Ribbons

1 pound Tempered Chocolate (page 378)

For the Chocolate Ganache Frosting

In a small saucepan, combine the heavy cream and sugar and bring to a simmer. Place the chocolate in a heatproof bowl and pour the hot cream mixture over the top. Rest for 1 minute, then whisk together until smooth. Transfer the mixture to a shallow baking dish and cover the surface with plastic wrap. Cool at room temperature until the ganache thickens to a frosting consistency.

For the Chocolate Syrup

In a medium saucepan, bring the sugar and ¾ cup water to a simmer. Remove from the heat and, using a hand blender, puree in the chocolate until smooth. Set aside to cool.

For the Chocolate Genoise Cake

Preheat the oven to 320°F. Grease the inside of a 3-quart stainless steel bowl with nonstick cooking spray and lightly coat with flour.

Fill one-third of a medium saucepan with water and bring to a simmer. In the bowl of an electric mixer, whisk to combine the eggs, yolk, and sugar. Set the bowl over the pot of simmering water. Continue whisking until the temperature of the mixture reaches 140°F. Remove from the heat and place the bowl on the mixer fit with a whisk attachment. Whip at medium-high speed until it cools to room temperature and forms ribbons as it falls from the whisk, about 5 minutes.

Sift the cocoa powder and the 1½ cups flour together into a medium bowl. With a rubber spatula, fold the dry ingredients into the egg mixture in 3 additions, until no streaks remain.

Fold in the milk and melted butter until just combined. Transfer the batter to the prepared 3-quart stainless steel bowl.

Place the bowl on a baking sheet and transfer to the oven. Bake for 1 hour, and check the cake by inserting a cake tester into the center. Once the tester comes out clean, remove from the oven and immediately invert the cake onto a cooling rack.

Once cooled, use a serrated knife to divide the cake into 3 even layers and set them on the rack. Brush each layer with about 2 tablespoons chocolate syrup per side to moisten.

Frost the top of the 2 bottom layers with enough ganache to equal the thickness of the cake layers. Stack the layers back together and frost the outside of the cake with the remaining ganache.

For the Chocolate Ribbons

Pour about ½ cup of chocolate onto a flat marble, glass, or stainless steel surface. Spread it into a 1-millimeter-thick rectangle, about 2 feet long by 6 inches wide. Allow the chocolate to set for 5 minutes, or until it is no longer liquid or shiny yet is still slightly soft. With a straight-edged stainless steel spatula held at a 45-degree angle, scrape the chocolate widthwise to form wavy ribbons. Transfer the ribbons to a tray and repeat the process until all the chocolate is used. Decorate the cake with the ribbons.

BASE RECIPES

STOCKS, SAUCES, AND PUREES

CHICKEN STOCK
MAKES ABOUT 1 GALLON

6 pounds chicken bones, wings, and/or trim, skinned, fat trimmed, rinsed, and patted dry

2 onions, peeled and cut into quarters

2 small carrots, peeled and cut into 2-inch pieces

1 stalk celery, trimmed and cut into 2-inch pieces

1 medium leek, trimmed, split lengthwise, and rinsed

1 head garlic, split in half

1 bay leaf

5 sprigs parsley

½ teaspoon white peppercorns

Put the chicken bones and 7 quarts of cold water in a tall stockpot and bring to a rolling boil. Add another 3 quarts very cold water and skim off the fat that rises to the top. Reduce the heat to a simmer and skim regularly for 10 minutes.

Add the remaining ingredients to the pot and simmer, uncovered, for 4 hours, continuing to skim. Drain the stock into a colander set over a bowl. Discard the solids, then pass the liquid through a fine-meshed sieve lined with cheesecloth, and discard the solids. Chill and store, covered, in the refrigerator for up to 1 week, or freeze and use as needed.

VEAL STOCK
MAKES ABOUT 1 GALLON

6 pounds veal bones, cut into 2-inch slices, fat trimmed, and rinsed

2 tablespoons vegetable oil

2 onions, peeled and quartered

2 small carrots, peeled and cut into 2-inch pieces

2 stalks celery, cut into 2-inch pieces

1 tablespoon tomato paste

4 ounces button mushrooms, trimmed, cleaned, and halved

6 cloves garlic, peeled and smashed

5 sprigs parsley

2 sprigs thyme

2 bay leaves

½ teaspoon white peppercorns

Place the bones in a large stockpot and cover with cold water. Bring to a boil, then strain the bones and rinse them with cold water; wipe the stockpot clean. Meanwhile, in a large sauté pan, heat the oil over medium-high heat and add the onions, carrots, and celery. Cook, stirring, for 5 minutes, or until they start to caramelize. Add the tomato paste and cook, stirring, for 5 minutes; set aside. Return the bones to the pot, add 6 quarts cold water, and simmer for 10 minutes, skimming away any foam that rises to the surface. Add the cooked vegetables, the mushrooms, garlic, parsley, thyme, bay leaves, and peppercorns. Simmer, skimming as needed, for 4 hours. Strain the stock through a fine-meshed sieve lined with cheesecloth and discard the solids. Chill and store, covered, in the refrigerator for up to 1 week, or freeze and use as needed.

VENISON CONSOMMÉ
MAKES 2½ QUARTS

8 pounds venison bones, chopped into 1-inch sections, and rinsed

1 bottle (750 ml) dry red wine

2 small onions, peeled, 1 halved and 1 diced

2 cups wild mushroom trim or halved white button mushrooms

1 cup diced leek

1 cup diced carrot

1 clove

5 juniper berries

3 thyme sprigs

1 bay leaf

1 pound venison meat trimmings, chopped

Salt and freshly ground white pepper

4 egg whites

Marinate the venison bones in the wine overnight.

Preheat the oven to 400°F. Strain the bones, reserving the wine, and transfer them to a large roasting pan. Transfer to the oven and roast for 30 minutes, or until browned. Place a heavy-bottomed sauté pan over high heat and add the halved onion cut side down. Cook, undisturbed, allowing the onion to blacken.

Transfer the roasting pan from the oven to a burner over medium heat and add the reserved wine. Bring to a boil, using a wooden spoon to release any browned bits from the bottom. Transfer to a large stockpot with the burned onion, mushrooms, ½ cup leek, ½ cup carrot, the clove, juniper, thyme, bay leaf, and 4 quarts of water. Simmer for 3 hours, skimming any foam that rises to the surface as needed. Strain the liquid through a fine-meshed sieve, discard the solids, and chill over ice.

In a food processor, combine the venison meat with the remaining leek, diced onion, and carrot, 1½ teaspoons salt, and ¼ teaspoon pepper; pulse several times to chop well. Add the egg whites and pulse until well combined and pasty. In a large heavy-bottomed saucepan, whisk to combine the meat mixture with the chilled broth. Bring to a simmer over medium heat, scraping the bottom of the pan twice to keep the meat from sticking. Then cook undisturbed; the mixture will begin to form a solid mass, or raft. Once the raft begins to rise to the surface, gently poke a hole in the top. Allow the consommé to gently simmer for 30 minutes, occasionally basting the raft by ladling the consommé from the hole. Adjust seasoning with salt and pepper. Carefully strain by ladling the consommé through a fine-meshed sieve lined with 3 layers of wet cheesecloth. Cool and reserve, chilled.

COURT BOUILLON
MAKES ABOUT 1 GALLON

5 tablespoons coarse sea salt

¼ cup black peppercorns

1½ tablespoons coriander seeds

2 star anise

6 medium carrots, peeled and sliced

4 onions, peeled and sliced

1 head fennel, sliced

10 cloves garlic, peeled

1 (1-inch) knob of ginger, peeled and sliced

1 bay leaf

2 basil stems

Peels and juice of 1 orange

1 cup dry white wine

½ cup white vinegar

Pour 1 gallon of water into a large stockpot and add the salt, spices, vegetables, orange peel and juice, and herbs. Bring to a boil, then reduce the heat, cover, and simmer for 20 minutes. Add the white wine and vinegar, simmer for 5 more minutes, then strain through a fine-meshed sieve. Use immediately or chill over ice and store, covered and refrigerated, for up to 1 week.

CHICKEN JUS
MAKES ABOUT 1 CUP

2 tablespoons canola oil

4 pounds chicken bones and/or wings, chopped into 1-inch pieces, rinsed, and patted dry

1 small onion, thinly sliced

1 stalk celery, thinly sliced

5 medium shallots, thinly sliced

6 cloves garlic, peeled and smashed

1 cup dry white wine

3 quarts Chicken Stock (page 368), or water

2 parsley stems

2 thyme branches

Heat the oil in a large Dutch oven over high heat. Add the bones and sear until browned on all sides, about 10 minutes total; remove and set aside. Strain all but 1 tablespoon fat from the pan. Add the onion, celery, shallots, and garlic to the pan and reduce the heat to medium. Cook, stirring, until the onions are translucent. Add half of the white wine and reduce, while scraping the bottom of the pan, until dry. Return the bones and cook with the vegetables, stirring for another 2 minutes. Add the remaining wine and the chicken stock (or water), stir, and bring to a boil. Skim any foam that rises to the surface and reduce the heat to a steady simmer. Add the parsley and thyme and simmer for 30 minutes, skimming regularly.
Strain through a colander set over a bowl and discard the solids. Then strain the liquid through a fine-meshed sieve into a saucepan. Simmer, skimming as needed, until reduced to 1 cup, or until thick enough to coat the back of a spoon.

Chill the jus over ice. Store refrigerated for up to 4 days, or freeze until needed.

SAUCE PÉRIGUEUX
MAKES ABOUT 1 CUP

1 tablespoon butter

1 small shallot, minced

1 tablespoon fresh or canned chopped black truffle

½ small clove garlic, minced

2 tablespoons Madeira

2 tablespoons truffle juice, optional

1 cup Chicken Jus (page 369)

2 tablespoons Chicken Stock (page 368)

Melt the butter in a small saucepan over medium heat. Add the shallot, black truffle, and garlic, and cook, stirring, until the shallot is translucent. Add the Madeira and truffle juice and reduce by half. Add the chicken jus and stock and bring to a simmer. Skim any foam that rises to the top. Keep warm or reserve, chilled, until ready to use.

BASIC MEAT JUS
(Can be used for pork, venison, veal, or lamb)
MAKES ABOUT 1 CUP

2 tablespoons canola oil

4 pounds bones and/or trimmings, cut into 1-inch pieces, rinsed and patted dry

5 shallots, peeled and thinly sliced

1 small onion, thinly sliced

1 stalk celery, thinly sliced

2 cloves garlic, peeled and smashed

1 cup wine, beer, or spirit that pairs with the dish

3 quarts stock (page 368 for Chicken or Veal Stock), or 4 quarts water

2 parsley stems

2 thyme branches

½ teaspoon white peppercorns, wrapped in cheesecloth and secured with butcher's twine

Heat the oil in a large Dutch oven over high heat. Add the bones and sear until browned on all sides, about 10 minutes total. Remove the bones, set aside, and strain all but 1 tablespoon fat from the pan. Reduce the heat to medium and add the shallots, onion, celery, and garlic. Cook, stirring, until the vegetables release their juices and the onions are translucent. Add half of the wine (or other beverage) and reduce until dry, while scraping the bottom of the pan. Return the bones and cook with the vegetables, stirring, for another 2 minutes. Add the remaining wine and the stock (or water), stir, and bring to a boil. Skim any foam that rises to the surface and reduce the heat to a low simmer. Add the parsley, thyme, and peppercorns and simmer for 45 minutes, skimming regularly.

Strain through a colander set over a bowl and discard the solids. Then strain the liquid through a fine-meshed sieve into a medium saucepan. Simmer, skimming as needed, until reduced to 1 cup, or until thick enough to coat the back of a spoon.

Chill the jus and store refrigerated for up to 4 days, or freeze until needed.

RABBIT JUS
MAKES ABOUT 1 CUP

2 tablespoons canola oil

If making the Spring Rabbit Rissolé, page 172:

Bones and forelegs from 1 rabbit (about 2½ pounds), chopped into 1-inch pieces, rinsed and patted dry

If making Rabbit Porchetta, page 38:

Bones and trimmings from 1 rabbit (about 2½ pounds), chopped into 1-inch pieces, rinsed and patted dry

½ small onion, chopped

1 shallot, chopped

½ small carrot, chopped

½ stalk celery, chopped

1 clove garlic, peeled and chopped

3 tablespoons riesling wine

2 quarts Chicken Stock (page 368), or water

1 sprig thyme

1 sprig mint

Heat the oil in a large Dutch oven over high heat. Add the chopped rabbit bones and trim and sear until browned on all sides, 6 to 8 minutes; remove and set aside. Strain any excess fat from the pan. Reduce the heat to medium-low and add the onion, shallot, carrot, celery, and garlic. Stir with a wooden spoon, scraping the pan to loosen any browned bits from the bottom. Continue cooking for about 4 minutes, stirring, until the vegetables are golden brown. Add the wine, bring to a simmer, and stir. Return the bones to the pan, pour in the chicken stock (or water), and bring to a boil. Skim any foam that rises to the surface, add the thyme and mint, and reduce the heat to a steady simmer for 30 minutes, skimming regularly.

Strain through a colander set over a bowl, discarding the solids. Then strain the liquid through a fine-meshed sieve into a clean saucepan. Simmer, skimming as needed, until reduced to 1 cup, or until thick enough to coat the back of a spoon.

Chill the jus and store refrigerated for up to 4 days, or freeze until needed.

MAYONNAISE
MAKES ABOUT 2 CUPS

1 egg yolk

1 tablespoon plus 1 teaspoon Dijon mustard

2 teaspoons lemon juice

½ teaspoon salt

2 cups grapeseed oil

1 tablespoon olive oil

Freshly ground white pepper

In a medium bowl set on a dish towel (to keep it from sliding), whisk the yolk, mustard, lemon juice, and salt until smooth. Slowly stream in the oils, while whisking vigorously, until emulsified and fluffy. If the mayonnaise is too thick, you can add a little water. Season with pepper. If it separates, you can put a tablespoon of water in a clean bowl and stream in the separated mayonnaise, while whisking vigorously to bring it together.

SYRAH REDUCTION
MAKES ⅓ CUP

1 bottle (750 ml) syrah wine

1 cup port wine

1 cup sliced shallots

1 teaspoon cracked black pepper

1 small bay leaf

2 sprigs thyme

In a large saucepan, combine all the ingredients over medium heat, bring to a simmer, and simmer until reduced to 2 cups. Strain through a fine-meshed sieve and continue reducing to ⅓ cup. Reserve, chilled, for up to 1 week.

SPINACH PUREE
MAKES 1½ CUPS

Salt

2 tablespoons butter

1 cup heavy cream

1½ pounds spinach leaves, stems picked

Freshly ground white pepper

Bring a large saucepan of salted water to a boil and place a bowl of ice water on the side. Place the butter in a small saucepan and brown it over medium heat. Add the heavy cream and simmer until reduced by half. Boil the spinach leaves for 3 minutes, or until very tender, and then chill in the ice water. Strain and squeeze the leaves dry and transfer them to a blender. Add the hot cream mixture to the blender and puree on high speed until very smooth. Season with salt and pepper and pass through a fine-meshed sieve. If not using immediately, chill in a bowl placed over ice.

GRILLED EGGPLANT PUREE
MAKES 2 CUPS

1 (3-pound) eggplant

¼ cup tahini

2 tablespoons lemon juice

2 tablespoons olive oil

1 teaspoon ground cumin

Salt

Heat a grill or cast-iron grill pan over medium heat. With a paring knife, poke a few holes in the eggplant, set on the grill, and cover with aluminum foil. Cook, turning on all sides and keeping covered until tender, 20 to 30 minutes. Transfer to a cutting board and, once cool enough to handle, peel off the charred skin. Quarter the flesh and use a spoon to scrape and discard the seeds. Transfer the flesh to a colander set over a bowl and allow the juice to drain at room temperature for 30 minutes. Chop the flesh and transfer to a blender. Puree with the tahini, lemon juice, olive oil, cumin, and salt until smooth. Reserve, chilled.

GARLIC PASTE
MAKES ½ CUP

2 heads garlic

Olive oil

Salt and freshly ground white pepper

Preheat the oven to 400°F. Slice off the top quarter of the garlic head. Sprinkle the exposed cloves with a bit of olive oil, salt, and pepper. Wrap in foil and bake for 45 minutes, or until soft and golden brown. Rest until cool enough to handle, squeeze out the cloves, and scrape them through a fine-meshed drum sieve. Reserve, chilled.

TRUFFLE COULIS
MAKES ABOUT ½ CUP

1 tablespoon butter

1 small shallot, minced

1¾ ounces black truffle shavings

2 tablespoons Madeira

¼ cup heavy cream

Salt and freshly ground white pepper

In a small sauté pan over medium heat, melt the butter and add the shallot and truffles. Cook, stirring, until the shallots are translucent. Add the Madeira and simmer until reduced by half. Cover with the heavy cream, season with salt and pepper, and very slowly simmer, covered, for 20 minutes, or until the truffles are tender. Puree and reserve, chilled.

APPLE SKIN CHIPS

Canola oil for frying

12 (3-inch-long) apple peels, edges squared

Powdered sugar as needed

Preheat the oven to 190°F. Fill one-third of a medium saucepan with canola oil and heat to 300°F. Place the apple peels in a bowl and dust with enough powdered sugar to coat. Fry, fully submerged, for 2 minutes, or until the skins stop bubbling but haven't colored. Drain onto a paper towel–lined tray, then flatten the skins in a single layer onto a parchment-lined baking sheet. Dry in the oven for 4 hours, or until crispy.

Cool and store in an airtight container.

ARTICHOKE CHIPS

Canola oil for frying

3 baby artichokes, peeled

Rice flour

Salt

Fill one-third of a medium saucepan with canola oil and heat to 300°F. With a mandoline, cut the artichokes lengthwise into $\frac{1}{16}$-inch-thick slices. Transfer them to a bowl and toss with rice flour to coat. Fry until crispy (you may need to do this in batches). Drain onto a paper towel–lined tray and sprinkle with salt; cool. Store in an airtight container.

BIRYANI MASALA SPICE MIX
MAKES ABOUT 1 CUP

10 cloves

10 green cardamom pods

10 black cardamom pods

2 tablespoons fennel seeds

6 tablespoons coriander seeds

2 tablespoons cumin seeds

1 (4-inch) cinnamon stick, broken into pieces

1 tablespoon Tellicherry peppercorns

1 teaspoon chili flakes

In a small, dry sauté pan combine the spices over medium-low heat. Toast while stirring constantly, until very fragrant but being careful not to let them burn, 4 to 5 minutes. Transfer the spices to a plate to cool. Pulse in a spice grinder to a fine powder. Shake through a fine-meshed sieve and store in an airtight container.

CRISPY SHALLOT RINGS
MAKES ABOUT 1 CUP

Canola oil for frying

1 medium shallot, peeled

Rice flour

Salt

Fill one-third of a medium saucepan with canola oil and heat to 300°F. With a mandoline, slice the shallot into $\frac{1}{16}$-inch-thick rounds into a bowl; separate the rounds into individual rings. Toss in enough rice flour to lightly coat. Fry the rings until crispy and lightly browned (you may need to do this in batches). Remove with a slotted spoon. Drain onto a paper towel–lined tray, sprinkle with salt, and cool. Store in an airtight container.

MELBA CROUTONS

4 to 6 (depending on recipe) very thin ($\frac{1}{16}$-inch) slices white bread

2 tablespoons olive oil

Salt and freshly ground white pepper

For seaweed croutons:

2 sheets nori, finely minced

Preheat the oven to 300°F. Cut the slices of white bread into desired shapes. Brush 2 Silpats or sheets of parchment paper with olive oil on one side. Place 1 on a baking sheet oil side up. Line the slices of bread on top in a single layer and sprinkle both sides with salt and pepper (and the nori, if using). Top with the second Silpat or sheet of parchment, oil side down. Top with another baking sheet and bake for 10 to 12 minutes, until crispy and lightly browned. Cool and store in an airtight container.

GARLIC CHIPS
MAKES ABOUT ½ CUP

10 large cloves garlic, peeled

Canola oil for frying

Salt

With a mandoline, cut the garlic cloves lengthwise into thin slices and place in a small saucepan. Cover with cold water, bring to a simmer, strain, and repeat twice. Strain and pat dry the slices.

Fill one-third of a medium saucepan with canola oil and heat to 250°F. Fry the garlic in 2 to 3 batches for 2 minutes each, or until the chips are a light golden brown, stirring occasionally if needed to keep them submerged. Strain onto a paper towel–lined tray and sprinkle with salt. Cool and store in an airtight container.

CANDIED WALNUTS
MAKES 2 CUPS

2 cups walnut halves

3 cups sugar

Canola oil for frying

Salt

In a medium saucepan, combine the walnuts, 3 cups cold water, and 1 cup of the sugar and bring to a simmer. Simmer, stirring occasionally, for 3 minutes; strain and repeat the process 2 more times. Strain onto a parchment paper–lined baking sheet and cool at room temperature.

Fill one-third of a medium saucepan with canola oil and heat to 350°F. Fry the walnuts in 3 batches until browned, and strain onto a paper towel–lined tray. Sprinkle lightly with salt and cool at room temperature. Store in an airtight container for up to 1 week.

FINE WHITE BREADCRUMBS
MAKES 2 CUPS

1 (2-pound) loaf white pullman bread

Line a baking sheet with a rack. With a serrated knife, remove the crust from the bread and cut it into 1-inch chunks. Arrange in a single layer on the rack and leave for about 24 hours in a dry location, until crispy throughout.

Pulse the bread in a dry blender or food processor to fine crumbs. Shake the crumbs through a coarse sieve. Transfer any large pieces back to the blender, pulse, and pass through the sieve. Store the crumbs in an airtight container for up to 1 week.

HERB CHIPS

1 tablespoon grapeseed oil

Italian parsley or nettle leaves, or other large smooth-surfaced herb leaves that can be laid flat

If using nettles, wear gloves to guard your skin from irritants. Tightly wrap a microwave-safe plate with a layer of plastic wrap so that the top is taut and elevated by the rim. Lightly brush the plastic with grapeseed oil. Arrange the leaves on the surface in a single layer, without touching, and cover them with another taut sheet of plastic wrap. Microwave on high for 25 seconds, remove the top plastic layer, and microwave 2 more times in 20-second intervals, or until the leaves are dried. Store covered at room temperature for up to 2 days.

SALSIFY SPIRALS
MAKES 10 TO 15 SPIRALS

Canola oil for frying

2 thick stalks salsify, peeled

Salt

Fill one-third of a large saucepan with canola oil and heat to 300°F. Use a mandoline to shave long, thin ribbons from the salsify. Fry the slices, making sure they stay submerged, until they become slightly translucent and soft. With tongs or a heatproof strainer, transfer the slices to a paper towel–lined plate. Raise the temperature of the oil to 350°F.

Put on 2 layers of latex gloves or sugar gloves. With a pair of tongs, submerge 1 strip of salsify in the oil until it starts to turn golden brown but is not yet crispy. Remove the strip from the oil, cool for a few seconds, and quickly and carefully wrap it in a spiral around a cylindrical knife steel or wooden spoon handle. Cool the spiral on the steel, then slide it off; it should be crisp. Continue

the process to make spirals with the remaining salsify strips. Sprinkle with salt and store in an airtight container for up to 2 days.

BREADCRUMB CUPS
MAKES 8 CUPS

1 cup duck fat

1 cup flour

3 medium eggs, beaten with 3 tablespoons water

2 cups Fine White Breadcrumbs (at left)

Canola oil for frying

Place a spherical Flexipan mold (we used a 96-form Flexipan Pomponettes Mold) on a flat surface and fill at least 16 cups with duck fat. Spread with a small metal spatula to level off the tops. Freeze until solid. Pop out 8 of the cups. Using an open flame, one at a time, lightly melt the flat surface of a loose duck fat cup and then adhere it to the top of one that remains inside the mold, forming a sphere. Repeat the process to make at least 8 spheres. Freeze the spheres until set and pop out of the mold.

Place the flour, eggs, and breadcrumbs in separate shallow bowls. Dredge the frozen spheres in the flour, dip into the egg, and then coat in the breadcrumbs; freeze. Roll in the breadcrumbs once more; return to the freezer. Working in small batches from the freezer, cut a 1/16-inch cap from the spheres.

Fill one-third of a large saucepan with canola oil and heat to 275°F. Fry the balls in 2 to 3 batches until the breadcrumbs turn golden brown and the duck fat melts into the frying oil. Drain the breadcrumb cups onto a paper towel–lined tray and cool. Store in an airtight container for up to 1 week.

TEMPURA BATTER
MAKES 3 CUPS

1½ cups rice flour

3 tablespoons cornstarch

¼ teaspoon baking soda

1¼ cups club soda, chilled

Sift the flour, cornstarch, and baking soda into a medium bowl and form a well in the center. Up to 1 hour before use, whisk in the club soda to the consistency of pancake batter. Reserve, chilled.

TUILE BATTER
MAKES 1 CUP

4 tablespoons butter, melted

2 tablespoons orange juice

1½ teaspoons salt

2½ tablespoons powdered sugar

¾ cup flour

3 egg whites

In a medium bowl, whisk to combine the butter, orange juice, salt, and powdered sugar. Whisk in the flour and then the egg whites to make a smooth batter. Store, refrigerated, for up to 1 week.

PASTA DOUGH
MAKES ABOUT 1 POUND

2 cups 00 pasta flour
(we recommend Gran Mugnaio)

10 egg yolks

¼ teaspoon salt

½ tablespoon olive oil

1½ tablespoons water

In an electric mixer fitted with a dough hook, combine the flour, yolks, salt, and olive oil and mix on low speed until well combined. Add 1½ tablespoons water, or as needed until the dough pulls together and clings to the hook. Continue kneading on low speed for 10 minutes. Remove the dough from the mixer and wrap tightly with plastic wrap. Refrigerate for at least 1 hour or up to 3 days before use.

BRAISED SHORT RIBS
SERVES 4

4 cups red wine

1 cup ruby port wine

4 bone-in 2-inch-thick short ribs

Salt

Cracked black pepper

Flour for dusting

2 tablespoons olive oil

1 medium onion, cut into small dice

2 carrots, cut into small dice

1 rib celery, cut into small dice

4 large shallots, peeled and split

1 small leek, white and light green parts only, diced and rinsed

1 head garlic, halved

4 sprigs thyme

1½ tablespoons tomato paste

1½ quarts Veal Stock (page 368)

Preheat the oven to 300°F. Pour the red wine and port into a large saucepan and boil until it reduces by half.

Pat the short ribs dry with paper towels, season them on all sides with salt and pepper, and dust them lightly with flour. Heat the olive oil over medium-high heat in a large heavy-bottomed Dutch oven. Sear the short ribs evenly on all sides, 3 to 4 minutes per side, until well browned (you may need to do this in batches). Remove the short ribs from the pan and set aside. Lower the heat to medium, remove all but 2 tablespoons fat from the pan, and add the onion, carrots, celery, shallots, leek, garlic, and thyme. Cook for 5 to 7 minutes, stirring occasionally, until lightly browned. Stir in the tomato paste and continue to cook for another 2 to 3 minutes. Add the reduced wine, browned ribs, and stock to the pot. Bring to a boil, cover tightly, and transfer to the oven to braise for 3 to 3½ hours, or until the ribs are fork-tender. Remove the pot from the oven and cool at room temperature for 20 minutes. Gently scoop the ribs from the pot and pull out their bones and tendons, being careful not to shred the meat. Return the ribs to the sauce and refrigerate overnight.

The next day, scoop out and discard any fat that has risen to the surface of the sauce. Remove the ribs, trim any remaining cartilage, and transfer to a heatproof dish. Heat the sauce, then strain through a fine-meshed sieve into a clean saucepan. Reduce to a consistency thick enough to coat the back of a spoon and pour over the ribs; cover. (*At this point the ribs and sauce can be reserved, refrigerated, for up to 4 days.*)

When ready to serve, place the covered dish in a preheated 325°F oven and cook, occasionally basting the meat with the sauce until heated through, about 30 minutes.

....

FOIE GRAS TERRINE
MAKES ONE 14-OUNCE TERRINE

1 fresh grade A foie gras
(approximately 19 ounces)

1 quart whole milk

Seasoning ratio (grams of seasoning per pound of foie gras):

7 grams salt

1.5 grams white pepper

1 gram sugar

31 grams Sauternes wine

Rinse the foie gras with cold water
and transfer to a large container. Add the milk and enough ice water to submerge. Cover the surface of the foie gras and liquid with moist cheesecloth to prevent oxidation. Cover and refrigerate overnight.

Rest the foie gras in the liquid at room temperature until it softens to a resistance similar to the fleshy part of your palm. Remove the foie gras from the liquid and pat dry. Pull apart the 2 lobes and discard the fatty tissue in between. Place a sheet of parchment paper on a flat surface and set the lobes on top, with the undersides facing up and pointed ends facing down. Using a butter knife, gently butterfly open and expose the veins just below the surface of each lobe, starting at the wider ends.

While holding the knife at a 45-degree angle, working from the wider top ends to the pointed ends of the lobes, scrape and push aside the foie gras from the veins to expose them as they branch and become smaller. Stop scraping once the small veins become too thin to separate from the foie gras. Using a paring knife, pick out the thick ends of the veins and gently lift them out. Use tweezers to extract any pieces of vein that are still attached.

Weigh the foie gras, measure the seasoning according to the ratio listed in the ingredients, and sprinkle evenly on both sides. Transfer the foie gras to a plate, cover, and refrigerate for 4 hours.

Remove from the refrigerator and rest at room temperature for 30 minutes. Stack the 2 lobes together with the smooth sides facing out and the wide ends meeting the pointed ends. Place a 3-foot sheet of plastic wrap on the counter, set the foie gras in the middle, and roll tightly to enclose, forming a cylinder. Tie off the ends and poke it all over about 20 times with a cake tester. Transfer to a sous-vide bag and vacuum-seal.

Using an immersion circulator, preheat a water bath to 144°F. Submerge the bag and cook until the internal temperature reaches 129°F, about 85 minutes.

Remove the bag from the water, rest at room temperature for 15 minutes, and then transfer to the refrigerator. Cool until the internal temperature reaches 77°F. Cut open the bag and remove the foie gras over a baking dish lined with a rack. Scrape any remaining fat from the bag or coating the foie gras into the baking dish. Line a terrine mold or 8½ x 4½-inch loaf pan with plastic wrap. Gently press the foie gras into the prepared pan and cover it with more plastic wrap. Cut a piece of cardboard or other flat, sturdy surface to fit the inside of the mold and rest on top. Place weights, such as canned goods, on top of the cardboard to evenly press the foie gras. Refrigerate the foie gras and extra fat from the baking dish overnight.

Transfer the reserved foie gras fat into a saucepan and melt until liquefied over medium heat. Strain the fat through a cheesecloth-lined sieve and cool at room temperature until opaque and slightly thickened. Remove the top layer of plastic from the foie gras and with an offset spatula, smooth the surface to flatten. Spoon a thin layer of fat on top of the foie gras to prevent oxidation. Extra fat can be reserved, chilled, for other uses. Store the terrine, chilled, for up to 2 weeks.

OILS, DRESSINGS, AND CONDIMENTS

TOMATO CONFIT
MAKES 40 "PETALS"

20 ripe plum tomatoes (about 6 pounds)

4 tablespoons olive oil

2 teaspoons salt

½ teaspoon sugar

4 cloves garlic, peeled, split, germ removed, finely sliced

10 basil leaves

4 sprigs thyme, leaves picked

2 bay leaves, torn into smaller pieces

Freshly ground white pepper

Preheat the oven to 200°F. Bring a large
pot of water to a boil and set a bowl of ice water on the side. Core the tomatoes and score their bottoms with an X. Boil the tomatoes in small batches for approximately 5 seconds to loosen the skins and then transfer to the ice water to chill. Peel the tomatoes, split them in half lengthwise, and scoop out their seeds with a spoon.

Line 2 baking sheets with aluminum foil. In a large bowl, toss the tomatoes with the oil, salt, sugar, garlic, herbs, and some freshly ground pepper. Arrange the tomatoes cut side down in a single layer on the baking sheets and scatter the rest of the ingredients around them. Bake the tomatoes 2 hours, flip them, and bake another 2 hours or until they have reduced in size by half and look dehydrated. Remove the baking sheets and cool at room temperature. Transfer the tomatoes to a non-reactive lidded container and pour any remaining oil from the pan over top. Store refrigerated up to 2 weeks.

GREEN HERB OIL
MAKES ABOUT ¼ CUP

Salt

8 ounces green herb leaves

¼ cup grapeseed oil

Bring a medium pot of salted water to a
boil and place a bowl of ice water on the side. Boil the leaves until tender, 2 to 3 minutes, then chill in the ice water. Squeeze dry and transfer to a blender with the grapeseed oil. Puree on high speed until very smooth and bright green. Transfer the contents to a saucepan and simmer until the liquid stops bubbling, making sure not to fry the greens. Line a fine-meshed sieve with a coffee filter and place over a dry bowl. Pour the oil into the filter and transfer to the refrigerator. Allow it to strain, undisturbed, for about 2 hours, then transfer the oil to a squeeze bottle and reserve, chilled.

....

MUSTARD VINAIGRETTE
MAKES 1½ CUPS

2 tablespoons Dijon mustard

1 teaspoon salt

5 tablespoons sherry vinegar

1 cup grapeseed oil

2 tablespoons olive oil

Freshly ground white pepper

In a small bowl, whisk to combine the
mustard, salt, and vinegar. Slowly stream in the oils while whisking, and season with pepper. Store, chilled, for up to 1 hour.

WALNUT GLAZE
MAKES ½ CUP

½ cup walnut oil (we recommend Huilerie Beaujolaise)

1⅔ teaspoons glycerin monostearate

In a small saucepan, combine the walnut
oil and glycerin monostearate and place over medium-low heat. Cook, stirring, just until the glycerin monostearate is dissolved. Chill over ice and store, refrigerated.

....

MOSTARDA CREMONA
MAKES ½ CUP

2 tablespoons honey

2 tablespoons lemon juice

3 tablespoons sugar

2 tablespoons Sauternes wine

½ teaspoon brunoised fresh peeled ginger

¼ teaspoon Szechuan peppercorns

½ teaspoon mustard seeds

½ teaspoon mustard powder

1 pinch of piment d'Espelette

½ tablespoon Armagnac

½ tablespoon mustard oil

3 firm red plums, pitted and diced

In a small saucepan over medium heat,
combine all the ingredients except the plums with 2 tablespoons water and bring to a simmer. Reduce for 5 to 8 minutes, to a syrupy consistency. Add the plums and cook over low heat, stirring occasionally, until the plums are tender but not mushy. Transfer the mixture to a nonreactive container, cover, and refrigerate. For best results, prepare 1 to 2 weeks in advance.

BLACK OLIVE MOSTO OIL
MAKES ABOUT ½ CUP

1 cup Moroccan dry-cured
black olives, pitted

½ cup olive oil

1 splash of Tabasco sauce

Preheat the oven to 190°F. Transfer the
olives to a foil-lined baking sheet and bake for
5 hours, or until crispy. Transfer the dehydrated
olives, olive oil, and Tabasco to a blender
and puree until smooth. Pass through a fine-
meshed sieve and store, chilled, for up to
1 month.

BUDDHA'S HAND CITRON CONFIT
MAKES ABOUT 3 CUPS

1 small Buddha's hand citron

¾ cup plus 1 tablespoon sugar

With a small knife, trim the fingers from
the citron and cut the remaining base into
4 wedges. Using a sharp mandoline, thinly
slice all pieces widthwise. Transfer the slices
to a medium saucepan and cover with cold
water. Bring to a simmer, strain, and repeat
the process twice. Strain and add the sugar
with 2 cups of water. Simmer for 1 minute,
stirring to dissolve the sugar. Remove from
the heat and store, chilled, in the syrup.

LEMON CONFIT
MAKES ¼ CUP STRIPS

1 lemon

¼ cup sugar

With a vegetable peeler, remove 1-inch
strips of lemon zest and trim away the white
pith. Julienne the strips, transfer to a small
saucepan, and cover with water. Bring to a
boil, strain, and repeat the process 3 times.
Return to the pan and add the sugar and
1 cup cold water; bring to a simmer. Simmer
for 1 minute. Transfer to a bowl and store the
lemon zest in the syrup, refrigerated.

PICKLING LIQUID
MAKES 1 CUP

1 cup rice vinegar

3½ tablespoons sugar

½ teaspoon salt

In a small saucepan, combine the vinegar,
sugar, and salt, and bring to a simmer.
Simmer until dissolved. Transfer to a nonreactive container and refrigerate, covered,
for up to 2 weeks.

CLARIFIED BUTTER
MAKES 1¾ CUPS

2 cups (4 sticks) butter

Place the butter in a small saucepan and
set over low heat. Cook, undisturbed, until it
begins to lightly simmer and form a white
froth at the surface. Remove from the heat
and let stand for 5 minutes. With a small
spoon, skim off the froth. Place a fine-meshed
sieve lined with cheesecloth over a bowl. Pour
the clear butter through the sieve, leaving the
milky solids in the bottom of the pan. Chill
and store, covered, for up to 2 weeks in the
refrigerator, or freeze and use as needed.

CHANTERELLE DUXELLE
MAKES ½ CUP

1 tablespoon butter

1½ teaspoons brunoised shallot

4 ounces chanterelle mushrooms,
cleaned and small-diced

Salt and freshly ground white pepper

Melt the butter in a medium sauté pan
over medium-low heat and add the shallot.
Cook, stirring occasionally, until translucent,
about 2 minutes. Add the mushrooms and
cook, stirring, over medium heat until tender
and any moisture they may have released is
evaporated. Season with salt and pepper.
Reserve, chilled.

BASE RECIPES FOR PASTRY

DARK CHOCOLATE GLAZE

4 sheets gelatin

½ cup plus 2 tablespoons
heavy cream

1 cup plus 1 tablespoon sugar

9 tablespoons unsweetened
cocoa powder (we recommend
Valrhona cacao paste block)

Soak the gelatin sheets in ice water for
10 minutes; squeeze dry. In a medium saucepan, combine the heavy cream, sugar, and
5 tablespoons water and bring to a simmer.
Remove from the heat and whisk in the cocoa
powder and gelatin until smooth. Pass through
a fine-meshed sieve and chill for at least
2 hours, or overnight. Store, covered, in the
refrigerator, for up to 1 week.

TEMPERED CHOCOLATE

1 pound 60% to 70% dark chocolate, chopped

Fill one-third of a large saucepan with
water and bring to a simmer. Place the chocolate in a heatproof bowl and set over the water,
stirring occasionally, until it reaches 113°F.
Remove the bowl from the heat. If a large
room-temperature marble is available, the
chocolate can be poured onto it and slowly
folded onto itself using 2 metal spatulas until
it cools to 84°F. Otherwise, it can be left in
the bowl and slowly stirred until the temperature comes down to 84°F. As you use the
chocolate, keep it at a liquid state (it should
not get any cooler than 80°F) by intermittently
stirring it over the simmering water. Be careful
not to let the temperature exceed 88°F, or
the chocolate will need to be tempered again.

VANILLA SABLÉ BRETON DOUGH
MAKES ABOUT
14 OUNCES DOUGH

¼ cup plus 1 teaspoon
powdered sugar

½ teaspoon salt

1⅛ cups flour

3½ tablespoons cornstarch

1 Tahitian vanilla pod, split
and seeds scraped

1 hard-boiled egg yolk

¾ cup (1½ sticks) butter, softened

In a medium bowl, whisk to combine the
powdered sugar, salt, flour, cornstarch, and
vanilla seeds. Pass the yolk through a coarse
sieve. In an electric stand mixer fitted with
a paddle, mix the butter until creamy. While
the machine is mixing on medium speed,
gradually add the dry ingredients. Add the
yolk and mix just until incorporated.

Scrape the dough from the bowl and, with
your hands, pat it into a 1-inch-thick rectangle.
Wrap in plastic and refrigerate for at least
4 hours or overnight.

ALMOND CRUMBLE

½ cup (1 stick) butter

9 tablespoons sugar

⅔ cup plus 1 tablespoon flour

⅔ cup plus 1 tablespoon almond flour

Preheat the oven to 350°F. In an electric
stand mixer fitted with a paddle, mix the
butter until creamy. Gradually add the sugar,
flour, and almond flour to the butter while the
machine is mixing on medium speed, until the
mixture looks like large crumbs. Line a baking
sheet with parchment paper and scatter the
crumbs over the top. Bake for 14 minutes, or
until golden brown. Cool and store in an
airtight container.

CROUSTILLANT TUILE POWDER

1 cup sugar

1 tablespoon powdered glucose

1 cup dry cake crumbs (reserved from Biscuit Mirliton, Sablé Breton, or Pistachio Dacquoise)

1 pinch of salt

Line a rimmed 18 x 13-inch baking sheet with a Silpat. Combine the sugar and glucose in a medium saucepan and melt, stirring occasionally, over high heat, until it reaches 355°F. Remove from the heat and stir in the crumbs and salt. Pour onto the prepared baking sheet and cool at room temperature until hardened, about 3 hours. With a blunt object, break the hardened sugar into small pieces and transfer to a food processor. Pulse into a fine powder and shake through a fine-meshed sieve. The powder can be stored in an airtight container for up to 2 weeks.

....

CARAMELIZED NUTS

⅓ cup sugar

1 cup peeled unsalted nuts, such as peanuts or pistachios

Salt, if needed

Line a baking sheet with a Silpat. In a heavy-bottomed medium saucepan, heat the sugar to 250°F. Stir in the nuts with a wooden spoon. Continue cooking the nuts over medium heat until the sugar turns from a frosted white color to a glossy caramel. Pour onto the prepared tray and spread into an even layer. If using the nuts for a savory preparation, sprinkle lightly with salt. Cool at room temperature until hardened. Transfer to a food processor and pulse into small pieces. Cool and store in an airtight container up to 1 week.

PULLED SUGAR

1 pound isomalt sugar

Water-based food coloring, as needed

In a large heavy-bottomed saucepan, melt the sugar over medium heat. Stir occasionally with a heatproof spatula until it reaches 338°F on a candy thermometer. Use a pastry brush dipped in cold water to clean the inside of the saucepan as it cooks to prevent the sugar from crystallizing.

Pour the sugar onto the middle of a large Silpat sheet. While wearing sugar gloves, lift the sides of the Silpat to fold the sugar back onto itself as it seeps to the edges. Continue folding the sugar in this manner until the temperature drops to 285°F. Add food coloring drop by drop and work it into the sugar by folding it in your gloved hands.

Begin to pull the sugar by grasping opposite sides of the melted sugar and, with even pressure, stretch it out to arm's length, then fold it back onto itself. Repeat this process at least 10 times until the sugar is glossy.

Place sugar under a sugar lamp (or heat lamp) and keep it on the Silpat as you cut off smaller portions to work into desired shapes.

To make thin sugar strands, pull a small mass of sugar into very thin ribbons. Quickly wrap around ring molds to make circles, or leave them straight to make sticks. Trim with scissors and transfer to a tray lined with parchment paper to cool.

If the sugar becomes too hard to mold, you can microwave it: Microwave on high for 30 seconds, and, wearing the gloves, check the texture. If it hasn't softened enough to be able to mold, continue microwaving on high in 10-second intervals. Be very careful, as hot pockets can form in the middle of the sugar mass.

Store the sugar in sealed containers at room temperature, with silica gel packets if possible.

CULINARY TERMS AND INGREDIENTS

Agar-agar A gelling agent derived from red algae; used by boiling in liquid until the solids dissolve.

Al dente A degree of cooking in which the food (normally pasta) has been just cooked through and firm but not hard. In Italian, "to the tooth."

Apple pectin A gelling agent derived from apples that causes a thickening characteristic of jams or jellies; used by boiling in liquid until the solids dissolve.

Baton A knife cut; a short thin stick, ranging from ½ inch to 2 inches in length and approximately ¼ inch in width.

Black garlic Sweet-tasting garlic heads that have been fermented in their skin in a moist, high-temperature environment.

Brik dough (feuille de brique) Also known as warka or malsouka; paper-thin pastry sheets often made made of flour, semolina, water, oil, salt, and vinegar or lemon juice.

Brunoise A knife cut; ¹⁄₁₆-inch-thick cubes.

Chiffonade A knife cut; leafy greens or herbs cut into long, thin strips.

Colza oil Oil obtained from the seeds of *Brassica rapa*, a variety of the plant that produces turnips. Also known as rapeseed oil.

Cornet A cone made from a parchment paper; useful for piping with a small tip.

Crème fraîche Thick fermented fresh cow's milk cream that contains about 28 percent butterfat.

Cuisson The act of cooking, or in some cases referring to the degree of cooking you would like to reach.

Dried fennel stems Stalks of a fennel bulb that have been dehydrated.

Fennel pollen A spice made from granules harvested from the buds of flowering fennel plants.

Finger limes A micro citrus that grows wild in Australia, with interior pulp consisting of "pearls," or citrus "caviar," and a flavor profile that is a blend of lemon, lime, and grapefruit.

Flan powder A thickening powder used for hot-process preparations such as pastry cream or flan.

Frenched A term used to describe a rack of meat that has had the meat, fat, and membranes connecting the individual rib bones removed.

Fromage blanc Also known as fromage frais, a slightly drained cow's milk cheese. We recommend Isigny Ste. Mère 40%.

Gaufrette A waffle cut made by using a mandoline fitted with a waffle plate and turning the food 180 degrees after each slice.

Glucose powder A simple sugar derived from corn used in ice cream and sorbets to avoid water crystallization.

Glycerin monostearate An emulsifying agent for oils, waxes), and solvents; dissolves in oil heated to 140°F.

Green peppercorns in brine Dried green peppercorns soaked in a brine of salt, water, and sometimes vinegar.

Gremolata Chopped herb condiment, often with olive oil and citrus or other acidic note.

Ice cream stabilizer A powder used to keep the creamy texture of ice cream and reduce ice crystallization. We recommend Sevarome 64G.

Isomalt A sweet crystalline substance derived from sucrose.

Julienne A knife cut; long thin strips, 1 to 2 inches in length and approximately ¹⁄₁₆ inch in width.

Kataifi dough Shredded phyllo dough.

Kombu Dried kelp often used in Japanese cuisine, found dried and needed to make dashi broth.

Lemon omani Also known as black lime; made from fresh limes boiled in salt water that are sun-dried until the insides turn black.

Lilliput capers Tiny Spanish capers, usually packed in a sherry vinegar salt solution.

Manouri cheese A semi-soft Greek goat or sheep's milk whey cheese.

Marcona almonds Almonds imported from Spain, with a smoother, more delicate flavor than California almonds. Usually sold salted and roasted.

Mince A very fine knife cut, smaller than brunoise.

Mirin Japanese rice wine with a lower alcohol content than sake, and consisting of 40 to 50 percent sugar.

Nettlesome cheese Cave-aged cow's milk cheese with a nettle-studded interior; made at Valley Shepherd Creamery in New Jersey.

Nori sheets Edible seaweed sheets made by shredding red algae and rack-drying; often used for sushi.

Oyster leaves Pale gray/green leaves with a salty and oysterlike flavor; native to Scotland and the British Isles.

Piment d'Espelette Chili pepper cultivated in the Basque region in France that has a delicate, perfumed heat.

Red seaweed salad In Japanese, *aka-tosaka*; a red seaweed, often sold salt-packed; can be rinsed and eaten as salad.

Red self-hardening clay Commonly available in 5-pound moist-form blocks at pottery supply stores; malleable red clay that can air-dry.

Sea cress Cultivated by Chef's Garden; a crunchy, juicy, smooth, and wild micro green with a hint of saltiness.

Small dice A knife cut; ¼-inch cubes.

Sous-vide French for "under-vacuum," a method of cooking food sealed in airtight plastic bags.

Soy lecithin powder Derived from soybeans, an emulsifying agent commonly used as a thickener and stabilizer, often used for blending watery liquids to produce foam.

Supreme A citrus segment without the white membrane, made by carving off the skin and pith and then cutting in between the sections.

Taggiasca olives Small, cured black olives from Liguria, Italy, with a firm bite and a sweet, fruity, and mild flavor.

Telicherry peppercorns Whole black peppercorns from the Indian Malabar coast that are left on the vine longer than other peppercorns, resulting in an earthy, pungent flavor.

Thai coconut Also referred to as young coconut; a coconut that is harvested before fully mature, with thin husks, filled with coconut water and gelatinous meat. Often sold with the husk removed and a pointed tip.

Tourné A knife cut made with a paring, bird's beak, or tourner knife by trimming the sides of a food into an oblong football shape.

Trimoline Also known as inverted sugar; a mixture of glucose and fructose in a heavy syrup form, often used to provide moisture to pastries.

Vegetable gelatin (carrageenan) Extracted from red seaweeds, used for thickening, stabilizing, and emulsifying. Provides a smooth texture and accentuates flavor.

Verjus or "verjuice" The pressed juice of high-acid, low-sugar unripened wine grapes.

Xanthan gum A natural powdered additive used as a thickening agent and/or stabilizer; derived from fermentation of glucose or sucrose by a bacterium.

Za'atar A Middle Eastern spice blend made of herbs, sesame seeds, and salt.

SOURCES FOR INGREDIENTS AND TOOLS

INGREDIENTS

Baldor Specialty Foods | www.baldorfood.com
Finger limes, hearts of palm

La Boîte | www.laboiteny.com
Vadouvan, Pierre Poivre, custom spice blends

The Chef's Garden | www.chefs-garden.com
Baby turnips, green pea shoots, micro basil, micro carrot tops, micro cilantro, micro Greek mint, micro red ribbon sorrel leaves, micro savory leaves, micro sea cress, micro wood sorrel leaves

The Chefs' Warehouse | www.chefswarehouse.com
Brik dough (feuilles de brique), flan powder, lilliput capers, Korean dried chili threads

Cinco Jotas | www.cincojotas.com
Pata negra (Iberico Ham)

The Cooking District | www.cookingdistrict.com
Colza oil, pistachio oil, Huilerie Beaujolaise walnut oil, Orleans mustard, Thiercelin Green Apple Mustard, Huilerie Beaujolaise cider vinegar, Melfor vinegar, Huilerie Beaujolaise raspberry vinegar

D'Artagnan | www.dartagnan.com
Game, poultry, duck fat, pork blood, tarbais beans

L'Epicerie | www.lepicerie.com
La Baleine salts, oils, extracts, honey, purees, syrups, Valrhona chocolate, gelatin sheets, gold dust, isomalt, feuilletine, xanthan gum, apple pectin, chestnut flour, piment d'Espelette, glucose powder, soy lecithin powder, agar-agar, trimoline, pistachio paste, coffee extract, Cacao Barry pailletté feuilletine

Hamakua Farms | hamakuafarms@hotmail.com
Fresh Hawaiian heart of palm

Kalustyan's | www.kalustyans.com
Tandoori paste, lemon omani, black garlic, dried fennel stems, five-spice powder, spices

Koppert Cress | www.koppertcress.com
Oyster leaves, purple shiso

Minus 8 Vinegars & Verjus | www.minus8vinegar.com
8 Brix red and white verjus

Murray's Cheese | www.murrayscheese.com
Cheese, Marcona almonds, fromage blanc, Vermont Creamery cultured farm butter

New York Cake | www.nycake.com
Gold luster dust

Olive to Oil | www.olivetooil.com
Manni Per Mio Figlio olive oil

Plantin | www.truffe-plantin.com
Black truffles, truffle juice

Potironne Company | www.potironne.com
Sarl Henri Maire escargot

River & Glen | www.riverandglen.com
Washington State steelhead trout caviar

Solex Fine Foods | www.solexfinefoods.com
Game, wild mushrooms, Scottish langoustines, wild lumpfish caviar, gourgane flour

Urbani Truffles | www.urbani.com
White truffles

Valley Shepherd Creamery | www.valleyshepherd.com
Nettlesome cheese

Williams Sonoma | www.williams-sonoma.com
Restaurant Lulu fig balsamic vinegar

TOOLS

JB Prince | www.jbprince.com
Chocolate forks, clear acetate sheets, Silpat sheets, scales, fine-meshed drum sieves (or tamis), fine-meshed sieves (or chinois), pastry tips, stem thermometers, various pastry cutter sizes, Flexipan molds, flat meat mallets, sugar gloves, sugar lamps, tweezers, food grinder attachments for KitchenAid mixer, cannoli forms, vegetable juicers, whipped cream makers (iSi), kougelhopf mold

Korin | www.korin.com
Knives, Japanese turning slicers (Chiba Peel S), Japanese sumi charcoal, Japanese cedar paper

Williams Sonoma | www.williams-sonoma.com
Knives, mixers, blenders, baking dishes, baking sheets, small electrical tools, cheesecloth, pots and pans, measuring tools, 8½ x 4 ½-inch loaf pans, hand tools, pastry bags, scales, pasta machines, food mills

ACKNOWLEDGMENTS

In the peaceful dining room, maître d's, sommeliers, and waiters move swiftly between tables to the sound of hushed conversations. In the kitchen, it's an intense organized pressure that pervades while the chefs dab precise finishing touches on plates. Without these talented men and women, without the hours spent together striving for excellence, I could not have brought you this book. I could not be where I sit now.

Thank you to:

First and foremost, my incredibly dedicated, tireless chef and culinary manager, AJ Schaller, for coordinating this book, by researching, planning, cooking with our chefs, styling, and editing. For the last ten years she has brought to the Daniel team her smile and efficient manner, at both the stove and the computer with equal dexterity.

Chad Brauze, a seasoned chef and mathematics student at Columbia University, who tested the recipes that make up this book. We know he gets the equations exactly right.

Jean-François Bruel, our energetic executive chef and pillar of strength and knowledge for the last decade, who lent his years of experience, creativity, and talent. He has an uncanny ability to lead the team while he teaches and shares constantly.

Eddy Leroux, our gifted chef de cuisine for the last decade, who always brings back from his travels around the world the most interesting spices and ideas. He is the troubadour of our culinary spice chest.

Our dedicated executive sous chef, Sébastien Mathieu, who blends traditional culinary history with a modern taste. The hardworking team of sous-chefs that have strengthened our brigade, led by Gregory Stawowy, who has collaborated with Soo Gil Lim, Roger Ma, Olivier Gagne, Alex Burger, Brian Loiacono, Arno Busquet, and Devin Broo, as well as the thirty-five chefs who maintain our daily level of high expectations and performance.

Part of my chefs' team, my loyal corporate chefs Fabrizio Salerni and Olivier Muller, who help us on a daily level to maintain our culinary standards. For the Iconic section, they brought both support and good humor!

■ ■ ■

For the sweet part of the book, under the expert guidance of corporate pastry chef Eric Bertoïa, pastry chef, Sandro Micheli, and his sous chefs, Samuel Allevard and Thomas Croizé, worked tirelessly to prepare, measure, and create our artful and delicious desserts.

As our chief steward, Toto Ourzdine, this gardien de la maison worked behind the scenes to ensure the flow of our fresh, daily ingredient deliveries.

In the dining room, our past general manager and current director of operations Michael Lawrence, for the past fifteen years, has worked persistently to maintain our company's standards. Our extraordinary service team is led by his successor, the young, poised, and professional general manager, Pierre Siue, who dons his white gloves to shave the truffles as only he can! He is assisted daily by Anthony Mathieu and our team of maître d's in the impeccable precision and consistency of service. Bernard Vrod, Elvir Dzananovic, Yannick Vrod, and John Winterman make sure that the room is resplendent every night. Pascal Vittu, our cheese steward, unveiled some of the hidden gems from his cheese cart so we could share them with you.

These twenty years would not have been the same without the watchful and elegant eye of our past public relations director, Georgette Farkas. Today she is succeeded by the bright Lauren Mueller, a very talented asset who brings years of marketing experience, assisted by Carla Siegel, who lends her skills and creativity to our business.

In the skybox, my multilingual personal assistant, Maisie Wilhelm, who, with boundless energy and happy spirit, manages my office with brio, tact, and diplomacy, even when I throw her curve balls.

Our master sommeliers, led by the very knowledgeable, passionate Rajeev Vaidya, bring their extensive talent and expertise in wine to our guests and educate our service staff tirelessly.

Daniel Johnnes, my longtime friend and the most Burgundian of all American sommeliers, who oversees our wine program, bringing his expertise in wine pairing and always contributing in a creative way to our wine-driven events at Daniel.

Mark Fiorentino, head baker, who thrice daily bakes our bread delights with lush crumb and rich crust.

My longtime managing partner and friend Lili Lynton, who was instrumental in the founding of Daniel twenty years ago, and still is my closest and finest adviser.

Joel Smilow, my guiding financial partner, who helped weigh risks and opportunities and always stirred us to make the best decisions. I owe him these twenty ambitious successful years of Daniel and give him a big thank-you.

Brett Traussi, whom I first met in 1985 while he was an intern at the Plaza Athénée, and is now our trusted chief operations officer. The Dinex Group is strengthened by his combination of know-how and intuition.

The captain of our finances, CFO Marcel Doron, who for twenty years has steered our ship on the perfect course, helping us run a successful business, advising our chefs and managers along the way.

Ryan Buttner, our assistant director of operations, who has seen it all since 2001, and keeps a keen eye on our growth.

We wouldn't be able to keep our team well staffed with motivated, ambitious, and fresh talent without the help of Cynthia Billeaud, our elegant human resources director of eight years.

The helpful, talented, and tenacious Kim Witherspoon, one of the finest literary agents in the culinary world.

To the team at Grand Central Publishing: Jamie Raab, Matthew Ballast, Pippa White, Tareth Mitch, Tom Whatley, Anne Twomey, and especially our wonderful and highly respected editor Karen Murgolo, for her dedication to this project and for the trust she bestowed on the Daniel crew.

∎ ∎ ∎

Sylvie Bigar, a dear friend, French accomplice, and passionate home cook with prolific food and travel writing experience, who has helped capture my voice and translate the kitchen life and emotions into meaningful words. Her wit, passion, and humor made her a delight to work with on this project.

My friend, the best-selling author and obsessive cook Bill Buford, who spent the last four years in Lyon studying French cuisine and whom I challenged to come cook with me the iconic dishes I learned as a young chef and always wished to re-create. It is rare for a chef to share a stove with such a literary academic who takes you on a journey with his words.

Thomas Schauer and Sahinaz Agamola-Schauer, for the friendship and joy of collaborating on our third book together, and their assistant, Jessica Ozment, the best possible photography team: talented, smooth, and precise. And to Gary Tooth, who brought simplicity and elegance to the design of this book.

Olivier Giugni, the expressive floral designer, who, with Carine Bonnet from L'Olivier, paints the flowery backdrop of our life at Daniel.

Michel Bernardaud for letting us dig into Bernardaud's wonderful china; Christofle for opening up their showroom so we could borrow their elegant flatware and silver; Quality Tableware for the Hering, Furstenberg, Raynaud, and Guy Degrenne china; James Robinson Antiques for allowing us to use their antique silver trays and settings for the iconic meals; Kaplan Prop Company for their help with the various pieces for the iconic and home dishes.

Abalone, Jade Tiger, Cauliflower Concassé, Caviar, 69–71

almonds
Almond Crumble, 378
Apricot and Lavender Clafoutis, Fresh Green Almonds, 242
in Dover Sole Ballotine à la Polonaise, 105–7
Flaked New England Cod, Tarbais Beans, Chorizo, Almond Cloud, 64–71
in Warm White Asparagus Salad, Poached Egg Dressing, 51

Alsace, menu and recipes, 335–41
Beer-Marinated Pork Rack with a Barley-Mustard Crust, 338
Kougelhopf, 341
Root Vegetable Baeckeoffe, 340
Wild Mushroom Tarte Flambée, 336

appetizers
Beaufort and Riesling Fondue Ravioli, Green Peppercorns, Sunchokes, 95–97
Black Truffle Oeuf en Cocotte, 92
Caraway-Cured Tai Snapper, Cucumber and Dill Broth, 19
Chilled Salmon à l'Oseille, 25–27
Chilled White Asparagus Soup, Wild Chervil, Chive Blossoms, 52
Citrus-Cured Fluke, Shiso Bavarois, Ponzu Gelée, 8–11
Crayfish Timbale, Cockscombs, Watercress Velouté, 54–57
Creamy Spring Garlic Soup, Petit Gris Beignets, 44–47
Eckerton Hill Farm Heirloom Tomato Tasting, 32–33
Foraged Herb Pyramid Agnolotti, Pata Negra, Nettlesome Cheese, 99–101
Frog Leg Fricassée, Kamut Berries, Spinach Puree, 72–73
Frog Leg Soupe en Croûte VGE, 61–63
Grand Aïoli, 352
Hazelnut-Crusted Maine Sea Scallops, Nettles, Swiss Chard, 76–77
Jade Tiger Abalone, Cauliflower Concassé, Caviar, 69–71
Langoustine and Uni Chaud-Froid, 21–23
Lobster Biryani Masala, Fresh Coconut Chutney, Spiced Sheep's Yogurt, 80–83
Miso-Glazed Sea Scallop Rosace, Brussels Sprouts, Crispy Rice, 84–85

Modern Salade Lyonnaise, Leeks, Lardons, and Oeuf Mollet, 360
Mussel and Cauliflower Velouté, 344
Nantucket Scallop Ceviche, Blood Orange Sauce, 13
Pea and Lettuce Velouté, Hickory Smoked Squab Breast, 48–49
Peekytoe Crab Rolls, Granny Smith Apple, Celery, Walnut, 5–7
Poached Carolina Shrimp, Summer Melons, Lemon Balm, 29–30
Rabbit Porchetta, Farmer Lee's Baby Vegetable Salad, 38–41
Soft-Shell Crab Tempura, Lemon Gremolata, Pickled Fresno Peppers, 75
Spanish Mackerel au Vin Blanc, Poached with Carrot Mousseline, Lettuce-Wrapped Tartar with Caviar, 15–17
Spot Prawn Croustillant, Hearts of Palm Tandoori, Kumquat, 78
Venison and Daikon Radish Mosaic, 35–37
Venison Consommé with Black Truffle, 58
Warm White Asparagus Salad, Poached Egg Dressing, 51
White Truffle Scrambled Eggs, 91
Wild Mushroom Tarte Flambée, 336

apples
Apple Skin Chips, 372
Grain-Crusted Venison, Lambic-Braised Red Cabbage, Honeycrisp Apples, 200–203
Peekytoe Crab Rolls, Granny Smith Apple, Celery, Walnut, 5–7
Slow-Baked Apple Mille-Feuille, Confit Honeycrisp Ice Cream, 230–31
in Tarte Normande, 348
Apple Skin Chips, 372
Apricot and Lavender Clafoutis, Fresh Green Almonds, 242

artichokes
Artichoke Chips, 372
Garlic-Studded Gigot with Artichokes and Watercress, 346
in Red Snapper "en Croûte de Sel," Harissa, Pistachio Butter, 108–11
Striped Bass in a Cilantro-Tapioca Pistou, Artichokes, Lemon Croquettes, 136–37
in Vermont Spring Lamb, Peas à la Française, 184–89

asparagus
Chilled White Asparagus Soup, Wild Chervil, Chive Blossoms, 52
Escalope Viennoise, Veal Quenelles, Green Asparagus, 176–79
Roasted Guinea Hen, Morel and Giblet-Crusted White Asparagus, Vin Jaune Jus, 165–67
in Spring Rabbit Rissolé, Mousserons, Fava Beans, 172–75
Warm White Asparagus Salad, Poached Egg Dressing, 51

avocadoes
in Eckerton Hill Farm Heirloom Tomato Tasting, 32–33
in Langoustine and Uni Chaud-Froid, 21–23
Squab Vadouvan Pastilla, Young Radishes, Avocado Chutney, 154–57

baby turnips
in Chilled Salmon à l'Oseille, 25–27
in Peppered Magret of Duck, Rhubarb Variations, 159–61
in Rabbit Porchetta, Farmer Lee's Baby Vegetable Salad, 38–41
Bacon-Wrapped Monkfish with Lobster, Fall Squash, Tellicherry Pepper Jus, 116–19
Baeckeoffe, Root Vegetable, 340
Banana, Chocolate, and Hazelnut Gâteau, Lime Confit, Vanilla-Lime Sorbet, 256–57

base recipes, 368–79
batter, dough, 374
dry pantry, 372–73
meats, 374–75
stocks, sauces, and purees, 368–71
Basic Meat Jus, 370

bass
Slow-Baked Sea Bass, Pommes Lyonnaise, Leek Royale, 113–15
Striped Bass in a Cilantro-Tapioca Pistou, Artichokes, Lemon Croquettes, 136–37

batters
Tempura Batter, 374
Tuile Batter, 374
Bavarois, Shiso, Ponzu Gelée, Citrus-Cured Fluke, 8–11
Beaufort and Riesling Fondue Ravioli, Green Peppercorns, Sunchokes, 95–97

beef
  Braised Short Ribs, 374–75
  Duo de Boeuf, Bone Marrow–Crusted
    Tardivo, Sweet Potato Dauphine, 209–11
  Tête de Veau en Tortue, 281–84
Beer-Marinated Pork Rack with a Barley-
    Mustard Crust, 338
beets
  in Citrus-Cured Fluke, Shiso Bavarois,
    Ponzu Gelée, 8–11
  in Rabbit Porchetta, Farmer Lee's Baby
    Vegetable Salad, 38–41
Beignets, Petit Gris, Creamy Spring Garlic
    Soup, 44–47
Biryani Masala, Lobster, Fresh Coconut
    Chutney, Spiced Sheep's Yogurt, 80–83
Biryani Masala Spice Mix, 372
Blackberry and Crème Fraîche Vacherin,
    238–41
black olives
  Black Olive Mosto Oil, 377
  Elysian Fields Farm Lamb Rack, Spiced
    Tomato Chutney, Summer Squash,
    Black Olives, 190–93
Black Truffle Oeuf en Cocotte, 92
Blood Orange Sauce, Nantucket Scallop
    Ceviche, 13
Braised Short Ribs, 374–75
bread, Daniel on, 42
Breadcrumb Cups, 373
Breadcrumbs, Fine White, 373
broccoli, in Soft-Shell Crab Tempura, Lemon
    Gremolata, Pickled Fresno Peppers, 75
broccoli rabe, in Grand Aïoli, 352
Brussels Sprouts, Crispy Rice, Miso-Glazed
    Sea Scallop Rosace, 84–85
Buddha's Hand Citron Confit, 377
Butter, Clarified, 377
Butter, Pistachio, Red Snapper "en Croûte de
    Sel," Harissa, 108–11

cabbage
  Grain-Crusted Venison, Lambic-Braised
    Red Cabbage, Honeycrisp Apples,
    200–203
  in Root Vegetable Baeckeoffe, 340
  Truffled Poularde, Chestnut-Stuffed
    Cabbage, Salsify, 162–63
Caille aux Raisins, Chanterelles, Sauternes
    Jus, 151–53

Canard à la Presse, 294–96
Candied Walnuts, 373
Caramelized Nuts, 379
Caraway-Cured Tai Snapper, Cucumber and
    Dill Broth, 19
carrots
  in Grand Aïoli, 352
  in Rabbit Porchetta, Farmer Lee's Baby
    Vegetable Salad, 38–41
  Spanish Mackerel au Vin Blanc, Poached
    with Carrot Mousseline, Lettuce-
    Wrapped Tartar with Caviar, 15–17
  in Vermont Spring Lamb, Peas à la
    Française, 184–89
cauliflower
  in Dover Sole Ballotine à la Polonaise, 105–7
  Jade Tiger Abalone, Cauliflower Concassé,
    Caviar, 69–71
  Mussel and Cauliflower Velouté, 344
caviar
  Jade Tiger Abalone, Cauliflower Concassé,
    Caviar, 69–71
  Spanish Mackerel au Vin Blanc, Poached
    with Carrot Mousseline, Lettuce-
    Wrapped Tartar with Caviar, 15–17
Cedar-Wrapped Kampachi, Romano Beans,
    Sauce Diable, 139–41
Celery, Walnut, Peekytoe Crab Rolls, Granny
    Smith Apple, 5–7
Ceviche, Nantucket Scallop, Blood Orange
    Sauce, 13
chanterelles
  in Black Truffle Oeuf en Cocotte, 92
  Caille aux Raisins, Chanterelles, Sauternes
    Jus, 151–53
  Chanterelle Duxelle, 377
  in White Truffle Scrambled Eggs, 91
charentais melons, in Poached Carolina
    Shrimp, Summer Melons, Lemon Balm,
    29–30
Chartreuse, 299–303
Chaud-Froid, Langoustine and Uni, 21–23
cheese
  Beaufort and Riesling Fondue Ravioli,
    Green Peppercorns, Sunchokes, 95–97
  Daniel on, 219
  in Eckerton Hill Farm Heirloom Tomato
    Tasting, 32–33
  Foraged Herb Pyramid Agnolotti, Pata
    Negra, Nettlesome Cheese, 99–101

in White Truffle Veal Blanquette, Polenta
    Taragna, Crosnes, 181–83
Cherries, Sweet Bing, Kirsch Chantilly, Sicilian
    Pistachio Ice Cream, 232–35
Chervil, Wild, Chive Blossoms, Chilled White
    Asparagus Soup, 52
chestnuts
  Contemporary Chestnut Mont-Blanc,
    258–61
  Truffled Poularde, Chestnut-Stuffed
    Cabbage, Salsify, 162–63
  Wild Hare à la Royale, 195–99
Chicharrones, Crispy, Five-Spiced
    Porcelet, Black Trumpet Mushrooms,
    204–7
chicken
  Chicken Jus, 369
  Chicken Stock, 368
  Modern Salade Lyonnaise, Leeks, Lardons,
    and Oeuf Mollet, 360
  Poulet à l'Estragon, Rice Pilaf and Yellow
    Wax Beans, 363
  Poulet en Vessie, 309–12
  Truffled Poularde, Chestnut-Stuffed
    Cabbage, Salsify, 162–63
  Volaille à Noelle, 305–6
chickpeas, in Elysian Fields Farm Lamb Rack,
    Spiced Tomato Chutney, Summer
    Squash, Black Olives, 190–93
Chilled Salmon à l'Oseille, 25–27
Chilled White Asparagus Soup, Wild Chervil,
    Chive Blossoms, 52
chips
  Apple Skin Chips, 372
  Artichoke Chips, 372
  Garlic Chips, 372
  Herb Chips, 373
Chive Blossoms, Wild Chervil, Chilled White
    Asparagus Soup, 52
chocolate
  Chocolate, Banana, and Hazelnut Gâteau,
    Lime Confit, Vanilla-Lime Sorbet,
    256–57
  Chocolate-Coffee Bar, Mascarpone
    Whipped Cream, 252–53
  Chocolate Praliné Palet d'Or, 249–51
  Cocoa-Dusted Dark Chocolate
    Bombe, 364
  Dark Chocolate Glaze, 378
  Tempered Chocolate, 378

Chocolate, Banana, and Hazelnut Gâteau, Lime Confit, Vanilla-Lime Sorbet, 256–57

Chocolate-Coffee Bar, Mascarpone Whipped Cream, 252–53

chorizo
   Flaked New England Cod, Tarbais Beans, Chorizo, Almond Cloud, 64–71
   Sweet Maine Shrimp–Coated Halibut, Chorizo, Crushed Garbanzo Beans, 121–23

Cilantro-Tapioca Pistou, Striped Bass in a, Artichokes, Lemon Croquettes, 136–37

Citrus-Cured Fluke, Shiso Bavarois, Ponzu Gelée, 8–11

Clafoutis, Apricot and Lavender, Fresh Green Almonds, 242

Clarified Butter, 377

Clay-Baked King Salmon, Fennel Royale, Caramelized Figs, 132–35

Cockscombs, Watercress Velouté, Crayfish Timbale, 54–57

Cocoa-Dusted Dark Chocolate Bombe, 364

Coconut Chutney, Fresh, Spiced Sheep's Yogurt, Lobster Biryani Masala, 80–83

Cod, Flaked New England, Tarbais Beans, Chorizo, Almond Cloud, 64–71

condiments, 376–77

confits
   Buddha's Hand Citron Confit, 377
   Grape Confit, 152
   Lemon Confit, 377
   Lime Confit, Banana, Chocolate, and Hazelnut Gâteau, Vanilla-Lime Sorbet, 256–57
   Tomato Confit, 376

Contemporary Chestnut Mont-Blanc, 258–61

Coulibiac, 287–92

coulis
   Charentais Melon Coulis, 30
   Huckleberry Coulis, 170, 171
   Plum Coulis, 36, 37
   Rhubarb Coulis, 160
   Sorrel Coulis, 26, 27
   Truffle Coulis, 371

Court Bouillon, 369

crab
   Peekytoe Crab Rolls, Granny Smith Apple, Celery, Walnut, 5–7

Soft-Shell Crab Tempura, Lemon Gremolata, Pickled Fresno Peppers, 75

Crayfish Timbale, Cockscombs, Watercress Velouté, 54–57

Creamy Spring Garlic Soup, Petit Gris Beignets, 44–47

Crispy Shallot Rings, 372

Crosnes, White Truffle Veal Blanquette, Polenta Taragna, 181–83

Croustillant Tuile Powder, 379

Cucumber and Dill Broth, Caraway-Cured Tai Snapper, 19

culinary terms and ingredients, 380–81

daikon radish
   in Peppered Magret of Duck, Rhubarb Variations, 159–61
   Venison and Daikon Radish Mosaic, 35–37

Daniel (restaurant). See Restaurant Daniel

Daniel at home. See home-cooked meals

Dark Chocolate Glaze, 378

desserts
   Daniel on, 262–63
   chocolate
      Chocolate, Banana, and Hazelnut Gâteau, Lime Confit, Vanilla-Lime Sorbet, 256–57
      Chocolate-Coffee Bar, Mascarpone Whipped Cream, 252–53
      Chocolate Praliné Palet d'Or, 249–51
      Cocoa-Dusted Dark Chocolate Bombe, 364
      Peanut Croustillant, Turrón Candy Ice Cream, 255
   Contemporary Chestnut Mont-Blanc, 258–61
   fruit
      Apricot and Lavender Clafoutis, Fresh Green Almonds, 242
      Blackberry and Crème Fraîche Vacherin, 238–41
      Fig, Pine Nut, and Mascarpone Custard Tart, 356
      Ice Wine Sabayon, Poached Yellow Peach, Red Currant, 246
      Kougelhopf, 341
      Poached Rhubarb, Vanilla Parfait, Michel Guérard's Sauternes-Rhubarb Ice Cream, 223–25

Raspberry and Yuzu Verrine, Swirled Sorbet, 236–37

Slow-Baked Apple Mille-Feuille, Confit Honeycrisp Ice Cream, 230–31

Strawberry Granité Rosace, Szechuan Peppercorn Sorbet, 244–45

Sweet Bing Cherries, Kirsch Chantilly, Sicilian Pistachio Ice Cream, 232–35

Tarte Normande, 348

Warm Ruby Red Grapefruit, Candied Pomelo, Bergamot Honey, 226–29

iconic French, 327–29

pastry, base recipes for, 378–79

dough
   Pasta Dough, 374
   Vanilla Sablé Breton Dough, 378

Dover Sole Ballotine à la Polonaise, 105–7

duck
   Canard à la Presse, 294–96
   Peppered Magret of Duck, Rhubarb Variations, 159–61

Duo de Boeuf, Bone Marrow–Crusted Tardivo, Sweet Potato Dauphine, 209–11

Eckerton Hill Farm Heirloom Tomato Tasting, 32–33

eggplant
   in Cedar-Wrapped Kampachi, Romano Beans, Sauce Diable, 139–41
   Grilled Eggplant Puree, 371

eggs
   Black Truffle Oeuf en Cocotte, 92
   Modern Salade Lyonnaise, Leeks, Lardons, and Oeuf Mollet, 360
   Warm White Asparagus Salad, Poached Egg Dressing, 51
   White Truffle Scrambled Eggs, 91

Elysian Fields Farm Lamb Rack, Spiced Tomato Chutney, Summer Squash, Black Olives, 190–93

Escalope Viennoise, Veal Quenelles, Green Asparagus, 176–79

escargots, in Creamy Spring Garlic Soup, Petit Gris Beignets, 44–47

fava beans
   in Crayfish Timbale, Cockscombs, Watercress Velouté, 54–57
   in Rabbit Porchetta, Farmer Lee's Baby Vegetable Salad, 38–41

in Seared Pacific Sable, Gourgane Panisse, Pickled Ramps, 124–27

Spring Rabbit Rissolé, Mousserons, Fava Beans, 172–75

in Striped Bass in a Cilantro-Tapioca Pistou, Artichokes, Lemon Croquettes, 136–37

fennel

Clay-Baked King Salmon, Fennel Royale, Caramelized Figs, 132–35

in Langoustine and Uni Chaud-Froid, 21–23

Loup de Mer on Herbes de Provence Citrus Salt, Fennel and Grape Sauce Vierge, 355

figs

Clay-Baked King Salmon, Fennel Royale, Caramelized Figs, 132–35

Fig, Pine Nut, and Mascarpone Custard Tart, 356

Fine White Breadcrumbs, 373

fish and shellfish

appetizers

Caraway-Cured Tai Snapper, Cucumber and Dill Broth, 19

Chilled Salmon à l'Oseille, 25–27

Citrus-Cured Fluke, Shiso Bavarois, Ponzu Gelée, 8–11

Crayfish Timbale, Cockscombs, Watercress Velouté, 54–57

Creamy Spring Garlic Soup Petit Gris Beignets, 44–47

Flaked New England Cod, Tarbais Beans, Chorizo, Almond Cloud, 64–71

Grand Aïoli, 352

Hazelnut-Crusted Maine Sea Scallops, Nettles, Swiss Chard, 76–77

Jade Tiger Abalone, Cauliflower Concassé, Caviar, 69–71

Langoustine and Uni Chaud-Froid, 21–23

Lobster Biryani Masala, Fresh Coconut Chutney, Spiced Sheep's Yogurt, 80–83

Miso-Glazed Sea Scallop Rosace, Brussels Sprouts, Crispy Rice, 84–85

Mussel and Cauliflower Velouté, 344

Nantucket Scallop Ceviche, Blood Orange Sauce, 13

Peekytoe Crab Rolls, Granny Smith Apple, Celery, Walnut, 5–7

Poached Carolina Shrimp, Summer Melons, Lemon Balm, 29–30

Soft-Shell Crab Tempura, Lemon Gremolata, Pickled Fresno Peppers, 75

Spanish Mackerel au Vin Blanc, Poached with Carrot Mousseline, Lettuce-Wrapped Tartar with Caviar, 15–17

Spot Prawn Croustillant, Hearts of Palm Tandoori, Kumquat, 78

iconic French dishes

Coulibiac, 287–92

Turbot Soufflé, 269–72

main courses

Bacon-Wrapped Monkfish with Lobster, Fall Squash, Tellicherry Pepper Jus, 116–19

Cedar-Wrapped Kampachi, Romano Beans, Sauce Diable, 139–41

Clay-Baked King Salmon, Fennel Royale, Caramelized Figs, 132–35

Dover Sole Ballotine à la Polonaise, 105–7

Loup de Mer, Tender Leeks, Ovoli Mushrooms à la Crème, 129–30

Loup de Mer on Herbes de Provence Citrus Salt, Fennel and Grape Sauce Vierge, 355

Red Snapper "en Croûte de Sel," Harissa, Pistachio Butter, 108–11

Seared Pacific Sable, Gourgane Panisse, Pickled Ramps, 124–27

Slow-Baked Sea Bass, Pommes Lyonnaise, Leek Royale, 113–15

Striped Bass in a Cilantro-Tapioca Pistou, Artichokes, Lemon Croquettes, 136–37

Sweet Maine Shrimp–Coated Halibut, Chorizo, Crushed Garbanzo Beans, 121–23

Five-Spiced Porcelet, Black Trumpet Mushrooms, Crispy Chicharrones, 204–7

Flaked New England Cod, Tarbais Beans, Chorizo, Almond Cloud, 64–71

Fluke, Citrus-Cured, Shiso Bavarois, Ponzu Gelée, 8–11

foie gras

Foie Gras Terrine, 375

in Grain-Crusted Venison, Lambic-Braised Red Cabbage, Honeycrisp Apples, 200–203

in Scottish Grouse Farcie, Poached Quince, Huckleberry, 168–71

in Venison and Daikon Radish Mosaic, 35–37

in Wild Hare à la Royale, 195–99

Foraged Herb Pyramid Agnolotti, Pata Negra, Nettlesome Cheese, 99–101

French classics. See iconic French dishes

Fresno Peppers, Pickled, Soft-Shell Crab Tempura, Lemon Gremolata, 75

Frog Leg Fricassée, Kamut Berries, Spinach Puree, 72–73

Frog Leg Soupe en Croûte VGE, 61–63

Garbanzo Beans, Crushed, Sweet Maine Shrimp-Coated Halibut, Chorizo, 121–23

garlic

Creamy Spring Garlic Soup, Petit Gris Beignets, 44–47

Garlic Chips, 372

Garlic Paste, 371

Garlic-Studded Gigot with Artichokes and Watercress, 346

Gourgane Panisse, Pickled Ramps, Seared Pacific Sable, 124–27

Grain-Crusted Venison, Lambic-Braised Red Cabbage, Honeycrisp Apples, 200–203

Grand Aïoli, 352

Grapefruit, Warm Ruby Red, Candied Pomelo, Bergamot Honey, 226–29

grapes

Caille aux Raisins, Chanterelles, Sauternes Jus, 151–53

Loup de Mer on Herbes de Provence Citrus Salt, Fennel and Grape Sauce Vierge, 355

Green Herb Oil, 376

Grilled Eggplant Puree, 371

Grouse Farcie, Scottish, Poached Quince, Huckleberry, 168–71

Guinea Hen, Roasted, Morel and Giblet–Crusted White Asparagus, Vin Jaune Jus, 165–67

Halibut, Sweet Maine Shrimp-Coated, Chorizo, Crushed Garbanzo Beans, 121–23

Hare à la Royale, Wild, 195–99

Harissa, Pistachio Butter, Red Snapper "en Croûte de Sel," 108–11

hazelnuts
Chocolate, Banana, and Hazelnut Gâteau, Lime Confit, Vanilla-Lime Sorbet, 256–57
in Chocolate Praliné Palet d'Or, 249–51
Hazelnut-Crusted Maine Sea Scallops, Nettles, Swiss Chard, 76–77
hearts of palm
in Lobster Biryani Masala, Fresh Coconut Chutney, Spiced Sheep's Yogurt, 80–83
Spot Prawn Croustillant, Hearts of Palm Tandoori, Kumquat, 78
Herb Chips, 373
Herb Pyramid Agnolotti, Foraged, Pata Negra, Nettlesome Cheese, 99–101
herbs, Daniel on, 87
Hickory Smoked Squab Breast, Pea and Lettuce Velouté, 48–49
home-cooked meals, xix, 333–64
Beer-Marinated Pork Rack with a Barley-Mustard Crust, 338
Cocoa-Dusted Dark Chocolate Bombe, 364
Fig, Pine Nut, and Mascarpone Custard Tart, 356
Garlic-Studded Gigot with Artichokes and Watercress, 346
Grand Aïoli, 352
Kougelhopf, 341
Loup de Mer on Herbes de Provence Citrus Salt, Fennel and Grape Sauce Vierge, 355
Modern Salade Lyonnaise, Leeks, Lardons, and Oeuf Mollet, 360
Mussel and Cauliflower Velouté, 344
Poulet à l'Estragon, Rice Pilaf and Yellow Wax Beans, 363
Root Vegetable Baeckeoffe, 340
Tarte Normande, 348
Wild Mushroom Tarte Flambée, 336
Huckleberry, Scottish Grouse Farcie, Poached Quince, 168–71

Ice Wine Sabayon, Poached Yellow Peach, Red Currant, 246
iconic French dishes, xix, 269–324
Canard à la Presse, 294–96
Chartreuse, 299–303
Coulibiac, 287–92
Jambon au Foin, 274–79

Pâté en Croûte, 317–19
Pot-au-Feu, 321–24
Poulet en Vessie, 309–12
Rillette, 315
Tête de Veau en Tortue, 281–84
Turbot Soufflé, 269–72
Volaille à Noelle, 305–6
ingredient guide, xix, 380–81
ingredient sources, 383

Jade Tiger Abalone, Cauliflower Concassé, Caviar, 69–71
Jambon au Foin, 274–79
jus
Basic Meat Jus, 370
Chicken Jus, 369
Rabbit Jus, 370

Kampachi, Cedar-Wrapped, Romano Beans, Sauce Diable, 139–41
Kamut Berries, Spinach Puree, Frog Leg Fricassée, 72–73
Kirsch Chantilly, Sweet Bing Cherries, Sicilian Pistachio Ice Cream, 232–35
Kougelhopf, 341
Kumquat, Spot Prawn Croustillant, Hearts of Palm Tandoori, 78

lamb
Elysian Fields Farm Lamb Rack, Spiced Tomato Chutney, Summer Squash, Black Olives, 190–93
Garlic-Studded Gigot with Artichokes and Watercress, 346
Vermont Spring Lamb, Peas à la Française, 184–89
Langoustine and Uni Chaud-Froid, 21–23
leeks
in Five-Spiced Porcelet, Black Trumpet Mushrooms, Crispy Chicharrones, 204–7
Loup de Mer, Tender Leeks, Ovoli Mushrooms à la Crème, 129–30
Modern Salade Lyonnaise, Leeks, Lardons, and Oeuf Mollet, 360
Slow-Baked Sea Bass, Pommes Lyonnaise, Leek Royale, 113
lemon
Buddha's Hand Citron Confit, 377
Lemon Confit, 377

Soft-Shell Crab Tempura, Lemon Gremolata, Pickled Fresno Peppers, 75
Lemon Balm, Poached Carolina Shrimp, Summer Melons, 29–30
lettuce
Pea and Lettuce Velouté, Hickory Smoked Squab Breast, 48–49
Spanish Mackerel au Vin Blanc, Poached with Carrot Mousseline, Lettuce-Wrapped Tartar with Caviar, 15–17
Veal Kidney à la Graisse, Mustard Seeds, Black Radish, Butter Lettuce, 213–15
lobster
Bacon-Wrapped Monkfish with Lobster, Fall Squash, Tellicherry Pepper Jus, 116–19
in Grand Aïoli, 352
Lobster Biryani Masala, Fresh Coconut Chutney, Spiced Sheep's Yogurt, 80–83
Loup de Mer, Tender Leeks, Ovoli Mushrooms à la Crème, 129–30
Loup de Mer on Herbes de Provence Citrus Salt, Fennel and Grape Sauce Vierge, 355
lovage, in Warm White Asparagus Salad, Poached Egg Dressing, 51
Lyon, menu and recipes, 359–64
Cocoa-Dusted Dark Chocolate Bombe, 364
Modern Salade Lyonnaise, Leeks, Lardons, and Oeuf Mollet, 360
Poulet à l'Estragon, Rice Pilaf and Yellow Wax Beans, 363

Mackerel au Vin Blanc, Spanish, Poached with Carrot Mousseline, Lettuce-Wrapped Tartar with Caviar, 15–17
Mascarpone Whipped Cream, Chocolate-Coffee Bar, 252–53
Mayonnaise, 370
meat
appetizers
Frog Leg Fricassée, Kamut Berries, Spinach Puree, 72–73
Frog Leg Soupe en Croûte VGE, 61–63
Hickory Smoked Squab Breast, Pea and Lettuce Velouté, 48–49
Pea and Lettuce Velouté, Hickory Smoked Squab Breast, 48–49

Rabbit Porchetta, Farmer Lee's Baby
Vegetable Salad, 38–41
Venison and Daikon Radish Mosaic, 35–37
base recipes. *See also* stocks
Basic Meat Jus, 370
Braised Short Ribs, 374–75
Foie Gras Terrine, 375
Rabbit Jus, 370
iconic French dishes
Canard à la Presse, 294–96
Chartreuse, 299–303
Jambon au Foin, 274–79
Pâté en Croûte, 317–19
Pot-au-Feu, 321–24
Poulet en Vessie, 309–12
Rillette, 315
Tête de Veau en Tortue, 281–84
Volaille à Noelle, 305–6
main courses
Beer-Marinated Pork Rack with a
Barley-Mustard Crust, 338
Caille aux Raisins, Chanterelles, Sauternes
Jus, 151–53
Duo de Boeuf, Bone Marrow–Crusted
Tardivo, Sweet Potato Dauphine,
209–11
Elysian Fields Farm Lamb Rack, Spiced
Tomato Chutney, Summer Squash,
Black Olives, 190–93
Escalope Viennoise, Veal Quenelles,
Green Asparagus, 176–79
Five-Spiced Porcelet, Black Trumpet
Mushrooms, Crispy Chicharrones,
204–7
Garlic-Studded Gigot with Artichokes
and Watercress, 346
Grain-Crusted Venison, Lambic-Braised
Red Cabbage, Honeycrisp Apples,
200–203
Peppered Magret of Duck, Rhubarb
Variations, 159–61
Poulet à l'Estragon, Rice Pilaf and Yellow
Wax Beans, 363
Roasted Guinea Hen, Morel and
Giblet–Crusted White Asparagus, Vin
Jaune Jus, 165–67
Scottish Grouse Farcie, Poached Quince,
Huckleberry, 168–71
Spring Rabbit Rissolé, Mousserons, Fava
Beans, 172–75

Squab Vadouvan Pastilla, Young
Radishes, Avocado Chutney, 154–57
Truffled Poularde, Chestnut-Stuffed
Cabbage, Salsify, 162–63
Veal Kidney à la Graisse, Mustard Seeds,
Black Radish, Butter Lettuce, 213–15
Vermont Spring Lamb, Peas à la
Française, 184–89
White Truffle Veal Blanquette, Polenta
Taragna, Crosnes, 181–83
Wild Hare à la Royale, 195–99
Melba Croutons, 372
Melons, Summer, Lemon Balm, Poached
Carolina Shrimp, 29–30
Miso-Glazed Sea Scallop Rosace, Brussels
Sprouts, Crispy Rice, 84–85
Modern Salade Lyonnaise, Leeks, Lardons,
and Oeuf Mollet, 360
Monkfish, Bacon-Wrapped, with Lobster,
Fall Squash, Tellicherry Pepper Jus,
116–19
Mont-Blanc, Contemporary Chestnut,
258–61
morels
in Crayfish Timbale, Cockscombs,
Watercress Velouté, 54–57
in Escalope Viennoise, Veal Quenelles,
Green Asparagus, 176–79
in Hazelnut-Crusted Maine Sea Scallops,
Nettles, Swiss Chard, 76–77
Roasted Guinea Hen, Morel and Giblet–
Crusted White Asparagus, Vin Jaune
Jus, 165–67
Mostarda Cremona, 376
Mousserons, Fava Beans, Spring Rabbit
Rissolé, 172–75
mushrooms. *See also* chanterelles; morels;
porcini mushrooms
in Beaufort and Riesling Fondue Ravioli,
Green Peppercorns, Sunchokes, 95–97
Five-Spiced Porcelet, Black Trumpet
Mushrooms, Crispy Chicharrones,
204–7
in Foraged Herb Pyramid Agnolotti, Pata
Negra, Nettlesome Cheese, 99–101
Loup de Mer, Tender Leeks, Ovoli
Mushrooms à la Crème, 129–30
Spring Rabbit Rissolé, Mousserons, Fava
Beans, 172–75
Wild Mushroom Tarte Flambée, 336

Mussel and Cauliflower Velouté, 344
Mustard Vinaigrette, 376

Nantucket Scallop Ceviche, Blood Orange
Sauce, 13
Nettles, Swiss Chard, Hazelnut-Crusted Maine
Sea Scallops, 76–77
Nettlesome Cheese, Foraged Herb Pyramid
Agnolotti, Pata Negra, 99–101
Normandy, menu and recipes, 343–48
Garlic-Studded Gigot with Artichokes and
Watercress, 346
Mussel and Cauliflower Velouté, 344
Tarte Normande, 348
nuts. *See also* chestnuts; hazelnuts; walnuts
Caramelized Nuts, 379

oils, dressings, & condiments, 376–77
olives. *See* black olives
onions. *See* pearl onions

parsnips, in Scottish Grouse Farcie, Poached
Quince, Huckleberry, 168–71
Pasta Dough, 374
pastry, base recipes for, 378–79
Pâté en Croûte, 317–19
Pea and Lettuce Velouté, Hickory Smoked
Squab Breast, 48–49
Peach, Poached Yellow, Red Currant, Ice
Wine Sabayon, 246
Peanut Croustillant, Turrón Candy Ice Cream,
255
pearl onions
in Caille aux Raisins, Chanterelles,
Sauternes Jus, 151–53
in White Truffle Veal Blanquette, Polenta
Taragna, Crosnes, 181–83
peas
Pea and Lettuce Velouté, Hickory Smoked
Squab Breast, 48–49
Vermont Spring Lamb, Peas à la Française,
184–89
Peekytoe Crab Rolls, Granny Smith Apple,
Celery, Walnut, 5–7
Peppered Magret of Duck, Rhubarb
Variations, 159–61
Pickling Liquid, 377
piment d'Espelette, Daniel on, 87
Pine Nut, Fig, and Mascarpone Custard Tart,
356

pistachios
  in Kougelhopf, 341
  Red Snapper "en Croûte de Sel," Harissa,
    Pistachio Butter, 108–11
  Sweet Bing Cherries, Kirsch Chantilly,
    Sicilian Pistachio Ice Cream, 232–35
plums, in Venison and Daikon Radish Mosaic,
  35–37
Poached Carolina Shrimp, Summer Melons,
  Lemon Balm, 29–30
Poached Rhubarb, Vanilla Parfait, Michel
  Guérard's Sauternes-Rhubarb Ice
  Cream, 223–25
Polenta Taragna, Crosnes, White Truffle Veal
  Blanquette, 181–83
Pomelo, Candied, Bergamot Honey, Warm
  Ruby Red Grapefruit, 226–29
Ponzu Gelée, Citrus-Cured Fluke, Shiso
  Bavarois, 8–11
Porchetta, Rabbit, Farmer Lee's Baby
  Vegetable Salad, 38–41
porcini mushrooms
  in Venison Consommé with Black Truffle, 58
  in Wild Hare à la Royale, 195–99
pork
  Beer-Marinated Pork Rack with a Barley-
    Mustard Crust, 338
  Five-Spiced Porcelet, Black Trumpet
    Mushrooms, Crispy Chicharrones,
    204–7
  Jambon au Foin, 274–79
potatoes
  in Dover Sole Ballotine à la Polonaise, 105–7
  in Five-Spiced Porcelet, Black Trumpet
    Mushrooms, Crispy Chicharrones,
    204–7
  in Loup de Mer, Tender Leeks, Ovoli
    Mushrooms à la Crème, 129–30
  in Root Vegetable Baeckeoffe, 340
  Slow-Baked Sea Bass, Pommes Lyonnaise,
    Leek Royale, 113
  in Sweet Maine Shrimp–Coated Halibut,
    Chorizo, Crushed Garbanzo Beans,
    121–23
Pot-au-Feu, 321–24
Poulet à l'Estragon, Rice Pilaf and Yellow Wax
  Beans, 363
Poulet en Vessie, 309–12
Prawn Croustillant, Spot, Hearts of Palm
  Tandoori, Kumquat, 78

Provence, menu and recipes, 351–56
  Fig, Pine Nut, and Mascarpone Custard
    Tart, 356
  Grand Aïoli, 352
  Loup de Mer on Herbes de Provence Citrus
    Salt, Fennel and Grape Sauce Vierge,
    355
prunes, in Venison and Daikon Radish Mosaic,
  35–37
Pulled Sugar, 379
purees
  Grilled Eggplant Puree, 371
  Spinach Puree, 371

quail
  Caille aux Raisins, Chanterelles, Sauternes
    Jus, 151–53
quail eggs
  in Chilled Salmon à l'Oseille, 25–27
  in Foraged Herb Pyramid Agnolotti, Pata
    Negra, Nettlesome Cheese, 99–101
Quince, Poached, Huckleberry, Scottish
  Grouse Farcie, 168–71

rabbit
  Rabbit Jus, 370
  Rabbit Porchetta, Farmer Lee's Baby
    Vegetable Salad, 38–41
  Spring Rabbit Rissolé, Mousserons, Fava
    Beans, 172–75
radicchio di Treviso, in Duo de Boeuf, Bone
    Marrow–Crusted Tardivo, Sweet Potato
    Dauphine, 209–11
radishes. See also daikon radish
  Squab Vadouvan Pastilla, Young Radishes,
    Avocado Chutney, 154–57
  Veal Kidney à la Graisse, Mustard Seeds,
    Black Radish, Butter Lettuce, 213–15
Ramps, Pickled, Seared Pacific Sable,
    Gourgane Panisse, 124–27
Raspberry and Yuzu Verrine, Swirled Sorbet,
    236–37
Ravioli, Beaufort and Riesling Fondue, Green
    Peppercorns, Sunchokes, 95–97
Red Snapper "en Croûte de Sel," Harissa,
    Pistachio Butter, 108–11
Restaurant Daniel, xii, xiii, xiv
  recipes from, ix, xix, 3–261
    appetizers, 5–101
    desserts, 223–61

  fish, 105–41
  meat, 151–215
  wine cellar, 145–46
rhubarb
  Peppered Magret of Duck, Rhubarb
    Variations, 159–61
  Poached Rhubarb, Vanilla Parfait, Michel
    Guérard's Sauternes-Rhubarb Ice
    Cream, 223–25
rice
  Miso-Glazed Sea Scallop Rosace, Brussels
    Sprouts, Crispy Rice, 84–85
  Poulet à l'Estragon, Rice Pilaf and Yellow
    Wax Beans, 363
Rillette, 315
Roasted Guinea Hen, Morel and Giblet–
    Crusted White Asparagus, Vin Jaune
    Jus, 165–67
romanesco
  in Dover Sole Ballotine à la Polonaise, 105–7
  in Jade Tiger Abalone, Cauliflower
    Concassé, Caviar, 69–71
Romano Beans, Sauce Diable, Cedar-
    Wrapped Kampachi, 139–41
Root Vegetable Baeckeoffe, 340

Sabayon, Ice Wine, Poached Yellow Peach,
    Red Currant, 246
Sable, Seared Pacific, Gourgane Panisse,
    Pickled Ramps, 124–27
salmon
  Chilled Salmon à l'Oseille, 25–27
  Clay-Baked King Salmon, Fennel Royale,
    Caramelized Figs, 132–35
  Coulibiac, 287–92
Salsify Spirals, 373
salt, Daniel on, 87
sauces
  Basic Meat Jus, 370
  Daniel on, 142
  Rabbit Jus, 370
  Sauce Périgueux, 369
  Syrah Reduction, 371
scallops
  Hazelnut-Crusted Maine Sea Scallops,
    Nettles, Swiss Chard, 76–77
  Miso-Glazed Sea Scallop Rosace, Brussels
    Sprouts, Crispy Rice, 84–85
  Nantucket Scallop Ceviche, Blood Orange
    Sauce, 13

Scottish Grouse Farcie, Poached Quince, Huckleberry, 168–71

Sea Bass, Slow-Baked, Pommes Lyonnaise, Leek Royale, 113

Seared Pacific Sable, Gourgane Panisse, Pickled Ramps, 124–27

seasoning, Daniel on, 87

sea urchin (uni), in Langoustine and Uni Chaud-Froid, 21–23

Sheep's Yogurt, Spiced, Lobster Biryani Masala, Fresh Coconut Chutney, 80–83

shellfish. *See* fish and shellfish

Shiso Bavarois, Ponzu Gelée, Citrus-Cured Fluke, 8–11

shrimp
    in Grand Aïoli, 352
    Poached Carolina Shrimp, Summer Melons, Lemon Balm, 29–30
    Sweet Maine Shrimp–Coated Halibut, Chorizo, Crushed Garbanzo Beans, 121–23

Slow-Baked Apple Mille-Feuille, Confit Honeycrisp Ice Cream, 230–31

Slow-Baked Sea Bass, Pommes Lyonnaise, Leek Royale, 113–15

snap peas, in Chilled Salmon à l'Oseille, 25–27

snapper
    Caraway-Cured Tai Snapper, Cucumber and Dill Broth, 19
    Red Snapper "en Croûte de Sel," Harissa, Pistachio Butter, 108–11

Soft-Shell Crab Tempura, Lemon Gremolata, Pickled Fresno Peppers, 75

sorrel, in Chilled Salmon à l'Oseille, 25–27

sous-vide, note on, xix

Spanish Mackerel au Vin Blanc, Poached with Carrot Mousseline, Lettuce-Wrapped Tartar with Caviar, 15–17

spicing, Daniel on, 87

spinach
    Frog Leg Fricassée, Kamut Berries, Spinach Purée, 72–73
    Spinach Purée, 371
    White Truffle Scrambled Eggs, 91

Spot Prawn Croustillant, Hearts of Palm Tandoori, Kumquat, 78

Spring Rabbit Rissolé, Mousserons, Fava Beans, 172–75

squab
    Hickory Smoked Squab Breast, Pea and Lettuce Velouté, 48–49
    Pea and Lettuce Velouté, Hickory Smoked Squab Breast, 48–49
    Squab Vadouvan Pastilla, Young Radishes, Avocado Chutney, 154–57

squash
    Bacon-Wrapped Monkfish with Lobster, Fall Squash, Tellicherry Pepper Jus, 116–19
    Elysian Fields Farm Lamb Rack, Spiced Tomato Chutney, Summer Squash, Black Olives, 190–93

stocks
    Chicken Stock, 368
    Court Bouillon, 369
    Daniel on, 142
    Veal Stock, 368
    Venison Consommé, 368–69

Strawberry Granité Rosace, Szechuan Peppercorn Sorbet, 244–45

Striped Bass in a Cilantro-Tapioca Pistou, Artichokes, Lemon Croquettes, 136–37

Sunchokes, Beaufort and Riesling Fondue Ravioli, Green Peppercorns, 95–97

Sweet Bing Cherries, Kirsch Chantilly, Sicilian Pistachio Ice Cream, 232–35

sweetbreads
    in Escalope Viennoise, Veal Quenelles, Green Asparagus, 176–79
    in White Truffle Veal Blanquette, Polenta Taragna, Crosnes, 181–83

Sweet Maine Shrimp–Coated Halibut, Chorizo, Crushed Garbanzo Beans, 121–23

Sweet Potato Dauphine, Duo de Boeuf, Bone Marrow–Crusted Tardivo, 209–11

Swiss Chard, Hazelnut-Crusted Maine Sea Scallops, Nettles, 76–77

Syrah Reduction, 371

Szechuan Peppercorn Sorbet, Strawberry Granité Rosace, 244–45

Tai Snapper, Caraway-Cured, Cucumber and Dill Broth, 19

tapioca pearls
    in Caraway-Cured Tai Snapper, Cucumber and Dill Broth, 19

Striped Bass in a Cilantro-Tapioca Pistou, Artichokes, Lemon Croquettes, 136–37

Tarbais Beans, Chorizo, Almond Cloud, Flaked New England Cod, 64–71

Tart, Fig, Pine Nut, and Mascarpone Custard, 356

Tarte Flambée, Wild Mushroom, 336

Tarte Normande, 348

Tellicherry Pepper Jus, Bacon-Wrapped Monkfish with Lobster, Fall Squash, 116–19

Tempered Chocolate, 378

Tempura Batter, 374

Tête de Veau en Tortue, 281–84

Timbale, Crayfish, Cockscombs, Watercress Velouté, 54–57

Tomato Confit, 376

tomatoes
    Eckerton Hill Farm Heirloom Tomato Tasting, 32–33
    Elysian Fields Farm Lamb Rack, Spiced Tomato Chutney, Summer Squash, Black Olives, 190–93
    Tomato Confit, 376

tool guide, xix

tool sources, 383

Truffled Poularde, Chestnut-Stuffed Cabbage, Salsify, 162–63

truffles
    Black Truffle Oeuf en Cocotte, 92
    Daniel on, 88
    Truffle Coulis, 371
    Truffled Poularde, Chestnut-Stuffed Cabbage, Salsify, 162–63
    Venison Consommé with Black Truffle, 58
    White Truffle Scrambled Eggs, 91
    White Truffle Veal Blanquette, Polenta Taragna, Crosnes, 181–83

Tuile Batter, 374

Turbot Soufflé, 269–72

turnips. *See* baby turnips

Turrón Candy Ice Cream, Peanut Croustillant, 255

uni (sea urchins), in Langoustine and Uni Chaud-Froid, 21–23

Vacherin, Blackberry and Crème Fraîche, 238–41

Vadouvan Pastilla, Squab, Young
    Radishes, Avocado Chutney,
    154–57
Vanilla Sablé Breton Dough, 378
veal
    Escalope Viennoise, Veal Quenelles, Green
        Asparagus, 176–79
    Tête de Veau en Tortue, 281–84
    Veal Kidney à la Graisse, Mustard
        Seeds, Black Radish, Butter Lettuce,
        213–15
    Veal Stock, 368
    White Truffle Veal Blanquette, Polenta
        Taragna, Crosnes, 181–83
Velouté, Mussel and Cauliflower, 344
venison
    Grain-Crusted Venison, Lambic-Braised
        Red Cabbage, Honeycrisp Apples,
        200–203
    Venison and Daikon Radish Mosaic,
        35–37
    Venison Consommé, 368–69
    Venison Consommé with Black
        Truffle, 58
Vermont Spring Lamb, Peas à la Française,
    184–89
Volaille à Noelle, 305–6

walnuts
    Candied Walnuts, 373
    Peekytoe Crab Rolls, Granny Smith Apple,
        Celery, Walnut, 5–7
    Walnut Glaze, 376
Warm Ruby Red Grapefruit, Candied Pomelo,
    Bergamot Honey, 226–29
Warm White Asparagus Salad, Poached Egg
    Dressing, 51
watercress
    Crayfish Timbale, Cockscombs, Watercress
        Velouté, 54–57
    Garlic-Studded Gigot with Artichokes and
        Watercress, 346
whelks, in Grand Aïoli, 352
White Truffle Scrambled Eggs, 91
White Truffle Veal Blanquette, Polenta
    Taragna, Crosnes, 181–83
Wild Hare à la Royale, 195–99
Wild Mushroom Tarte Flambée, 336

wine
    Caille aux Raisins, Chanterelles, Sauternes
        Jus, 151–53
    Daniel on, 145–46
    Ice Wine Sabayon, Poached Yellow Peach,
        Red Currant, 246
    Poached Rhubarb, Vanilla Parfait, Michel
        Guérard's Sauternes-Rhubarb Ice
        Cream, 223–25
    Roasted Guinea Hen, Morel and Giblet–
        Crusted White Asparagus, Vin Jaune
        Jus, 165–67
    Spanish Mackerel au Vin Blanc,
        Poached with Carrot Mousseline,
        Lettuce-Wrapped Tartar with Caviar,
        15–17
    Syrah Reduction, 371

Yellow Wax Beans, Poulet à l'Estragon, Rice
    Pilaf and, 363

zucchini, in Elysian Fields Farm Lamb Rack,
    Spiced Tomato Chutney, Summer
    Squash, Black Olives, 190–93

Daniel Boulud, a native of Lyon, France, is considered one of America's leading culinary authorities and is one of the most revered French chefs in New York, the city he has called home since 1982. Boulud is best known for New York's Daniel, the Michelin three-star Relais & Châteaux restaurant. He is also chef/owner of db Bistro Moderne, DBGB Kitchen and Bar, Bar Boulud, Café Boulud, Boulud Sud, and Épicerie Boulud, as well as restaurants in Miami and Palm Beach, Florida, and internationally in London, Singapore, Beijing, Montréal, and Toronto. He is the author of seven cookbooks; the recipient of three James Beard Foundation awards, including Outstanding Chef (1994) and Outstanding Restaurant (2010); and was named a Chevalier de la Légion d'honneur (2006) by the French government. Boulud has served on the board of directors of Citymeals-on-Wheels since 2000, becoming co-president in 2013, and is also co-founder and chairman of the Bocuse d'Or USA Foundation.

Sylvie Bigar is an International food and travel writer whose work has appeared in the *New York Times*, *Saveur*, *Food Arts*, *Departures*, *Travel & Leisure*, *Town & Country*, *National Geographic Traveler*, on bonappetit.com, and elsewhere. She writes a food and travel blog, sbigar.com; and tweets as Frenchiefoodie. Her next book explores identity and cassoulet. Born in Geneva and fluent in three languages, Bigar has three passports, but she calls New York home.

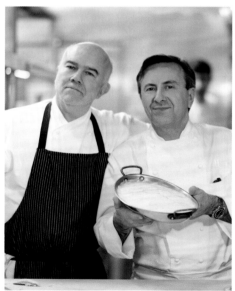

Bill Buford is the author of *Heat: An Amateur's Adventures as a Kitchen Slave, Line Cook, Pasta Maker, and Apprentice to a Dante-Quoting Butcher in Tuscany* and *Among the Thugs*. He has been a staff writer and the fiction editor of the *New Yorker* and was the founding editor of the literary magazine *Granta*. In 2008, he moved to Lyon, France, with his wife, Jessica Green, and their two children, and lived there for five years, learning the French kitchen, which will be the basis of his new book, provisionally entitled *Dirt*.

Restaurant Daniel
60 East 65th Street
New York, NY 10065

www. danielboulud.com

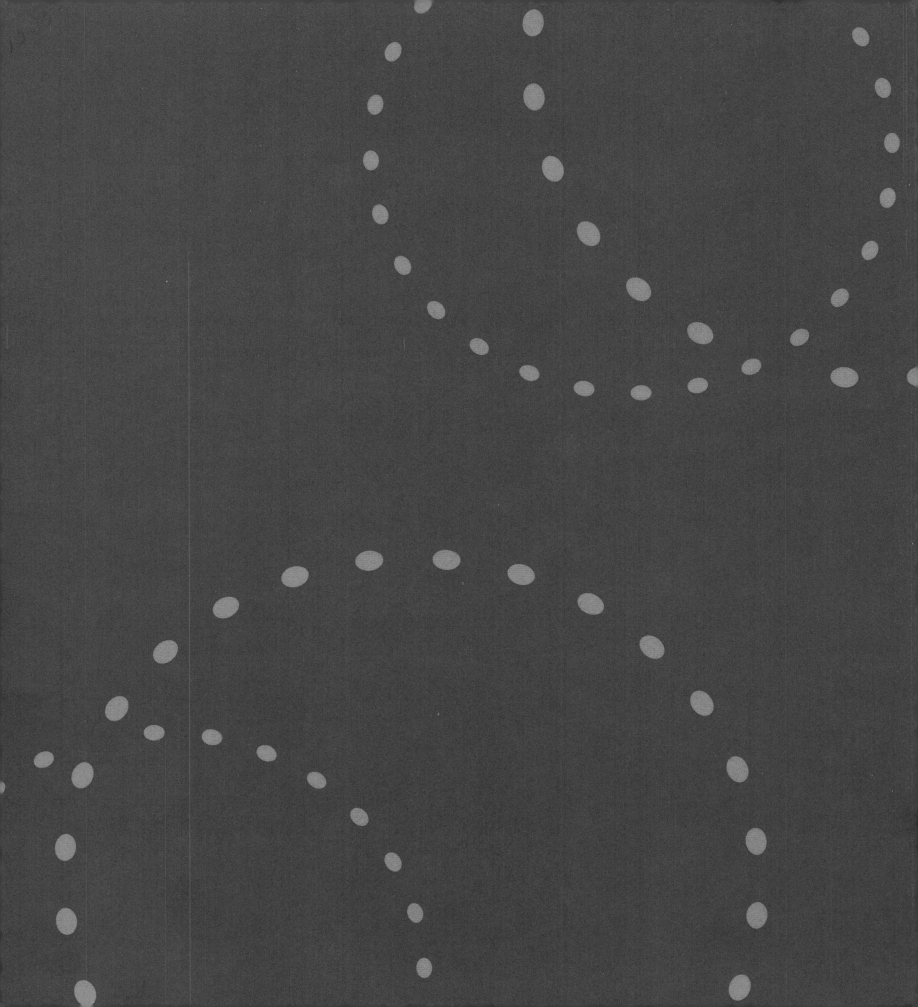